MORE THAN A GAME

MORE
THAN A GAME

*The Story
of Cricket's Early Years*

JOHN MAJOR

Harper*Press*
An Imprint of HarperCollins*Publishers*

HarperCollins*Publishers*
77–85 Fulham Palace Road,
Hammersmith, London w6 8jb
www.harpercollins.co.uk

Published by HarperCollins*Publishers* 2007

4

A catalogue record for this book is available from the British Library

ISBN 13 978-0-00-718364-7
ISBN 10 0-00-718364-X

Set in PostScript Linotype Minion with Janson and
Castellar Display by Rowland Phototypesetting Ltd,
Bury St Edmunds, Suffolk

Printed and bound in Great Britain by
Clays Ltd, St Ives plc

This book is proudly printed on paper which contains wood
from well managed forests, certified in accordance with
the rules of the Forest Stewardship Council.
For more information about FSC,
please visit www.fsc-uk.org

Mixed Sources
Product group from well-managed
forests and other controlled sources
www.fsc.org Cert no. SW-COC-1806
© 1996 Forest Stewardship Council

To Norma, Elizabeth, James and Luke

Contents

Illustrations

Charles Lennox, second Duke of Richmond, a keen gambler with a lifelong love of cricket. Mezzotint by John Faber Jr, after John Vanderbank. *(Courtesy National Portrait Gallery, London)*

Sir William Gage, whose estate Firle in East Sussex was one of the cradles of eighteenth-century cricket. *(Courtesy of the Firle Estate Trustees)*

Cricket being played in 1743 at the Artillery Ground in Finsbury, London. *(The Roger Mann Collection)*

Lionel Sackville, first Duke of Dorset, one of the great early patrons of the game. Portrait by Sir Godfrey Kneller, 1717. *(Private Collection, © NTPL/John Hammond)*

Charles Sackville, second Duke of Dorset. Portrait by Rosalba Carriera. *(Private Collection, © NTPL/John Hammond)*

Frederick Louis, Prince of Wales, an enthusiastic early patron of cricket. Portrait miniature by Gaetano Manini, 1755. *(© Ashmolean Museum, University of Oxford/The Bridgeman Art Library)*

The Duke of Cumberland, a better judge of a soldier than a cricketer. Portrait by David Morier. *(© Private Collection/Philip Mould Ltd/The Bridgeman Art Library)*

A match at Moulsey Hurst, on the banks of the river Mole in Surrey. *(The Roger Mann Collection)*

'Lumpy' Stevens, the most deadly underarm bowler of his day. *(The Roger Mann Collection)*

Sir Horace Mann, the most amiable of cricket's early benefactors. *(The Roger Mann Collection)*

John Frederick Sackville, third Duke of Dorset, the third in a line of great cricketing patrons. Portrait by Sir Joshua Reynolds, 1769. *(Private Collection, © NTPL/John Hammond)*

The Countess of Derby plays cricket with other ladies at The Oaks, in Surrey, in 1779. *(The Roger Mann Collection)*

John Nyren, whose memories of Hambledon have given us a vivid
  picture of early cricket. *(The Roger Mann Collection)*
An eighteenth-century cricket match, possibly at Hambledon. *(The
  Roger Mann Collection)*
A page from a sketchbook by George Shepheard, showing some of the
  Hambledon cricketers. *(The Roger Mann Collection)*
The Bat and Ball Inn on Broadhalfpenny Down, Hambledon. *(The
  Roger Mann Collection)*

'Silver Billy' Beldam joined the Hambledon club in 1785, and lifted the
  art of batting to a new level of style and elegance. *(The Roger Mann
  Collection)*
Lord Winchilsea, a key founder of the MCC who encouraged Thomas
  Lord to acquire its first ground. *(The Roger Mann Collection)*
*Cricket Played by the Gentlemen's Club, White Conduit House, Islington
  in 1784. (The Roger Mann Collection)*

An engraving, after Thomas Rowlandson, depicting a match between
  the ladies of Hampshire and Surrey at Newington in 1811. *(The Roger
  Mann Collection)*
The canny Yorkshireman Thomas Lord, who left the world's most
  famous cricket ground as his memorial. *(The Roger Mann Collection)*
William Ward, a central figure in securing Lord's place as the
  headquarters of cricket. *(The Roger Mann Collection)*

Benjamin Aislabie, first Secretary of the MCC. *(The Roger Mann
  Collection)*
Lord Frederick Beauclerk: avaricious, ill-tempered, hypocritical, and
  adept at bending the rules. *(The Roger Mann Collection)*
Fuller Pilch, the finest batsman of his day, and 'single-wicket
  champion of England'. *(The Roger Mann Collection)*
John Wisden, the founder of the *Almanack* and a fast round-arm
  bowler. *(The Roger Mann Collection)*
The Scorer, by Thomas Henwood (1842). *(The Roger Mann Collection)*
Alfred Mynn and Nicholas Felix before their famous single-wicket
  contest in 1846 for the title 'champion of England'. *(The Roger Mann
  Collection)*
William Clarke, the finest underarm bowler of them all, and the
  founder of Trent Bridge cricket ground. *(The Roger Mann Collection)*

Clarke's All-England Eleven of 1847. *(The Roger Mann Collection)*

The All-England Eleven on the move in 1851, by Nicholas Felix. *(The Roger Mann Collection)*

George Parr, who succeeded Clarke as leader of Nottinghamshire and the All-England Eleven. *(The Roger Mann Collection)*

The first English overseas touring team. George Parr's men gather on deck before their 1859 voyage to North America. *(The Roger Mann Collection)*

H.H. Stephenson's English team arrives in Melbourne on Christmas Eve 1861. *(The Roger Mann Collection)*

Tom Hayward and Robert Carpenter, two fine Cambridgeshire batsmen of the 1860s. *(The Roger Mann Collection)*

Arthur Haygarth, whose *Cricket Scores and Biographies* is the bedrock of our knowledge of the years 1744 to 1878. *(The Roger Mann Collection)*

The 1880 Australians, the first visitors to play a Test match in England. *(The Roger Mann Collection)*

Charles Alcock, whose immense backstage contribution to cricket warrants a higher place in the mythology of the game than history has yet given him. *(The Roger Mann Collection)*

Alfred Shaw, who bowled the first over in Test cricket. *(The Roger Mann Collection)*

Edward Mills Grace, W.G.'s elder brother and one of the most formidable cricketers of his day. *(The Roger Mann Collection)*

W.G. Grace poses with Harry Jupp of Surrey. *(The Roger Mann Collection)*

Three of the remarkable Studd brothers, two of whom played Test cricket for England. *(The Roger Mann Collection)*

'The Demon' – Frederick Spofforth, the first of the great Australian bowlers. *(The Roger Mann Collection)*

The Hon. Ivo Bligh led the English team which recovered the Ashes in Australia in 1882–83. *(The Roger Mann Collection)*

Lord Harris batting at Lord's for the Lords and Commons Eleven against the touring Canadians in 1922. *(The Roger Mann Collection)*

The Ideal Cricket Match, by Sir Robert Ponsonby Staples (1887). *(The Roger Mann Collection)*

Acknowledgements

Few books have been written without advice and help from many different quarters, and this one is no exception. My thanks are heartfelt and wide-ranging.

Throughout my life I have devoured each and every book that came within my reach, and in doing so I came across contradictions in some of the accepted tales of early cricket. The genesis of this book was twofold: I wanted to separate fact from fiction, and to dig as deep as I could into the history of the game; and in doing so, to understand more about the lives and ambitions of the early pioneers. Since I was writing in the margins of extensive travelling, it soon became clear that I needed help with research, and, as the first of many kindnesses, David Rayvern Allen suggested I approach those peerless authorities on early cricket, John Goulstone and Roger Packham. Their encyclopaedic memory of facts and source material proved invaluable. No question relating to the game was too obscure for them to pursue, and I am enormously grateful to them both. Similar thanks are due to Piers Warburton, who joined the research team to check and unearth documentation on times past, in order to place cricket in its historical and social context.

The list of those who, in turn, gave their time, thought and effort to my research team is too long to detail, but I offer them all my grateful thanks. Among those who helped me directly, I would like to mention Trevor Jones at The Oval; Peter Wynne-Thomas at Trent Bridge; Keith Hayhurst at Old Trafford; and Adam Chadwick, Neil Robinson, Glenys Williams and Ken Daldry at Lord's. Staff at the British Library proved – as ever – that there was no piece of literature, however obscure, that they could not source, and Norma Crane of Medway Archives unearthed some early pamphlets of great value.

Among former parliamentary colleagues, Sir Robert Atkins MEP and Sir Michael Marshall were especially encouraging and helpful. Both made suggestions I adopted, and provided information from their own private archives. Michael, although very sick throughout my writing, remained characteristically enthusiastic and wrote and telephoned with ideas. Alas, he will never see the finished product.

As word spread that I was writing a history of cricket, I was enormously touched by the many letters I received from members of the public, sharing their own detailed knowledge of the game – most of which proved to be extremely useful. Conversations with Roger Knight, former captain of Surrey and Chief Executive of the MCC, offered invaluable help, as did archival information from another long-standing friend, Mrs Pat Wheeler.

In my office, Arabella Warburton read and reread the text with the eyes of a lay person to remove jargon, and suggested the reordering of early drafts. Kay Knipe, Anne Stenson and Vanessa Burgess shared the burden of deciphering my manuscript, and amended and re-amended the drafts so often that they could practically recite large chunks of it.

At HarperCollins, Michael Fishwick gave me early encouragement to embark on this project, Richard Johnson gave me every incentive to continue, and Robert Lacey edited the manuscript with the same skill and precision he demonstrated during the writing of my autobiography. Their input was invaluable.

Throughout the last year my family has endured endless weekends of writing, with the same degree of patience they showed when the red boxes held me hostage during my years in government. As an author herself, Norma was always swift to empathise with the agonies of writing, assuring me that the occasional writer's block would always clear.

Any errors in the book are entirely my own, as are any and all opinions expressed. If, when the last page is turned, you have derived even half as much pleasure in reading it as I have in writing it, I shall be a happy man.

John Major
London, January 2007

Preface

All my life cricket has been a joy. My sister taught me the game when I was very young, and it met a need that has never gone away. She would bowl to me as I clutched a tiny bat and tried to defend the wicket chalked on our garage door. I was rather embarrassed by my sister's tutelage until I learned that W.G. Grace had been taught under the eagle eye of his mother. That made me feel better, but not play better.

I have only a dim recollection of those early days, and of watching the local village side whilst my father enjoyed a game of bowls. He preferred Drake's game to Hutton's; but I turned my back on the bowling green and my eyes to the cricket square.

There was no coaching at my primary school, but we did play cricket. I can still relive one incident that has the power, over half a century on, to bring a hot flush of embarrassment to my face. It was a game in which for the first time I wore full whites, pads and gloves, and had my own bat. I was expected to score runs, and that made me even more nervous – caring *too much* rarely produces the best outcome, as I was to learn later in life. I strode to the wicket, took guard, carefully looked at the field placings, and prepared for the first ball. I played forward and felt the ball hit the middle of the bat. But the boy at first slip appealed, and the umpire/teacher squinted down the wicket, raised his forefinger theatrically and gave me out, leg before wicket. I was mortified, and without thought, stuttered, 'But, but, I hit it!'

Uproar ensued. 'Out,' snarled the umpire/teacher. 'Out. Off' – he was now waving his arm like a windmill – 'Off you go.' He was right, of course, that I should not have questioned his decision. He was not right to mutter 'Bloody boy,' as, head down, I walked off, shamed and burning with injustice. That teacher's angry face is imprinted forever on my mind; it is not a happy memory. But not even he could turn me away from cricket.

We are led to believe that our character is formed in our earliest years. I believe that. Joy and pain are at their sharpest when they are new. I remember trying to hide my deep disappointment that my parents were never able to see me play cricket. They had many reasons not to do so – chronic ill health, worry, the struggle to make modest ends meet when the week outran the money. They were old, too. When I was six my father was seventy, and my mother closer to fifty than forty. Both smoked, and their poor health was made worse by the foul habit. It would kill my mother in the end, but for many years before that, hacking coughs and shortage of breath were a daily occurrence. And they were exotics: our neighbourhood did not house many ex-trapeze artists, gauchos, jugglers, card-sharps or speciality dancers, and even as a boy I knew my parents were not to be judged by the usual criteria.

Once, I was certain they would come. Our school team was due to play close to our home, and I wrote out instructions for my parents on how to get there – out of our gate, turn right, then right alongside the brook, a further turn right where I went bird-nesting, and there we would be, in a field to the left. I was captain, and set a field with myself at cover-point and midwicket so that I had a clear view of the entrance gate, but neither of my parents came. My father had been doubtful anyway. He was losing his eyesight, although as a nine-year-old I was not aware of that. And my mother, who had gamely promised to come, was too ill with her interminable bronchitis. As I carried old Dr Robinson's prescription to the chemist the following morning, I vowed I would never smoke.

Years later, Alec Bedser told me that his mother never saw him, or his twin Eric, play cricket. Not that Mrs Bedser was without opinions. When Alec took eleven wickets in his first Test match at Lord's, the press asked for her views of her son. 'Which one?' 'Alec,' they said. 'Why Alec?' 'He's just taken eleven wickets in a Test on his debut,' they explained. Mrs Bedser was forthright: 'That's what he's paid for, isn't it?'

As a child, cricket entered my bloodstream, and it has given me a lifetime of enjoyment and solace. Yet there are pessimists about the game. As long ago as 1932, C.P. Snow was moaning: 'These days, a man of taste can only go to an empty ground and regret the past.' The same dreary view can often be heard on county grounds today, as hindsight flourishes with the aid of rose-tinted spectacles.

I have never understood why we see the past as a Golden Age. It's a false image. There was little golden about Victorian England, when children were sent scurrying up chimneys to clean them. Or Restoration England, when every portrait shows a closed mouth because a smile would have revealed rotten or blackened teeth. A cool analysis of the past will temper the rosing of the spectacles. The same is true of cricket: there have been many golden days, but the aspic of old photographs can hide the worst of times as well as the best.

As a game, cricket is complex. People who have never played are apt to say, 'I don't understand it.' Much the same was said about the Impressionists, although there was nothing complicated about their art: as Claude Monet put it, 'I simply looked at what the universe had to show us and used my brush to give an account of it.' So too with cricket: it delights the eye and touches the soul. Part of this is physical: the smell of linseed oil on willow, the feel of ball on bat, the pleasure of holding a shiny new red ball, the clatter of disturbed stumps, the snick and catch that turns heads, and, on the best of days, the scent of newly-mown grass under the warmth of the rising sun. There is no cricketer alive who has not enjoyed these sensations, and cherished the memory of them. Lucy Baldwin, a fine cricketer and wife of Prime Minister Stanley Baldwin, put it well: 'The crack of bat against ball amid that humming and buzzing of summer sound is still to me a note of pure joy that raised haunting memories of friends and happy days.' Romantic tomfoolery? Perhaps. But cricket is that sort of game, and it would lose much of its charm if it were not.

One does not have to be talented to be besotted by cricket, as a thousand village games prove each summer. I first saw this at school. One boy, whose anonymity I shall protect, practised in the nets for hours – and often, I suspected, in front of a mirror – for every batting movement ended in a pose of classical perfection. No cricket whites were ever more neatly pressed, or pads or boots whiter, or bat more beautifully oiled, and when, head high, he strode out to the wicket, he oozed class and confidence. Alas, the image was false: he put so much into the elegance of every stroke that he overlooked the need to hit the ball, and all too soon would turn in surprise to look at his shattered stumps. He left the crease swiftly yet gracefully, nodding in congratulation to the bowler, head still high, bat tucked under arm, pulling off his batting gloves as if, for all the world, he was returning to the pavilion in triumph.

He was never downhearted. As he took his pads off, he would tell us all that he had been beaten 'in the flight' or 'off the pitch'; and, theorists all, no one suggested he had, again, just missed a straight one. He knew the theory of cricket. He knew the statistics. He knew the spirit in which the game should be played, and he revelled in it. Runs or not, it was joy enough for him to be on a cricket pitch. I don't know if he ever read A.A. Milne, but his poem had him exactly right:

> But what care I? It's the game that calls me –
> Simply to be on the field of play;
> How can it matter what fate befalls me,
> With ten good fellows and one good day!

I was so lucky that cricket was played at my grammar school; it was, with rugby, the only activity that made the experience bearable. During one game the pitch was positioned within striking distance of some enticing windows, and the temptation to put the ball through one of them was irresistible. The prize was to be a pint of illicit beer

– I was only fourteen at the time, and such devilment appealed. A cross-batted heave missed the main target but did crash through an adjacent church window. The tinkle of glass brought a great cheer. It was enough: a triumph was celebrated.

Not long afterwards a heavier drink, scrumpy, caused more trouble. I drank a little too much, and as I travelled home it began to extort its revenge. I arrived safely, but when my father opened the door I was on my knees barking at him. I thought it was funny. He did not. Only my mother's intervention saved me from being banned from cricket.

I was no cricketing prodigy, but nor was I a complete mug. I had my days, and they remain precious memories: 50 runs in a house match, with the winning hit a straight four that whistled past the bowler's nose; 33 runs scored in three overs to win a game on a day when every hit seemed to find the boundary; 7 wickets for 9 runs, including a hat-trick, in a Colts game, when four of the runs scored off me were an edge that, half a century on, I still know that an even half-alert fielder should have caught in the slips. A meagre return for my love of the game, you might think, but only if you don't know cricket. Runs, wickets and catches are all very well, but they don't capture the fun of it all, the camaraderie, the hopes, the mini-triumphs and disasters, the wins, defeats and close finishes, the sunny days and the wet ones, all memories every cricketer locks away for the dark months when the summer game is in hibernation.

When my father finally lost his eyesight and all his money in the early 1950s, our family were uprooted from our modest bungalow in Surrey to two rooms of a multi-occupied Victorian relic in Brixton. The accommodation lacked finesse, but it was within walking distance of the Kennington Oval at a time when Surrey had the greatest county team of them all. I camped out at The Oval during the summer holidays as a devoted spectator. It cannot have been so, but memory insists that the sun always shone and Surrey always won. And what a feast they offered. Peter May's bat rang like a pistol shot, and the suffering ball bounced back from the pavilion pickets before a fielder had even moved. May's batting once got me into a frightful scrape.

I had borrowed my father's precious gold stopwatch to time how long it took a May off-drive to reach the boundary, and in pressing the stop button it slipped from my fingers and smashed open on the terracing. The innards sprang out. The watch looked terminally sick. So did I as I confessed all to my father. 'Tell me,' he said, gingerly holding the watch by a broken spring, 'about Peter May.'

May was one of many great players in that Surrey team. Tony Lock, menace shining from his bald pate, bowled the unplayable ball and caught the impossible catch. Jim Laker ambled gently to the wicket, but his off-breaks spun and spat at the batsman. The thin man, Peter Loader, was fast as a whippet; and Alec Bedser, the great medium-pacer, stately as a galleon, tormented batsmen with nagging accuracy and a leg cutter no other bowler has ever matched. Decades later he told me he discovered the leg cutter by accident, and had taken two years to perfect it. 'It's a leg spinner, really,' he confided, 'but you need *these* to bowl it properly.' Thereupon he held up the enormous Bedser hands and chuckled. These were golden days of sun and shadows, Tizer and sandwiches, and I shall never forget them.

The 1950s were also a time of massive immigration to England from the West Indies, and many of the new Britons settled in Brixton. The house we lived in was for a time multi-occupied *and* multi-racial, and it provided a good primer on poverty for a future Conservative Prime Minister. I knew the immigrants as neighbours. I lived with them. I played with their children. I shopped with them in Brixton market. I saw them for what they were: men and women seeking opportunity and a new life in a land immeasurably more wealthy than the ones they had left behind.

Others, more fearful, more suspicious, saw them in a harsher light. They feared for their jobs and their livelihoods. They were frightened of possible turmoil in their neighbourhoods. Bigots and foolish men inflamed these fears. Pessimists predicted trouble. Brixton became a powderkeg of racial discontent. People waited for it to blow. Waited for the riots, the lawlessness. They waited in vain. The new Britons settled in. The dire predictions of conflict proved to be wrong.

In my youthful innocence, I wasn't surprised. Instead of inciting fear, the bigots and pessimists should have gone to The Oval, where, when the West Indies played, it was carnival time: the atmosphere was noisy and full of fun as the crowd enjoyed glorious days of cricket. For those in the packed ground the painful reality of life in Brixton was put aside, even though at close of play it was still there. Prejudice and hardship were daily companions to the new Brixtonians. Dr Johnson, who knew London two hundred years earlier, had it right: 'This mournful truth is everywhere confessed/Slow rises worth, by poverty depressed'.

Slow rises worth – but it did rise. And the West Indians' cricket, the way they played and the way the team conducted themselves in victory, did much to help. A few years earlier they had taken on England at her own game, in her own country, at the very headquarters of cricket. And they beat her on merit. Perhaps no win in cricket ever had such social significance as Ramadhin and Valentine's destruction of England at Lord's in June 1950. A big hundred by Clyde Walcott set it up; it was then won by the charm and guile of the cricketing sophisticate's delight: the art of great spin bowling. It was intelligent cricket – the West Indies out-thought England as well as outplayed them. As a result, all West Indians walked a little taller in their tough lives because their national cricket team had lifted their morale. No wonder the calypso rang out in celebration: 'Cricket, lovely cricket', indeed!

This is a classic illustration of the power of cricket. It can uplift whole communities – whole nations even – or cast them down. And because cricket is played largely in the mind, and reflects the society from which the cricketers spring, it can imprint the character of that nation indelibly upon the minds of those who watch the way in which a national team plays.

When not at The Oval, I spent hour upon hour defending a Brixton lamp-post against the bowling of any passer-by. Only my half-brother Tom and our mutual friend Butch were regulars, and only bad light, in the form of nightfall, stopped play. In 1966 my love of playing the game reached a premature end when a car accident in northern Nigeria left me with a leg so shattered it was almost lost; but that did not mean I would never again pick up a bat.

As Prime Minister, in 1991 I attended a meeting of Commonwealth Heads of Government in Harare and opened the batting in a charity match with the Australian Prime Minister, Bob Hawke. The previous evening Bob had entertained his fellow heads of government with a selection of Australian and trades union songs, most of them unrepeatable, as we shared more beers than was wise. The following morning, since I had not held a bat for years, I had a net before the game. As I looked around the lovely Wanderers ground, I was flattered to see that it was filling with spectators, although my Press Secretary Gus O'Donnell, never one to let hubris pass unchallenged, did wonder aloud whether they might have come to see their local hero Graeme Hick, who was due to bat at number three.

Bob Hawke and I opened to gentle bowling, and began to settle down, with Bob stealing the bowling towards the end of each over. I didn't mind: it was a joy just to be there. We tapped the ball here and there, and ran our singles. After a few overs the wisdom of the Hawke strategy was revealed: 'Off you go,' said the umpire, waving us off the pitch as he added, rather pointedly, 'It's time for the real cricketers.' A roar of applause greeted our departure.

Hawke had scored over 20, while I had less than 10. 'Did you know we didn't have long?' I asked him as we trudged back to the pavilion. 'Jeez, yes,' he admitted, a Cheshire-cat-sized grin splitting his craggy features. 'Didn't you know, John? Arrh, heck – I thought you did.' Not for the first or the last time, I noted that Australians play hard.

Our host in Zimbabwe was the President, Robert Mugabe, in the years before he encouraged militants to force out white farmers and steal their property. In 1991, Mugabe talked to me fondly of cricket. 'It civilises people and creates gentlemen. I want everyone to play cricket in Zimbabwe. I want ours to be a nation of gentlemen!' From beyond the grave, Lord Hawke would have approved, though he, like me, would have regarded land theft as most definitely 'not cricket'. Hawke would have disapproved too of the mismatch between

Mugabe's sentiments and the outcome of his policies: his government all but destroyed Zimbabwean cricket.

Forty years after I first visited The Oval, I came to know the Surrey club from the inside. During my years in government The Oval was a sanctuary where cares were put aside. Upon the morrow of defeat in the 1997 general election I bade my farewells to Downing Street and the Queen and headed to The Oval for a leisurely lunch and a soothing afternoon of cricket. Nor did the balm fail me: 'You had a rough decision, mate,' called out a gnarled regular, before turning to more important matters. 'This boy is a good bat.' Indeed he was: it was a young Combined Universities batsman, Will House, later of Sussex, who played a fine cameo innings. Since leaving office I have been able to step back into the pleasures of cricket as if it had never been interrupted by the rude reality of politics.

No one has ever had a sufficient gift of tongues to do justice to the charm of cricket. In fact we cannot even be sure how – or when – the game began. Folklore tells us that generations now gone would pause as they passed some insignificant village game, simply to see how the next ball fared, and then, uplifted and enlightened, pass on their way. Observation tells us that people do so still. So we know the fascination of cricket from its birth. We know, too, its historic moments and its famous players. But how did cricket come to be built into the warp and weft of the English language? How did it develop into the favourite pastime of a large part of the English-speaking world? Why – in all sport – does cricket possess a literature that no other can match? Why do grown men babble of games they never saw and cricketers who died a hundred years before?

A wet day makes a conversationalist of the most taciturn cricket-lover. One rain-drenched hour at The Oval was filled with a discussion about Don Bradman's last Test innings, when the great man was bowled second ball by Eric Hollies for a duck in the final Test of the 1948 series. It is a story every cricket-lover knows, and, cheated of cricket, we were debating at which end the Don was batting. Someone turned to Arthur Morris, the former Australian Test batsman, who was listening silently as he sipped a glass of red wine. 'Surely, you must know, Arthur? Were you in that team?' asked an ignoramus. Raman Subba Row, the former England batsman, who knows his history, choked. 'Yes,' said Arthur, sipping placidly. 'I was at the other end when Don was out. I scored 196.'

There is a postscript to this story. As Bradman returned to the pavilion he was stopped in the Long Room by Field Marshal Montgomery, once captain of cricket at St Paul's school, who had famously encouraged his troops to 'hit Rommel for six'. Montgomery barked at him, 'Sit down, Bradman, and I will tell you where you went wrong.' The absurdity of anyone telling the most prolific run-getter of all time how to bat apparently escaped the old soldier. Bradman revealed this vignette in a letter to the Surrey Club many years later; he did not mention whether he had taken the opportunity to criticise the Field Marshal's battle plan at El Alamein, but probably he did not. This was wise, as Montgomery was never plagued by self-doubt. A man who can say, 'As God said – and, on the whole, he was right . . .' is not a man to be crossed. Bradman was prudent to keep his own counsel. Moreover, he was courteous even when a sharp response was justified.

I discovered this for myself that same rainy day at The Oval. I had never met Bradman, but I did occasionally speak to him on the telephone. As we debated his last innings during one of the showers, Raman remembered it was the Don's birthday, and someone suggested I phone him with our congratulations. I did so. As we spoke, I described the day's cricket and the wretched weather. 'How is it in Australia?' I asked. 'Dunno,' came the reply. 'It's two o'clock in the morning here.'

Sir Donald Bradman is from the aristocracy of cricket. He is one of the rare breed of cricketing knights, all of whom are from the upper class of talent. But the honours system is haphazard, ultimately at the whim of subjective judgements and sometimes perverse. In the more class-conscious Victorian age, even W.G. was overlooked. As Prime Minister, I wished to put right some injustices. I could not simply award honours, but I could nominate for the appropriate independent scrutiny committee to adjudicate.* My first nomination for consideration was Harold Larwood, one of England's greatest fast bowlers, who had been disgracefully treated by the cricketing establishment after the notorious 'bodyline' series against Australia in 1932–33. He had been driven out of Test cricket for obeying his captain's instructions.

The Scrutiny Committee were startled at a nomination for a cricketer who had ceased playing nearly sixty years earlier, and I daresay sucked their teeth before deciding to award Larwood an MBE – below tariff, I thought, but welcome nevertheless. I had a further small list of names, but thought it proper to proceed cautiously, a decision I came to regret, for the Grim Reaper struck before I did, and my other nominations came too late.

When Harold Larwood was awarded his honour, I received a message that he wished to speak to me. I telephoned him in Australia, and learned something of the generous mind of cricketers. Within two minutes he was talking not of himself but of Jack Hobbs and his skill in batting on treacherous wickets. Larwood spoke with affection of Hobbs, as well as awe, and that conversation remains imprinted on my mind for the generosity of spirit it showed. It is a trait that is uplifting in all walks of life.

The statistics of cricket are a total fascination to the aficionado. For years my Cabinet colleague Peter Brooke and I used to pose one another abstruse cricket questions across the Cabinet table, or in restaurants, or on any occasion we met. Peter's knowledge of cricket is encyclopaedic: who else could name any cricketing parson who scored a hundred before lunch at Bangalore during the Indian Mutiny? My old friend Robert Atkins, an MP once and then an MEP, has telephoned me each Sunday morning for years to discuss the state of English cricket and bemoan the loss of Corinthian values. Sometimes he even talks of politics: he bemoans the loss of Corinthian values there, too. But not every politician is a cricket-lover.

When I was Prime Minister Cabinet met on Thursday mornings,

* As anyone can now do under reforms I instituted in 1993.

at the same time as Test matches began. In those days Cabinet debated policy and took decisions, so the meeting stretched on until lunchtime. From time to time folded messages would be brought in to me by the Duty Clerk. I would read them before passing them to Robin Butler, the Cabinet Secretary, a descendant of the great Victorian cricketer Richard Daft, and from him they would cross the table to the Chancellor, and later President of Nottinghamshire County Cricket Club, Ken Clarke. Grimaces or smiles would follow. These notes drove my Deputy Prime Minister Michael Heseltine, who sat on my left, to distraction. Prime Minister, Cabinet Secretary, Chancellor ... was sterling crashing? Was there a crisis? A ministerial resignation? No: they were the Test scores: disbelievingly, Michael filched the notes from my blotter for the Heseltine Papers.

Cricket can be a bridge between opposites. The late Bob Cryer, a very left-wing Labour MP, would always stop to talk cricket with me. John Redwood, a very right-wing Conservative MP, who in 1995 attempted with a great deal of gusto to pitch me out of No. 10, would do the same if, by miscalculation, we found ourselves at the same dining table in the Commons. Even the journalist Simon Heffer, a persistent and hostile critic, was able to summon up a bleak smile if we passed one another at the idyllic cricket ground at Wormsley Park in Buckinghamshire that was Paul Getty's pride and joy.

Cricket can also bind friendships. When the Conservative Party lost the election in 1997, John Howard, Prime Minister of Australia, and his wife Janette were among my first visitors: as a consolation John presented me with that Australian symbol, a baggy green cap: it is a treasured possession. Four years later I was talking about cricket caps and helmets to the old Australian Test all-rounder Sam Loxton. 'Helmets,' scoffed Sam. 'I didn't even wear a helmet at Tobruk!' In 2005, when we met at Lord's during the Ashes tour, a chortling Sam presented me with an authentic Australian helmet. I was forever grateful we'd talked of helmets, not protectors – although I doubt Sam wore one of those at Tobruk either.

A love of cricket is for everyone. As the great batsman K.S. Ranjitsinhji pointed out early in the twentieth century:

> Go to Lord's and analyse the crowd. There are all sorts and
> conditions of men there round the ropes – bricklayers, bank
> clerks, soldiers, postmen and stockbrokers. And in the pav-
> ilions are QCs, artists, archdeacons and leader-writers. Bad
> men, good men, workers and idlers, are all there, and all at
> one in their keenness over the game . . . cricket brings the
> most opposite characters and the most diverse lives together.
> Anything that puts very many kinds of people on a common
> ground must promote sympathy and kindly feelings.

That has been my experience, too. A few years ago I was invited to
the beautiful island of Barbados to deliver the annual Frank Worrell
Lecture. The following evening a galaxy of Caribbean cricketers –
Everton Weekes, Clyde Walcott, Garry Sobers, Wes Hall, Charlie
Griffith, Richie Richardson – attended a dinner for me at the British
High Commission. Cricket conquers all differences, and I – an ex-
Conservative Prime Minister – enjoyed some memorable (to me, at
least) cricketing exchanges with the old West Indian opener Alan
Rae, whose politics were very different. No one cared, and someone
on that lovely evening, Wes Hall I think, referred to cricket as 'the
happy game'. You can't play cricket if you're unhappy, and you can't
be unhappy if you *do* play cricket was a maxim that met general
approval over the rum punches and the laughter. It has certainly been
true in my own life.

In fact, cricket can unlock *all* the emotions. On the day, after
sixteen barren years, that England regained the Ashes at The Oval in
2005, I watched the crowd spontaneously and joyously sing 'Jerusa-
lem' and 'Land of Hope and Glory'. There are precedents for such a
display. When Jessop scored a famous hundred to win the final Test
against Australia at The Oval in 1902, the spectators hurled their
bowler hats to the sky in ecstasy. We may be sure that many were
lost. So too at Jack Hobbs's first innings at The Oval after passing
Grace's record of 126 career centuries in 1925. Amid the applause the
Yorkshire captain called for three cheers for Hobbs and then, Yorkshire being Yorkshire, dismissed him for a beggarly eight runs. The
emotion displayed that day was affection for a great cricketer. When

Boris Karloff, an enthusiastic amateur wicketkeeper, visited The Oval, Surrey weren't sure what to do with him. He was watching the cricket avidly from the balcony when, in reply to a polite enquiry from an anxious host, he muttered in that inimitable voice: 'Wonderful. I think I'm dead and gone to heaven!'

Karloff was a character. Cricket attracts them. I was on The Oval balcony with another, Sir George Edwards – then around ninety years of age – when a guest asked the old man, rather pompously, what he remembered of the war and what, if anything, he'd done in it. George smiled bleakly. 'I helped design the Wellington bomber,' he said, 'if that counts.' I treasure that moment. It was an understatement: George did more than that. He worked with Sir Barnes Wallis on the 'bouncing bomb' that destroyed the great German dams but which, in early tests, kept sinking. George, a keen cricketer, knew why. 'It's underspin, not overspin,' he explained. Barnes Wallis relented – and the Dam Busters took out the Möhne, Sorpe and Eder dams with a leg-break.

'History is bunk,' supposedly said Henry Ford, who never played cricket. That is not my criticism. A number of fine writers have already told the story of cricket. Is there more to be gained by treading on the old turf? I believe so. There are myths to dispel, neglected areas to be examined, for the history of cricket is often seen in a vacuum, as if it developed unaffected by the turbulent history of the nation that gave it birth. But from its earliest days, to the recent tremors of match-fixing and corruption and the innovation of technology-aided umpiring, the game has held up a mirror to the temper of the nation.

Moreover, what of the cricketers? Too often, they appear in one-dimensional form only: all that is known is their on-field exploits. But what were they like? Who were they? What did they do after the cricket years were over, and their eyes dimmed and their sinews stiffened? What was happening off the field as they played cricket? How was the world changing? How did people live? What were their recreations? Cricketers had a flesh-and-blood existence outside the game, and however imperfectly, I shall try to bring alive the mosaic of times past in order to present a more rounded picture of them and the nature of their lives.

Cricket, once first among English games, is no longer so, as the winter sports of football and rugby grow in popularity. It must fight for its future. Even the cricket season seems to shrink annually as football eats away at both ends of the season. By the autumn equinox on 22 September the season is dead and gone, even though, theoretically at least, the sun is still above the horizon for twelve hours every day. Even the refraction of the sun's rays, caused by the earth's atmosphere, which gives the British Isles an extra six minutes of daylight, cannot compete with the commercial imperatives that lengthen the football season.

And yet – cricket *is* different. It is a team game made up of individual contests. Batsman and bowler are locked in gladiatorial combat. One must lose. Each batsman faces alone the hostile intent of every member of the fielding side, all seeking to dismiss him, with the sole support of his batting partner at the other end of the pitch. He knows his contribution may decide the outcome of the match. And can any other game provide a father figure for a nation to match W.G. Grace, who turned a country-house sport into an international obsession – and who is still recognised by his initials alone nearly a hundred years after his death? No, it cannot. Can any other game offer a pre-eminent genius so far above the normal run of talent as Don Bradman? No, again.

In its first 450 years, cricket has besotted wise men and fools. Its fairy godparents were gambling and drink. Its early enemies were Church and state. And yet, it has brought together beggars and royalty, thrown up a rich array of characters, invaded literature and art, and evolved from primitive beginnings to the sophistication of the modern game.

Although cricket is of the very essence of England, the skills of Bradman and Sobers, of Hadlee and Tendulkar, are evidence that the game has far outstripped the land of its birth. England no longer owns cricket. Like radar, penicillin, electricity, the steam engine, railways, the jet engine, computers and the worldwide web, cricket is an English invention – an export as potent as the English language itself. At one level it is a game and no more; at another it helped cement an Empire and bind a Commonwealth. Its legacy is a fellow-ship of cricket-lovers across continents and through generations. In the world of sport, it is the greatest story ever told.

It began a long time ago.

1

The Lost Century of Cricket

But we don't know how long. The search for the birth of cricket has been as fruitless as the hunt for the Holy Grail: neither can be found.

What is cricket, at its most basic? It is a club striking a ball: so are golf, rounders, baseball, hockey and tennis. So are the ancient games of club-ball, stool-ball, trap-ball, stob-ball, each of which some scholars have been keen to appropriate as 'early cricket'. The nineteenth-century pioneer historian the Reverend James Pycroft asserts, without proof, that 'Club-ball we believe to be the name which usually stood for cricket in the thirteenth century.'* His case, however, collapses in the light of later evidence, and the great mid-nineteenth-century cricketer Nicholas Felix (a pseudonym – his real name was Nicholas Wanostrocht) was more likely right when he wrote: 'Club ball is a very ancient game and totally distinct from cricket.'

The paucity of early mentions of cricket has led to some far-fetched assumptions about games that *might* have been cricket, but probably are not. The poet and scholar Joseph of Exeter is said to have written in 1180:

> The youths at cricks did play
> Throughout the merry day.

If they did so, no one else noted it for hundreds of years. This claim has other defects, too: the couplet sounds more eighteenth-century than

---

* In this he echoes the eighteenth-century historian Joseph Strutt, who suggested that 'the manly exercise of cricket' originated from club-ball.

twelfth, and all Joseph's known writing is in Latin. In any event, in 1180 Joseph was on his way to the Third Crusade as an official chronicler, and thoughts of 'youths' and 'merry days' may not have been uppermost in his mind.* We can dismiss Joseph of Exeter. Even less likely is the evidence of an eighth-century monk, Eustatius Constacius, that cricket was played in Florence for the entertainment of Parliament.

Much ink has been spilled by historians over an entry, in 1300, in the wardrobe accounts of King Edward I referring to the sixteen-year-old Prince of Wales, the future Edward II, playing 'creag' and other sports with, as some have suggested, his childhood friend the lamentable and doomed-to-a-bad-end Piers Gaveston. It is evident that 'creag' is a game, but it requires a mighty leap of faith to claim that it was cricket; the kindest judgement that can be made upon this romantic assumption is 'not proven'. In any event, could the villainous Gaveston have been a forefather of cricket? I hope not, and fortunately I think not.

Thomas Babington Macaulay wrote of history that 'It is sometimes fiction. It is sometimes theory.'** In the absence of concrete evidence, of documentary proof, of contemporary records, his maxim holds true of the genesis of cricket. It *may* have been played under another name earlier than we know, but since its birth is shrouded in legend and mystique, we cannot be certain. The silence of antiquity *suggests* that the game was not played in ancient times, but does not *prove* that it was not. It is probable that games such as club-ball were ancestors of cricket, but they cannot be acknowledged as the game itself, and should not be assumed to be so. As the fourteenth-century philosopher William of Occam wrote: 'Things not known to exist should not be postulated as existing.' This is a good principle for soundly-based history. Although the mists and myths are enticing, the truth is more prosaic: cricket evolved from instincts and games as old as man himself.

---

* He later produced an epic on the Crusade entitled *Antiocheis*.
** Macaulay was never short of opinions. When he was a precocious toddler, his aunt enquired after a minor ailment and drew the reported response: 'I thank you, Madam, for your solicitous inquiry. The agony has somewhat abated.'

But when? Here we may be on firmer ground. 1598 was a memorable year. The weather was foul that winter, and on 21 December, in a mini-ice age, the Thames froze. A week later, in a snowstorm, men of the Chamberlain's Company of Actors, led by Richard Burbage and armed in case of unwelcome interruptions, dismantled a theatre in Shoreditch, loaded it onto wagons and transported it through Spitalfields and Bishopsgate to a waterfront warehouse. From there it was ferried across the Thames to be rebuilt on a new site. They called the new theatre the Globe, and the players' favourite son, William Shakespeare, had part-ownership of it.

That Christmas Shakespeare had a new play, *Much Ado About Nothing*, which the players performed at Court for Queen Elizabeth I. A similar view might have been held about a contemporary court case over land ownership. Mr John Derrick, otherwise a forgotten English gentleman, testified to a Guildford court that: 'Being a scholler in the ffree schoole of Guldeford hee and diverse of his fellows did runne and play there at creckett and other plaies.'* W.G. Grace cast doubt on this in his *Cricket* (1891), and suggested that a local historian may have inadvertently substituted 'cricket' for 'quoits'. It is not clear why he thought this. As Mr Derrick was a coroner, it is likely that his deposition was accurate. And as he was then nearly sixty years of age, he would have been a young scholar around 1550–60, thus giving us a precious date by which cricket was being played.

It is not surprising that cricket attracted little contemporary attention, for greater matters were afoot. Within a few years of the death of Henry VIII in 1547 a mighty struggle for souls was raging as the religion of the state swung from Protestant (under Edward VI) to Catholic (under Mary), and back to Protestant once more (under Elizabeth I). Henry VIII had been sufficiently even-handed to persecute Protestants and Catholics alike, but his children were more discriminating, and burned, hanged or imprisoned only their

---

* The relevant extract from the deposition is shown in full, as the works of some early historians, notably H. S. Altham's classic *A History of Cricket* (1926), contain errors of transcription. Altham also refers to Derrick as 'Denwick'.

religious opponents. Predictably, in the midst of the carnage cricket did not get a look-in. Nonetheless, Derrick's deposition suggests that the game existed, under its current name, during the 1550s, although it cannot have been widespread. It may not have fitted into the lifestyles of the middle and upper strata of society. Behind the mullioned windows men drank beer for breakfast before hunting wildlife on uncultivated heaths and shooting pheasant, duck, partridge and snipe, while their womenfolk gossiped over needlework, wrote letters, read, and supervised the kitchen. Large families were commonplace, but half of all children failed to reach adulthood, and none, it seems, played cricket. The game makes no appearance in Shakespeare,* Jonson or Marlowe, there is no known reference to it in mid-sixteenth-century statutes, nor does it appear in surviving memoirs or letters of the time. Not even Brer Rabbit in his briar patch managed such a low profile. Cricket must have been played only by a minority, probably peasants, and even then spasmodically, to have remained so unnoticed and unrecorded.

Or, sometimes, *mis*-recorded. A contemporary reference to the England of Queen Mary reads as follows:

> They make there, divers sort of puppet works or Babyes, for to bring up children in vanitee. There are made likewyse, many kyndds of Bales, Cut-Staves, or Kricket-Staves, Rackets, and Dyce, for that the foolish people should waste or spend their tyme there-with, in foolishness.

This reference to 'Kricket-Staves' is a real trap. The text was written by a Westphalian, Hendrick Niclaes, who lived in England during Queen Mary's reign, where his name was anglicised to Henry Nicholas. A deeply religious man, a Protestant, who disapproved of pleasure, he founded a sect that gained a foothold in Cambridgeshire and Essex. For this initiative he was imprisoned by Queen Mary and released by Queen Elizabeth, following which he sensed the tenor of the times and wisely returned home to Cologne. Niclaes was the

---

* But see *Coriolanus*, Act I, Scene I: 'What's work, my Countrymen in hand?, Where go you, with bats and clubs?' The game is unlikely to be cricket.

author of religious tracts, and it is one of these, *Terra Pacis*, published in Amsterdam – probably in 1575, but written earlier – and translated from its original Base-Almayn (Low German being his native tongue in Westphalia), which contains the reference to 'Kricket-Staves'. But it is a mistranslation: the original word was '*kolven*', meaning 'clubs': Niclaes was referring to one of the many forms of club-ball. Despite this, the English version of *Terra Pacis* does have a legitimate claim to fame. It was thought to have inspired John Bunyan as the former tinker lay in Bedford prison eighty-five years later, when he began *The Pilgrim's Progress*, his enduring allegory of travel 'from this world to that which is to come'. If so, Herr Niclaes deserves an honoured footnote in the histories of religion and of literature – but not of cricket.

As young John Derrick enjoyed his boyhood cricket, England was astir. The mid-1500s were years of peril: England's relationship with its northern neighbour Scotland had broken down, reawakening the dangers of a Franco–Scottish threat to the realm. The economy was weak, the coinage debased, the Protestant–Catholic dispute unsettled, Puritanism was emerging and there were dangers aplenty on every front. It was an age calling for great men and great deeds, and Elizabeth was lucky: Cecil and Walsingham guided policy, and, when not wreaking havoc on our enemies, Raleigh, Drake and Hawkins stood guard on England's shores, while Marlowe, Jonson and Spenser joined Shakespeare in pouring genius onto parchment.

In the midst of this tumultuous century an unknown rural genius, somewhere in the Weald of south-east England, tweaked some ancient game and cricket was born. As anonymous as his ancient forebear the inventor of the wheel, he would have gained immortality had his name become known. Alas, it did not, though his shade can rest content that he built a game for all time.

Primitive cricket was a pastime for the grassroots of English life, and was unburdened by the sophistication of years to come. It did not have eleven players a side. Nor were there two umpires. No one wore whites. There were no recognised field placings. Rules of play were haphazard. There were no six-ball overs. Runs were recorded by innumerate peasants who cut notches on a stick. Accepted laws lay far in the future. But the essentials of the game were already evident. A player with a bat, oddly misshapen by today's standards, defended a crude wicket, squat and without a middle stump, against another player with a ball who 'bowled' underarm and attempted to break the wicket to 'put out' the batsman.

We can conjecture more. The 'batsman' faced the bowler more square-on than side-on, with the 'bat' held well away from his unprotected legs; with that stance he must have hit the ball mainly on the leg side. The theory of 'side-on' batting, with the left elbow pointing down the wicket, was far away – as indeed was side-on overarm bowling, with the lead arm used for balance and as a direction-finder. Such refinements were over two hundred years away from this crude sixteenth-century forerunner of the game we know today.

The Elizabethan age died in the early hours of 24 March 1603, and James VI of Scotland succeeded to the English throne as James I. It was a turbulent time, during which resistance to the absolute rule of kings was to grow, and with it the demand for greater liberty. Some antipathy had begun to emerge in Elizabeth's reign, but she was wise enough to know when to offer what was desired before it was forced from her – on the question of monopolies, for example. James had no such gift, and his errors of judgement paved the way for revolution. He was graceless and merciless towards his opponents, among whom were the adherents of the infant sect of Puritanism, which had plagued him in Scotland. His response was to persecute them,* but *they* grew in strength and *he* grew in unpopularity. A cinder was smouldering that would lead to revolution.

The new Stuart age of the seventeenth century opened a lost century for cricket. Other interests prevailed. Wigs were coming into fashion. *Hamlet*, the greatest of all ghost stories, made its debut in 1600, and the East India Company was founded, to become in time a building block of the greatest empire the world had ever seen.

---

* At a conference at Hampton Court between Anglicans and Puritans in January 1604, James backed the Anglican bishops. Shortly afterwards, a hundred Puritan ministers were dismissed from their livings.

Nonetheless, cricket was spreading slowly. Its cradle was Kent, Sussex and Surrey, but it rarely merited public attention, and what scraps we know of it come from court hearings, inquests, church records and the pitiful number of letters and diaries that have survived the years.

It was a bloody age for the birth of a graceful game. Two years into the new reign of James I, in 1605, Guy Fawkes and his co-conspirators were hanged, drawn and quartered for conspiring to blow up Parliament: it was thought not to be cricket. Or, more likely, cricket was not thought of at all, for the game is not even mentioned in the *Book of Sports* (1618). It was known to the authorities, however, and frowned upon, although playing it at the wrong time attracted only minor penalties. But penalties there were.

The Church, refreshed by the new King James Bible (1611), was severe on defaulters. Sunday was for worship, and perhaps a day of rest. It was *not* a day for enjoyment. Cricket, when the Church was not condemning it as 'profane', was deemed to be fun, and fun was not to be had on the Sabbath. A string of cases in Sussex and Kent opens a window on seventeenth-century attitudes and casts a search-light on the infancy of cricket.

On Easter Sunday, 1611, Bartholomew Wyatt and Richard Latter chose cricket in preference to divine service at Sidlesham church in Sussex, outraging the churchwardens. The Archdeacon too was furious. Such a heinous sin merited punishment, and at a consistory court held in Chichester Cathedral the two men admitted their guilt, and were fined twelve pence and ordered to pay penance. They did so, but a greater penalty was to come. A year later, both men were married in Sidlesham on successive days, but for one of them there was to be no happy ever after: the new Mrs Latter died within three months, and Richard Latter by 1616. It was, thought the faithful, divine retribution.

The unfortunate Richard Latter was very likely related to the Latters of the adjoining parish of Selsey, and thirty-one years later the travails of young Thomas Latter provide a further indication that the game was passed down the generations. Thomas had hit Henry

Brand of Selsey on the head 'with a cricket batt', testified Henry's sister Margaret at Arundel quarter sessions in January 1648. It is unclear whether the cause of the fatal injury was malicious or accidental, but since Margaret accepted twenty-six shillings' compensation for her brother's death it is likely that it was no more than a mishap. It is not known if the episode dampened the Latter family enthusiasm for cricket, but it would not be surprising if it had. It must have been terrifying to face the quarter sessions accused of causing a death.

This was not a unique case. Twenty-four years earlier, at nearby Horsted Keynes in 1624, Jasper Vinall died in a bizarre accident. He and his friend Edward Tye were playing cricket when Tye hit the ball straight up in the air and attempted to hit it again as it fell. As he did so, Vinall, seeking to catch the ball, ran in behind his back and was struck heavily on the forehead by the flailing bat (value ½d, as the inquest noted). The coroner's jury acquitted Tye of malice and brought in a verdict of misadventure – proper in law, no doubt, but death by enthusiasm would have been more apt. The moment of taking a catch at cricket is one of total absorption and pure joy, and in that exultant mood poor Jasper was robbed of life.

Although the Church was generally prickly about cricket, there were exceptions. The 'old churchwardens' of Boxgrove, Sussex – Richard Martin Senior and Thomas West – were in hot water in 1622 for 'defending and mayntayning' the playing of cricket by their children.* Their arraignment in the church was clearly the end of a long saga, for the children had apparently been given 'sufficient warning' to desist and had ignored it; even worse, they played in the churchyard and 'used to break the church windowes with the ball'. It was also contended that 'a little childe had like to have her braynes beaten out with a cricket batt', although there was no evidence that such an incident had occurred. Nonetheless, a zealot thought it *might*, and the charge sheet was lengthened. The intriguing element of this case is the fathers' encouragement of the game, which suggests that they too had played cricket as children – probably around 1580–90.

* The children were William Martin, Richard Martin Junior and Raphe West, playing with two friends, Edward Hartley and Richard Slaughter.

The Church authorities continued to look on with disapproval. It seemed evident to them that not only was the game a thoroughly bad influence on godliness, it was thoroughly dangerous as well. Miscreants continued to be punished. In 1628, East Lavant in Sussex was a hotbed of mischief. At an ecclesiastical court in Chichester on 13 June, Edward Taylor and William Greentree were charged with 'playing at cricket in tyme of divine service'. Their defences differed. Taylor admitted that he was 'at a place where they played at cricket both before and after evening prayers but not in evening prayer time'. It did him no good: he was fined twelve pence for non-attendance at church and ordered to confess his guilt before the entire congregation of East Lavant church on Sunday, 22 June, in the following terms:

> Whereas I have heretofore highly displeased Almighty God in prophaning his holy Sabbath by playing at Crickett thereby neglecting to come to Church to devine service. I am now hartily sorry for my said offence desiring you here present to accept of this very penitent submission and joyne with me in prayer unto Almighty God for the forgiveness thereof saying Our Father which art in heaven . . .

Greentree was more brazen. He denied the offence until the court heard evidence to the contrary from the churchwarden. Faced with this deposition, Greentree offered a partial confession that 'he hath bene some tymes absent from Church upon the Sabbath day in tyme of divine service and hath bin at cricket with others of the parishe'. He was sentenced to return to court on 20 June, but no further records survive.

The ritual of apology must have made some members of the congregation very uncomfortable, for eight other men from the same village faced a similar charge only one month later. All received similar sentences, and the rigmarole of public penance was repeated, although the evidence suggests that it was not very effective.

By the 1630s the joyless spirit of Puritanism began to creep over the land. Its nature is exemplified in the life of the Reverend Thomas Wilson, an extreme Puritan who was appointed to the living of

Otham, near Maidstone, in 1631. Forty-one years later his biography was written by an admirer, George Swinnock, who wrote of Maidstone: 'Maidstone was formerly a very prophane town, insomuch that I have seen Morrice dancing, Cudgel-playing, Stool-ball, Crickets, and many other sports *open and publickly* on the Lords Day ... the former vain sinful customes of sports were reformed before his coming.'* The Reverend Wilson's career was mixed. He was suspended from his living in 1634 by the vehement anti-Puritan Archbishop Laud (1573–1644), and left Otham for Maidstone, accompanied by some of his flock. The warm welcome he received from like-minded souls suggests that Maidstone was not entirely populated by 'prophane' lovers of fun.

A further biography of another Puritan, Richard Culmer, by his son, also named Richard, reveals that he was suspended as Rector of Goodnestone, Kent, in 1634 for refusing to read the *Book of Sports*. Known as 'Blue Dick' for his eccentric habit of wearing a blue gown, the vengeful Reverend Culmer denounced the alleged informant who caused him to be suspended at Goodnestone so fiercely that he was imprisoned in the Fleet Prison for libel.** Around 1639 this joyless cleric was made assistant to the Reverend Austin of Harbledown parish, near Canterbury, where he rapidly became detested for seeking to suppress Sabbath sports and drunkenness. The parishioners of Harbledown were made of sterner stuff than those who had issued apologies so lamely in other places. In Harbledown, instead of penance, the cricket-loving parishioners provoked 'Blue Dick' by 'crickit playing before his door, to spite him'. I daresay they succeeded.

But 'Blue Dick' was not easily swayed from his convictions. He reproved the cricketers privately, and then – since this had no effect – publicly. The cricketers remained defiant, but cunning replaced provocation and they moved their game to 'a field near the woods'

---

* Some historians mistakenly attribute the damning of Maidstone to Wilson himself rather than Swinnock, for example David Underdown in *Start of Play* (2000), and Derek Birley in *The Willow Wand* (1979) and *A Social History of Cricket* (1999).
** If he was imprisoned for libel, the offending denunciation should have been written. However, I can find no record of it: possibly 'libel' was used sloppily, and the offence was actually slander.

in a remote part of the parish that was well away from prying eyes. It did not work. A suspicious Culmer sent his son to investigate, but Richard Junior was forced to retreat rapidly, followed by a hail of stones thrown at him by the irate cricketers. Time draws a veil over how, or whether, the stand-off was resolved.

The Reverend Culmer does not disappear from history – nor does his fanaticism. In 1643, in true Puritan style, he was appointed to destroy 'irreligious and idolatrous' monuments in Canterbury Cathedral. This was a task to his taste, and he set to with a will and wrecked much of the fifteenth-century stained glass with his own hands. Later, he conspired to have the rector of Minster ejected from his living and was himself appointed to it: at once he began to squabble with his new parishioners. His behaviour became ever more eccentric, and on one occasion he swarmed up the church steeple by night and removed the cross from the spire. The local parishioners were by now used to the exploits of their rector, and simply observed that to finish the job properly he should have pulled down the entire church, since its ground shape was itself a cross. The Reverend Culmer may stand forever as an icon of religious intolerance, and given the tenor of the times, his cricket-loving parishioners were lucky that he proved so ineffective.

The Puritan ambition, even pre-Cromwell, to create a devout nation gave power to the Church that was too often misused by fanatics. Social conditions added to the influence of the clerics. In the first half of the seventeenth century, the entire population of England was a mere 4 to 4½ million, of whom nearly 80 per cent lived south of the Humber, mostly in parishes of four to five hundred souls. The members of these small communities looked to their cleric and their squire for social and moral guidance, and rarely travelled beyond their own village. Most people were poor. Incomes were low and rents were high. Hardship was a daily reality. But where life was wretched, an early Poor Law existed to bring relief from distress. The Privy Council encouraged justices of the peace to find work for the poor so that the worst poverty was confined to the *anciens régimes* of Continental Europe.

In 1638 the Honourable Artillery Company was presented with land at Finsbury in London that would in time become one of the most famous of the early cricket grounds. Intriguing mentions of cricket abroad now begin to appear from time to time: Adam Olearius' *Voyages and Travels of Ambassadors* (1647; English translation 1662) suggests that in Persia (now Iran) a form of cricket was played. If so, it has yet to enter the sporting bloodstream of the nation, and it is hard to imagine Mullahs and Ayatollahs looking any more kindly on the game than did seventeenth-century Puritans. It is more likely to be a confusion in the translation.

In England, cricket-lovers continued to be prosecuted, the court hearings they faced being among the handful of mentions of the game during the seventeenth century. More Sabbath-breakers faced the archdeaconry court in Midhurst, Sussex, in 1637, when eight players were fined and ordered to make public penance. It is a tribute to cricket that it survived such disapproval.

If the misbehaviour of parishioners shocked the Church elders, they were dumbfounded when one of their own, the Reverend Henry Cuffin, was charged in 1629. Cuffin, a young curate of Ruckinge, Kent, and presumably as godly as his cloth, was censured for playing cricket 'in very unseemely manner with boyes and other very meane and base persons of our parrishe to the great scandal of his Ministerie and offence of such as sawe him play at the said game'. His defence was a stiletto in the ribs of those who peppered the charge with the unsuitability of the curate consorting with 'very meane and base persons'. Not so, said Cuffin, he had been playing with 'persons . . . of repute *and* fashion'. And moreover, he added that he 'doth diligentlie serve the Cure of Ruckinge'. It is not clear whether Reverend Cuffin would have accepted the charge meekly if he *had* been playing with the peasantry, but the presence among his fellow cricketers of 'persons of repute' made him belligerent in his defence. There is no record that he was censured, fined or ordered to make public penance, but the whole episode, apart from casting a light on the class-consciousness of the time, tells us that the peasants' game was moving upmarket.

A few years earlier, in 1625, an ill and near senile King James I had died unlamented, and his son, more talented and fitted for the throne in every way but one, succeeded him as Charles I. But his one defect was fatal – a stubborn determination to exercise absolute rule in an age when the spirit of the nation was for greater democracy. Charles did not seem to care, or perhaps even to notice, that his behaviour was draining support from the monarchy. He caused offence to friend and foe alike, making no effort to humour Parliament or people. He courted widespread disapproval by marrying a Catholic, Henrietta Maria of France, agreed only reluctantly to the Petition of Right, and declined to address grievances. He made promises only to break them. He persecuted the Puritans, who were mutilated, imprisoned and forced to flee the country.* But the cropping of ears, branding of bodies and slitting of noses increased dissent rather than deterring it. The struggle became severe, culminating in the Civil War, the execution of the King in 1649 and the birth of the Commonwealth with Cromwell at its head and Puritanism as its faith.

Oliver Cromwell is one of the great figures of English history, and he held a special fascination for me as by far the most illustrious Member of Parliament for my own constituency of Huntingdon. He and I are the only Members from that seat – thus far – to head a government. Cromwell became leader after a civil war in the country; I became leader as a civil war erupted within the Conservative Party. In each case, our enemies were implacable. Cromwell, General of the New Model Army and Lord Protector of the Commonwealth, was said by his foes to have enjoyed a boisterous youth. Whether this is true or not, his adult life was uneventful until, in his forties, he was propelled to the forefront of English life. As a private man he was commonplace. As a General, he was superb. As Lord Protector, his virtues and failings were on a grand scale; he can be mentioned with justice alongside Caesar and Napoleon.

The downside of Puritanism was that it robbed the Church of charity and put a premium on cant and piety. The prigs were in

---

* For example, in 1637 the Star Chamber sentenced three Puritan writers to imprisonment and to have their ears cropped for libelling bishops.

control. Lives were disrupted. Theatres were closed. Drama was stigmatised. The arts were restrained, and an anti-clerical feeling took root that would one day welcome the restoration of the monarchy. During the years of the Commonwealth poetry was the only art that prospered, thanks to the mighty imagination of Milton. It is an anomaly that Milton was a supporter of Puritanism: he was so by default, in his opposition to the excesses of an autocratic King. But neither his blindness, nor his gout, nor his many disappointments and hardships, could dim his advocacy of the liberty of the press and the elimination of prejudice, or his belief in taxation by the people, not the crown. He did not advocate the freedom to play cricket, or even deign to notice the game. Milton's nephew Edward Phillipps was, however, familiar with cricket. In a poem written in 1658, entitled 'Treatment of Ladies as Balls and Sports', he wrote: 'would that my eyes had been beaten out of my head with a cricket ball the day before I saw thee'. He was not always so averse to women, his preferred recreation being more basic: 'Ellen, all men command thy eyes/ Only I command thy thighs,' he wrote in 'The Art of Wooing and Complementing' (1655).

The Church, in its rigorous crackdown on Sunday cricketers, was a mild pre-echo of a Puritan ethic that sank deep into the British soul. It is, after all, not all that many years ago that professional cricket was prohibited on Sunday, as the spirit of the Lord's Day Observance Society held sway with much of contemporary opinion. Puritanism was tough on recreation, and it is unsurprising that cricket was targeted: the austere piety of the Puritans' beliefs, and their determination to make people devout, was bound to be in conflict with the exuberant joy of a ball game.*

But the courts did not always convict. At the Kent assizes held at Maidstone on 27 July 1652, six men of Cranbrook were accused of playing 'a certain unlawful game called cricket', but were acquitted as, to the horror of the Church, the justices ruled that the game was not unlawful. It was a rare blemish for the killjoys that was soon to

---

* In Ireland, the Major-General banned 'krickett'. 'Sticks' and 'balls' were ordered to be burnt by the common hangman; the players were not.

be corrected at Eltham, Kent, in 1654, when seven players were fined two shillings each by the churchwardens for playing on the Sabbath. Four parishioners of Hunton, Kent, were similarly charged in 1668. Even after the restoration of Charles II and the end of Puritan government in 1660, some of the old attitudes still prevailed. In May 1671 Edward Bound was held to be 'in contempt of the law of England' and 'a bad example to others' for playing cricket on a Sunday. However, he was luckier than earlier miscreants, and was exonerated under the General Pardon Act.

Cricket remained largely an amusement of village peasants. There are mere glimpses of the game through the lost seventeenth century. In 1611, Randle Cotgrave's French–English dictionary translated 'crosse' as 'a cricket staffe' and 'crosser' as 'to play at cricket', thus fuelling the occasional claim, surely erroneous, that 'criquet' is of French origin. Nor is it the case, as often claimed, that 'criquet' was played in France in 1478 before spilling across the Channel. There is no medieval text identifying 'criquet' as a game, since it was not: 'criquet' was, and is, the French name for an insect similar to a grasshopper, just as 'cricket' is in English. Moreover, an examination of the original text that has misled historians shows that the word 'criquet' was not actually used at all: it was in fact 'etiquet', meaning a 'small stick'. The text reads: 'une lieu où en jouoit a la boulle pre d'une ataché ou etiquet' ('a place where people were playing at boulle near a stake or peg' – 'boulle' probably being the game of boulles, or a forerunner of it, which to this day remains so popular in France).*
A further indication that cricket did not originate in France comes from a Swiss visitor, César de Saussure, one hundred years later, who reported, 'The English are fond of a game they call cricket.'** The English, not the French.

Even in the midst of Church and state persecution cricket began to take root, although, as with the earlier John Derrick case, it is sometimes only legal action that preserves a record of it. In May 1640,

* See Leonard Hector, 'The Ghost of Cricket Walks the Archives', *Journal of the Society of Archivists*, Vol. IV, No. 7, 1973, pp.579–80.
** Quoted in, for example, Derek Birley's excellent *The Willow Wand* (1979).

as the Civil War drew nearer, civil disputes still exercised the courts. A suit of trespass was brought in the King's Bench Division in which the plaintiff, Robert Spilstead, alleged trespass on his land near Chevening, Kent, during which cattle did 'bite the sprouts and young shootes thereof and ... tread and consume his grasse', and the defendants, Robert Shell and Michael Steavens, 'did spoile and subverte his ground with carriages' as well as 'take and carry away 400 of hoppoles'. In response, the defendants pleaded that the rector of Chevening owned the tithes of all the woods growing in the parish, and that they were merely farming them for him. A complicated argument about boundaries and jurisdiction then followed in which, to support his case that the damaged coppice was within his ownership, Spilstead gave evidence that 'about 45 years since there was a football playing and about 30 years since a cricketting* betweene the Weald and Upland and the Chalkehill'.

There is evidence that cricket may have begun climbing up the social scale by the 1640s, notwithstanding the distractions of the Civil War. On 29 May 1646 four gentlemen of 'prophane' Maidstone – William Cooper, Richard Marsh, Robert Sanders and Walter Francklyn – lost a game of cricket on the open common at Cox Heath, three miles south of the town, to two young Royalists, Thomas Harlackenden and Samuel Filmer. The nature of the game – and the politics of the victors – must have brought the Reverend Thomas Wilson close to apoplexy but it aroused great excitement in Maidstone. A bet on the outcome was laid – cash for candles, and when the loser failed to hand over the candles, court action followed.

Early fiction began to notice cricket, and it is one of 'the games of Gargantua' in an English translation of the works of Rabelais. But fiction can mislead as well as inform, and it did so with confident assertions that cricket was played in venerable colleges by the mid-seventeenth century. Although it is possible that it may have been, it is by no means certain. A reference to cricket at Winchester College in 1647 is based on an undated Latin poem, 'De Collegio Wintoniensi',

---

* A term especially associated with the Sevenoaks–Tonbridge area until the nineteenth century.

by Robert Mathew, a scholar who left the college that year. It relates how boys climbed a hill to play a game involving a ball ('*pila*') and bat ('*bacillo*') which *may* have been cricket, but he makes no mention of that name. A later reference to cricket at Winchester, circa 1665, is total fiction. It derives from a purely conjectural account of a boy's schooldays in W.L. Bowles's *The Life of (Bishop) Thomas Ken*, published in 1830, which imagines how

> our junior, 'the tear forgot as soon as shed', if it has ever for a moment been on his youthful cheek, is at ease among his companions of the same age; he is found, for the first time, attempting to wield a cricket bat; and, when his hour of play is over . . .

This piece of nineteenth-century fiction was seized on as evidence that cricket was played at Winchester and Eton in the mid-seventeenth century. This *could* be so, but fiction cannot be accepted as *bona fide* evidence.*

Nor can faulty memory. Writing about the genesis of club cricket, the *Cricketer Spring Annual* of 1933 records: 'Fifty years ago, an aged villager, close on 90 years . . . recollected seeing an old print, then hanging in a wayside cottage, showing "Cricket on ye old Green", and giving an approximate date of 1685.' This cannot be correct, since prints of cricket matches became available only in the 1740s, so even if this unlikely tale has a basis in fact, the picture referred to could not date before the middle of the eighteenth century.**

I am puzzled, too, by Altham's assertion in *The History of Cricket* that 'with the restoration [of Charles II in 1660], in a year or two it became the thing in London society to make matches and to form clubs'. If Altham is right I can find no evidence of it. So far as I can determine there is no record of a cricket match being played in London before the 1700s, and no mention of a club until 1722, sixty-two years after the Restoration.

Not that life was dull during the reign of Charles II. Popular

* Although it has been, for example in H.S. Altham's *The History of Cricket* and Ashley Mote's *The Glory Days of Cricket* (1997).
** Nonetheless, the date of 1685 appears in David Underdown's *Start of Play*.

history recalls the King as a merry monarch, easy-natured and lasci-
vious, and a welcome antidote to the pious Puritans. Charles would
have agreed with the American George Nathan that 'Women and
Englishmen are actors by nature,' since he lifted an old prohibition
and permitted women to act on the stage. Prior to his edict, women's
roles had been played by soft-featured young men, fearful that their
voices would break and their careers be over. The way was open for
Margaret Hughes, probably the first legitimate professional actress,
who became mistress to Charles I's nephew Prince Rupert, and went
on to gamble away a fortune.

More famous names soon followed, including 'a mighty pretty
woman' (according to Dr Johnson, a keen observer), who had probably had a relationship with the notorious libertine and poet Lord
Rochester when very young. 'Nelly, my life, tho' now thou'rt full
fifteen', rhymed Rochester, before becoming more explicit. Nell
Gwynne made her debut in Dryden's *The Indian Emperor* at the King's
Theatre in 1665, and was soon to catch the King's eye. Cricketers should
be grateful she did, for as we shall see, descendants of Charles II and
Nell were to play an important part in the history of the game.

By 1660 the Puritans were universally loathed, and the bells rang
to welcome home the King. An ultra-Royalist House of Commons,
eager to restore power to Charles, invited him home from exile. The
loyal populace lined the streets in welcome, and soon cheered and
roared as thirteen regicides of Charles I were brutally done to death.
To satisfy the mob the half-rotted corpses of Cromwell and Thomas
Ireton were dug up to be spat on and hanged. Three of the regicides
had been captured in Holland, and handed over to face execution by
one of the most unprincipled adventurers in English history. George
Downing, an itinerant preacher, became a chaplain in Sir Thomas
Fairfax's Puritan army before worming his way into Cromwell's
favour. As Scoutmaster General– Cromwell's top spy – in Scotland
he was well paid, and he invested his money wisely. He married well,
too, into the powerful Howard family, and was appointed British
ambassador to The Hague, to which his Letter of Credence was
written by Milton: 'A person of eminent Quality, and after a long

trial of his Fidelity, Probity and Diligence, in several and various negotiations, well approved and valued by us.'

In The Hague Downing spied on Royalists, including the future Charles II and his sister, the Princess of Orange. But his loyalties were elastic, and upon Cromwell's death this Puritan favourite turned coat and became an avid Royalist. The cynical and worldly Charles exploited him as his own spy, and later, for services rendered, appointed him a Baronet. But nothing was ever straightforward with Downing. After a while he fell out of favour, was committed to the Tower of London, released, and then turned to speculative building. One street, on the edge of what was once known as Thorney Island, near Whitehall, still carries his name – Downing Street.

The nation's fondness for the King did not last once his greed and self-indulgence became common knowledge. Within a few years the great diarist Samuel Pepys was noting of an alliance formed with Holland and Sweden that it was 'the only good public thing that hath been done since the King came into England'. Nor did anything match it in the years that followed, and it is fortunate that the nation never learned that its dissolute King was willing to take a pension from its arch-enemy, the King of France. Yet even without that knowledge, faithful Royalist support began to crumble. Events did little to help the King. For the average Londoner life was miserable. Grime was everywhere, as every household, shop and factory burned coal. Clothes, rarely changed, went grey, then black. The plague of 1664 – the fifth in under fifty years – and the Great Fire of London two years later devastated the City.

To public dismay, in 1673 the King's brother James married a Catholic, Mary of Modena. In 1678 Titus Oates developed the fantasy of a Popish plot by Jesuits to murder the King and burn London. The dissolute Parliament, in which Members were bribed and corrupted, was finally dissolved after eighteen years and a new Commons, hostile to the King, elected. Thrice dismissed, it was thrice re-elected. Charles died in 1685, muttering, 'Let not poor Nelly starve,' but with no words of comfort for his country, and his brother came to the throne as James II.

In the midst of these dramas there are mentions of cricket, which was now beginning to attract spectators. The quarter sessions in Maidstone on 28 March 1668 were attended by Sir Roger Twysden, who observed in his notebook: 'there was no great matter of consequence. A question was started whether an excise man could exact money from a poor person [who] at an horse-race or kricketing sold a bushel or two of malt made into drinks.' The Justice waived the excise duty on 'kricketing', which must have brought more agony to the Thomas Wilson school of morality – as must a further decision to allow the sale of ale to spectators. Sport and alcohol were about to begin a long-term relationship. So too were sport and gambling. In July 1697 'a great match at cricket was played in Sussex; they were eleven of a side, and they played for fifty guineas apiece'. In the seventeenth century that was a large sum of money – but it would soon be dwarfed.

The game was growing more popular. Thomas Lennard, who became Lord Dacre just before his eighth birthday, was an early spectator. In 1674 he married Anne Palmer, an illegitimate daughter of Charles II and the Duchess of Cleveland, and as son-in-law to the King was further ennobled as Earl of Sussex. His wife, only twelve years old at the time of her marriage, had such a wild temperament that by the age of fifteen her husband had removed her from Court to Hurstmonceaux Castle in Sussex. In June 1677, no doubt seeking a few quiet hours, the Earl drew £3 from his accounts to attend 'the crekitt match at Ye Dicker', a stretch of common land near to the castle.

It seems the young Countess was not seduced by cricket, because later that same year she deserted her husband to join her mother in Paris. Here life looked up for her when she *was* seduced by the British ambassador, the future Duke of Montagu. In the early 1680s she returned to her husband, with whom she had little in common. A few years later Sussex supported William of Orange in the 1688 Revolution, while she sided with her uncle, the deposed King, James II, then in exile at St-Germain. It must have been a real Jack Spratt marriage, for their views differed on every matter. Nor would she have been pleased when the Earl's extravagance and gaming losses compelled him to sell his estates.

But, so far as we know, their relationship never led to 'riot and battery'. This was the conviction obtained against Thomas Reynolds, Henry Gunter and a widow, Eleanor Lansford, for battering Ralph Thurston while 'being only spectators at a game of cricket'. The cause of the assault is not known, but it is most likely to have been a dispute over a bet: if so, they would have been wiser to have paid up, as did Sir John Pelham, Bart, who lost 2s.6d. in 'a wagger about a cricket match at Lewis' in 1694.

Five years later, philosophers were muscling in on the game. The text in 1699 of *The World Bewitched*, by Edward Ward, contains a dialogue between two Astrologers and the Author, in which it is asserted that: 'Quoits, cricket, nine-pins, and trap-ball will be very much in fashion, and more tradesmen may be seen playing in the fields, than working in their shops.'

As the seventeenth century came to a close, the British navy was carrying traders, missionaries and the game of cricket to many parts of the world – a naval chaplain on HMS *Assistance*, Henry Teonge, recorded a game of 'crickett' near Aleppo as early as 6 May 1676. In England, the game was widening its appeal. Cricket was moving beyond its base camp around the Weald. London, then the greatest city in Europe, was beginning to appreciate it. Noble families were beginning to patronise the game. Spectators, gamblers and publicans welcomed it as a vehicle for their interests. The press – then, as now, with a London bias – newly freed from censorship, was on hand to publicise it, or more typically the antics of prominent supporters and the size of their bets on matches.

For cricket, money was to be the root of all progress. As the eighteenth century dawned, most of the wealth of England was in the hands of a small number of families, who by and large had few time-consuming responsibilities and ample leisure in which to enjoy their good fortune. The age of the patron was not far away.

2

The Early Patrons

In 1700 England was on the eve of an empire that would carry to the world a language, a system of law, a parliamentary tradition and, more prosaically, team sports – above all cricket. The growth of this empire was not preordained, the product of no grand design, but the natural consequence of free trade, self-interest and fear. Its roots reached far back, but we may usefully trace it from the birthdate of cricket – the early age of Elizabeth.

From that time, trade had played a crucial role in extending British ambitions. Imports of sugar, coffee and tobacco from Virginia, and tea – by the mid-seventeenth century on its way to popularity – all whetted the appetite for more trade and greater overseas possessions. Industry and commerce expanded steadily, but by 1700 England was still only a middle-ranking power. By contrast, France had an economy twice the size of England's and a population nearly four times as large, whereas India – destined to become a British possession – had nearly one-quarter of the trade of the entire world. The wider world was far away from England's damp island: it took up to seven weeks to sail to America against the winds, nine weeks to Barbados, and six months to round the Cape of Good Hope en route to Calcutta. But events and sea power were to shape a momentous century. No one could have dreamed what lay ahead.

In the English villages, peasants and craftsmen were finding a wider market for their produce in the towns and cities. Basic crops of wheat, barley and rye went to make bread for the masses. Barley had a wider use: it made malt for the beer and ale that had long been the drinks of England, except in the cider districts of the western counties. Even children drank weak beer, since it was often healthier than impure water. The roads were dire, which restricted the movement of men and materials. Waterways and rivers were used as highways. West Country cheeses were carried to London by sea. When harvests were plentiful, surplus corn was exported. As trade grew, so did profits for the merchants who reinvested in agriculture. The Industrial Revolution lay half a century ahead, and England still enjoyed a truly beautiful landscape. The desecration of forests for timber, coal and housing had not yet begun. Swamps and wildernesses were being tamed for agriculture, and population growth had not yet marred the land with the scars of development.

Other than in a handful of villages, no one was much bothered about the infant game of cricket. Greater events, far away from the cradle of the game, were shaping the future. But cricket was putting down roots. It was still a rustic sport, poorly endowed and, so far as we know, confined to the south of England. Teams had no set number of players. Rules were haphazard, and varied from village to village. Dress was variable. Bats were curved. Two stumps – most likely so-called because the primitive game was played with the stumps of trees as a wicket – were still the norm. Bowling was underarm and along the ground (hence 'bowling'), Drake-style, but faster. The concept of the carefully-prepared modern cricket square was unknown, and wickets were pitched on bumpy, grassy surfaces that were unpredictable and could cause nasty injuries. It would be another hundred years before anyone wore protective leg or shin pads, even though a serious injury could cost a rural player his livelihood.

In the early 1700s these hardy players had no concept of the changes that lay ahead for their game as they nursed their bumps and bruises. For the eighteenth century would see the establishment of a governing body, albeit self-appointed, the first laws codified, the game spread through and beyond the southern counties of England, scores and records kept spasmodically, and the style of cricket evolve. Even ladies' teams were formed. Cricket would emerge from its infancy.

Early in the new century the game was adopted by influential patrons, and became a welcome distraction in London. The capital may have been the centre of wealth and the leader in fashion, but daily life was harsh for the majority of its citizens. The London of early cricket was a town of unpaved streets and open sewers, where garbage and bodily waste were tipped from the windows of leaky, broken-down slums in which eight to ten of the poorest people would huddle in a single unheated room. In the worst quarters, decrepit houses quite literally fell down on their dwellers' heads. In such conditions life expectancy was low and infant mortality huge. Children slept in the streets, clothed only in rags, and no one was safe out at night if the gin shops had been busy in the evening – as usually they had.

For most of the sick, folk remedies were all that were on offer, and superstitious nonsense was widely believed: it was thought efficacious to apply a live toad to the kidneys to treat a urinary infection, or a hanged man's hands to a cyst. But some tangible improvements to health care were being made. Philanthropists founded hospitals in the major towns and cities. In London, new hospitals – including maternity hospitals – were established to supplement St Bartholomew's and St Thomas's, which had served the capital for six hundred years. Guy's and Westminster Hospitals were born out of private philanthropy, but the demands of healthcare also led to the foundation of St George's and the London and Middlesex Hospitals, all of which opened their doors between 1720 and 1745. And such a licentious age brought the Lock Hospital into being – it cared for sufferers from venereal diseases. The Foundling Hospital, another new arrival, cared for destitute children and raised funds through a public lottery.

For all its primitive nature, London was a vibrant city, and enjoyed greater pre-eminence in the nation than ever before or after in its history. In 1700 it boasted two thousand coffee shops, where the rich smell of roasted coffee offset the stench of unwashed bodies and the reek of tobacco. Coffee shops became a centre of social life, where gossip and news were exchanged. One coffee-house keeper,

Edward Lloyd, set up a pulpit for shipping news, and Lloyd's of London was born. Each shop had its own clientele. The Cocoa Tree Chocolate House attracted Tories, while Whigs would be found at St James's. Poets favoured Wills Coffee House, and the clergy gathered at Truby's. Aristocrats played cards at White's Chocolate House, where professional gamblers waited to fleece them.

London's streets were alive with vendors selling flowers, milk or newspapers; there were bootblacks, domestic servants on errands and porters carrying everything from letters to heavy burdens. Elms lined many of the streets, but so did household waste and effluent. Residents had to endure the stench of livestock being driven to market – or to the abattoirs on Tower Hill. The animals battled with the fashionable modes of transport: sedan chairs carried by 'chairmen' who feared that the new invention of umbrellas would cut their trade,* and hackney carriages drawn by horses. The River Thames was covered with ships, boats and barges of all kinds, and the smell of fish leaving Billingsgate would linger in the air.

Cleaner air could be enjoyed either by walking beyond London to the rural villages of Hampstead or Kentish Town, or in the 'lungs' of the city – Hyde Park, Green Park, Kensington Gardens or St James's Park, where society strolled in their finery hoping to see and be seen. London drew people in like a magnet, and by 1730 had 6–700,000 inhabitants, compared with only 20–30,000 in Birmingham, Manchester and Sheffield. Dr Samuel Johnson, a native of Lichfield, with a modest population of three thousand, would say of his adopted home: 'When a man is tired of London, he is tired of life.' It was a tribute to the vibrancy of a town that was, among other things, embracing cricket with enthusiasm.

It is, perhaps, not surprising that it did so. Leisure for the masses was limited and often violent. Cockfighting was brutal but popular. Bare-knuckle boxing, often in the yards of taverns or in Marylebone fields, competed with cricket as a rising entertainment. It began as a

* Jonas Hanway (1712–86) is credited with inventing the umbrella, but this is doubtful: in 1710, two years before Hanway was born, Swift wrote: 'The tuck'd up seamstress walks with hasty strides/While streams run down her oil'd umbrella's sides' ('City Show').

spectator sport in the 1730s, with the great Jack Broughton as the main attraction. Broughton wrote the primitive 'rules' of the ring, and was sponsored by the cricket-loving, Scots-bashing Duke of Cumberland, who even built a theatre in which to stage his main bouts. Ahead for boxing lay Daniel Mendoza, Tom Cribb and a long line of champions who would further popularise the sport.

An even more violent entertainment was execution day at Tyburn. It was a holiday: shops were closed, stands were erected for spectators and the condemned were drawn through the streets in carts. Life was cheap for the very poor, and often the judicial system robbed them of it for modest offences. In the fifty years from 1690 the number of offences carrying the penalty of death by hanging rose fourfold, to 160: sheep stealing, minor theft, any number of offences against property, all carried a capital sentence. The criminal code was barbarous for a nation that was among the least violent in Europe.

Cricket was not a civilising influence in the bustle of eighteenth-century London – such a Victorian notion lay far ahead. Early cricket sponsors came from dubious sources: pubs and breweries eager to sell their product, and rich patrons attracted by the scope for gambling. These early patrons are elusive figures. Little is known of their character and lifestyle, and such scraps as are available offer only a partial portrait. Nonetheless, early newspapers, court cases over wagers, and memoirs of the great families enable us to piece together some of the jigsaw. The midwives of cricket were a mixed bunch: some mad, some bad, and some idle. All would have vanished into obscurity but for their promotion of cricket.

At the time the more raffish gentry took up the game, it was growing in popularity in rural areas. The Church, its old enemy, remained as hostile as ever, but the public were warming to the spectacle, and matches often attracted huge crowds. A rough and tumble, or an illegal affray, was a frequent accompaniment to a competitive game or an unsettled bet, and in a violent age that may have been an added attraction.

All this made news, and the early newspapers – soon to be joined (in 1706) by the first evening paper, the *London Evening News* –

lapped it up. Reports in the *Post Boy*, the *Postman* or the *Weekly Journal* were sparse, but then as now, trivia made good copy, and the size of bets laid and the rivalries between aristocrats were widely reported. Attractive games were advertised by sponsors, often inn-keepers keen to attract a thirsty crowd, and tended to be between teams of eleven or twelve players, though there is no clue as to why that number was settled upon. In every (advertised) instance the match was arranged to accommodate a wager:

> These are to inform Gentlemen, or others, who delight in cricket playing, that a match of cricket, of 10 Gentlemen on each side, will be play'd on Clapham Common, near Fox-Hall [Vauxhall], on Easter Monday next, for £10 a head each game (five being design'd) and £20 the odd one.

Such an advertisement, from the *Post Boy* of 30 March 1700, is typical, but even the 'gentlemen' players were not always regarded with respect. A burlesque poem of 1701 parodied a Tunbridge beau:

> It's true he can at cricket play,
> With any living at this day,
> And fling a coit or toss a bar,
> With any driver of a car:
> But little nine-pins and trap-ball,
> The Knight delights in most of all.
> Conceiving like a prudent man,
> The other might his honour stain,
> So scorns to let the Publick see,
> He should degrade his Quality.

'He should degrade his Quality' – this was pure snobbery from the author, who evidently believed that cricket should remain a 'peasant's game'. But not all poems were written to mock. Five years later, in 1706, the far more elegant pen of William Goldwin published *Musae Juveniles*, a collection of poems in Latin, one of which, '*In Certamen Pilae*', describes a cricket match, giving evidence of the nature of the contemporary game as well as confirming that it was played at Eton when he was a pupil there in the 1690s. Goldwin later became vicar of St Nicholas, Bristol, and his famous poem tells us much about early cricket. His lines reveal that batsmen had curved bats, and the ball was a leathern sphere, thus confirming that early cricket employed the leather casing for balls first adopted by the Romans nearly two thousand years earlier. The umpires (there were two) officiated whilst 'leaning on their bats', and the scorers 'cut the mounting score on sticks with their little knives'. Batsmen could be caught out by a fieldsman who 'with outstretched palms joyfully accepts [the ball] as it falls'. Finally, Goldwin refers to the 'rustic throng', thus telling us that cricket was a spectator sport from the outset, and that its first supporters were rural working men.

While matches between 'gentlemen' were growing in popularity, more impromptu games were also thriving on common land at Chelsea, Kennington, Walworth, Clapham and Mitcham, as well as on rural grounds around the Weald. The rustic cricketers were not always welcome. As the *Postman* warned on 5 April 1705:

> This is to give notice to any person whatsoever, that they do
> *not* presume to play at foot-ball, or cricket, or any other sport
> or pastime whatsoever, on Walworth Common, without lease
> of the Lords of that Manor . . . as they will answer the same
> when they are sued at law for so doing.

The name, Walworth Common, implies that it was common land, but the lords of that manor felt otherwise. They wished to discourage cricket, as did their allies the Church, who were only too happy to promote propaganda against it. A contemporary pamphlet recounted the tale of four young men unwise enough to play cricket on a Sunday. As they did so, a 'Man in Black with a Cloven-foot' rose out of the ground. The Devil, for it was said to be he, flew up into the air 'in a dark cloud with flashes of fire', but left behind him a very beautiful woman. Two of the players lost interest in the game and stepped up to kiss her. This was a bad move. The young men fell down dead: it was, after all, the Sabbath. Their companions, shocked at the result of such sin, ran home, appropriately to Maidenhead, where they lay in a 'distracted condition'. The local minister prayed with them, and in church preached a sermon on the theme 'Remember the Sabbath Day to Keep it Holy' (Exodus 20, Verse 8). For good measure, he denounced cricket as a 'hellish pastime' – thus explaining to the congregation why the Devil was so attracted to it. At the inquest into the deaths of the two unfortunate youths, the coroner and the jury attributed their fate to 'the last judgement of God, for prophaining his Holy Sabbath'. In cricket's infancy, such poppycock resonated among the ill-educated peasantry. No one even considered a more likely cause of death: the players were struck by lightning, and the beautiful woman was a figment of the fevered imagination of a sunny day.

More eminent men than these rustic boys found themselves the victims of pamphlet propaganda. In May 1712 a broadsheet, *The Devil and the Peers*, attacked the Duke of Marlborough and an unidentified peer for playing a single-wicket match in Berkshire. This was real villainy, for the match was on a Sunday – *and* for a wager of twenty guineas. The unidentified peer, 'who went to Eaton School', was most likely Marlborough's son-in-law Francis Godolphin, known by his courtesy title Lord Railton. Godolphin won, but – for even hostile pamphleteers must fawn over a Duke – not before His Grace had 'gave 'em several Master strokes'. Marlborough was, after all, a national hero, and Sunday or not, master strokes were master strokes. Despite his sycophancy to Marlborough, the sour old pamphleteer predicted that the 'Sabbath-Breakers will not escape the Hands of Justice'. He was wrong: not even the Church dared to move against the Duke, who heavily outgunned minor officials, as well as the pamphleteer.

So, of course, did the early patrons, all of whom had wealth or title, or both, to bolster their immunity from potential attackers. This is fortunate for cricket, since otherwise the spoilsports might have won the day. Aristocratic patronage began to lend a social respectability to cricket that it badly needed. Stow's *Survey of London* (1720) mentions cricket as no better than football, wrestling, bell-ringing, shovelboard and drinking in alehouses as an amusement of 'the more common sort', but this slur would soon become redundant. Samuel Johnson played cricket at Oxford University in 1729, and Horace

Walpole refers to cricket at Eton between 1727 and 1734.* Eton cricket also features in a poem entitled 'The Priestcraft or the Way to Promotion' printed in 1734 'behind the Chapter House in St Paul's churchyard' and written by an eighteenth-century angry young man, J. Wilford, who offers tongue-in-cheek advice to 'the inferior clergy of England' about how to behave at the forthcoming election. In the midst of his rant he unwittingly confirms that cricket was of rising interest:

> No more with Birch, let Eton's pupils bleed;
> No more with learned lumber stuff their head,
> Her rival fee! Like Nursery of Fools,
> Who practice Cricket, more than Busby's Rules.

Clearly, the aristocracy's fascination for cricket was being reflected in the schools and universities to which they sent their children.

Three early patrons stand above the rest: Edward Stead, a sponsor of Kentish cricket, and two sponsors of Sussex, the Duke of Richmond and Sir William Gage. Stead (1701–35) lived the proverbial 'short life but a merry one'. In his teens he inherited large estates in Kent, but he soon set about losing his fortune at cards and dice, to which, along with cricket, he was addicted. 'The devil invented dice,' said St Augustine, but Stead was not listening. He was so reckless that at the age of twenty-two he was forced to mortgage some of his lands to repay his gambling debts and raise capital.

By night Stead played the tables. By day he abandoned them for cricket, and formed his own team, 'Stead's Men', or sometimes 'Men of Kent'. Throughout the 1720s he arranged and played in many games – with mixed fortunes. On one occasion, Stead's men were in a winning position when their Chingford opponents refused to finish the game. The cause of their refusal is unknown, but as a large wager depended on the result, Stead went to court to get his money. His plea was heard by the aptly-named Lord Chief Justice Pratt, who, it

* Walpole (1717–91) was the fourth Earl of Orford and third son of Prime Minister Robert Walpole. A sometime MP for Callington, Castle Rising and King's Lynn, he is most remembered for his letters and memoirs.

was reported, 'not understanding the [rules of the] game, or having forgot', simply ordered the match to be finished from where it left off, and made no order that Stead should be paid the sum due on the wager. There is no record of whether the game was ever completed or the wager settled. Nor do we know if the insolent journalist who doubted the Lord Chief Justice's competence was fined for contempt.

But the ruling that the game should be finished had a favourable repercussion for cricket, if not for Stead. When, a week later, in Writtle, Essex, a zealous justice of the peace summoned a constable to disperse a few innocent locals playing the game, a cricket-lover wrote indignantly to the press with the unanswerable question: was it legal to play cricket in Kent *at the order of the Lord Chief Justice* – but not legal to play in Essex?

With or without his guineas, Stead played on. In August 1726 the 'Men of London and Surrey' faced him for twenty-five guineas at Kennington Common. Two years later his team was matched against the Duke of Richmond for 'a large sum of money' at Cox Heath. In the same year Stead and another of cricket's early patrons, Sir William Gage, played an eleven-a-side game for fifty guineas at the Earl of Leicester's park at Penshurst. Stead's men won after leading by 52 to 45 on the first innings. The final margin of victory is not recorded. It was the third occasion that summer that the 'Men of Kent' had defeated the Sussex team.

This fixture seems to have been a popular event, for the teams were rivals again the following year at Penshurst, when Gage obtained his revenge and won back double his money. The star of the game was a groom of the Duke of Richmond, Thomas Waymark, who 'turned the scale of victory by his agility and dexterity'. Undeterred by this defeat, Stead, whose enthusiasm was greater than his success, played on – the gambler's 'win some, lose some' mentality being his natural instinct. In August 1730 he and three other gentlemen played, and lost, against four men of Brentford for a 'considerable wager' in the deciding match in a series of three.* In June 1731 his '11 Gentlemen

* The earlier matches had been played at Westerham on 28 May and at Kew Green on 4 June.

of Kent' lost to '11 of Sunbury', and thirty guineas changed hands. On 4 September a further (unknown) sum was wagered on a Surrey and Kent game, but a severe rainstorm washed out the fixture when Surrey, with three men to bat, needed twelve runs to win. The drenched cricketers agreed to a rematch, and Stead's guineas were temporarily saved.

Stead was a graceful loser, and his nonchalance won him powerful friends. In August 1733 his team was matched against one raised by Frederick Louis, the Prince of Wales, the eldest son of George II, for a plate valued at £30. The game was played at Moulsey Hurst, Surrey, and the Prince's men won. The contest was repeated in 1735, when Stead backed a London club against the Prince's 'Surrey' team, and gained a narrow win by one wicket. It was to be the gambler's last throw: Stead died a month later near Charing Cross, having done much to popularise early cricket.

One of Stead's familiar opponents, Sir William Gage, succeeded to a baronetcy in 1713, at the age of eighteen. Nine years later he was elected to the Commons as MP for Seaford, which he retained until his death twenty-two years later. His estate, Firle in East Sussex, was one of the cradles of cricket, and it is likely that he learned to love the game as a boy. Apart from contests against Stead, Gage's 'Sussex XI' were familiar opponents of the Duke of Richmond, the Earl of Middlesex, Lord John Sackville and the Prince of Wales. A letter to Richmond written by Gage on 16 July 1725 catches the flavour of the times:

> My Lord Duke,
>
> I have received this moment Your Grace's letter and am extremely happy Your Grace intends as the honour of making one [presumably a game, but possibly also a wager] on Tuesday, and will without fail bring a gentleman with me to play against you, one that has played very seldom for these several years. I am in great affliction from being shamefully beaten yesterday, the first match I played this year. However, I will muster up all my courage against Tuesday's engagement. I will trouble Your Grace with nothing more than I wish you success in everything but ye cricket match.

The wording of the letter suggests that the approach for either a game or a wager came from Richmond, and may have been for a single-wicket contest. Gage is keen to assure the Duke that he and his partner are in neither good form nor practice, although whether this was really the case or was intended to entice a larger wager is unclear. The fact that Gage tells Richmond he has only just played his first game of the year, with the season so well advanced, suggests, if true, that he may have been engaged on parliamentary duties.

Other games against Richmond were certainly between teams of eleven a side, for one, at Lewes in August 1730, was postponed because the Duke's most accomplished player, his groom Thomas Waymark, fell ill. It is likely that Richmond was being cautious as the wager was high. In any event, the match was off.

Gage's enthusiasm for cricket is summed up in a letter from John Whaley to Horace Walpole in August 1735, after he had seen Gage's Sussex team beat the Gentlemen of Kent: 'They seem as much pleased as if they had got an Election. We have been at Supper with them all and have left them at one o'clock in the morning laying betts about the next match.' Where bets were concerned, return matches were common courtesy, and later in the month the Earl of Middlesex, supported by his brother Lord John Sackville and nine other gentlemen, defeated Gage and his Sussex colleagues to secure their revenge and – perhaps – recover their money.

The combination of cricketing rivalry and betting could be combustible. In July 1741 Slindon beat Portslade in a game attended by Gage and the Duke of Newcastle. On 5 August, Gage wrote to Newcastle to report the aftermath:

> ... the night of the cricket match after Your Grace left the field there was a bustle occasioned by the cry of 'Calves head' being resented by some of Your Grace's friends and some hearty blows were given ... the Western cricketers that had left the hearing of it returned with their cricket batts and dealt some heavy blows which carried the victory ... I am glad the cricket match was over before this happened.

Sometimes the blood flowed during a match. The *Old Whig* reported on 1 July 1736 that 'two famous Richmond men' were playing two London men, Mr Wakeland (a distiller) and Mr Oldner, when one of the Richmond men (who were not named) was badly injured. The ball 'hit up against the side of his nose, broke his nose, hurt his eye, and bruised his face . . . he lost a great quantity of blood'. 'Notwithstanding this accident some Human Brutes who laid [bets] against the Richmond men, insisted he should play . . . after his nose was set, and his face dressed, and one side tied up, [he] attempted to play again.' It was gallant but unavailing. The blood flowed again, and the match had to be rescheduled.

In its long history, cricket talent has often passed from father to son – for example, in recent years the Pollocks, Cowdreys and Stewarts, among others– and this phenomenon was evident with the greatest of the early patrons, the Sackville family. Three Sackvilles were prominent supporters of cricket, and a second wave was to follow. Lionel Sackville was created first Duke of Dorset in 1720, and in his pomp maintained his own 'cricketing place' at Knole near Sevenoaks: it was the first ground to be regularly mown, rolled and cosseted in preparation for cricket. There is no record of how often games were played at Knole, but Dorset employed as a gardener Valentine Romney, who according to the *Kentish Gazette* 'was held to be the best cricket player in the world'. It was, of course, a 'world' still confined to the Home Counties of England, but the Duke's employment of Romney bore testimony to his enthusiasm, which was inherited by his sons Charles and John.

In 1734, at the age of twenty-three, Charles Sackville, bearing the courtesy title of Earl of Middlesex, was elected Member of Parliament for East Grinstead, the family borough, but the embryonic politician had a far greater enthusiasm for cricket than for government. One year after his election he was seen at cricket matches, in the company of the Prince of Wales, more often than in the Commons. The two men raised teams to play one another, and in one encounter Sackville's team won by four wickets for a prize of £1,000,* even though

---

* Kent (Sackville) *vs* London and Middlesex (Prince of Wales) on 12 and 30 July 1735.

the Prince had employed Cook of Brentford, reckoned to be one of the best bowlers of the day. A return match at Bromley Common saw Sackville win by ten wickets. The Prince's team batted first and scored 73, a reasonable score on the bumpy wickets of the day, but it was easily topped by Sackville's Kent, who amassed 97. When London collapsed in the second innings for 32, Kent needed only a mere 9 runs for a comfortable win. A contemporary report gives a flavour of the social niceties when a Prince of the realm was involved. The Earl and his team were in place by 11 a.m., together with a multitude of spectators, but the stumps were not pitched until the Prince arrived two hours later, having driven leisurely to the ground in a one-horse chair. At the end of the game, pandemonium ensued as the Prince departed. The large crowd, boisterous and refreshed with strong ale, mingled together and 'a great deal of mischief was done, by some falling from their horses, or others being rode over . . . and one man was carried off for dead as HRH passed by'. It must have been mayhem.

Middlesex was an easy-natured character, who loved fun, was open-handed and lavished substantial sums of money on opera as well as cricket. Not everyone approved. In 1743 the acidic Horace Walpole wrote to his friend Horace Mann:

> There is a new subscription formed for an Opera next year to be carried on by The Dilettanti, a club, for which the nominal qualification is having been in Italy and the real one being drunk: the two chiefs are Lord Middlesex and Sir Francis Dashwood who were seldom sober the whole time they were in Italy.

This was a harsh judgement, but standard fare for Walpole, who did not always escape unscathed himself. One victim jeered that 'he used to enter a room as if he were stepping on a wet floor with his hat crushed between his knees'. In short, he minced. Perhaps Walpole's sharp tongue was a weapon of self-defence. If so, he was exercising it again on 4 May 1743:

> Lord Middlesex is the impresario and must ruin the House of Sackville by a course of these follies. Beside what he will lose

this year, he has not paid his share of the losses of the last, yet
he is singly undertaking another for next season, with the
utmost certainty of losing between £4000 and £5000.

Not everyone was so censorious – or ungrateful. Years later, an
obituarist praised Middlesex as 'a leading Patron of Opera'. Walpole
would have scoffed, and it beggars the imagination what he might
have written of the scale of present-day opera subsidies. The Duke of
Dorset shared Walpole's analysis of his son's opera ventures, for he
advised the King *not* to subscribe: if the son fell out of favour with the
monarch, the father had no intention of doing so. Walpole dripped
contempt: 'Lord Middlesex is so obstinate that this will probably only
make him lose £1000 more.'

Such episodes infuriated Dorset, who sought a steadying influence
for his wayward heir. He found one in Grace Boyle, the daughter
of Viscount Shannon, whom Middlesex married, no doubt under
duress, in 1744. Grace was no beauty – she was unkindly described as
'low and ugly but a vast scholar', and 'very short, very plain, very
yellow, and a vain girl, full of Greek and Latin'. She seems an unlikely
bride for the pleasure-loving Middlesex, but Dorset was pleased to
have tied his son down: in relief, he settled £2,000 a year on him.
Unfortunately, Middlesex didn't tie Grace down, and she became the
mistress of the Prince of Wales, which suggests either that the Prince
loved fine minds or that Grace was less plain than her detractors
claimed. Or perhaps not – the historian Thomas Babington Macaulay
claimed, rather spitefully, that the Prince of Wales often quitted 'the
only woman he loved [his wife] for ugly and disagreeable mistresses'.
In any event, Middlesex may have had other things on his mind: the
first cricket laws were framed that same year.

The old Duke died in 1765, and Middlesex succeeded to the Dorset
title. Sackville manuscripts were soon recording bills for cricket bats
(at 2s.6d. each) and cricket balls (at 3s.6d. each). But the new Duke's
final years were unhappy; he passed them as a 'proud, disgusted,
melancholy, solitary man', and his behaviour became irrational and
unbalanced. When Grace died in 1763 he lived with a girl he hoped
to marry, but was thwarted when his family prevented the match,

citing his unstable mental state. The second Duke of Dorset died in 1769, disillusioned, insolvent, mad, and a widower.

His brother John followed an eerily similar path. He entered Parliament even younger than Middlesex, being elected for Tamworth at only twenty-one years of age. He sat in the Commons for thirteen years, but, the family preference being strong, cricket took priority over his parliamentary duties. He played for his brother's teams, as well as those he arranged himself. As an Equerry to Queen Caroline from 1736 he too came to know the Prince of Wales well, and in 1737 the two of them arranged what the *London Evening Post* called 'the greatest match at cricket that has ever been contested'. The game, held on 15 June at Kennington Common, was one of the social events of the year. A pavilion was erected for the Prince, and the press of humanity was so great that one poor woman, caught in the crowd, had her leg broken. Her pain was alleviated with a generous gift of ten guineas from the Prince. Lord John Sackville had assembled a fine team, and Kent won comfortably. A return match was arranged, but Kent won again, by an innings.

In June 1744 Sackville gained a small measure of immortality by taking a crucial catch as Kent beat England by one run at the famous Artillery Ground in London. The poet James Dance, alias James Love (a name he adopted after marrying a Miss Lamour), described it in 'Cricket: An Heroic Poem', published on 5 July that year:

> Swift as the falcon, darting on its prey,
> He springs elastick o'er the verdant way;
> Sure of success, flies upwards; with a bound,
> Derides the slow approach and spurns the ground.
> Prone slips the youth, yet glories in his fall,
> With arm extended shows the captive ball.

In other words, Lord John took a running catch and fell over. The description of the event was a bit floral, and the poet confessed in one of his mock-scholarly footnotes that 'though this description may a little exceed the real fact, it may be excused as there is a great deal of foundation for it'. If so, one wonders why the apologetic footnote was penned.

In that same year there were tricky hurdles for Lord John to face off the field. Two days after his mistress Frances Leveson-Gower gave birth to his child at Woburn Abbey, her irate parents compelled them to marry. Sackville's cricketing friend the Prince of Wales soothed the ruffled in-laws and offered to make up Lord John's allowance from his father to £800 a year, which was accomplished by appointing him a Lord of the Bedchamber. It was a much-needed sinecure, for lack of funds was a constant burden for this impecunious second son. He had hoped to inherit the Sussex estates of his elderly great-uncle Spencer Compton,* valued at £3,000–£4,000 per annum, but upon his expected benefactor's death he received nothing. His great-uncle may have feared the money would be squandered.

A lost inheritance, an unwanted child and a hasty and unwelcome marriage were not the sum total of Lord John's misfortunes. The taint of mental instability was as strong in the Sackville genes as the love of cricket. In 1746, as a Lieutenant Colonel in the 2nd Foot Guards, he was arrested for desertion as his regiment was about to embark for overseas service. He was released to confinement in a private lunatic asylum, and hustled abroad by his embarrassed family. In 1760 Lord Fitz Maurice reported that Sackville was eking out an existence in Lausanne, 'living on a poor allowance and but very meanly looked after. He was very fond of coming among the young English at Lausanne, who suffered his company at times from motives of curiosity, and sometimes from humanity. He was always dirtily clad, but it was easy to perceive something gentlemanlike in his manner and a look of birth about him, under all his disadvantages. His conversation was a mixture of weakness and shrewdness, as is common to most madmen.' When told his brother Lord George had been dismissed from the army in 1759 for failing to obey an order to advance at the Battle of Minden, John immediately responded, 'I always told you my brother George was no better than myself.' Unstable or not, he seems to have had an accurate self-image.

John Russell, Duke of Bedford, was related by marriage to Lord

* The Earl of Wilmington, who succeeded Sir Robert Walpole as Prime Minister in 1742.

John Sackville, and shared his enthusiasm for cricket. In 1741, before six thousand spectators, his team played a match at Wotton, Bucks, against a side raised by Richard Grenville, brother-in-law of Pitt the Elder. Grenville was obviously keen to win, for he paid his players two guineas each, but he lost the game, and no doubt his bets too. Ralph Vernay, a critic of gambling, wrote: 'These matches will be as pernicious to poor people as horse races for the contagion spreads.' Bedford also lost two games at Woburn Park to teams raised by the Earls of Sandwich and Halifax, but he was successful a year later in beating a London side at the Artillery Ground. The following year, 1743, London had their revenge, winning two matches, the latter at the Artillery Ground for five hundred guineas. Nothing daunted, the Duke played on and continued to sponsor games at Woburn Park until at least 1756.

The Prince of Wales was not the only cricketing enthusiast with royal blood. Charles Lennox, the second Duke of Richmond (1701–50), a grandson of Charles II and his French mistress Louise de Kérouaille, later Duchess of Portsmouth, was among the most important of the early patrons. Introduced to cricket at an early age, he became a lover of the game, patron of matches, sponsor of players and father and grandfather of significant figures in cricket history. At the age of eighteen, as Lord March, he was married to a thirteen-year-old girl in settlement of a gambling debt. The cynical ceremony over, the bridegroom toured Europe and the child-bride returned to her education. Five years later, on the eve of a formal reunion, they met by chance and were entranced with one another. They enjoyed a long and idyllic marriage before Richmond died at the age of forty-nine; his Duchess, the once child-bride Sarah, survived him by less than a year. His friend Lord Hervey, often the possessor of a wicked tongue, wrote in his *Memoirs*:

> There never lived a man of more amiable composition; he was kindly, benevolent, generous, honourable and thoroughly noble in his way of acting, talking and thinking; he had constant spirits, was very entertaining and had a great deal of knowledge though, not having had a school education, he was a long while reckoned ignorant by the generality of the world.

It was a kindly and apt epitaph, and surprising too, from a man once described by Alexander Pope as 'a painted child of dirt that stinks and stings'. The Duke of Richmond would have been flattered by the tribute, but more pleased, perhaps, that both his sons were able cricketers.

In his prime the Duke was fastidious about how his team was turned out. In 1726 he paid for 'waistcoats, breeches and caps' for his cricketers, and two years later burdened them with 'yellow velvet caps with silver tassels'. Apart from these sartorial touches he was also meticulous about the rules under which he played, and two games against a Mr Alan Brodrick – one to be played in July 1727 in Surrey, the second in August in Sussex – saw these spelled out in great detail. The pitches were of twenty-three yards; a player falling sick during the match could be replaced; any player voicing an opinion on any point of the game would be turned out, with, of course, the exceptions of the Duke and Mr Brodrick; each side should provide one umpire; batsmen must touch the umpires' stick for every run or it would not count; and no player could be run out unless the wicket was broken by a fielder with the ball in his hands. From these Articles of Agreement (reproduced in full as Appendix 1, page 399) we see glimpses of how conformity began to be reached in the rules of cricket.

Richmond was a keen gambler. Some of his wagers were for a comparatively modest twelve guineas a game, but he was apt to take on far larger bets, although accepting only a percentage of them personally: for example, in April 1730 he and four others shared a wager for a hundred guineas on a game in Hyde Park. In August 1731 he sponsored two matches for two hundred guineas a time against a Middlesex XI led by a Mr Chambers (probably Thomas Chambers, a forebear of the great nineteenth-century MCC figure Lord Frederick Beauclerk). Chambers won the first match on 16 August, and was winning the return on the twenty-third when the allotted time elapsed and it was declared drawn. The latter game drew thousands of spec-tators, including many 'persons of distinction of both sexes'. It ended with the near-obligatory affray, in which, as *Fog's Weekly Journal* reported, 'The Duke and his cricket players were greatly insulted by the mob at Richmond and some of the men having their shirts tore off their backs: and 'tis said a law suit will commence about the play.'

Richmond's love of cricket was lifelong. Ten years later, in 1741, his correspondence is full of cricket chat as he writes about the Sussex County by-election. There was a lot of cricket in Sussex in June of that year. On the tenth he confides to the Duke of Dorset: 'My steward is now going about the parishes, he has been at a cricket match today.' Four days later, Richmond writes to the Duke of Newcastle that 'Sergison [Thomas Sergison, the Tory candidate] was expected last night at Westdean and 'tis believed he will go to a great cricket match in Stansted Parke tomorrow between Slyndon and Portsmouth.'

To the Duke of Newcastle he added that Sergison was 'attended by Lisbon Peckham* and four or five of the Chichester Tory's, butt did not ask for one vote, and I don't believe could have made one if he had asked. I got Tanky** to come in order to swell and look big at him but Sergison never appeared before us, butt went off as soon as we came.' So he may have done, but the episode was not over, as a further letter to Newcastle on 29 July revealed: 'have you heard that Sergison treated his people the night of the cricket match at Portslade and that there was a bloody battle between them and the Slyndoners but the last came off victorious tho' with some broken heads' – a reference to the match attended by Newcastle and Sir William Gage.

Slindon – 'poor little Slyndon', as Richmond referred to it – was a favourite side of his, for he wrote again to the Duke of Newcastle apologising that he would be late for a meeting because he wished to see Slindon play 'the whole County of Surrey' at Merrow Down. A postscript notes gleefully that 'wee have beat Surrey almost in one innings'. This correspondence suggests that cricket was not an isolated amusement in Sussex in 1741, but that a series of matches were played, that they were not all sponsored, that they could draw large crowds,

* Henry Peckham, nicknamed 'Lisbon' because of his interest in the wine trade, notably port, was a merchant and three-time Mayor of Chichester. He was the grandfather of Harry Peckham, who was to help revise the Laws of Cricket thirty-three years later.
** The Earl of Tankerville, whose grandson was also to be on the committee revising laws with Harry Peckham.

and that Richmond was an enthusiast for the game itself, irrespective of whether wagers were involved. Cricket was becoming a settled part of rural life and a proper subject for aristocratic correspondence – even by-election candidates attended games as part of their campaigns.

But Richmond has more information for us yet. In 1745 he was one of the backers of three games between Surrey and Sussex,* the accounts of which are preserved in the Sackville manuscripts at Maidstone:

To 12 gamesters at the Artillery Ground And Moulsey Hurst @ 3 guineas each	£37–16s–
To 10 gamesters on Bury Hill, 9th Sept	£10–10s–
To Martin of Henfield on ditto	£ 2– 2s–
To Adam Newland for going to fetch him	10s–
To the scorer	10s–6d
To half the bill of expenses paid by Mr Smith	£10– 9s–
	£61–17s–6d

The above bill to be paid for in the following proportions:

Duke of Richmond 40	£24–15s–
Lord Sackville 20	£12– 7s–6d
Mr Taaf 20	£12– 7s–6d
Duchess of Richmond 10	£ 6– 3s–9d
Lord Berkeley 10	£ 6– 3s–9d
	£61–17s–6d

Richmond and Lord John Sackville were old allies as patrons, but that did not inhibit Lord John from rebuking the Duke about his team selection: 'I wish you had let Ridgway play instead of your stopper behind, it might have turned the match in our favour.'

Two of the other sponsors of the Surrey–Sussex games, 'Mr Taaf' and the Duchess of Richmond, merit special mention. Theobald Taafe

---

* At the Artillery Ground, London, and Moulsey Hurst in August, and at Bury Hill on 9 September.

(c.1708–80) was an Irishman with aristocratic connections and a long purse, having married a wealthy Englishwoman. Sometime MP for Arundel as a Whig, he was a boon companion in 'riot and gaming' of the Duke of Bedford and Lord Sandwich. Horace Walpole, that censorious correspondent, wrote to Horace Mann on 22 November 1751:

> He is a gamester, usurer, adventurer, and of late has divided his attentions between the Duke of Newcastle and Madame de Pompadour, travelling with turtles and pineapples in post-chaises to the latter, flying back to the former for Lewes races – and smuggling burgundy at the same time.

Walpole had a fine disregard of the laws of libel. But perhaps he was right, for later that year Taafe was charged with robbing a gambling associate in Paris and thrown in prison. He was released after representations by the British Ambassador, but his constituents in Arundel were unimpressed: he came bottom of the poll at the next election in 1754. Thereafter he became notorious as a gambler, libertine and confidence trickster, and was twice more imprisoned in France, including a spell in the Bastille.

As for the Duchess of Richmond, the Goodwood accounts reveal that she bore the costs of staging cricket matches, which suggests that she had absorbed a love of the game from the Duke. In July 1741 she writes him: 'If there was a leisure day I should be glad to get Slindon and East Dean ready to play at cricket.' The very next day she writes: 'Send a servant as soone as you can to lett Robert Dearling at East Dean know he is to get the people att your house on Saturday and the same person must afterwards go to John Newland with the same message.' Newland was almost certainly John Newland of Slindon, one of three brothers who played for England against Kent in 1744. Nor was the Duchess's interest short-term. In July 1747 the *Whitehall Evening Post* was clearly referring to her when it reported of a ladies' match: 'They play very well ... being encouraged by a lady of high rank in their neighbourhood, who likes the diversion.'

The dukes were not the highest-born enthusiasts for cricket: that accolade belongs to Frederick Louis, Prince of Wales (1707–51), known to history as 'poor Fred'. The eldest son of George II and Queen Caroline, from his childhood his life was a constant and deadly feud with his parents, with mutual dislike evident on both sides. The underlying cause of the bitterness between them is unknown, but we can conjecture. Certainly the fact that Frederick was educated in Hanover, and barely saw his parents between the ages of seven and twenty-one, cannot have helped. As an adult he lived in an unimpressive house in the unfashionable area of Leicester Fields (now Square). It was a time of Whig domination, in which Tories were regarded as the enemies of the ruling family and excluded from preferment: only Whigs were ennobled or created baronets. Prince Frederick courted the out-of-favour Tories, welcomed them to his home, and opposed Whig policy. All of this must have hugely irritated the King – which was, of course, its purpose.

When the Prince put politics aside he turned to cricket, and matches with such as Stead, Gage and the Sackvilles. He was first seen at a cricket ground at Kennington in 1731, after which his interest blossomed. At the end of a game between Surrey and Middlesex at Moulsey Hurst in July 1733 he paid a guinea to each player for their skills, although that afternoon cricket was only the forerunner of the entertainment. As the Prince prepared to leave a hare sped past him, pursued by soldiers. The terrified animal took to the nearby Thames for sanctuary but, undeterred, the soldiers jumped in and caught her before she had swum to the safety of deep water. A joyous water battle ensued as the soldiers fought over the captured hare, to the vast amusement of the onlookers. The fate of the hare is unknown.

Such diversions whetted the Prince's appetite for the game. At Moulsey Hurst in June 1735 he backed Surrey and other country men against London in an eventful contest. London's finest bowler, a Mr Ellis, dislocated his finger and was replaced by the famous Cook of Brentford. It was a bad day for fingers, for one of the Prince's team also damaged a digit, retired for a while and then returned to the crease, but failed to score many runs.* The London team won,

---

* The injured man was Wood of Woodcote, a member of an avid cricketing family who formed nearly all of the Surrey team that beat Kent at Duppas Hill, near Croydon, in 1731.

with Mr Wheatley, a distiller, and a Mr Dun leading them to victory.

The Prince played his first match (the Prince and ten noblemen vs London) at Kensington Gardens in 1735, aged twenty-eight, and two years later, in June 1737, was leading a team against the Duke of Marlborough for 'a considerable sum'. The Prince's team won, and in July were due to play for £500 against the same opponents, but the game was apparently abandoned following the birth of his eldest son the day before. It was a birth that typified the enmity that now existed between the Prince and his parents: his wife was staying at Hampton Court, but when she was 'in her birth pains' he removed her so that his child was not born in a palace in which the King and Queen were resident. He was not alone in his hostility: his parents fully returned it. The King's view of Frederick was that he was 'a monster and the greatest villain ever born', while Queen Caroline confided to the Prime Minister Sir Robert Walpole, 'You do not know my filthy beast of a son as well as I do.' Shortly after her grandchild was born the Queen died, and the royal family's tangled personal relationships were once more exposed. 'You must remarry,' the dying Queen told her husband. 'Non, j'aurai des maîtresses' ('No, I shall have some mistresses'), he replied, in a staggering example of boorishness. 'Ah, mon Dieu,' signed the Queen, 'cela n'empêche pas' ('My God, that needn't stop you').

Although the Prince was more frequently a spectator than a player, often bringing distinguished guests with him,* in a game at Cliveden, his home in Buckinghamshire, sometime in 1749 he received a heavy blow on his side from a cricket ball. When he died two years later while dancing at Leicester House, that blow was widely thought to be the cause of the abscess that killed him. Following the wretched Jasper Vinall (see page 24), his was another death attributed to cricket. It is probable that his father did not miss 'poor Fred', and another of his late mother's assessments of him echoes through the ages: 'My dear firstborn is the greatest ass, and the greatest beast in the world, and I heartily wish he was out of it.'

---

* For example, the Prince and Serene Highness of Hesse in June 1746.

Out of it he now was, but propriety required the King to order full mourning. All public amusements ceased. Ladies dressed in black bombazine and plain muslin, while men wore black cloth (with adornments or decorations), plain muslin cravats and black swords. Both sexes wore muffled chamois leather shoes. This ostentatious display continued for six months. 'Deep' mourning lasted a week, 'full' mourning for three months, and, farcically, 'second' mourning for a similar time, during which grey could replace deepest black. One effect of this charade was to destroy sales of silk, and thus rob fifteen thousand workers in Spitalfields of their jobs. Cricket showed more genuine respect to the Prince, with a game in his memory at Saltford Meadow near Bath in July 1751.

While Frederick had been alive and enjoying his cricket, his younger brother William Augustus, Duke of Cumberland (1721–65), had been involved in more savage business. Much of Scotland had never been reconciled to the Act of Union with England in 1707, and in 1745 the Jacobite cause raised its standard once more. 'Bonnie' Prince Charlie landed in the Western Isles, and within three months was ruler of most of Scotland. His army marched, winning victories as far south as Preston, but gained few adherents either in the low-lands of Scotland or in England. At Derby they halted and turned to march back to Scotland, pursued by the English under Cumberland. In April 1746 Cumberland destroyed the Scots at Culloden, and the Jacobite revival ended. The English pursued the rebels with ferocity, accompanying Cumberland's victory with merciless slaughter that earned the enduring epithet 'Butcher' for their commander. So hated was he that when Dr Johnson visited Bedlam, he found an inmate tearing at his straw in the belief that he was punishing Cumberland for his cruelty to the Scots. If he had visited Jonathan's Coffee House at Temple Bar he would have seen some more cruelty: it was decor-ated with the severed heads of Scots rebels. They remained on display for years. None of this seems to have impacted upon the cricket patrons, who rejoiced at the defeat of the Scots and welcomed Cumberland to their number.

There is no doubt that Cumberland was merciless in his pursuit of those who were seeking to turn his father off the throne, and his porcine features and eighteen-stone bulk added to the image of ruthlessness. The reality that he was also a brave and innovative commander, with an eye for merit among his soldiers (he promoted Howe, Coote and Wolfe) and a record of solid if unspectacular reforms of army procedures, is buried in the small print of history.

At leisure, Cumberland loved horse-racing, cards, the fine arts, especially Chelsea china, and when not soldiering he was a frequent spectator at cricket. In one of his early forays, in August 1751, his team was beaten by an innings by a side raised by Sir John Elwell, Bart, an opponent who was better known for his love of fox-hunting. But in the same month Cumberland's team was victorious against Lord Sandwich in what may have been a return match, for a letter from Robert Ord to the Earl of Carlisle dated 13 August reports the ironic outcome of an earlier encounter:

> You see in the papers that Lord Sandwich has won his match at cricket against the Duke, but what I think the best part of the story is not told here. The Duke, to procure good players on his side, ordered 22, who were reckoned the best players in the Country, to be brought before him, in order for him to choose 11 out of them. They played accordingly, and he chose 11. The other 11, being affronted at the choice, challenged the elect to play for a crown a head out of their own pockets. The challenge was accepted; and they played before the Duke and the elect were beat all to nothing.*

It seems, at least for the first match, that Cumberland was a finer judge of soldiers than of cricketers.

Horace Walpole's disapproving correspondence unmasks another noble cricketing sponsor. Henry Bromley, Lord Montford, became a peer in 1741 when George II allowed his mistress Lady Yarmouth to sell two peerages to raise funds. Bromley immediately raised teams to play Lord John Sackville, and was sufficiently active in society to catch Walpole's attention, as he wrote to Horace Mann in June 1749:

---

* Quoted in Eric Parker, *The History of Cricket* (1950).

'I could tell you of Lord Montford's making cricket matches and fetching up parsons by express from different parts of England to play matches on Richmond Green; of his keeping aide-de-camps to ride to all parts to lay bets for him at horse-races . . .' The bets were lost, and Montford wasted his fortune, but he lacked neither courage nor style. When he realised he was £30,000 (about £3 million today) in debt he made his will, read it carefully three times and then went into the next room and shot himself through the head before his lawyer had left the house.

Another notorious gambler, William Douglas, Earl of March (1725–1810), put his knowledge of cricket to good purpose. He entered into a wager that he could convey a letter a certain number of miles within a given time, which, since the distance was faster than horses could travel, was deemed to be impossible. But March was cunning: he enclosed the letter within a cricket ball and had it repeatedly thrown around within a circle of eminent cricketers, easily covering the distance. It was sharp practice, but he won his guineas.

John Montague, Earl of Sandwich (1718–92) – famous for the invention of the snack bearing his name – features in cricket history as the cricket-lover to whom James Dance dedicated his 1744 'Cricket: An Heroic Poem' (see page 53). He was also the subject of some satirical verses written by Sir C.H. Williams which appeared in the *Place Book for the Year, 1745*:

> Next in lollop'd Sandwich, with negligent grace
> For the sake of a lounge, not for love of a place
> Quoth he, 'Noble Captain, your fleets may now nick it,
> For I'll sit at your board, when at leisure from cricket.'

Sandwich, who was a Lord of the Admiralty at the time, kept up his cricketing activities alongside his official duties. In June 1751 he organised three matches against the Earl of March for the sum of a thousand guineas, the winner requiring two victories. Both Sandwich and March played in the games, and Sandwich's team of 'eleven gentlemen from Eaton [sic] College' were dressed in silk jackets and velvet caps to add to the spectacle. They also 'took constant exercise' to prepare themselves. The result of the first match is unrecorded, but Sandwich won the second and March the third, so the fate of the guineas is unknown. As an added attraction, a further entertainment that appealed to all classes was laid on: there was cockfighting between each match, at which spectators shouted their bets as the blood and feathers flew. It was an odd accompaniment to cricket, but cock-fighting remained a hugely popular sport.

Sandwich maintained an active interest in playing cricket until at least 1766, when he was in his late forties. As George Montague wrote to Horace Walpole in October that year:

> Lord Sandwich would play at cricket when he was at Sir George's this summer with his eldest son, against Sir George and the youngest Sir George caught him out left handed before he got one, went in, fagged him fourteen times till the Earl was not able to run any or move, but paid his money and went to bed.

'Sir George' was Sir George Osborn, Bart (1742–1818). Sandwich was a tall, vigorous man who when not playing cricket was an active member of the notorious Hell Fire Club. He certainly lived up to its reputation: after his long-suffering wife finally left him in 1755 he had three sons by a mistress who was murdered by a deranged clergyman in 1779.

Cricket had entered the bloodstream of the aristocracy, and a relative handful of patrons, enthusiasts for cricket and betting, did much to popularise the peasant's game. Until 1750 most teams were known by the name of their home town or parish, or by the identity of their patrons. There are references to a few cricket clubs: in 1718–19 the Rochester Punch Club Society in Kent had been formed, and was playing a London side. A Clapham Club appeared in 1731, and by 1735 there were at least two clubs in London – a Westminster Club that played its home games at Tothill Fields, and an Artillery Ground side, which also played under the loose nomenclature of the 'London Club'. Another London club was playing home games at Lamb's Conduit Fields by 1736, and in 1745 and 1747 advertisements in the

Norwich Mercury invited 'lovers of cricket' to 'subscribe their names for the ensuing season'. The enthusiasts of Norwich clearly took the game very seriously: spectators were warned 'not to bring dogs along with them', for 'if there was any interruption . . . by them in the game . . . all such dogs will certainly be killed on the spot'. The poor animals found chasing the ball irresistible, thus hindering play.

It was a fierce threat from enthusiasts of a game growing in fame. In 1755 cricket would even earn a mention in Dr Johnson's new dictionary. 'Cricket', defined Johnson, is 'a sport of which the contenders drive a ball with sticks in opposition to each other' – accurate insofar as it went, but inadequate. Soon the game would be far better-known.

3

The Later Patrons

By the middle of the eighteenth century, cricket was poised for changes that would make it the game we know today. It was emerging from its infancy in a small world of contrast and paradox. The fortunate few lived pampered lives. A lady of means would dine in mid-afternoon before going out to the theatre, following which she would play card games at a friend's house, at which dancing might begin at a late hour with the arrival of the male guests. Her male counterpart could be expected to breakfast late, possibly with friends, and then visit one of London's two thousand or so coffee houses to gamble, read or discuss business and politics. He might shop before dining in the late afternoon and visit the theatre at around 6 p.m. Wife, mistresses or friends might occupy his evening. From such a society came the patrons of cricket.

But life was very different for most people. Incomes were dreadfully low. Half of all families in England lived on less than £25 per annum. The 'nearly poor' families of tradesmen and builders might have £40 a year with which to keep a large family, but £50 a year turned a family into consumers. Many families bought only second-hand clothing, thus enabling them to dress above their income. Clothes might make up half of a man's net worth, for few owned houses or possessed material wealth. The limit of ambition for most was sufficient clothes and food, and a rented roof. Twenty people died each week of starvation in London. Life expectancy was under thirty-seven years for the population as a whole, but even less for

Londoners, with their unhealthy diet and insanitary and overcrowded homes.

Against this background of such social inequality, the second wave of cricket patrons carried the game to a wholly new dimension. When their work was done, the great Hambledon teams had earned immortality and the MCC had begun its long domination of the game. These patrons were few in number, but their influence was lasting. Another Sackville, the third Duke of Dorset, and Sir Horace Mann were the fount from which Kentish cricket flourished, while the Earl of Tankerville was a prominent sponsor for Surrey.

Sir Horace, a Kentish landowner and lifelong devotee of the game, was the most amiable of all the early benefactors. In 1765, at the age of twenty-one, he inherited around £100,000 (about £10 million today) from his father, a clothier who had amassed his fortune from army contracts. Ten years later his wealth was supplemented when his uncle Horace Mann Senior – the long-time recipient of the acid-infused letters of Horace Walpole – made over his estates in return for an annuity. This act of generosity made the young Horace one of the richest landowners in Kent. He married Lucy Noel, a daughter of the Earl of Gainsborough, in April 1765, and rented Bourne Place, a delightful mansion midway between Canterbury and Dover. Among the first summer visitors welcomed by Horace and Lucy were the Mozart family from Austria, including their talented nine-year-old son Wolfgang Amadeus. Young Wolfgang, probably the greatest child prodigy in history, had already toured Europe, met Marie Antoinette, played at the royal Courts in London and Vienna, and composed minuets and symphonies. Upon hearing a pig squeal, his musical ear absorbed the noise and his infant tongue proclaimed, 'G sharp.'

The Mozarts must have talked of music and their plans, and Horace, in imparting his own views, may have been lyrical about his preparations to build a cricket pitch in his grounds. At the age of twenty-two Horace founded the Bourne Club, and set the team up to play in Bourne Paddock, in front of his mansion. He laid out an attractive ground, described by John Burnby in 1773 as having 'smooth grass ... laid compleat ... a sweet lawn, with shady trees encompass[ed] round'. It was a beautiful setting. Bourne Paddock was to host many famous cricket encounters and inspire great nostalgia among those who knew it. Almost seventy years later, in 1840, the *Kentish Telegraph* recalled whimsically that 'In our hot days . . . this manly game met with great patronage at Bourne Place, and there are yet a few of our contemporaries left, who would give a little to throw away their cares and crutches, and renew those old recollections of Sir Horace and his merry friends.'

And merry they were, for the open-handed Horace and Lucy Mann entertained with style. Every match day was a great event. A game between teams styled 'Hampshire' and 'All-England' in August 1772 gives some flavour of the scene. A large ring was formed beyond the boundary, where booths offered food and drink. Seats and benches were set out to enable spectators to enjoy the game in comfort, and grandstands were erected for the elite, who included many prominent figures of the county. It must have been a magical occasion, with fifteen to twenty thousand spectators on the first day. The match lasted two days, each of seven hours' duration, with 'England' winning a hard-fought game by one wicket. One attraction for the crowd was that cricket was developing 'stars', and in this game two of the greatest, whom we shall meet later, were in the opposing teams: 'Lumpy' Stevens caused astonishment by clean-bowling John Small, which according to the *Kentish Gazette* 'had not been done for some years'.

Not all games were on such a grand scale. Between the opening of the new ground and 1771 the Bourne Club played all over Kent, as far afield as Cranbrook, Wrotham, Leigh, Dartford and Tenterden; that they endured the difficulties of travelling such distances by horse and cart is a tribute to the enthusiasm of the players and the growing popularity of the game. In May 1768 Mann took his team to London for a five-a-side game at the Artillery Ground, where they were beaten by Lord John Sackville after a two-day contest. One month later, on 10 June, the Bourne Club travelled to Westerham and lost to a combined Westerham and Caterham team by 14 runs: this game is memorable insofar as it was the first time that the full score of an eleven-a-side game was published in a newspaper, the *Kentish Post* of 11 June.

The interest of the press reflected the rising interest of the public. Bourne Paddock was becoming famous. A 'numerous and genteel company of spectators' was there on 28 and 29 August 1771 for a game against Middlesex and Surrey. The popular enthusiasm for cricket was so great that a competing event, a benefit for the actress Mrs Dyer, had to be postponed – which, no doubt, caused her intense frustration.

Apart from Mann's liberality, a further reason for the popularity of games at Bourne Paddock was that, year upon year, he engaged the most eminent cricketers to play in his team. An early acquisition was Richard Miller,* who made his first known appearance against '22 of Dover' in 1771. John Burnby regarded Miller as 'of England's cricketers, the best'. He was a batsman, famous for scoring 95 for Kent against Hampshire in 1774, which remained Kent's record score for nearly fifty years. John Nyren, the most celebrated chronicler of cricket's early days, remembered him as 'a beautiful player, and always to be depended upon; there was no flash – no cock-a-whoop about him, but firm he was, and steady as the pyramids'.

A later arrival was James Aylward, son of a Hampshire farmer, who played for his own county until 1779, and in 1777 batted from 5 p.m. on Wednesday to 3 p.m. on Friday to score 167 against England – at the time the highest score ever made. He is shown on the scorecard as batting at number ten, but in fact he opened the innings: the scorecard is a tribute to social class – gentlemen first, professionals next and rustics last. Aylward was a rustic. He played for Mann for four years from 1780, until he became landlord of the nearby White Horse inn and was awarded catering rights at Bourne Paddock; he continued thereafter as both player and caterer. He also served Mann as bailiff, a post for which he was, Nyren observed, 'but ill qualified'.

A few years after Aylward's arrival, John Ring, one of the best batsmen of the day, was added to Mann's team's strength. Ring was

---

* Not 'Joseph', as is sometimes stated; nor, as is also claimed, was he employed by Dorset or Tankerville.

short – no more than five feet five inches – thickset, and played in Bourne Paddock for many years before an accident at cricket practice cost him his life. Apparently his brother George was bowling to him when a ball reared and broke his nose. While recuperating he caught a fever and died. Other lesser-known figures such as the May brothers – Dick the bowler and Thomas the batsman – also spent time in Mann's employ: spectators were rarely without famous figures to attract them to Bourne Paddock.

The genial Horace Mann had other preoccupations in the early summer of 1772. His uncle, Horace Mann Senior, was installed as a Knight of the Bath, and his nephew acted as his proxy while he was overwhelmed with ceremonies. Young Horace organised a magnificent ball in his uncle's honour and, extraordinary though it may seem today, was awarded a knighthood for his work as deputy to his uncle. His wealth and social position no doubt aided his preferment. The contemporary diarist John Baker notes Horace's knighthood with no surprise at its cause, and then goes on to paint a vivid picture of the general atmosphere at a game of cricket on 23 July 1772:

> to cricket match at Guildford between the Hamilton [he means Hambledon] Club ... and Sir Horace ... Buller of 'White Hart' had a very good stand with benches above one another over his booth ... the booth below had so many ladies and gentlemen we could not get seats ... but I found a small booth where we had a good dinner and good cider and ale.

Baker returned the next morning, but the second day was less satisfactory:

> Rode to cricket match before ten, began at half past ten ... Dined today at Butlers [possibly a misprint for Buller, or some other proprietor] booth; no ladies but one only – who was in Stand in brown riding habit. Much worse dinner than in little booth yesterday and ordinary half crown and pay for liquors (with waiters and all it came to a crown) and the whole with better dinner and better liquors [was] but half crown yesterday.

As Baker's postscript shows, he was not alone in his irritation at having to pay *more* money for a *less* satisfactory meal:

> Yesterday, Mrs Cayley complained, the ladies – though invited
> – were all called on for a crown for their ordinary and one
> shilling for tea. At which, they were surprised and offended,
> thinking they were all at free cost from the invitation.

Bourne Paddock raised no such hackles. In July 1773 a grandstand was erected for a Kent vs Surrey match, won comfortably by Surrey, and Sir Horace's popularity inspired two poems in his honour. In 'Surry Triumphant', John Duncombe described his performance at the wicket:

> At last, Sir Horace took the field,
> A batter of great might,
> Mov'd like a lion, he awhile
> Put Surrey in a fright.
>
> He swung, 'till both his arms did ache,
> His bat of season'd wood,
> 'Till down his azure sleeves the sweat
> Ran trickling like a flood.

As Sir Horace scored only 3 and 22, and Surrey won by 153 runs, the poem is a little over the top – but perhaps Sir Horace's hospitality flowed through the poet's veins, and much may be forgiven for that. If so, it flowed through other veins too. John Burnby wrote in 'The Kentish Cricketers' (1773):

> Sir Horace Mann, with justice may
> Be term'd the hero of the play
> His gen'rous temper will support
> The game of cricket's pleasing sport.
>
> And few there are that play the game
> Which merit a superior name
> He hits with judgment, throws to please
> And stops the speedy ball with ease.

The clue to this sycophancy may lie in the poet's tribute to 'gen'rous temper', since Sir Horace's highest known score was 23, and his five innings that season yielded a mere 44 runs. We may surmise that the two poets were not dog-lovers, for they make no mention of the fact that at Bourne Paddock, people 'were desired to keep their dogs at home, otherwise they will be shot'.*

In 1774, fate cast a shadow over the idyllic life of the Manns. The year started well for Sir Horace: his growing prestige earned him membership of the famous committee that revised the laws of cricket at the Star and Garter (see page 104), and at the age of thirty he was elected the Member of Parliament for Maidstone. But any hopes of combining sport and politics were soon cast aside: Lucy was taken ill, and Sir Horace moved his family to the warmer climate of the Continent, at the home of his uncle in sunny Florence. But Lucy's health did not improve, and after three years' absence from his new constituency Sir Horace offered his resignation. It was not accepted. Lucy's condition worsened, and she died in February 1778. The grief-stricken Sir Horace did not return home until November of that year. Lucy had been the love of his life, and he would never remarry.

On his return to England he sought solace in his other great love, cricket, but no longer as a player. Sir Horace played in only one more game, scoring 0 and 1 for Six of Kent against Six of Hants at Moulsey Hurst in August 1782. He did however resume his role as patron and benefactor, sponsoring a five-a-side game against the Duke of Dorset and hosting a Kent–Surrey game at Bourne Paddock, both in June 1779, before returning to Italy. For the next eight years this lost and restless soul was a constant traveller, and as Horace Walpole noted in 1783, 'he makes no more of a journey to Florence than of going to York races'.

During Sir Horace's spells in England, Bourne Paddock was a lively place due to cricket and his continued largesse. When 'Hampshire' with Lumpy Stevens played 'All-England' for a thousand

---

* Presumably the dogs, not the people.

guineas in July 1782, one spectator, Lady Hales – a near neighbour – wrote to her friend Susan Burney:

> Tomorrow Sir Horace Mann begins his fetes by a great cricket match between His Grace of Dorset and himself, to which all this part of the world will be assembled ... many out of compliment to Sir Horace, who is never so happy as when he has all the world about him, and as he gives a very magnificent Ball and Supper on Friday, it would not be polite to attend that – without paying a compliment to his favourite amusement.*

This letter speaks well of Lady Hales's sensitivity, and paints a vivid picture of the occasion. 'All this part of the world will be assembled', and Sir Horace 'is never so happy as when he has all the world about him', whether it be for the game itself or his post-match entertainment. But Lady Hales was wrong in one respect: Sir Horace and the Duke of Dorset were backing 'All-England', leaving Hampshire gentlemen to back their own county.

It seems that Sir Horace attempted to offset his loneliness following the loss of Lucy with these great events: certainly his reputation for hospitality grew in the 1780s, and his good nature and open-handed way of life earned him many admirers. After a Kent against All-England game in August 1786, the *Kentish Gazette* reported not only that a multitude had attended the game, enlivened by 'the very splendid appearance of ladies', but that

> the very generous and liberal hospitality so conspicuous at Bourne House, does infinite honour to the very respectable and benevolent owner who, whilst he is patronising in the field the manly sport of cricket, is endeavouring to entertain his numerous guests with the most splendid entertainment in his house.

The Kent–All-England game was an annual event and a social highlight. It was repeated in August 1787, with the usual post-match ball (on this occasion in a new room built for the purpose) to which all the principal families of the county were invited. Among the guests

* Quoted in Lord Harris and F.S. Ashley-Cooper, *Kent Cricket Matches* (1929).

was the Marquess of Lansdowne, who as Lord Shelburne had been Prime Minister a few years earlier.

When his uncle died in 1786 Sir Horace inherited a baronetcy, together with the family seat at Linton Park. Four years later he left his beloved Bourne, the house and the cricket ground that had provided him with so much happiness over the years, and moved to Linton. But Linton failed to capture his heart as Bourne had done, and Sir Horace lived there only briefly before offering it to his daughter and son-in-law. Thereafter, he divided his time between far smaller homes at Egerton and Margate.

Politics re-entered his life. Sir Horace had retired from the Commons in 1784, but in 1790 he was re-elected for the constituency of Sandwich, which he would represent for the following seventeen years. Cricket, however, was a passion he couldn't assuage, and at leisure in Margate he once again turned to arranging matches as well as watching them. He helped promote clubs, and was a prominent member of the newly formed Marylebone Cricket Club (see page 106), and when Kent played the MCC at Lord's in August 1791 the *Kentish Chronicle* noted that Sir Horace was a spectator and 'remained the whole day at the ground with his book and pencil' – presumably either scoring or, just possibly, noting wagers. On 20–22 July 1807, at a game between twenty-three of Kent and thirteen of England at Penenden Heath, near Maidstone, it was recorded: 'that old amateur of the bat, Sir Horace Mann, was present every day and dined at the ordinary, which was sumptuously furnished and well attended' (for more on this match, see pages 128–9).

His cricketing afterlife was not easy: his open generosity exceeded the means with which he could subsidise it. As early as 1767 his uncle was worrying, and with good cause, that he would dissipate his fortune. By the 1780s he was wagering huge sums on matches, borrowing from relatives and raising money against the security of the Linton estate. By 1800 he was heavily in debt to local traders and farmers. As an old man, in 1808, he was declared bankrupt.

His enthusiasm for the game never dimmed, and John Nyren, writing several decades later, recalled Sir Horace at a match at

Hambledon, 'walking about, outside the ground, cutting down the daisies with his stick – a habit with him when he was agitated'. It is a lovely image, and one with which we might leave the life of the greatest, and most amiable, of the early benefactors. Horace Mann's kind and generous spirit had done much to promote the early growth of the game. His contribution was immense.

Sir Horace was not the only patron presiding over the growth of late-eighteenth-century cricket: both the Earl of Tankerville (1743–1822) and the Duke of Dorset (1745–99) – the third in the great line of cricketing Sackvilles – helped build its popularity.

Tankerville, an old Etonian introduced to cricket at school, inherited his earldom at the age of twenty-four. He was, according to Nyren, 'a close and handsome man, about 5' 8" in height', with a lively temper that was not always kept in check. After a fracas with a coachman in 1774 he was rebuked in the St James's Chronicle as 'renowned for nothing but cricket playing, bruising and keeping of low company' – a harsh judgement for a man who was at the time Chairman of the East India Company's Court of Directors. Three years earlier he had married Emma, daughter of Sir James Cole-brooke, and settled at Mount Felix, 'a large plain edifice of no archi-tectural pretensions whatever' in Walton-on-Thames. Tankerville was a keen sportsman, and maintained a cricket ground at Byfleet that was suitable for practice but inadequate for formal games: these he staged at Laleham Burway or Moulsey Hurst, both of which were within easy reach of Mount Felix. Although never a great player, he was an important sponsor of cricket, most notably of Surrey.

He first appears as a cricketer on the eve of his marriage, playing for the Cobham Club against a Mr Vaughan and the Dorking Club in a series of three matches in August and September 1771. Tankerville lost the series, watched by a great multitude of spectators who thronged the fields and refreshment marquees to gamble large sums on the outcome. Notwithstanding that defeat he was a successful batsman who 'distinguished himself in the field in a capital manner'.*

* G.B. Buckley, *Fresh Light on Eighteenth Century Cricket* (1935).

His highest score of 45 for England against Hampshire at Guildford in 1777 may seem modest these days, but was creditable on the wickedly uneven pitches of the time.

As a patron, Tankerville employed two of the finest contemporary cricketers to boost his team. Edward 'Lumpy' Stevens (1731–1819), son of an innkeeper, was discovered by a cricket-loving brewer, a Mr Porter, and as his skill blossomed he became Tankerville's gardener at Mount Felix in the early 1770s. Lumpy, as described by Arthur Haygarth, was a 'thick made round shouldered man', widely regarded as the premier bowler in England, who according to John Nyren had a capability to 'bowl the greatest number of length balls in succession . . . of all men within my recollection'. Tankerville once won a bet of £100 (about £10,000 at today's prices) that Lumpy could hit a feather placed on the pitch at least once in four balls. Such accuracy made him a legend, and he was deadly on unprepared wickets to any batsman with poor technique. Lumpy remained a top-class bowler well into his fifties, and did not retire until 1789. When he died thirty years later, his old patron Tankerville, in a gesture that speaks well of him, erected a gravestone for Lumpy in Walton-on-Thames churchyard; the two had shared many cricketing exploits, and Tankerville had not forgotten his protégé. Nor had others: the Duke of Dorset commissioned a portrait that can still be seen at Knole. Lumpy was an early cricketing legend.

Another of Tankerville's cricketing employees, William Bedster, was a batsman who served as his butler for around five years from 1777. He first appears, misreported as 'Belsted', at a game between England and Hampshire at the Artillery Ground. Tankerville had received a severe blow below his knee and was forced, in 'excruciating pain' to quit the field. Bedster fielded in his stead and – the laws being elastic at the time – was then permitted to open the batting with Tankerville, who had clearly recovered. They put on 49 between them, a large opening stand for the time. After leaving Tankerville, Bedster played for Berkshire and Middlesex before becoming landlord of a public house in Chelsea.

As Tankerville was a leading member of the aristocracy, his

sporting preoccupation was not universally well regarded at a time when England was at war with the American colonists. An anonymous tract published by John Bew lampoons Tankerville and Dorset. The author was scathing about the two men he calls 'The Noble Cricketers', and introduces the insulting poem with the sarcastic observation that it is 'a testimonial of my regard'. In his preamble he urges the two peers to 'For God's sake, fling away your bats, kick your mob companions out of your house and, though you can do your bleeding Country no service, cease to accommodate insult on [top of] misfortune, by making it ridiculous.' After this pugnacious invective, the poem continues:

> O Muse, relate the mighty cares that fill
> The Souls of D..s.t and of T..k..v.lle,
> From glory far, at Folly's shrine they fall,
> Leag'd with the wond'rous Wight, yclept Sam Small,*
> With Lumpy, Horseflesh** and a score beside,
> Scum of St Giles's, and their Lordships pride
> Where mob-encircled, midst th' Artillery ground
> Pimps, Porters, Chimney Sweepers grinning round,
> Far from the Cannon's roar, they try at cricket,
> Stead of their country, to secure a wicket,
> There, mad for praise, they glutton-like devour
> The nauseous flattery, which those Panders pour.
> And lo! their ragged partners of the field
> Seem as well pleas'd the Bat, as Blade, to wield,
> As well on Cakes, as Carnage to regale.

Whether Tankerville saw these lines is uncertain, but he retired from cricket in 1781 to enter politics, where his behaviour soon aroused controversy. At first all went well: he took a junior position in Lord Shelburne's brief administration, lost it under his successor the Duke of Portland, but returned to government when the twenty-four-year-old William Pitt the Younger became Prime Minister in December 1783. Two years later, in an attempt to expose corruption, Tankerville

---

* Poet's error: he means the batsman John Small.
** Poet's error: he means Hogsflesh, a bowler from Hampshire.

accused a colleague, Lord Carteret, of using public funds to buy his own personal household effects, but could not sustain the charge, and was dismissed from the government. When a subsequent report, ironically requested by a relative, Charles Grey, later the author of the Great Reform Act, cleared Carteret of wrongdoing, it ended Tankerville's hopes of a successful political career. He consoled himself by amassing one of the world's largest collections of seashells.

After his retirement from politics Tankerville emerges only intermittently into the public gaze, most famously in 1794, when he fought a duel with Edward Bouverie – and wounded him – for making unwelcome advances to his daughter Ann. His cricketing past was not forgotten, however. In 1801 the *Morning Herald* printed lines that, despite having few claims to literary greatness, must have been a welcome antidote to the cruel caricature John Bew had published so many years earlier:

> To serve the King for pure good will,
> The motto is of Tankerville,
> It is a sentimental tenet
> Of the illustrious house of Bennet
> May each, to his succeeding son,
> Act always as the Father's done
> Perhaps you'll think 'tis here no matter
> That he's an independent batter,
> And, at the famous game of cricket,
> Keeps the best guard before the wicket,
> When match'd against the playing men
> He beats nine of them out of ten
> Making, if at the work he labours,
> More runs and notches than his neighbours.

Tankerville's time at the heart of cricket was far shorter than Horace Mann's, but his role in promoting the game, especially during Mann's frequent absences abroad, earns him an honoured place among those who embedded cricket as part of the English way of life. In 1805, when he was in his early sixties, he was described by Thomas Creevey as a 'haughty, honourable man . . . communicative and entertaining with a passion for clever men, of which he considers himself to be one, though certainly unjustly'. Lady Tankerville, the former Emma Colebrooke, fares rather better: she *was* credited with being very clever, and with having 'as much merit as any woman in England', but 'like her Lord, was depress'd and unhappy'. If true, it is a sad postscript.

The third Duke of Dorset, John Frederick Sackville (1745–99), was the finest cricketer of the later patrons. He was an instinctive ball-player, with a good eye and a fine temperament. His talent was evident at Westminster School, where he was regarded as 'the best [player] of his time at cricket and billiards'. He also played tennis and fives to a high standard. As a man, he was well-made, five feet nine inches in height with a habit when at ease, according to John Nyren, of standing with his head tilted to one side. Despite his social position he was an empty-headed playboy, 'not in possession of any brains', according to contemporary opinion. But he was a kindly man. Like many aristocrats, he had assets aplenty but not much 'ready money'. Nonetheless, he spent lavishly, sometimes on the poor, but more often on his own amusements.

Although not handsome, Dorset had pleasant features, an agreeable manner and a natural dignity. But Nathaniel Wraxall, in his *Posthumous Memoirs* (1836), concurs with his critics that he did not possess 'superior abilities' – except at cricket, where eye and wrist coordination made him the finest gentleman all-rounder of his time. Twice in 1773 he bowled out six batsmen in a single innings, and one year later hit 77 runs for Hampshire at the Vine, Sevenoaks. These were prodigious feats for the time, and John Burnby, the cricket-loving poet, was on hand to record them in 'The Kentish Cricketers':

> His Grace the Duke of Dorset came,
> The next enroll'd in skilful fame,
> Equal'd by few, he plays with glee,
> Nor peevish seeks for victory.
> His Grace for bowling cannot yield,
> To none but Lumpey in the field:
> And far unlike the modern way,

Of blocking every ball at play,
He firmly stands with bat upright,
And strikes with his athletic might,
Sends far the ball, across the mead,
And scores six notches for the deed.

Burnby's description suggests that Dorset, then twenty-eight, was an attacking batsman who stood upright at the crease with his bat raised from the blockhole, much as Victor Trumper and Graham Gooch were to do many years later. And if it is a true judgement that he yielded at bowling to 'none but Lumpey', he was certainly a pre-eminent all-rounder.

In 1768, as Lord John Sackville, he organised a game between the old boys of Westminster and Eton – for whom the diarist William Hickey was longstop. It was not one of Hickey's finest hours. He failed to attend the pre-match practices, despite being informed of them, and awoke on the morning of the match with a nasty hangover in 'a cheap lodging house near Drury Lane'. The contest was for a wager of twenty guineas a player, with the amount to be given by the losers to the poor of the parishes of Moulsey and Hampton – a generous gesture. Any player failing to turn up was to forfeit the same sum.

Hickey, feeling wretched but anxious to save his guineas, hurried home to change his clothes, collect his mare from the stables, and embark at a gallop to Moulsey Hurst. The wickets were due to be pitched at eleven o'clock, and Hickey had to ride twelve miles in forty-five minutes or forfeit his money. He made it with moments to spare, but noted that he had 'a horrible headache and sickness', the classic symptoms of over-indulgence. Having arrived barely in time to play, he did not distinguish himself, although after a hard match his team did win. It should have been less of a struggle. Hickey recalled:

the Westminsters insisted we should have won easier had I played as usual, but I was so ill at the time that I let several balls past me that ought not to have done so ... When we adjourned – a magnificent dinner was prepared, no part of

which could I relish, even Champagne failed to cheer me; I
could not rally ... The moment the bill was called for, and
our proportions adjusted and paid, I mounted my mare, and
in sober sadness gently rode to my father's [house] at
Twickenham.

One warms to Hickey for his unsparing account of his own shortcomings.

After succeeding to the dukedom at the age of twenty-four Dorset
embarked on a 'grand tour' of Europe, and for two years played no
cricket at all. He was accompanied by his mistress, Nancy Parsons, a
strikingly attractive woman who either enjoyed cricket or thought it
prudent to pretend to do so; in any event, upon her return from the
tour she attended matches with the Duke, to the delight of the
cricketers. Apart from her physical attractions, Nancy had something
of a reputation – she was formerly the mistress of the Duke of Grafton
– and the players were keen to gawp at her. John Nyren relates a tale
which illustrates the easy relationship that the players enjoyed with
the leading patrons.* Apparently his father Richard was eager to meet
the lovely Nancy, and the Earl of Tankerville, who was present at a
Hambledon game, cheerfully engaged her in conversation so that
Nyren could join him. It was a kindness that Richard Nyren never
forgot.

From early in his cricketing career the Duke of Dorset was a focus
of interest to spectators. In a game in which Kent beat a combined
Sussex and Hampshire team at Guildford in August 1772, great sums
were wagered upon whether the Duke or an opponent, the cricketing
vicar at Westbourne, the Reverend Edward Ellis, would score most
runs: it was the Duke, who scored 21 in a single innings, while the
Reverend Ellis made 16 in two innings.

As well as being a fine cricketer himself, Dorset employed
top-class players to strengthen his teams. One, John Minchen, alias
Minshull (1741–93),

---

* It was published in the *Town*, 21 October 1832, but censored from Nyren's book *The
Young Cricketer's Tutor* (1833).

was a capital hitter, and a sure guard of his wicket . . . however, not an elegant player; his position and general style were both awkward and uncouth; yet he was as conceited as a wagtail, and with his constantly aping what he had no pretensions to, was, on that account only, not estimated at the price at which he rated his own merits.

That at least was the view of Nyren, who was not an admirer of Minshull's behaviour, even though he grudgingly conceded his cricketing ability. And well he might, for Minshull scored the first recorded century in cricket, 107 for Dorset's XI against Wrotham on 31 August 1769. Six weeks later Dorset engaged him, nominally as a gardener, to work at Knole for eight shillings a week. Minshull remained at Knole for only three years, but during that time he cemented his reputation, as the *Kentish Gazette* reported on 8 August 1772:

> On Wednesday last a game of cricket was played [at the Vine, Sevenoaks] between eleven gentlemen of Sevenoaks and eleven of Wrotham and Ightham, which was determined in favour of the former by 56 notches. In this match a remarkable bet of thirty shillings to a guinea was laid, that the united parishes got more notches than the noted Minshull . . . but the famous batsman got 58, and the united parishes but 56.

Minshull was a fine acquisition, but not the only one to catch the Duke's eye. A more engaging personality was the labourer William Bowra,* engaged as a gamekeeper at Dorset's manor at Seal and Kemsing in 1778 for five, later seven, shillings a week. This modest sum secured a fine talent whom the Duke would cheer on while he was batting – 'Bravo, my little Bowra!' was a familiar cry from the boundary at the Vine. After the Duke's death Bowra remained a favourite of the Duchess, and she brought him to Knole, where for the rest of his life he worked as a gamekeeper.

In the 1770s the rules and tactics of cricket were continuing to take shape. Dorset, Tankerville and Mann were at Sevenoaks in July 1773 when Richard Simmons, reputed to be the finest fieldsman of

* Pronounced 'Borrer'. He is sometimes confused with a locksmith of the same name.

his day, stood sufficiently close to the Hampshire batsmen to intimidate them. A fortnight later the Duke was playing at Laleham Burway when his opponents attempted to do the same to him. The Duke complained, but to no effect until one of his attacking strokes felled a close fieldsman. Such aggressive fielding was set to become an everyday part of cricket.

Another important change in the game emerges in the diary of Richard Hayes of Cobham, who watched Dorset play at Sevenoaks Vine for All-England against Hampshire on 25 and 26 June 1776. Hayes records the Duke bowling the opening over – 'Four balls. Not a run got' – though Hampshire went on to score the respectable total of 241. All-England scored a mere 105 and lost heavily, with the Duke bowled for a paltry 6 runs. Hayes's diary contains two little gems of information. He wrote: 'They talk of having 3 stumps,' and noted also that 'by playing with broad bats ... it is a hard matter to hit the wicket'. Both these anomalies were soon to be corrected, and the later patrons would play a part in doing so.

The concept of three stumps has an air of modernity about it, but cricket still had its savage days. When Kent played Essex at Tilbury Fort in 1776, a row arose over the eligibility of one of the Kent team. Essex declined to play, and a fight ensued. One of the Kent men shot and killed an Essex player, and in the chaos that followed an old invalid was bayoneted and a soldier shot dead. Essex then fled, and the Kent team made off in boats. In a violent age, even such incidents did not diminish the enthusiasm for the game.

By 1777 Dorset had long since parted from the delectable Nancy Parsons, who married Viscount Maynard. Dorset's new mistress was a fellow aristocrat, the Countess of Derby, which created a great scandal. This did not bother either of them. The Countess decided to arrange a ladies' cricket match, and Dorset is said to have been the author of a letter published in a society magazine, although if so, his purpose in writing it seems ambiguous:

> Ladies, while you are eagerly pursuing the round of court
> pleasures and cutting out new figures for fashion, permit me
> to add to your entertainments a novelty of no less singularity

than those which of late so amply diverted your little society. Divert yourselves, then, for a moment of much importance, cast aside your needles and attend to my essay.*

After this patronising opening paragraph – 'cutting out new figures for fashion . . . your little society . . . cast aside your needles' – which would have earned him social crucifixion in the twenty-first century, the Duke – if indeed he really was the author – raises his game and entices women to become involved in cricket:

> Though the gentlemen have long assumed to themselves the sole perspective of being cricket players, yet the ladies have lately given a specimen that they know how to handle a ball and the bat with the best of us, and can knock down a wicket as well as Lord Tankerville himself. The enclosed drawing, which I thought proper to make for your information is a true representation of a cricket match played lately in private between the Countess of Derby and some other Ladies of quality and fashion, at the Oaks in Surrey, the rural and enchanting retreat of her Ladyship.

Having baited the hook, the author of the letter comes to the point, but cannot resist putting his tongue in his cheek:

> What is human life but a game of cricket? And, if so, why should not the ladies play at it as well as we? Beauty is the bat, and men are the ball, which are buffeted about just as the ladies' skill directs them. An expert female will long hold the ball in play: and carefully keep it from the wicket; for, when the wicket is once knocked down, the game of matrimony begins and that of love ends . . .

If Dorset, who had a lengthy string of mistresses, was indeed the author, as claimed by the magazine, it is unlikely that the double entendres were an accident. We shall never know whether the letter was a genuine attempt to encourage women to take up cricket, or a vehicle to poke fun at those scandalised by the Duke's relationship with the Countess.

* Quoted in the *Sporting Magazine*, 1803.

When France intervened to support the American colonists in the War of Independence, Dorset became a Colonel in the West Kent militia, and his participation in cricket began to fall away. After the war ended, in 1783, he was appointed Ambassador to the Court of Versailles, and he never again played top-class cricket. But his enthusiasm did not wane. While in France he played casual games for pleasure, despite a pompous rebuke from *The Times*, which frowned upon 'his associations with the inferior orders in pursuit of his favourite amusement, cricket'. *The Times* was in a grouchy mood: apart from castigating Dorset, it noted that horse-racing in Paris was on the wane and cricket was replacing it, but that the French 'could not equal the English in such vigorous exertions of the body'. The French were soon to show on the battlefield that their exertions were formidable. It was an early example of what, 150 years later, Churchill would say was '*The Times*' ability to be wrong on every major issue'.

Throughout his five years as Ambassador, Dorset spent a part of every summer in England, where he was able to enjoy some cricket. He carried his enthusiasms back to Paris, and supposedly presented Queen Marie Antoinette with a cricket bat that she 'kept in her closet'.* He finally returned home to England in 1789, amidst the first stirrings of the French Revolution but before the violent disruption became widespread. The real terror lay ahead. Myths arose about Dorset's homecoming. Serious historians** have alleged that his ambassadorial role 'ended in farce', when he invited Tankerville to bring a cricket team to play in Paris to placate anti-British feeling. At Dover, it is said, they 'encountered Dorset scurrying ignominiously the other way'. An earlier version suggests that he wrote not to Tankerville, but to William Yalden, then landlord of the Cricketer inn at Chertsey, an old Surrey cricketer, and that it was his eleven at Dover.† In fact the whole story is nonsense. Dorset did not 'scurry ignominiously' from Paris. He had written to the Foreign Secretary,

---

* According to *The Times*, 17 December 1789, it was preserved as a 'relique' (sic) of British prowess.
** e.g. David Underdown in *Start of Play*, pp.153–4.
† Arthur Haygarth, *Cricket Scores and Biographies*, Vol. 1 (1862).

the Duke of Leeds, in July 1789, seeking permission to return. As he had warned other British residents in Paris to leave, it seems unlikely that he would at the same time have invited a cricket team to France. It makes a good story, but it is fiction. Dorset left France on 8 August 1789, four weeks after the outbreak of the Revolution. He reached Dover on 10 August, continued to Bourne Place, dined with Horace Mann and, to celebrate his homecoming, spent the following day watching Kent play Surrey.

After his return Dorset married an heiress less than half his age – he was forty-six – and soon afterwards ceased to support cricket. The news of the bloody events in France, including the execution of Marie Antoinette, preyed on a mind already predisposed to melancholy. Sadly, the wayward Sackville gene that had robbed his forebears of their sanity was active once more. During the 1790s Dorset became progressively more morose and penny-pinching, in sharp and unhappy contrast to the gay enjoyment of his free and easy youth. He died a virtual recluse in 1799. His cricketing glories were long behind him, but not forgotten: he left the Vine 'for the use of cricketers'.

On their village greens the players may have noted these great events, but their attention would have been diverted by the more peaceful revolution that had taken place in their smaller world of cricket. The immortal Hambledon Club had been formed, enjoyed its greatest days, and set a shining example for all cricket to follow. To ensure that it did so, the game now acknowledged a governing body that would wield its authority for the next two centuries: the Marylebone Cricket Club had been formed.

4

The Men Who Made Cricket

In Terence Rattigan's screenplay for the film *The Final Test* (1953), an ageing cricketer, Sam Palmer, is dismissed for nought in his last innings. Unimpressed by his father's fame, Palmer's son Reggie, an aspiring poet, hero-worships Alexander Whitehead, a literary icon. But unbeknown to Reggie, his idol is a long-time admirer of Palmer. When Whitehead learns the identity of Reggie's father, he accepts an invitation to dinner to meet him. Both Palmer and Whitehead are tongue-tied by the eminence of the other, until the conversation turns to cricket. The poet tells the cricketer – to his astonishment – that he envies him his profession. 'I,' says Whitehead, 'am a creative artist. I will be judged on my work because I leave a record. *You* – on the other hand – will see your legend grow. You are like Paganini, Nijinsky and Garrick: one day you'll sit on Mount Olympus between Don Bradman and W.G. Grace.'

In this, Rattigan touches on a central truth. Reputations grow in the memory. This is especially true of cricket. Lovers of the game tend to view its past romantically, however crusty they may otherwise be. Just as the fictional Sam Palmer would 'see his legend grow', so have the reputations of the early cricketers and their sponsors. Nonetheless, we can say with absolute certainty that the years of the later patrons, Mann, Tankerville and Dorset, were formative ones for cricket. By 1750 the game had taken root; forty years on, technique and style had evolved, famous grounds had been laid out, detailed scores were kept, the rules had been codified and a governing body was in place. Further changes lay ahead, but in its essentials modern cricket had been born, and clubs were spreading far beyond its narrow birthplace of the Weald. Two of them were to have a lasting impact.

Hambledon, about fifteen miles north of Portsmouth, is an ancient Hampshire village whose cricket expertise ensured that its history is now more legend than fact. Many believe that the game was first played at the village's Broadhalfpenny Down, despite the reality that its genesis is at least two hundred years earlier. Yet Hambledon has become myth, and – as ever – myth has become reality. The myth sprang, unintended, from the pen of one man. John Nyren was born at Hambledon in 1764, the son of Richard Nyren, captain of the Hambledon team, guardian of their cricket ground and, until about 1771, proprietor of the Bat and Ball inn on Broadhalfpenny Down. From the age of twelve young John watched the Hambledon team, at the time when they were in their heyday and he was at his most impressionable. His love and admiration for Hambledon cricket was never to leave him, and over fifty years later, in 1833, he published *The Young Cricketer's Tutor*,* which in its final chapters included his recollections of the great days of Hambledon.

The book is a charming portrait of his heroes, infused with romanticism as Nyren recalls, no doubt with advantages, the deeds they did. It is a boyhood memory of men and their successes, in which virtues are recalled, fun is revisited and any failings, squabbles and miseries left unrecorded. It is a cricketing fairy story, a fusion of King Arthur and Robin Hood, and its simple recitation of good men and great events is a delight. *The Young Cricketer's Tutor* is *the* source reference for mid-to-late-eighteenth-century cricket, for no other comparable record exists. It carried the Hambledon team – or, more accurately, teams, for their glory days exceeded thirty years – into legend. The 'great' games were big social events. A pavilion, 'the Lodge', was erected for members, and the boundary was circled with tents for the teams and for catering: with flags flying, it was a colourful sight. Hambledon cricket was not just a game, it was big business.

* 'Collected and edited by Charles Cowden Clarke'. It is probable that Cowden Clarke wrote the book as a 'ghost', but the memories are Nyren's.

The team was professional and well-paid, the bets were large, and the logistics of feeding and watering twenty thousand spectators were formidable.

No doubt the team's fame is merited, even if Nyren does gild the lily. It was a remarkable collection of individuals. Every season they met for practice on the first Tuesday of May and each Tuesday thereafter. As their fame grew, even their practice days attracted crowds of spectators.

In the mid-1770s the two premier bowlers were Tom Brett and the left-handed Richard Nyren. Brett, a farmer, dark-haired and strong, was the fastest bowler of his day, and famed for his accuracy. Nyren, a Slindon man and nephew of the great cricketer Richard Newland, was the undisputed leader of the team in all matters: batsman, bowler and, despite his stout build, 'uncommonly active' in the field. Off the field he was a hard-headed businessman, mine host of the Bat and Ball, who advertised matches to attract crowds to the game and thereafter to his inn, where he sold 'punch to make hair curl' at twopence a pint. John Nyren remembers his father as 'the head and right arm' of Hambledon cricket, adding that he 'never saw a finer specimen of the thoroughbred old English yeoman'. In those few affectionate words the character of Richard Nyren stands out: did any father ever receive a finer tribute from his son?

The second-string bowlers were William Barber, who took over the Bat and Ball from Richard Nyren in 1771, and the unfortunately named William Hogsflesh – 'staunch fellows', Nyren tells us, 'and thorough going', which conjures up an image of honest yeoman cricketers with no intellectual pretensions. Nyren characterises a later bowler, Lambert (or possibly Lamborn; he is sometimes confused with William Lambert, an early-nineteenth-century Surrey player), known as 'the Little Farmer', as something of a bumpkin, without intelligence but with talent. Lambert was in fact a shepherd, and had the natural gift of bowling underarm off-breaks. He practised these aiming at sheep hurdles, but it was only when he was told where to pitch them by Richard Nyren that he tumbled out Kent and Surrey batsmen 'as if [they were] picked off by the rifle corps'.

The finest of the early batsmen was John Small Senior, a pioneer of forward play, renowned as the best judge of a short run – a skill perhaps learned from his specialist fielding positions at the equivalents of the modern-day cover point or midwicket. Small was the Hambledon version of the 'senior pro', whom Richard Nyren consulted on tactics and cricket law; he also entertained the team with his fiddle and double bass, and made bats and balls in the off-season. It was Small who developed a new straighter bat with a marked shoulder at the head of the blade. This was a great improvement, but it was still unsprung – such refinements lay far ahead.

Behind the stumps, the wicketkeeper – with no protective pads or gloves – was Tom Sueter, handsome and easy-natured by temperament, who must have stood up to Brett's fast bowling for he 'stumped out' many a batsman. He was also an accomplished left-handed batsman. Sueter was popular, 'a pet of all the neighbourhood'. A chorister in Hambledon church with a sweet tenor voice, he often sang solo or led team songs in the dressing room, and afterwards as they drank their ale at the Bat and Ball. His partner in harmony was George Lear, counter-tenor, middle-order batsman and, his chief role in the team, longstop to Sueter's wicketkeeping.

New players arrived to strengthen the team over the years. Noah Mann, short and swarthy as a gypsy, would ride twenty miles each way on horseback to practice every Tuesday: a fleet-footed, agile man, he batted and bowled left-handed and was an excellent fielder. Poor Noah came to a sad end: after a convivial evening he fell onto the smouldering ashes of a fire, and died of his injuries. He was only thirty-three. Years later, his son would umpire one of the most fateful games in cricket history (see page 132).

Even among the working men of the team, the two Walker brothers, Tom and Harry, stood out as 'unadulterated clod hoppers'. But they were difficult to dismiss and utterly without nerves – valuable attributes in a cricketer. Harry was a dashing batsman, quite unlike his brother. 'Old ever-lasting' Tom, who once faced 170 balls for one run, was hardly an advocate of brighter cricket. He did, however, make the first century on the first Lord's pitch (which was subsequently partially covered by Dorset Square): 107 for MCC against Middlesex – followed by four other hundreds on the same ground. Nyren's description of Tom Walker is memorable:

> a hard, ungainly scrag-of-mutton frame; wilted, apple-John face; long spider legs, as thick at the ankles as at the hips; the driest and most rigid limbed chap; his skin was like the rind of an old oak, and as sapless. He moved like the rude machinery of a steam engine in the infancy of construction and, when he ran, every member seemed ready to fly to the four winds.

A second set of brothers, George and William Beldham, brought forth the greatest batsman cricket had yet known. 'Silver Billy' Beldham had been taught by a gingerbread baker, Harry Hall, and he had learned well. Hall, from Farnham – the very cradle of cricket – may have been the first batsman to realise the full potential of playing forward. Hall was not a great player, but he batted side-on, with his left elbow up and a straight bat, which meant he could play down the line of the ball and hit to the off side of the field in a manner that had previously been impossible. Beldham was a keen pupil, and in the game in which Tom Walker scored the first hundred at Lord's, he scored 144. 'Silver Billy', an instinctive ball player, was a star from the moment of his arrival at Farnham in 1780 at the tender age of fourteen. He was engaged by Hambledon in 1785, aged nineteen, and played his first 'great' game two years later. Beldham was a batsman of elegance and style, a savage hitter with a particularly fine cut; a fine fielder in the slips and a competent medium-pace bowler, he lived for ninety-six years, played cricket for forty of them, and his memories, faithfully recorded by Pycroft in a famous conversation in *The Cricket Field* (1851), cast light in his old age upon the times in which he played.

Many other talented cricketers were part of these Hambledon teams: James Aylward (see page 70), the rustic who in 1777 scored 167 over three days, at the time the highest score in cricket; John Wells, a baker and a brilliant fieldsman, built like a cob horse and known as 'Honest' John; the Freemantle brothers, John and Andrew; Tom

Scott; John Small Junior; Richard Francis; Tom Taylor; William Fennex; Richard Purchase; and finally – but by no means least – the man who changed cricket forever: David Harris.

The name of David Harris does not convey the magic of a Sydney Barnes, a Harold Larwood or a Shane Warne, but his role in changing the face of cricket was greater than any of theirs. As Tom Brett left Hambledon, Harris arrived, to become the pioneer in that most fundamental of cricket skills, bowling on a length – and nothing was ever the same again.

Early bowling was underarm and along the ground, as in the ancient game of bowls: the ball, therefore, did not rear up, and the stumps did not need to be of any height. But in a 1744 codification of the laws the stumps were both heightened and narrowed. They became twenty-two inches in height and only six inches in width, and were adorned with both a proper bail and a popping crease. The target for the bowler was suddenly very different, and the concept of 'length' bowling became possible: a ball could pitch and rise and still hit the stumps, rather than passing safely over them.

From this much followed, and Harris practised summer and winter to perfect his new style. He was accurate and difficult to score off, and his best deliveries rose to trap unprotected fingers against the bat handle. Such 'length' bowling was a tricky prospect for the batsman: for a start it was no longer possible to play with the old-fashioned curved bat resembling a hockey stick. In or around the 1750s, therefore, the modern bat, or a near replica, was born, with a flat and square-faced front. Even so, the batsman's plight remained dire if he stood within his crease and attempted to swat every ball to leg in the traditional manner.

Before the advent of the new bat, forward defensive strokes were unknown, as they were all but impossible with the 'hockey-stick' shape. But against bowling pitched on a length it became essential, as did an array of strokes familiar today but unknown in the mid-eighteenth century. David Harris not only changed bowling, but batting too, as batsmen adapted to face the new threat to their wicket.

On one occasion Harris was presented with a gold-laced hat for an outstanding bowling performance. So far as we know he did not take three wickets in three balls on that occasion, but this incident *may* be the origin of the action, adopted in the 1850s, of presenting a hat to a bowler who accomplishes that feat. Or it may not, for in his wonderful series of novels purporting to be the adult memoirs of the cad Harry Flashman, immortalised in Thomas Hughes's *Tom Brown's Schooldays* (1857), George Macdonald Fraser gives a different explanation. In *Flashman's Lady* (1977), Flashman, by trickery of course, dismisses the great cricketers Felix, Pilch and Mynn in three balls, and is presented with a hat by Mynn. It is pure fiction of course, but for all we know something similar may have occurred. One day, hopefully, a researcher may uncover a hidden piece of cricket history to reveal the truth.

John Nyren's recollections of Hambledon give us a vivid picture of early cricket that is unavailable elsewhere ... and yet one longs for more. His narrative is rich in character studies of the players, but silent upon their lives and views. What did this mixture of honest yeomen and simple rustics think of the society in which they lived? How did they react when they left Broadhalfpenny Down to play matches in the sprawl of London? Did they know anything of the political turmoil of the wars against France, of the American Revolution and the fall of Lord North's government? What opinions did they have of twenty-four-year-old William Pitt the Younger becoming Prime Minister? Did they know Captain James Cook had discovered Australia? Nyren is silent on all these issues.

There may also be errors in his account of the changing game itself. Under Articles of Agreement signed for a game in 1727 (see Appendix 1, page 399), runs were scored when the batsmen crossed and touched the umpire's stick. In *The Young Cricketer's Tutor* Nyren refers to a 'block hole' between the stumps which the batsman had to touch to register a run – this was before the introduction of the popping crease. Thus, in this version of run-scoring, bat and fingers might collide – painfully for the fingers – when an attempt was made to 'run out' the batsman before, like a badger, he was safe and 'in his ground'. Unlike the 'umpire's stick', the 'block hole' theory of how runs were registered has no other contemporary confirmation: it *may* be right, but it is based only on Nyren's 1833 manuscript. It seems an unlikely tale to invent, so possibly both methods were in use for a time, perhaps by different clubs; but the 'umpire's stick' has the better historical pedigree.

Nyren may have misled us also about the size of the stumps. In the early eighteenth century, pictorial evidence suggests that wickets were about six inches wide, although the height varies: a 1739 engraving by Gravelot, a Frenchman, seems to show a height of around twelve inches, whilst in a 1743 painting by Hayman they appear to be the twenty-two inches approved in the 1744 codification of the laws. Yet, writing in the 1830s, Nyren refers to a manuscript he had seen which claimed that 'about 150 years since' – i.e. about 1680 – wickets were twelve inches high and twenty-four inches wide. No one has ever found this manuscript or any corroborating evidence.

Events caused two further innovations that were to last. In May 1775, five of Kent were playing five of England at the Artillery Ground, London. John Small Senior, in his prime as a batsman, was facing Lumpy Stevens, without doubt the pre-eminent bowler of the day. Fourteen runs were needed for victory – and were got. But before they were, Lumpy beat Small's defence three times, only to see the ball pass between the two stumps without disturbing either of them or the single bail. Morally, Small was out, he had been beaten, but as the wicket was undisturbed, he batted on. This was so patently unjust that from then on a third, central stump was added to prevent the ball passing straight between the wicket. By 1776 the press were reporting that 'it had been decided to have 3 stumps to shorten the game'. They were half-right: three stumps, yes – but to end an anomaly, not to shorten the game.

Another lacuna in the rules was exposed by a piece of sharp practice some time in the early 1770s. Thomas White of Reigate (not, as sometimes claimed, Shock White of Brentford), a regular England player, strode to the wicket carrying a bat as wide as the stumps – and, very possibly, a smile that was even wider at this attempted mischief. Nothing like this had been seen before, or would be seen again for two hundred years, until in 1979 Dennis Lillee tried, unsuccessfully, to use an aluminium bat during a Test match against England in Perth. The concept of such a wide bat was so at odds with the spirit of the game that it was soon outlawed, and as John Nyren, noted: 'An iron frame, of the statute width, was constructed for, and kept by, the Hambledon Club, through which any bat of suspected dimensions was passed, and allowed or rejected accordingly.'

In this fashion the laws continued to evolve, and though they were not yet universally applied, they soon would be. The intriguing question is, who determined and enforced the laws? It is probable, in pre-MCC days, that clubs such as Hambledon set the rules, and they simply became common usage.

The belief that Hambledon was the fount of cricket is by no means the only misconception about the club: the many myths of Hambledon would require Sherlock Holmes to unravel them all. They have, over the years, bamboozled even eminent and serious cricket historians such as Harry Altham, Derek Birley, David Underdown and R.S. Rait Kerr. In setting out what I believe to be misconceptions, made in the light of information available at the time, I mean no disrespect to those who related them as fact.

The history of Hambledon Cricket Club is shadowy from its inception, the date of which is itself a matter of controversy. Birley and Altham assert that the club was playing by 1756, but this is very questionable. It is true that the first known reference to Hambledon and cricket appears in that year – but not to a Hambledon Club. On 28 August 1756 the *Public Advertiser* reported a five-a-side match, for £20 a side, between five gentlemen of the parish of Hambledon and five named others at the Artillery Ground, London. It added that on the following Monday an eleven-a-side game would be played between the Dartford Club and eleven gentlemen of the parish of Hambledon, this being the deciding match between the teams for £50 a side. However, one cannot assume that this is *the* Hambledon Club. Dartford is referred to as a club, but Hambledon is twice described explicitly as a parish. It cannot be asserted confidently from this that Hambledon had yet formed a club, although a number of historians have done so. The minutes of the Hambledon Club, held at the Hampshire Record Office in Winchester, almost complete from 1772 to 1786, when the club was at its peak, contain no mention of the law-making responsibilities which some writers have attributed to it at this time, and nor has any yet turned up in contemporary newspapers.

The confusion appears to arise from a document, in the hands of the MCC and dated 1771, which purports to limit the width of cricket bats to 4¼ inches, a law which was to come into force in 1774. This paper bears the signature of three people who were believed to be Hambledon cricketers – yet in fact none of them was a member of the Hambledon Club. It may be one of the many cricketing fakes produced to supply a market avid for 'historic' documents. But even if the document is genuine, it does not establish the Hambledon Club as lawmakers. We do know – after the Thomas White incident – that three Hambledon cricketers signed a *club* rule over bat sizes, but that does not signify that they were rule-makers for all cricket controversies. In any event, when the 1774 rule revision took place Hambledon officials were present, and no doubt they urged the inclusion of a rule on the maximum size of bats.

At the beginning of the Hambledon Minute Book is a curiosity that teases over two hundred years later. 'By order of the Club, May 1st, 1781', a number of standing toasts are presented, presumably for formal dinners. After proper acknowledgement to royalty, there are toasts to the 'Hambledon Club', 'Cricket' and 'The President'. All these were standard fare, but in the midst of the cricketing toasts is the oddity – a toast to 'The Immortal Memory of Madge'. Who or what is 'Madge'? Is it an acronym? If so, for what? Was 'Madge' an early financial supporter? If so, I can find nothing to identify him. Was 'Madge' a woman, perhaps an abbreviation for Margaret? Or was it an in-joke among the club members that can no longer be deciphered? The possibilities are infinite, but the answer is hidden: we may never know.

Other club records are more revealing. There is a famous scene in the 1939 film *Goodbye, Mr Chips*, starring Robert Donat, in which the old schoolmaster Chips recalls punishing a boy for changing his marks in a Latin test from a 0 to a 9. A similar exaggeration is evident in estimates of the membership of the Hambledon Club. It has been claimed that 'assiduous researchers' have discovered that at its peak the club had 157 members; however, the researchers were neither assiduous nor accurate. All they did was to add up every subscriber over the twenty-five years between 1772 and 1796, and assume that sum total was the peak membership.* This is patently absurd: some would have withdrawn from membership, some would have died, and in any case many of the names are duplicated. The earliest surviving annual subscription list, for 1791, contains only fifty-two current members, and nothing in the club's minutes suggest that the figure ever much exceeded that.

There is also uncertainty about the identity of the club's founders. Altham speculated that the Reverend Charles Powlett was, if not the founder, at least the principal architect in developing the club. His assessment is that Powlett, assisted by Philip Dehany (sometimes inaccurately spelt 'Dehaney'), was prominent, together with others who had been pupils of Westminster School in the 1740s. Later writers have concurred, yet this can only be conjecture – we do not know, and it is equally likely that the founders could have been Thomas Land (1714–91), a minor patron of cricket, or John Richards (c.1737–1819), a Hambledon resident and the first treasurer of the club.

Land lived at Park House, a mile to the east of Hambledon village, beside the lane leading to Broadhalfpenny Down, and served as a local justice of the peace. He is possibly first mentioned in connection with Hambledon in the *St James's Chronicle* in September 1764, which refers to a game between the Gentlemen of Chertsey and Gentlemen of Hambledon called 'Squire Lamb's Club'. For 'Lamb' one could read 'Land', and by this date Hambledon is being referred to as a club. For the record, Hambledon won, although Chertsey were successful in a rematch. I can find no record of the outcome of a third and decisive game.

---

* Listed in F.S. Ashley-Cooper, *The Hambledon Cricket Chronicle 1772–96* (1924).

Land is mentioned in the version of the club song written by the Reverend Reynell Cotton, master of Hyde Abbey School, Winchester,* probably in 1772, and authorised in 1781:

> Then why should we fear either Sackville or Mann,
> Or repine at the loss of Bayton and Land?

This suggests that by then he had severed his connection with the Hambledon Club. None of this is conclusive. It is possible that 'Squire Lamb's Club from Hambledon' is not the Hambledon Club but a short-lived predecessor. Perhaps 'Lamb' is not 'Land'. The absence of references to Land in later years counts against him. So far as I can see, there is no mention of him in the club minutes, and his obituary in the *Hampshire Chronicle* of 27 June 1791 refers to him as a 'celebrated fox hunter' but does not mention cricket. He is therefore a possible founder only, and the case for him is as speculative as is that for Powlett and Dehany.

By 1767 the Hambledon Club's existence can be established. From the early minutes we know the names of thirteen gentlemen who were definitely members, and twelve others who *may* have been by 1772; but returning to Altham's claim that it was founded by former Westminster pupils, only four certainly attended that school, of whom only two were there in the 1740s. The club's members from 1772 onwards were highly influential: they included thirteen who either had, or were to inherit, titles, fourteen clergymen, and ten who were to become Admirals. Three members elected in the 1780s – Richard Barwell (1782), John Shakespeare (1784) and Laver Oliver (1786) – had gained riches in India. Hambledon had a lot of clout. Over a twenty-year period the club's Presidents included the Duke of Chandos, a future Duke of Richmond, and the Earls of Northington, Winchilsea (twice) and Darnley, as well as Lord John Russell. However, the eminent members from far away were outnumbered by those from nearer home. Over half of the initial twenty-five, who did not include Land – another strike against him as founder – lived within easy distance of Broadhalfpenny Down, which suggests that

* And President of the Hambledon Club in 1773, and possibly in 1774 too.

the club was simply founded by a group of local gentlemen. This is a less glamorous paternity than legend has suggested, but it is probably accurate.

Another uncertainty relates to the management of the club. Altham implies that Powlett 'piloted' Hambledon through 'at least one crisis', and that when the club folded in 1796 he was 'the last to abandon the sinking ship'. This is creditable if true, but it conflicts with the known facts. There is no record of Powlett attending *any* of the club's final meetings, nor of his being a subscriber for their last season. It seems that he sank before the club.

John Richards, however, did not, and he was the central figure in running the club throughout its heyday. Richards was about twenty-nine years of age when he settled in Hambledon in 1766, buying 'Whitedale', a large house just outside the village. Five years later he made his only known appearance as a cricketer, playing for Gentlemen of Hampshire against Gentlemen of Sussex at Broadhalfpenny Down. He is a type familiar to cricket history – the lover of the game with little skill at actually playing it. From the outset he seems to have been club treasurer, and thus financial executor of the club's wishes. He was the club's factotum, loyal and ever-present, as is reflected in a series of references from the club's minutes: in 1773 he was asked to check the expense of a conveyance to carry the team to away matches and then, later that year, to purchase it from surplus funds; in 1780 tobacco was ordered to be held in his safekeeping; in 1784 he was supervising alternatives to a 'booth' on the club's new ground at Windmill Down; and in 1787 he was asked to provide 'six spitting troughs' and a 'hogshead of the best port . . . to drink immediately'.

Richards was active in many local causes, and in 1772 was one of three nominees for Sheriff of Hampshire. He seems to have been as passionate about politics as cricket: in 1775 he helped found the Hampshire Club 'for the support of public liberty', acting sometimes as its steward, while in 1780 he was chairman of a meeting which adopted a petition against Lord North's government, promoted by his fellow Hambledon member Philip Dehany. He filled local government posts such as Surveyor of Highways, and though not himself a farmer, invented, according to the *Hampshire Repository*, 'several useful ploughs and implements of the drag and harrow, and a machine to weigh draft'. He was an energetic and inventive man who loved shooting, and thought little of walking six hours with his gun slung over his shoulder. In the midst of all these other pursuits he remained a faithful member of the Hambledon Club, and was one of only three subscribers who attended its final meeting before it was wound up in late 1796. But even then his stamp on the club did not end: his son, the Reverend Richard Richards, served as vicar of Hambledon for forty-one years, and was a member of the reformed club in the early nineteenth century.

Despite exaggerations of its historical significance, there is no doubt that Hambledon made a notable contribution to cricket. Although the image of Broadhalfpenny Down painted so fondly by John Nyren is an enduring one, it is misleading, since the Hambledon Club did not only play there. After the Duke of Dorset complained about the 'bleakness of the spot' the club moved on: the Duke's word was law. From 1778 many home games were switched to Stoke Down, fifteen miles to the north, and in 1782 the club began to use Windmill Down, much closer to the village, for their fixtures. This ground remained in use until the 1830s, and was the site of the first brick pavilion, where in 1784 the minutes instructed that 'a bell be hung in the Lodge under direction of the Stewards' – perhaps the first ever bell to signal the start of a game.

Other improvements were made too. In September 1784 three of the members were authorised to 'make such alterations to the "booth" as they think proper', and, more intriguingly, to erect a 'dulce lenimen for the Ladies'. This term occurs three times in classical Latin (once in Horace's *Odes* and twice in Ovid's *Metamorphoses*), and broadly means 'a sweet and healing consolation' – a charming description of an early purpose-built, on-site lavatory. Hambledon was always a very welcoming club to the ladies: as early as 1773 it bought green baize to cover the chairs in the 'Ladies tent'. By the early 1790s there was such pride in the club among its members that on match days they wore their own uniform of a sky-blue coat with a black velvet collar and the letters 'CC' (denoting Cricket Club) engraved on the buttons. Occasional games were still played at Windmill Down, but between 1777 and 1795 there was rarely more than one 'great' game a year – the sole exception being 1783, when two games were played. There were none at all in 1780, 1784, 1785 and 1794.

In July 1794 that old Hambledon warhorse Tom Walker lit a fuse that would smoulder for thirty years: he began to experiment with round-arm bowling, which gave him additional pace and an original line of attack. To test this new form of bowling, a match was played at Dartford between sides led by Walker and David Harris. Walker's team (scoring 130 and 59) defeated Harris's (76 and 60) by 53 runs, with only 'Silver Billy' Beldham (27) putting up significant resistance to Walker's new style of bowling. But the rustic Walker did not enjoy a social position that enabled him to press his case. Hambledon, although not the lawmaker of the game, said no to round-arm bowling, and that was the end of the matter. Walker went back to batting, and to bowling slow lobs. The conservatism that has so often governed cricket set the experiment quietly aside. Nonetheless, a seed had been sown.

In 1796 the original Hambledon Club was dissolved,* but not before leaving behind yet another small mystery that may never be solved. The club minutes record the presence of the revolutionary Tom Paine at a cricket match (Hambledon, East Meon and Petersfield vs Portsmouth) at Windmill Down on 29 August 1796, and specifically refer to him as 'Author of the Rights of Man'. If true this is remarkable, for had Paine been arrested in England at that time he would have faced the death penalty, in all its grisly horror, for treason. Madcap and reckless he may have been, but surely not to this extent, especially as earlier that month he is known to have declined to sail from France to America for fear of being picked up by a British warship patrolling the Channel. Theories abound as to what he was doing at Hambledon, but none convinces.

* The club was revived in 1806, but never again attained the eminence of earlier years.

In many ways Hambledon and Hampshire were synonymous on the cricket field, and the teams that represented them were apt to bear either name. It seems that the Hambledon members welcomed the dual description, for a club minute of 17 September 1782 refers to 'those players who intend to play in the County matches this year', and ruled that they should receive 'four shillings if winners and three shillings if losers'.

The Hambledon Club is pre-eminent because we *know* about it. But, out of the mists, some other clubs began to appear. An 'Old Sussex Cricketer' writing in 1882 claimed that there was 'a very strong club at Oakendene, near Cowfold' between 1790 and 1815.* No such club can be found under that name, but if for 'Oakendene' one can substitute 'Ockenden', the mystery may be solved. Ockenden Farm divides the Sussex villages of Cowfold and Twineham, and a club certainly thrived under the name of Ockenden from 1798 to 1811. Moreover, such sources as exist reveal that it played challenge matches and included well-known 'given' players in its team. At a match in August 1807 the 'county' shows Cowfold and Twineham with 'Silver Billy' Beldham in its team, as well as the famous all-rounder William Lambert and the long-hitting civil servant E.H. Budd, one of the leading amateur batsmen of the day. The Cowfold and Twineham Club disappears in 1811 without apparent reason, and was never reformed. It is probable that there are many more such stories which have been lost in the annals of time.

Be that as it may, Hambledon playing on Broadhalfpenny Down will forever catch and hold the imagination, and even if I feel a killjoy for dismissing some of the myths that have come to surround the club, I believe there is still ample evidence for it to be recognised as an important part of early cricket history.

In the years during which the Hambledon star rose and fell, the small world of cricket widened – and so did the cast of enthusiasts who came together to form the most famous club in history: the Marylebone Cricket Club.

* 'Sussex Cricket, Past and Present', *Cricket*, 13 July 1882.

For two hundred years, from its inception, the MCC was the most influential voice in cricket. But like Hambledon's, its birth is clouded in uncertainty. In the run-up to the formation of the MCC, cricket was growing in the rural areas and taking root in London. Clubs were springing up. Rich and powerful patrons were arranging games as a vehicle for gambling, bringing a source of income to ground landlords, brewers, caterers and cricketers alike. The press was reporting cricket more widely, sometimes with full scorecards. But amid this activity, controversies were arising over such matters as the width of the bat, the need for three stumps and the general rules of the game. The fracas at Sevenoaks in 1773 when a fielder, Richard Simmons, huddled so close to the batsman it was thought to be intimidating has already been mentioned. These controversies needed adjudication by a governing body whose judgement would be accepted by all. There was no democratic structure to elect such a body, and no one whose writ would run, other than the rich and powerful patrons whose enthusiasm and money had promoted the game for over half a century.

Thus far, regulation had been rather informal. Rules were set out in 1744, although this may have been merely a revision, or a codification, of existing practice. It is, however, certain that in 1774 a group of noblemen and gentlemen met at the Star and Garter in Pall Mall to revise the laws of cricket.* The Star and Garter was a fashionable watering hole – and one with notoriety in its history. Nine years earlier the fifth Lord Byron, grandfather of the poet, had dined there with a neighbour, William Chaworth. For several hours they had dined well, but not wisely, when a fierce quarrel broke out about – absurdly – the number of hares on Chaworth's estate. Byron's manic temper was let loose; he was not known as 'the wicked Lord' without reason. An upstairs room was acquired in which to settle the dispute in candlelit privacy, but tempers rose ever further, swords were drawn, and in a duel Byron killed his friend. He was immediately

* This revision contains the first known mention of 'leg before wicket'. However, there is no record of any LBW dismissal in a game until 1795, when the Hon. John Tufton was out to J. Wells for 3 runs while playing for England against Surrey at Moulsey Hurst.

charged with murder, but as a member of the House of Lords he claimed the right to be tried in Westminster Hall before 250 of his fellow peers. The trial was a sensation. Byron had often been the object of scandal, and now he was on trial for his life. Special galleries were erected for the crowds, thousands of tickets exchanged hands at six guineas a time, and all London society attended in their finest attire, having risen early to be present for the 7 a.m. start. The spectacle lasted only one long day, and at 6 p.m. Byron – dressed in mourning as a tribute to his dead friend – was acquitted of murder but convicted of manslaughter. Through a legal loophole he went free. Days later he was back in the House of Lords, and returned to his wayward life.

From the Star and Garter, the trail of the noblemen and gentlemen is muddied. In May 1775 there is a reference in the *Public Advertiser* to a game to be played by the 'Noblemen and Gentlemen of the Cricket Club' – but no precise name for the club is given. They reappear again, described in the *Morning Post* as members of the 'Grand Cricket Club', in October 1778, when they established a fund to reward cricketers who distinguished themselves in county matches. This patronage implies wealth and power, although the identity of the benefactors is unknown. In 1784 the 'Cricket Club of Noblemen and Gentlemen' was based at Willis's, a fashionable club in King Street, St James's. Its membership included Lord Winchilsea, a nobleman of the old school who became President of Hambledon in 1787. By the following year, 1785, the club had switched its formal meetings to the Star and Garter, where the *Morning Post* reported that the members dined at 5.30 p.m. on 30 May.

It is likely, but not provable from known documents, that this string of reports relates to the same group of cricket-loving enthusiasts. Now comes a conundrum that is crucial, but about which we can only conjecture. In the Record Office at Leicester there is a large broadsheet in four sections. One section is entitled: 'Rules of the Cricket Club' (that name again), while the other three are 'Committee', 'List of Subscribers of the Cricket Club' and, foremost of all, 'The Laws of Cricket, revised at The Star & Garter, Pall Mall, February

25th, 1784'. Here is the mystery: the names on the membership list suggest an earliest possible date of 1786,* but the heading duplicates the title of the laws published in 1774 – is '1784' a misprint, or are the rules a reprint from 1774? We cannot be certain, but the club rules make for fascinating reading (see Appendix 2, page 401). A 'stock purse' was built up of fees for dinners, and smaller sums from which club expenses were met. There are strict injunctions on membership and behaviour. None but 'gentlemen' can play. No one shall dispute the umpire's decision, upon penalty of a guinea fine. Only members and guests can enter the committee tent, and no horses or carriages are to be admitted to the cricket ground. It is all very clear-cut.

The membership of the club was impressive: 144 names, easily the largest known membership of any eighteenth-century cricket club. Nor were they any Tom, Dick or Harry: among them were the Duke of Dorset and Sir Horace Mann, together with twenty-two peers, including Viscount Maynard, husband of that vivacious and peripatetic paramour, the former Miss Nancy Parsons. A five-man committee presided: the Earl of Berkeley, Sir Peter Burrell, the Hon. Captain Monson, the Hon. Lionel Damer – a Sackville on his mother's side and cousin of the Duke of Dorset – and, as treasurer, the great Hambledon stalwart the Earl of Winchilsea.

The club played its cricket near White Conduit House, a round building with adjoining pleasure gardens north of Pentonville Road. On the edge of open country lay an open space – White Conduit Field – and it is here that the 'Lordling Cricketers' had their ground. They were not popular visitors, and on 22 June 1785 the *Daily Universal Register*, the forerunner of *The Times*, admonished them:

> It is recommended to the Lordling Cricketers who amuse themselves in White Conduit Fields, to procure an Act of Parliament for enclosing their play area, which will not only prevent them being incommoded, but protect themselves from a repetition of the severe rebuke which they jointly merit, and received on Saturday evening from some spirited citizens

---

* One of those on the list, 'Lord Dare', is probably in fact Lord Dacre (there was no 'Lord Dare'), who succeeded to the title in that year.

whom they insulted and attempted *vie et armis* to drive from
the footpath, pretending it was within their bounds.

This conjures up a vision of an embarrassing encounter as jaywalkers,
very possibly including the author of the press report, crossed the
cricket ground. Clearly the play area was unsatisfactory, and as a
result a cricketing legend enters the scene.

One of the regular spectators, employed as an occasional bowler
and general attendant, was a twenty-eight-year-old Yorkshireman
who combined a love of cricket with a bustling business acumen:
Thomas Lord (1757–1832). Both Winchilsea and Charles Lennox*
offered patronage to Lord if he would open a private ground. The
site Lord chose was situated on part of modern Dorset Square, just
north of Marylebone Road, extended to cover modern Ivor Place,
much of Boston Place and one-third of Marylebone Station, and was
in every way superior to White Conduit Fields. It was on a seven-acre
field that, apart from the playing surface, would hold over two thousand spectators and still leave sufficient space for a covered recess
under which refreshments could be served. The playing surface –
unsurprisingly – was uneven, but the ever-resourceful Lord assured
his patrons that it would be laid out like a bowling green for the 1787
season.

Before the season began, the club held an opening meeting at its
usual venue, the Star and Garter, on Monday, 30 April, followed by
dinner at 5.30 p.m. Despite the impending change of ground, no
change of name was proposed, and the club continued to be known
as the White Conduit Club. However, Lord – remembering the jaywalkers at the previous venue – fenced in his new ground to ensure
privacy. On 21 May 1787 a match was played between the White
Conduit Club and the County of Middlesex 'in the new cricket
ground, the New Road, Mary-le-Bone'. On 31 May and 1 June Middlesex again played on the ground, beating Essex by 93 runs.

* In May 1789 Lennox (1764–1819), later fourth Duke of Richmond, fought a duel on
Wimbledon Common with the Duke of York over a promotion that had been given to
Lennox in the Duke's regiment without the Duke having been consulted. Neither was
hurt in the duel.

Winchilsea and Lennox must have been delighted. Winchilsea's patronage was acknowledged in the *World* later that season, when it reported a game between the club and an England side. He is credited with 'good nature and liberality' as well as the generosity to ensure that Lord made a net profit. Lord was a lucky man: apart from a guaranteed income, he was much praised for the facilities he provided – which happened to abut a tavern of which he was the lessee. He was a shrewd son of Yorkshire.

The name of the White Conduit Club could not last, and on 30 July 1787 Lord's new ground staged a game between eleven gentlemen of the Mary-le-Bone Club and the Islington Club. This *may* be the debut of the MCC, as the Mary-le-Bone Club was probably the old White Conduit Club under a name that reflected the site of its new ground, but we cannot be absolutely certain. In any event, the White Conduit Club was playing as the Marylebone Club from the following season, 1788. Confusingly, the first MCC match was against a team designated as 'the White Conduit Club' – whom they beat by 83 runs.

The MCC has long claimed 1787 as its foundation date, and this may well be correct, but there is no irrefutable evidence in support of their contention. Although we can assume that the Mary-le-Bone Club that played against Islington was the renamed White Conduit Club, it could have been a wholly separate team using Thomas Lord's ground. No definitive evidence is available. Nonetheless, 1787 has entered history as the birthdate of the MCC, and fifty years later, in 1837, a grand jubilee match was held between the 'North' and 'South' of England to commemorate this anniversary. This apparent corroborative evidence is unconvincing: none of the players or officials involved in 1787 was still alive, nor were any of the founding club members, and any records were destroyed in the fire of 1825 (see page 145). Although we know that Lord's ground opened in 1787, we cannot be certain that the MCC was formed at the same time.

The club's initial membership is equally uncertain. Altham says that the Earl of Tankerville was 'one of the leading spirits in the White Conduit and Marylebone Clubs', whereas Rait Kerr asserts that he was a member of the MCC and Hambledon. So far as I can discover, he was a member of neither. Birley says that Tankerville, the Earl of Sandwich and the Duke of York were members of the MCC, but once more, I can find no proof of this.

Evidence is available, however, for the proposition that the MCC was accepted as the voice of authority from the outset. When, in 1788, a dispute over cricketing law arose between teams from Leicester and Coventry after a batsman hit the ball twice to protect his wicket, it was 'submitted to the first reputed cricket society in the Kingdom', namely, the MCC. Three years later, nine MCC members were invited to adjudicate over a dispute in a match at Hambledon on 13–15 July 1791 between England and Hampshire. The MCC was in business.

5

Cricket Spreads: Early Roots

The MCC was an aristocratic body. In its early days the most regular spectators were the Duke of Dorset and Charles Lennox (the future Duke of Richmond); a selection of peers including Winchilsea, Darnley, Cardigan and Lord Frederick Beauclerk; and other high-ranking individuals such as Colonel (later General) Bligh, the Hon. John and Henry Tufton, Sir Horace Mann, the Hon. Thomas Twisleton, and Messrs Charles Anguish, Louch, Powlett and George Dehany.* They were often joined by the Marquess of Hertford, Lord Thanet and, from time to time, the Duchess of Richmond, Lady Wallace and 'other ladies', although the feminine contingent were merely guests, and the MCC began – as it remained for so long – a male enclave.

Beyond the small world of cricket there was little interest in the birth of the MCC. Certainly for the next twenty years there would be many distractions. Britain was in a ferment of change. The Industrial Revolution, fifty years into its stride in the 1790s, was changing the way of life in town and country. In industrial areas the textile, iron, coal and metal trades had revolutionised production to meet a demand boosted by the fear, and then the reality, of war against France. In the two decades to 1800, war and industry would fuel a fourfold increase in the production of pig iron. In the first three years of the new century, forty-seven new blast furnaces were built to supply munitions, bridges, nails, vats, iron chains – and even pipes

* Not Philip Dehany of Hambledon fame.

for the infant gas industry. In London a network of docks was being constructed. By 1815 Hull was building a port to rival Liverpool and London.

As commerce boomed, so did shipping, with a thousand vessels a year being built. Between 1795 and 1805 the mercantile fleet grew by one-third. The navy built warships to fight France, and four thousand mature trees were sacrificed for each one. Large quantities of forest were cut down: Scotland and north-west England lost nearly all their trees. The price of timber soared, and in counties where there was no coal for heating, and few trees left to burn, cold food was the normal diet.

Steam power was making an impact. In 1802 the *Charlotte Dundas*, the first steam-powered canal boat, was in operation, and a decade later two hundred passengers at a time were being carried by a steam vessel on the Limehouse canal, while a steam packet was under construction that would travel from London to Calais at the eye-watering speed of twelve miles per hour.

Even so, the majority of jobs were still on the land. Agricultural prices rose, as the growing population (10.9 million, according to the 1801 census) needed to be fed, and this problem worsened when war with Napoleon cut back the imports of foreign corn. Land – even marginal farming land – was enclosed, as farming enjoyed a boom period due to inflation. But not all farmers prospered. For small-holders and their village workforces, the future was precarious. Many farms were too tiny to be profitable without wartime inflation, and new inventions such as the threshing machine reduced the need for labour. The plight of the rural poor was dire, and parish funds supplemented their wages to enable them to eat – in 1801 a Suffolk labourer earned nine shillings a week, and received a further six shillings in Poor Relief. This had the perverse effect of subsidising employers, who were able to keep wages low. War allied to industrial and agricultural turbulence was a heady brew, and brought hardship and discontent to millions of the urban and rural poor. Even when peacetime beckoned, their plight worsened.

Seventy-five years earlier the sharp eye of Daniel Defoe had observed class distinctions as he rode around England, but he had rejoiced in the underlying harmony of the social fabric: this was now about to crack. The well-to-do had been terrified by the French Revolution, which raised a spectre they feared and poisoned their minds against the underclass, however justified their grievances might be. As each month passed, the impact of war and Industrial Revolution began to chip away at the cohesion of society and widen the gulf between rich and poor, town and country. The rise of the meritocracy gained pace, and as the new industrialists tasted power and success they became less willing to defer to those who regarded themselves as their social superiors. The aristocracy, the meritocracy and the working man were all at odds. A storm was gathering, and the time was ripe for change.

Cricket could not be immune from the impact of war and social upheaval, although in its own modest fashion it meandered on, providing the old, familiar relationship between men far apart in wealth and rank. But for some years it did only meander. Historians have speculated that the decline in the amount of cricket played at this period was a side-effect of the Napoleonic Wars, and there may be some truth in this. Certainly earlier wars had such an impact. A summary of all known cricket matches during the Seven Years War (1756–63) shows a decline in the number of games from thirty in 1755, one year prior to war, to ten in 1761.* But this is a partial explanation only. Young men were not conscripted for the war (apart from a few press-ganged sailors), and neither armies nor navies were particularly large. Nevertheless, some credence can be given to the negative impact of the Napoleonic Wars. Hambledon subscription lists survive from 1791 to 1795, and they reveal how many members enlisted in the army or navy and went abroad: in 1791 none were lost to the club; in 1792 one; in 1793 six, two going abroad (presumably with the army) and four to sea. Six were also lost in both 1794 and 1795.

The historian Arthur Haygarth, the most avid researcher in all

* J. Carter, *Cricket Quarterly*, Vol II, No. 3, 1964. pp.161–71.

cricket, devoted his life to disinterring information about the game. In his *Cricket Scores and Biographies* (1862) he discovered that the MCC played twenty-four games in 1800, falling to seven in 1803, then rising slightly before falling again to only two in 1811 and 1812, before a steady growth back began. Similarly, a record of 'England' matches reveals eight in 1800, two in 1802, and a total in single figures (often only one a year) until 1825. A similar pattern is evident in a study of Sussex cricket over the same period.

Cricket-lovers had never welcomed the interference of the military in their game. In 1758, when the Superintendent of the Lines at Chatham had refused to let local people play cricket he received a letter threatening to murder him. Two years later there was outrage when a powder magazine was built on the cricket field at Gosport. Not all military officers were so insensitive. Before the Battle of Quiberon Bay in 1759, the British commander Sir Edward Hawke (a forebear of Lord Hawke, the eminent Victorian cricketer and administrator) had no reservations about the game. A sailor wrote home from the *Namur*: 'I take this, being the first, opportunity to inform you of my welfare. We live here very happily, have extreme fine weather, go ashore very often and play at cricket.'*

Affection for cricket was not at the expense of patriotism. When county militias were reformed in 1778 a contemporary song, 'The Man of Kent', celebrated the event and the role of cricketers:

> When Royal George commanded
> Militia to be raised,
> The French would sure have landed,
> But for such youths as these;
> Their oxen stall and cricket ball,
> They left for martial glory,
> The Kentish lads shall win the odds
> Your fathers did before ye.

While this song singled out Kent, the militias were nationwide, although Kent's location left it a likely front line in the event of

* *Norwich Mercury*, 7 June 1759.

invasion. Concern was such that even the cricket ground at Coxheath was requisitioned as a military camp. The commander-in-chief did not live a tented life on manoeuvres, but resided at old Sir Horace Mann's house while he was abroad. No doubt he was visited by the Duke of Dorset, who served as Colonel of the West Kent militia, although surprisingly there is no record of his regiment playing cricket. Other regiments, however, certainly did – for example, the officers of the Cinque Ports Corps played against Portsea Island in July 1781, and against the Bucks militia the following month.

There is evidence that cricket clubs were depleted by the demands of war. The diary entry of Richard Hayes of Cobham for 10 July 1778 suggests that the seafaring traditions of Chatham had an adverse impact on the team: 'Meopham Fair to the cricketing. The club is many of them gone to sea. No wonder they was beat.' It may be that in the 1790s the great bowler Lumpy Stevens was enlisted. A letter from 'A Kentish Cricketer', dated 20 May 1793 and published in the *Sporting Magazine*, reports that Ensign Hamilton of the 3rd Regiment, a member of Sevenoaks Vine Cricket Club, had a cannonball diverted from his head by an unnamed Sergeant, linked a day later in the *Maidstone Journal* to Lumpy. The report suggests that Lumpy might have thought 'his province invaded by the Sergeant who so dextrously caught the cannon-ball'. This story reeks of good-natured banter in which Lumpy's celebrity as a bowler was the subject of a jovial comparison to the nimble fielding skills of the Sergeant with an altogether more deadly ball.

War, then, was a factor in impeding the previously steady growth of cricket. So was social turbulence as families gave priority to their livelihood, and leisure featured lower among their priorities. There is one other factor that inhibited the growth in the number of games played, and would continue to do so until well into the nineteenth century. Travel options were still primitive. Travelling on horseback was tiring and slow for individuals, and inconceivable for whole teams, even in carts. One alternative, travelling by stagecoach, was expensive, slow and painful. In the 1750s it took six days to travel from London to Newcastle, four and a half days to Manchester and two days to Birmingham. Coaches were faster by the 1780s, but London to Newcastle was still three days' hard journeying, while Manchester took twenty-eight hours, and Birmingham nineteen. Nor were such journeys comfortable as a German tourist, Karl Philipp Moritz, testified in 1782, having ridden, as many did, on the outside of the coach:

> The getting up alone was at the risk of one's life, and when I was up, I was obliged to sit just at the corner of the coach, with nothing to hold by, and a sort of little handle fastened on the side . . . the moment that we set off, I fancied that I saw certain death await me.

Matters did not improve once the stagecoach got into its stride:

> The machine now rolled along with prodigious rapidity, over the stones through the town, every moment we seemed to fly into the air; so that it was almost a miracle that we still stuck to the coach and did not fall . . . When we came to get down hill, then all the trunks and parcels began as it were, to dance around me . . . I was obliged to suffer this torture . . . till we came to another hill again, when [I was] quite shaken to pieces and sadly bruised.

It is no wonder cricketers sought fixtures in their own locality.

The perils of travel were so intense that coaches were known as 'God permit', the unspoken thought being 'God permit I arrive safely' – a reasonable prayer, as they sometimes overturned and pitched their passengers off. Many stagecoach travellers arrived bruised and beaten at their destination. More expensive, but faster and safer, were post-chaises, which carried only two passengers compared to a stagecoach's six or eight. But they were an option only for the minority of the population, and certainly not for rustic cricketers.

The game of cricket had travelled further than individual teams were able to do, and had spread widely by the time the MCC was formed. Before 1700 it can only be proved that it was established in a handful of towns and villages in Surrey, Sussex and Kent; there is no record yet uncovered of it having spread north of the Thames by that date.

Cricket spread westward first, to Hampshire, although – possibly due to a lack of local newspapers – there are no references to the game there until 1729, when a combined Surrey, Sussex and Hampshire team played Kent; local teams in Hampshire can first be traced in the 1740s. But early references to West Country cricket are sparse and contradictory. In 1776 the *Salisbury Journal* refers to cricket being 'but lately introduced in these parts', yet other evidence suggests it was well-established. Records reveal that in 1772 a team of players from the Hampshire villages of Ringwood and Fordingbridge, and Downton in Wiltshire, opposed the 'noted players' from Milford in Hampshire.

Similar evidence comes from Dorset, where the game was sufficiently popular in the 1730s for twelve men of Dorchester to challenge all-comers 'to play at cricket for twelve pairs of gloves, value one shilling'.* It seems that the attraction of a bet, however modest, added spice to cricket far beyond the circle of the great patrons.

In September 1729 the *Weekly Journal* reported that an eleven-a-side game was played in Gloucestershire for a purse of twenty guineas, and nearby in 1769 the 'young gentlemen' of Cirencester were 'introducing the manly game of cricket into this county, where it has been hitherto unknown'. Other games are recorded at Durdham Down, Bristol (Bristol vs London), in 1752, and in 1769, again at Bristol, where the actor William Powell, a great rival to David Garrick, died after catching a cold that turned to fever after he had been playing or watching cricket on a chilly day.

Somerset was staging cricket in the 1770s. A local diarist, John Yeoman, refers to it in 1774 as a game which 'children play in our County', but in some places it was being played by adults. The village of Bruton played Redlinch in 1772 at Wincanton, and in 1795 men and youths of Bath played at Claverton Down, where, it was reported, 'the novelty of this manly exercise, in a regular match, drew together

---

* *Sherborne Mercury*, 9 May 1738.

a great number of spectators'. By 1819 a Bath Club was active, and the rise of club cricket began in the county, as it did in Gloucestershire, where isolated matches can be traced as early as a hundred years before.

Cricket was recorded in one south-western market town in 1773 by the novelist and diarist Fanny Burney, then only twenty-one, who wrote from Teignmouth in Devon of 'a grand cricket match . . . the cricket players dined on the Green, where they had a boothe erected, and a dinner from the Globe'. And at Falmouth a club existed where members gave 'a very elegant entertainment to the ladies'. However, regular inter-parish cricket is not known to have reached Devon or Cornwall until the 1820s.

Cricket did not spread evenly across whole counties, but was adopted in small villages or towns where local enthusiasts promoted the game. When Stockton opposed Stockton Downs in 1799 it was reported as 'an event so novel in the county of Wiltshire'. Yet it was not *that* novel: only a few miles away, Calne, Devizes, Salisbury and Marlborough had been merrily playing cricket for a quarter of a century. So had Westbury, from 1783.

In many counties – Hereford, Worcestershire, Shropshire, Cheshire, Lancashire, Cumberland, Westmorland, Staffordshire – there are virtually no eighteenth-century references to cricket. The pace quickens in the nineteenth century, and the invaluable *Bell's Life* reports in 1829 that although '2 or 3 years ago' cricket was scarcely known in Cumberland, 'now there are eight strong clubs'. Similarly, from the early 1820s regular – probably annual – fixtures were played between clubs in Liverpool and Manchester.

Cricket spread northwards from its south-eastern cradle, travelling east of the Pennines up to Northumberland. In his book *The History of Cricket* (1997), Peter Wynne-Thomas traces bats being manufactured at Welbeck Abbey, the Nottinghamshire seat of the Duke of Portland, as early as 1748. By the 1770s Nottingham was fielding teams against Sheffield, while in the latter decades of the eighteenth century cricket 'societies' had been formed in Newark, Bingham and Southwell. The *Leicester Journal* of 17 August 1776 advertises a 'great match' between Barrow-on-Soar and Mountsorrel, but does not report the outcome.

There are even earlier traces of cricket in Northumberland and County Durham. Records exist of the game being played at Raby Castle in 1751, and a 'great match' between the gentlemen of Gateshead and Newcastle ended in an easy victory for the former in mid-June 1753. At Hexham in January 1766 the river was frozen so solidly that a sheep was roasted upon it and the meat sold at twelve pence a pound to a numerous company 'who afterwards played at cricket', while others danced.* In eighteenth-century Hexham, hardy cricketers did not restrict the game to the summer.

Yorkshire too was enjoying cricket by the mid-century. It was played at Stanwick in 1751, and in 1773 West Auckland played Scruton at Piercebridge. Two years later, Colburn and Hipswell, near Richmond, contested a match that drew 'a great number of spectators who had fine diversion'. But Yorkshire cricket may already have had a long history. The court roll relating to Hillham, fifteen miles east of Leeds, notes in 1620: '*terr in loco voc Crickitt*', which *seems* to mean 'known to the locals as a cricket ground'. Although this cannot be wholly relied on without corroborating evidence, it does suggest an earlier genesis for cricket in Yorkshire than research has yet uncovered. A more reliable record is *The History and Antiquities of Richmond*, published in 1821, which looks back at 'various games and pastimes', and includes cricket as an amusement of 'the lower class of people'. This designation of cricket as a traditional game of the rural population hints at it having been played for some time, and not introduced from outside by travelling gentry. But once more, this is not definitive evidence.

Outside England, cricket was being played in Wales by local gentry at Carmarthen by 1783. The following year the *Hereford Journal* reported that a 'Swansea Cricket Meeting' had been fixed on 6 May for the first occasion of the season 'according to last year's resolutions'. The subscribers were invited to meet at the Bathing House

---

* *Felix Farley's Bristol Journal*, 25 January 1766.

to appoint a steward for that day, and a treasurer for the season. Welsh cricket then vanishes from view until its re-emergence in the 1820s, by which time clubs had been set up in Pontypool, Cardiff, Usk and Newport.

The earliest definitive accounts of cricket in Scotland are from the records of the leading aristocrats. In the 1780s, strangers were banned from the estate of the Duke of Hamilton – a brother-in-law of Sir Peter Burrell, a grandee of the White Conduit Club – on days when he was playing cricket. The Duchess too, the former Miss Elizabeth Ann Burrell, was a cricket enthusiast; she had met the Duke at a match in 1777 at the Oaks, Woodmansterne, Surrey, between the Countess of Derby XI and Ladies of Quality and Fashion. Miss Burrell scored more 'notches' than any other lady, and the Duke, mightily attracted by her face and form, married her in the close season. Other leading figures in Scotland were devotees of the game. Viscount Cathcart, a native of Surrey, and his brother-in-law the Duke of Atholl, played in a match at Shaw Park, Alloa, in 1785. Four years later the Gordon Castle Club included in its team for a match against the 55th Regiment the Marquess of Huntly (a future Duke) and his brother-in-law Charles Lennox – who scored 136, the first ever century in Scotland. A distant cousin, Lord Strathavon, yet another aficionado of the White Conduit Club, also played. The English connection was promoting the game in Scotland, and more eminent Englishmen would try to do so later. Lord Palmerston, the future Victorian Prime Minister, was at Edinburgh University in the early 1800s. When he failed to find enough people to 'muster up' to play cricket he turned to golf – 'A poor game compared to cricket, but better than nothing,' opined his Lordship. It was not a judgement endorsed by many Scots – then or now.

For anyone to 'muster up' a team to play cricket, facilities were needed, although we know very little of how cricket grounds at the time were functioning. Some famous venues disappeared. In 1780 a new lease banned cricket on the venerable Honourable Artillery Company site in London where so much early cricket had been played. Horace Mann's ground at Bourne Paddock continued to stage matches, but many others depended on being adjacent to hostelries: even Hambledon had been a neighbour to the Bat and Ball before matches moved from Broadhalfpenny Down to Windmill Down in 1782. 'Mr Siddle's new cricket ground at Deptford' in Kent was staging matches by 1748, followed by others at Gosport in Hampshire (1760), West Hill at Hastings, in Sussex (1769), Kevington at St Mary Cray in Kent (1768), Shipdham in Norfolk (1770), Linchmere in Sussex (1771) and Chatham in Kent (1772). None of these was allied to an inn or hotel.

As soon as it was formed, the MCC took precedence over all other clubs – even Hambledon. It had prestige, rank and the endorsement of cricket's leading sponsors. Membership was highly prized. In 1793 the prolific playwright and dramatist Frederick Reynolds was enjoying a huge triumph with his comedy *How to Grow Rich*, but in 1827 he would write in his memoirs:

> Notwithstanding this success, and my natural propensity towards the drama, yet it at this period only afforded me a secondary pleasure. The love of a mere pastime – of cricket was the first; and at length increased to such a height, that the day I was proposed as a member of the Marylebone Club, then in its highest fashion, I waited at the Portland Coffee House to hear from Tom Lord the result of the ballot with more anxiety than I had experienced the month before, while expecting the decision of the audience on my new play. Being unanimously elected, I immediately assumed the sky-blue dress, the uniform of the club, and soon thoroughly entered into all the spirit of this new and gay scene.

And gay, in the traditional sense, it was: the MCC presented the grave and serious face of authority to the world outside, but members did not take themselves seriously. Reynolds spills the beans about their facetious behaviour. Often it was schoolboy humour: Charles Anguish emptied a colleague's snuffbox and substituted hellebore, thus causing an unstoppable fit of sneezing in the midst of a toast. Reynolds does not identify the victim, except to note that he was a Member of Parliament speaking at a dinner for his electors. Sarah Siddons, the great tragedian, witnessed this comedy and much enjoyed it, but one guest sourly remarked: 'Sir, I can see no humour in a man who owes me three guineas.'

Even the much-loved Sir Horace Mann suffered from pranks. A fellow MCC member extracted mottos from bon-bons set in front of Sir Horace at dinner, and substituted *bon mots* of a riper and coarser nature. The courtly Sir Horace, blissfully unaware, began to read one of them aloud to the lady sitting beside him before stopping abruptly, tearing up the offending piece of paper and fleeing the room in shame. The lady remained to titter, blush and fan herself while the whole room chuckled.

Reynolds recalls that Charles Lennox was at his best after a few drinks: 'His Grace was most *himself* when *not himself*.' Lennox, whether himself or not, was a practical joker, as Reynolds discovered when offered the loan of a horse to ride to a cricket ground. The horse had been trained to be averse to red coats, and when Reynolds met some soldiers it became ungovernable and he was pitched to the ground. Lennox was vastly amused, and as Reynolds was lucky enough to survive intact, his whimsical good humour was able to be recorded for posterity.

Some MCC members stood aloof from the buffoonery. The bachelor Lord Winchilsea was 'too punctilious', and if Lords Thanet and Darnley had a frivolous nature, they hid it from public gaze. So did Lord Frederick Beauclerk, of whom more later, to whom frivolity was unimaginable. Lord Cardigan, whose son would lead the Light Brigade to disaster in the Crimea, was often a target of 'the wags', though Reynolds is silent on the details.

Tomfoolery apart, it was cricket that bound the members together. Lord Frederick Beauclerk stood 'unrivalled' as a cricketer, claimed Reynolds, who played a single-wicket match against him and was permitted ten innings to a solitary one by Beauclerk. Reynolds hit a few 'high, home and easy' balls, but was unable to bowl out his opponent, who won easily and pocketed the guineas. A second single-wicket match against another fellow MCC member, Henry Tufton, ended more dramatically: Reynolds hit the ball into Tufton's arm with such force that a bone was broken. After medical treatment the genial victim informed his persecutor: 'Reynolds, Lord Frederick has never *fractured* anything but *wickets*, so play him.'

Reynolds regarded his cricketing days as his happiest, and he played with many of the top players around the turn of the nineteenth century, including on one occasion the 'celebrated, formidable [David] Harris':

> In taking my place at the wicket, I almost felt as if taking my ground in a duel . . . and my terrors were so much increased by the mock pity and sympathy of Hammond, Beldham, and others round the wicket, that when this mighty bowler, this *Jupiter tonans*, hurled his bolt at me, I shut my eyes in the intensity of my panic, and mechanically gave a random desperate blow, which, to my utter astonishment, was followed by a loud cry all over the ring of 'run, run'.
>
> I did run; and with all my force; and getting three notches, the Duke of Richmond, John Tufton, Leigh, Anguish, and other arch wags, advanced and formally presented to me twenty-five sixpences in a hat, collected from the by-standers, as 'The Reward of Merit.' Even Lord Winchelsea, and Sir Horace Mann, contributed to this, and then all playfully commenced promoting a new subscription, which only stopped, because I could not stop the next ball. To my great joy, up went my stumps, and out I walked; certainly with some little *éclat*, being the first member of the club, who had been considered a regular player, i.e. paid for his services.

The 'mock pity' of the close fielders and the collection of sixpences for the wealthy Reynolds hint at the revelry of the MCC's early members.

Although the MCC had become the leading force in cricket, it did not yet have a settled ground. On 17 August 1810 the final game was completed* at Thomas Lord's Dorset Fields ground, as the lease expired: a team designated the 'Old', its members being thirty-eight years of age or more, beat the 'Young' by ninety runs. The astute

---

* The game began on 24–25 July, but its completion was deferred until 17 August because of rain.

Thomas Lord had foreseen that the lease would not be renewed, and had rented two fields on the St John's Estate, upon which he prepared a ground for 1809; for that season he had two grounds in use. The new ground was adopted by the MCC in May 1811, but was never popular, and a mere three games were played on it in two years. Then fate intervened when Parliament fixed a route for the Regent's Canal that flowed through the ground, and its role in cricket was over.

Lord was undaunted, and laid out a third ground, upon eight and a quarter acres of land rented in nearby St John's Wood for £100 per annum. It opened on 22 June 1814 with a match, almost certainly organised by Lord Frederick Beauclerk, in which MCC beat Hertfordshire by an innings and 27 runs. Beauclerk, 'Squire' George Osbaldeston, E.H. Budd and William Ward all played in the inaugural game. Lord's had found its permanent home.

6

The Round-Arm Rebellion

Although social conditions inhibited the growth of cricket during the early years of the nineteenth century, it was poised to grow from its rural cradle into an international obsession. The old patrons Winchilsea and Mann, and lesser-known benefactors such as Lords Yarmouth and Darnley, bowed out of cricket history. Lord Frederick Beauclerk, who first appeared in the 1790s, would be a key figure in the future. So too would William Ward and James Dark, whose futures would be interwoven with that of Lord's. Billy Beldham, John Small Junior, Tom Walker, William Fennex, John Wells and Robert Robinson were still playing, and George Osbaldeston, E.H. Budd, Thomas Beagley and William Searle began to come to the fore. John Willes was experimenting with a new form of bowling that would change the laws of cricket. Babies in their cradles, Nicholas Felix, Alfred Mynn and Fuller Pilch, would raise skills to a higher level.

In 1811 the women of Hampshire played the women of Surrey, and Thomas Rowlandson was on hand to draw a famous caricature of the occasion. Beneath an apparently dormant surface, the future of cricket was taking shape. Overseas, cricket was being played in Sydney, Australia. British prisoners of war were enjoying the game in Argentina, and St Anne's Cricket Club was flourishing in Barbados. The first known century in India was scored by R. Vansittart at Calcutta in 1806, for Old Etonians vs Rest of Calcutta. The game continued to spread. Officers of the Artillery Mess were playing in Cape Town in 1808, while in the United States Boston boasted its own cricket club. Games were soon being played at Green Point Common in Cape Town – still in use today – and in Naples, where a local club attracted French and Neapolitan members. In the next decade, officers of the Brigade of Guards played near Brussels, watched by the Duke of Wellington, before facing Napoleon at the Battle of Waterloo. Cricket can be traced to Tasmania, Valparaiso (Chile), Ontario, South Carolina and Gibraltar. Much of the spread mirrored the campaigns of the British Army and navy, but when the forces departed, cricket often stayed on.

The first book on cricket technique, Thomas Boxall's *Rules and Instructions for Playing at the Game of Cricket*, was published in 1801, and Samuel Britcher's books of scores – effectively early *Wisdens* – had been in circulation since 1790. A book with a section on cricket, translated from German, was published in Denmark as early as 1801. The game was strong in the public schools, with Eton, Harrow and Westminster contesting matches at Lord's. It is likely that Eton and Harrow had been playing an annual fixture at Lord's since the turn of the century, although 1805 is the first game for which scores are known. The poet Lord Byron, despite his lame foot, scored 7 and 2 for Harrow, although he later boasted of rather larger scores to his old friend Charles Gordon. It may be that his memory was befuddled, for as he freely admitted, the teams became drunk after the match and ended up at the Haymarket Theatre where, being young gentlemen out on a spree, they kicked up a fuss and made themselves thoroughly unwelcome.

While they did so, the army and navy engaged in a more deadly battle with France, and the government wrestled with domestic turbulence. New inventions cost jobs, and unrest among the workforce led to violence. In 1811 factory machines were destroyed in riots at Nottingham and the government, fearful of revolution, acted to make destruction of property a new capital offence. Harshness stood in for enlightened policy.

Other changes were more benevolent. Vast improvements in medicine and nursing were under way: bacteria were isolated, immunisation cut disease, and anaesthetics came into use. Other benevolent changes would improve the lifestyles of the mass of the population. Leisure time increased. The rise of the symphony orchestra began. New instruments, such as the woodwinds so beloved of Mozart, were added to orchestras. In 1808 Beethoven's Fifth Symphony added yet more instruments: trombones, piccolos and contra-bassoons swelled the orchestra, and as the century advanced cornets, tubas and additional percussion became more commonplace. It was all a far cry from the joyful singing at the Bat and Ball to the solitary fiddle of old John Small.

War and social conditions slowed the advance of cricket, but it was not about to wither. An 'England' team played thirty-five games in the first seven years of the century, although the range of opponents was limited, and most of their fixtures were against Surrey, Kent, Hampshire or the MCC. The same cricketers, albeit disguised as amateur 'Gentlemen' and professional 'Players', also began a rivalry at Lord's in 1806 that would endure for 156 years, until the distinction became obsolete and the fixture was abandoned. On the poor pitches of the time, some games produced miserly scores: Kent were bowled out for only 6 runs against Bexley. In all encounters, underarm bowling held sway. It was soon to be challenged by a more formidable proponent than the old Hambledon rustic Tom Walker.

The birth of round-arm bowling has its own legends. One, widely accepted, is charming, though dubious. John Willes, a handsome, wealthy landowner with property in Kent and Sussex, lived life to the full. He was also an individualist and, it would seem, could be some-thing of an awkward cuss. Much of our knowledge of him comes from the recollections of his nephew Edward Hodges, whose affec-tionate tales must be treated with the scepticism that is always wise when fond reminiscences masquerade as history. Hodges tells us that Willes was a reckless rider to hounds, a good boxer, a keen shot and an erratic suitor. He once eloped in a coach-and-four with a young lady from Harrietsham – a tale that cries out to be a limerick – but her father pursued them on horseback, pistol in hand, and returned her, unmarried, to the family home. When taxed with this tale by the young Hodges, Willes reacted with a fury that did not lessen when he was told that the story originated from a lady friend. It may have been true, or merely gossip, but it gives a flavour of an eccentric, spontaneous man of high temper, unrestrained by convention.

Willes was a keen cricketer who practised in a barn at Tonford, near Canterbury, with his sister Christiana (not 'Christina', as is often thought) and a dog trained to recover the ball. Christiana, Edward Hodges recalled, threw the ball to Willes round-arm, since her voluminous hooped skirts prevented her bowling in the familiar underarm fashion. Although this tale offers a truly delightful picture, and cannot be disproved, nor can it be relied upon, even though Christiana Willes was Hodges' mother. The winter practice in the barn must have been in the years immediately before Willes bowled round-arm in public, which would fix their date at between 1800 and 1806. Unfortunately for the story, at that time, as any devotee of the screen adaptations of Jane Austen – or of Thackeray's *Vanity Fair* – will know, hooped skirts were no longer in vogue.

A variant of the 'Christiana' genesis emerges in 1886, in a letter from 'R.H.W.', a former cricketer:

> I will just send you what Lord Verulam told me about the origin of round-arm bowling. One Knight, a south-country bowler, used to practise with his sister to keep his hand in, and his sister bowled to him in turn. As she put no steam on, he asked her to shy the ball, which she did in the way women usually do shy, that is without using wrist. He observed that the pace improved, and that there was no 'jerk', which was rigorously *defendu* in those days, and he tried the bowling himself, and found he could get great pace, a twist from the leg, and much more rebound. He laid the matter before Lord's Committee, and the style was at once legalized and adopted. This, Lord Verulam said, was about 1829, and I think we have proved that pretty correct, quite near enough.*

Well, not really. The tale is muddled, and is so similar to the more popular theory that I suspect it is an old man misrecalling a tale from his youth. 'One Knight, a south-country bowler' refers to Mr Knight

* *Cricket: A Weekly Record of the Game.*

of Alton, who features in the Reverend Pycroft's early history *The Cricket Field* (1851). We shall return to him shortly, for he was to have a significant role in revolutionising cricket, and came from an unexpected lineage. In the meantime, Pycroft offers yet another version of how round-arm bowling was introduced:

> Just before the establishment of Mr Willes' round-hand bowling, and as if to prepare the way, Ashby came forward with an unusual bias, but no great pace. Sparkes bowled in the same style; as also did Mathews and Mr. Jenner somewhat later. Still the batsmen were full as powerful as ever, numbering Saunders, Searle, Beagley, Messrs. Ward, Kingscote, Knight. Suffolk became very strong with Pilch, the Messrs Blake, and others of the famous Bury club; while Slater, Lillywhite, King and the Broadbridges raised the name of Midhurst and of Sussex. Against such batsmen every variety of underhand delivery failed to maintain the balance of the game, till Broadbridge and Lillywhite, after many protests and discussions, were so successful in establishing round-arm that it was long called 'Sussex bowling'.

Whatever the truth of its birth may be, the facts of the introduction of round-arm bowling to cricket are clear. At some point in or before 1806, John Willes began to bowl in the round-arm style in local games in Kent; no doubt his social status, together with his fiery temper, discouraged any opposition to his doing so. But opposition there was, and it would prove to be formidable.

In July 1807 Willes was one of 'Twenty-three of Kent' who played against 'Thirteen of All-England' at Penenden Heath, near Maidstone. The game, widely trailed as the 'greatest match' to be staged in Kent for twenty years, with a purse of a thousand guineas to the winner, was eagerly awaited, and many bets were laid. When Willes bowled, it would become famous. The *Morning Herald* reported:

> The straight arm bowling, introduced by John Willes Esq, was generally practised in the game, and fully proved an obstacle against getting runs in comparison to what might have been

got by the straight-forward bowling. This bowling met with great opposition.

The wording of this report – 'The straight-arm bowling ... was generally practised' – suggests that Willes was not alone in bowling round-arm during the game. Kent won by 162 runs, so it was obviously effective. Nonetheless, the new style must have been startling to the spectators. From the inception of cricket they had been accustomed to underarm bowling. Now they were seeing the bowler's arm being raised and the ball propelled not from under the arm, but with a slinging, scything action from shoulder height.

We will never know if the players and spectators at Penenden that day were content to embrace the new style of bowling, but it soon became clear that others were emphatically opposed to it. It is easy to understand their hostility. The action of round-arm bowling must have generated much greater pace than batsmen were accustomed to facing. Moreover, it changed the angle of attack, and did so on pitches that were uneven and grassy, and against batsmen without any protective clothing. Critics condemned the new style as unfair and dangerous. It slowed run-scoring (which had in fact never been fast) and tilted the advantage decisively from batsman to bowler. It would have been surprising if it had not aroused great passions.

And yet, after the initial press report on the game at Penenden Heath, there are no contemporary records of what happened next. It seems unlikely that the formidable Mr Willes simply abandoned his new style of bowling. But for years nothing is reported. Writing sixty years later, in 1868, Charles Box suggested in *The Theory and Practice of Cricket* that Willes was often barred from matches, and that most cricketers were bitterly opposed to round-arm bowling. Whenever Willes played – and his nature was such that it is unlikely he would have been easily dissuaded from doing so – games were said to have been brought to an end by uproar and spectators invading the pitch. However, these are post-hoc recollections made decades later, not contemporary reports.

Superficially, the lack of contemporary reports seems strange, but these were not normal times. In 1805 Napoleon had planned to invade England, observing that the Channel was 'nothing but a ditch'. If he had done so, Kent was a likely landing ground, and in the circumstances John Willes's exploits on the cricket field might not have been of primary interest to the press. Of course, the invasion never came. Sadly for Napoleon, the 'ditch' was patrolled by the Royal Navy. After years of invasion fears the British Army, aided by the Prussians, finally defeated him at Waterloo in 1815. A generation of peace lay ahead. Everywhere, innovation ushered in a new world. Stephenson built his first locomotive in 1814, the miner's safety lamp was invented by Humphry Davy, gas lighting was installed in Piccadilly and Dr James Blundell would pioneer the first human blood transfusion at Guy's Hospital. It was not evident at the time but, post-Waterloo, Britain's military might and industrial genius would lead her to an empire of unprecedented power.

Britain's embrace of free trade, technology and flexible labour markets accelerated her transformation from an agrarian to an industrial society. But although these changes laid the foundations for Britain's hundred-year global domininance, they ignited industrial unrest and fierce campaigns for social and political change. This should not have been surprising. After Waterloo nearly 300,000 soldiers and sailors flooded on to the job market, to find only mass unemployment. Heroes one day, they were hungry the next. Bad harvests and trade depression added fuel to widespread grievances. For many, bread and cheese was the staple diet, and meat was a luxury. The next few years, before the economy took an upturn in the 1820s, brought Britain closer to revolution than at any time in her history. Marches, rallies and secret plots filled the minds of the discontented, and fear of insurrection never left the government. The clamour for parliamentary reform, lower taxes and relief from poverty grew ever louder. Instead, the agitation of country Members of Parliament led in 1815 to a Corn Bill to protect marginal farming, which forced bread prices up, causing huge distress. Once more, it was the poor who suffered. It was a witches' brew of troubles.

The Corn Laws were just one factor driving the cause of reform.

The main political thrust came from credible and well organised labour movements. Pitt's Combination Act of 1800 had been intended to outlaw collective bargaining by both masters and men, but in practice masters could combine and workers could not. Yet the Corn Laws, Poor Laws, agrarian hardship, high taxes and poor factory conditions created a compelling case for labour to unite to negotiate fairer working conditions from employers. In 1818, delegates representing spinners and weavers travelled to London to set up 'a general union of trades'.

In the midst of such times, we should not be surprised that cricketing disputes were not widely covered in the media. Even so, the mystery remains: did Willes desist from bowling round-arm? We don't know. But it is certain that round-arm bowling persisted, for at the instigation of Lord Frederick Beauclerk and William Ward, two of the mandarins of cricket, the MCC passed a law to ban it in 1816. Such a ban can only have been necessary if the controversy was still simmering. However, the new Law 10 was poorly drafted, and brought confusion rather than clarity. Umpires were puzzled as to how to interpret it fairly, and as a result round-arm bowling did not disappear altogether. In any event, the MCC could make laws, but had no real power to enforce them.

If, at a distance of two hundred years, it seems odd that the law was not swiftly redrafted in a way that was clear to all, we should recall how difficult it is for the interpretation of *any* law on bowling actions to be beyond dispute. The dispute over 'chucking' in recent years (in the cases, for example, of Tony Lock and Muttiah Muralitharan) has shown us how opinion can be fiercely divided over the legitimacy of bowling actions.

Thus the dispute simmered on. Despite the primacy of the MCC, there was no formal first-class structure, nor meetings of governing bodies. As a result, although frowned on by many, round-arm bowling continued – and prospered – in rural and informal games. Willes and his supporters actively promoted it. Other bowlers adopted it. Umpires approved its use where both sides agreed. The MCC disapproved, but simply looked on. As Willes built up momentum, hoping to face down the traditionalists, conservative opinion-formers waited for the moment to pounce. A crunch was inevitable.

It is likely that the showdown, which took place six years after the passing of Law 10, came about by mutual agreement. Round-arm bowling had never been seen at Lord's, by far the most important ground, where it would have come under the gaze of the most power-ful figures in cricket. This was a class-conscious age: the servants might carouse and misbehave in the servants' hall, but never in the master's study. A match at Lord's was now arranged for 15 July 1822, when round-arm bowling would feature, and be judged.

The game was set up with all the formality of a High Court trial. For the defence, John Willes brought a Kent team in which he and William Ashby would bowl round-arm. For the prosecution, the MCC team took the field with William Ward, Frederick Beauclerk, E.H. Budd and the genial Benjamin Aislabie – the arch-conservatives of cricket, who believed that the new style deformed the game they loved. As judges came two old players, now umpires: Harry Bentley (see pages 286–8) and Noah Mann, son of the old Hambledon rustic who had burned to death in a fireside accident after some jovial drinks. Everyone knew what was at stake, and it would be astonishing if the umpires had not been primed for the impact of their decisions.

The MCC won the toss and elected to bat. As the opening bats-men, Nicholas and Lane, came to the wicket, all the attention was focused on the umpires. Ashby bowled the first over – four balls only – and was not called for a no ball. Noah Mann evidently accepted that his action was legitimate. Round-arm bowling had passed the first part of its crucial test. Willes must therefore have gripped the shiny red ball with high hopes as he prepared for the second over, but these were to be dashed when umpire Bentley called 'No ball.'

Willes saw that, for all his efforts, he had been lured into a trap: he had done all he could, prepared and plotted meticulously, yet an umpire at Lord's had declared his action to be illegal. He had lost his gamble. Round-arm bowling had been outlawed at the high court of cricket. Frustrated, angry and racked with disappointment, this passionate man deserted his team, marched from the pitch, mounted his horse and galloped from Lord's vowing never again to play cricket. However, he did not, in Harry Altham's compelling phrase, 'ride away out of Lord's and out of cricket history'. Far from it. Soon he would take up umpiring, promoting matches and coaching cricketers – not least in fielding, where his team from the tiny Kent village of Sutton Valence where he settled practised until they had 'blood on their hands'. He would live to see his argument won: within a mere three years he would discover, and coach, one of the great icons of cricket, Alfred Mynn – and Mynn would bowl round-arm.

The traditionalists had won the first skirmish with ease, but the reformers did not accept that the struggle was over. In the counties round-arm bowling had become popular, and the campaign to legalise the action gathered pace. William Lillywhite and James Broadbridge excelled in the new style, and ensured that Sussex became the team of the decade. In tandem they were a formidable pair: the subtle accuracy of the slow-medium Lillywhite bowling round the wicket, and the faster pace of Broadbridge, tormented batsmen. Lillywhite, a tiny man in tall hat, black bow-tie and broad cotton braces, was recognised as the finest bowler of the era – the 'Nonpareil' – and averaged over two hundred wickets a year. The adoption of round-arm bowling by such an eminent player was a significant boost for the reformers, and remained so, for Lillywhite was still bowling in great matches (and his own benefit match) a quarter of a century later. After he left Sussex following a dispute, old enmities over his bowling style were put aside and he joined the playing staff at Lord's. Later he became the first professional coach at Winchester College. On his death he was buried in Highgate cemetery, where a monument was erected over his grave by 'the noblemen and gentlemen of the MCC' who, at the last, claimed him as one of their own.

That was not the case in the 1820s, but the gradual spread of round-arm bowling was forcing conservative opinion to rethink its opposition. The traditionalists, however, had powerful advocates on their side. Thomas Lord, as ever, clung to the past. William Ward continued to be resolutely opposed, perhaps, as E.H. Budd unkindly noted, because he couldn't bat against it. Other dissenters included

William Denison, the foremost cricket writer; Frederick Beauclerk – but only, some said, when he had to face it; and John Nyren, son of Richard, the old captain of Hambledon, who feared it would change the character of the game. These attitudes did not spring from a rosy-eyed view of the past: those who held them simply opposed what they feared.

The schism was sharp, but events were forcing the diehards on the defensive. The reformers needed an advocate, someone of standing who could, with pen and tongue, bridge with guile and diplomacy the irreconcilable differences that were tearing cricket apart. A solution was needed that would spare the embarrassment of those who ruled cricket and were seeing their edict ignored. Fortunately, such a man was at hand. George Knight was a round-arm bowler of some skill. More importantly, he had intellect, cool judgement and a gift for words that must have been genetic. For Knight was not the name with which his father had been born. That name was altogether more famous.

Fifty years earlier in Hampshire, a parish rector, the Reverend George Austen, tended his flock and supplemented his meagre living from pastoral duties by educating boys in his rectory. These were the great days of Hambledon Cricket Club, and for recreation the students played cricket. It is likely that the vicar's own children joined in, including his eldest daughter Jane – Jane Austen.

The Austen family had modest means in a world in which wealth, property and social position were all. Jane Austen wrote six of the greatest novels in the English language, but did not enjoy huge success in her own lifetime. Her first published novel was *Sense and Sensibility* (1811), but that was not the first she had written. It was preceded by *First Impressions*, which was rejected and only published in 1813, after huge revisions and with a new title, *Pride and Prejudice*. After her death in 1817 she became iconic. Kipling rhymed:

> Jane lies in Winchester – blessed be her shade!
> Praise the Lord for making her, and her for all she made!
> And while the stones of Winchester, or Milsom Street, remain
> Glory, love and honour unto England's Jane.

Not all were enamoured. Mark Twain, not a fan, wrote: 'Every time I read *Pride and Prejudice* I want to dig her up and hit her over the skull with her own shin-bone.'

But the Austen family have a claim upon history that goes beyond literature. In 1783 Jane's elder brother Edward was adopted by a wealthy distant cousin, Thomas Knight of Godmersham, and in 1812 Edward Austen officially became Edward Knight. Edward had married in 1791, and he and his wife Elizabeth had eleven children. Four of the boys, Edward, George, Henry and Brook, were to play first-class cricket: Edward and George for both Kent and Hampshire, Brook for Kent and Henry for Sussex. It is George, Jane Austen's favourite nephew, who is the 'One Knight, a south-country bowler' referred to in Lord Verulam's inaccurate memory of the origin of round-arm bowling. And it was the same George Knight who was to take up the cudgels with the MCC in the quest to legalise round-arm bowling.

George Knight's interest in cricket arose in his childhood. The game was a favourite pastime for the Knight boys at home, and later at Winchester College. If, as Lord Verulam recalled, young George's sister bowled to him, another prospect arises: might not his famous aunt, Jane Austen, have done so as well?

The Austen/Knight cricketing dynasty went far beyond Aunt Jane's four nephews: Edward's sons Wyndham (Kent) and Philip (Cambridge University and Gentlemen of Kent) played first-class cricket, as did his grandson Sir Evelyn Bradford (Hampshire). His brother Henry also had grandsons who played first-class cricket – Lewis D'Aeth (MCC) and Edward D'Aeth (Oxford University). Jane's elder brother James had seven cricketing grandsons, of whom four, her great-nephews, played first-class cricket: Cholmeley and Charles Austen-Leigh for MCC, Spencer for Sussex and Arthur Austen-Leigh for Gentlemen of England. Somewhere in the Austen genes there must have been that precious gift for hand–eye coordination that marks out a talent for ball games.

Even Jane's niece Fanny had cricketing connections: her brother-in-law was Henry Knatchbull (Kent and Oxford University), while her own sons included H.T. Knatchbull-Hugessen (President of Kent

County Cricket Club) and William Knatchbull-Hugessen (Kent). Another of Fanny's sons was Edward, first Lord Brabourne, whose son Cecil played first-class cricket (Kent and Cambridge University). Elizabeth Knight, Jane Austen's niece, was the mother of another President of Kent CCC, Ernest Rice.

Even that is not the sum total of the Austen family legacy to first-class cricket. The four Knight brothers had first cousins, William and John Deedes, who played first-class cricket for Kent, and Sir Brook Bridges, twice elected President of Kent CCC. William also became President of the MCC. There is one final – and rather poignant – Austen connection to cricket. Jane never married, but she did accept an offer of marriage from Harris Bigg-Wither, only to change her mind overnight: Bigg-Wither's grandson became a prominent cricketer in north Hampshire.

Despite this galaxy of Austen family cricketing connections, it is Jane's nephew George who left the most indelible mark. In 1827–28 George, a member of the West Kent Club, played for Kent as a hard-hitting batsman and round-arm bowler. An old poem describes his skills:

> As a bowler first rate, as a bat far from vile,
> And he bowls in the new march of intellect style.

Recollections of George Knight suggest a player sufficiently talented to play five times between 1827 and 1837 for the Gentlemen in their annual fixture against the Players. His highest score in a top-class match was 50 runs at Lord's in 1825, ironically for the arch-conservative Mr William Ward's XI against Mr H. Lloyd's XI. Despite his evident gifts George did not, apart from cricket, live up to the family talents: 'He was,' said his nephew Lord Brabourne, 'one of those men who are clever enough to do almost *anything*, but live to their lives' end very comfortably doing *nothing*.' It is a damning assessment of an able man, but it ignores the mark George left on cricket, where – with Lillywhite and Broadbridge – he popularised round-arm bowling and changed the game forever.

Outside the MCC a compromise to the problem was being sought.

When Kent played Sussex at the Vine, Sevenoaks, it was agreed that the bowling should be neither 'a throw nor a jerk', but that the ball must be delivered either underarm or with a straight arm below the shoulder. Slowly but surely round-arm was forcing its way into cricket, although under the strict laws of the game it remained illegal. At the beginning of 1827 George Knight embarked on a campaign to persuade the MCC to repeal Law 10 and replace it. He set out his case in letters to the *Sporting Magazine*.

In his first and most important letter, of 15 January 1827, he gave notice that he would seek a change in the law. He prepared the ground with care. No law, he reminded the readers, had ever existed to set out the manner of bowling. Underarm bowling had served the game well until batting techniques improved, but was now ineffective: this lack of balance between bat and ball was causing cricket to decline. Nor was round-arm bowling novel, since it had been in common use for a decade. This bedrock of his argument was supplemented with a half-truth intended to spare embarrassment to the MCC if they changed Law 10. Knight argued – with the subtle drafting skills of his Aunt Jane – that round-arm bowling had only been outlawed when, in a match at Brighton, a bowler had raised his hand above his head. The MCC were correct, Knight wrote, to act against overarm bowling, but not round-arm. He would propose only to legalise round-arm. This presentation of the MCC having banned round-arm in error as they dealt with a greater evil was a dubious, but expedient, component of a seductive case in which Knight was seeking allies without provoking opponents.

He had another hurdle to overcome: the attack on round-arm bowling had focused on the claim that it was throwing, not bowling. Knight demolished this with ease: 'To call [round-arm] throwing is ridiculous. If a man were to attempt throwing a hundred yards . . . would he deliver the ball with his arm extended horizontally?' Since the answer to this was evidently no, the 'throwing' advocates were forced on the defensive. Knight concluded by promising that a subsequent letter would contain a definition of an appropriate law.

Knight's argument fell on the controversy like an unexploded bomb, but demolition experts were swift to respond, and the argument raged on. Undaunted, Knight prepared his case further at his estate at Godmersham Park, and wrote a second letter on 15 February 1827. He set out the inadequacy of the existing law, noting that a bowler might bowl from one end 'at Mary-le-bone itself' and have his deliveries accepted as legal by one umpire, yet might bowl with the same action from the other end and be no-balled by the second umpire. Since this was absurd, and yet was known to be true, Knight's case for some change in the law was unarguable. He went on to advocate the change he sought, once more deferring to the wisdom of the MCC. The Kent and Sussex matches, he pointed out, were 'played according to the very law, word for word, which I now propose, having been made with the express conditions, and chiefly for the purpose of trying its efficacy'. The umpires, he noted, had found this law to be clear-cut and easy to enforce. The message was clear: Knight's law worked, and the existing Law 10 did not.

He concluded by seeking to address the criticism that batsmen would be injured by a style of bowling that would increase the pace of the ball. In doing so, he returned to the adage that cricket was a 'manly' game: 'It has been said "this bowling will break our shins and knuckles"; to which I answer, that the first maxim I remember as a boy was, "Never be afraid of the ball." Men are not made of brown paper: I have seen many kinds of bowling I could not play, but never one I would not face.' This assertion undermined one of the better points of the traditionalists' case, and turned it into an object of scorn: it was a cunning conclusion to Knight's campaign.

As the round-arm controversy rumbled on, three 'experimental' games were agreed between 'England' and 'Sussex', in which the county team would be permitted to bowl round-arm but the England XI would not. The games were played at Sheffield, Lord's and Brighton, and – since old habits died hard – a side bet of a thousand guineas a side was laid to sweeten the occasion.

At Sheffield on 4 June 1827, Lillywhite and Broadbridge led Sussex to a comprehensive seven-wicket win over an all-professional England team. At Lord's the England team included the amateur George

Knight and William Ashby, two leading proponents of round-arm bowling, together with an implacable opponent, William Ward. There is no evidence that Knight or Ashby bowled round-arm, although they both took wickets; but Sussex won once more, by three wickets. The likelihood that Knight and Ashby bowled conventional underarm is confirmed by an extraordinary statement issued at the close of the game by the eight professionals of the England side, including Ashby. They asserted that they would 'not play the third match . . . unless the Sussex bowlers play fair – that is, abstain from throwing'. This was an odd intervention, since the games had been set up precisely to test round-arm bowling. Moreover, it is a mystery how Ashby could have signed such a declaration, and how George Knight could have permitted it to be issued. It is possible that Ashby was overborne by his fellow professionals, and that Knight did not know about it until after it had been issued: in any event the professionals soon backed down, and the third game at Brighton went ahead. This time Knight did bowl round-arm, and England, despite a lamentable first innings total of 27, won the game by 24 runs.

The impact of round-arm was evident, although the MCC committee was still in no mood to sanction it. But the walls of resistance were crumbling. The experimental games were sandwiched by other matches that year in which round-arm bowling was used. The Gentlemen and Players met twice at Lord's: in the first game, played before the experimental matches, round-arm bowling was permitted, although George Knight was no-balled repeatedly, including for one delivery with which he bowled Thomas Beagley, the finest left-handed batsman of the day. In the second game round-arm bowling was banned, and of twenty-four balls bowled by Knight, only four were allowed.

At Lord's the diehards seemed still to be prevailing, but after a lengthy meeting of the MCC in May 1828, the pressure for reform carried the day. The law was amended to permit the hand being raised as high as the elbow, and the back of the hand was allowed to be uppermost, with the arm extended horizontally. George Knight had won.

The victory must have been very sweet for John Willes, now settled in Sutton Valence to a life of hunting, shooting and coaching the village cricket team. Sutton Valence and its neighbours were cricketing rivals, and on match days he would entertain the teams at close of play in a liquid and lavish fashion. Edward Hodges recalls the players raising their glasses of whisky and brandy to serenade their patron's love of hunting:

> There was Spero, Spendigo, Bonnylass and Truelove,
> And Ruler that never looked behind him.

Willes sought out talent in the local villages, and one youth caught his eye: a young giant, blessed with the natural gift of pace but raw and wildly inaccurate. His name was Alfred Mynn, and he and his cricketing brother Walter were the sons of a farmer at Harrietsham – a village without a cricket team. It is likely that young Alfred only began to play the game in his late teens.

Willes noted Mynn's strength of arm and shoulder, cut down his lengthy run-up to a mere six paces, and preached to him the virtues of accuracy. This was not easy for the round-arm bowler. Underarm bowling – and the overarm bowling that lay thirty-five years in the future – relied on the arm pointing straight down the wicket as the ball was released. But round-arm bowling did not: at the point of delivery the arm was horizontal to the shoulder and an arm's length wide of it, which made accuracy difficult. Willes set Mynn to practise, practise, practise, and his protégé was keen not to disappoint, although control of line and length did not come easily. But Willes was patient; he knew he had uncovered a rare talent.

In 1835 a further concession was made, allowing the bowler to raise his hand to shoulder height, although it was re-emphasised that the ball must be bowled, and not 'thrown' or 'jerked'. Once more, the law of cricket had caught up with reality, and the scene was set for the era of round-arm bowling and the emergence of the first superstar of cricket: it would be the village lad that Willes had coached – Alfred Mynn.

7

The Mandarins of Lord's

The rebellion over round-arm bowling was not the only preoccupation of the MCC at this time. Although Thomas Lord had settled his ground on its final, famous site in 1814, more drama lay ahead. In 1824 that astute Yorkshireman saw another opportunity to increase his personal wealth: he formed a plan to build houses upon the perimeter of the cricket field. This would have been disastrous for Lord's, had not a fairy godfather been at hand. The benefactor was William Ward, cricketer, businessman and MCC member, who was so horrified to learn of the proposal that he sought out Lord and bought his leasehold interest for £5,400.* In doing so Ward not only protected the environment of the ground for cricket, but left the perimeter free for cricket-related improvements that would follow decades later.

In the year that he saved Lord's from the builders, William Ward was thirty-seven years of age. A tall, powerfully-built man, he was coming to the twilight of a formidable career in top-class cricket, but had a further twenty years of minor games still ahead. Ward straddled an era, having made his debut for England at Lord's in 1810, when Surrey were still fielding an elderly 'Silver Billy' Beldham in their team. Ward never forgot this, for Beldham took a catch to dismiss him for nought. In his early career Ward batted against underarm

---

* Until recently it was thought that Lord's plan to build houses was formed in 1825, and that Ward's purchase price was £5,000. Recent data provided by the Eyre Estate suggests that 1824 and £5,400 were the actual date and sum.

bowling, but as he matured, and despite his robust opposition, round-arm bowling prospered in Kent and began to predominate everywhere.

In his prime, between 1816 and 1828, Ward's scores were prodigious, the most famous being a mammoth innings of 278 for MCC, compiled over nearly two days against Norfolk, admittedly not a strong team, in 1820.* In that game a seventeen-year-old Fuller Pilch, destined to become the premier bat in England, made his debut at Lord's for 'Norfolk', who were in fact the Holt Cricket Club under the county's name. Ironically, Fuller's brother William dropped a caught and bowled chance off Ward when he had scored only 20, and a third Pilch, the eldest brother Nathaniel, scrambled for another catch that just evaded his reach. No one made an issue of the missed chances, for as Nathaniel commented philosophically, 'In a long innings there's always something.' Ward had many long innings, including 162 and 40 not out for MCC against the Artillery Club at Lord's in 1824 (it must have been an above-average pitch: Saunders scored 156 not out for the Artillery Club). He was famous for using a weighty four-pound bat, was a fierce striker of the ball in front of the wicket, and on at least four occasions scored the phenomenal total of 200 runs or more in a single match, while throughout his long career he was never dismissed twice for nought in any class of cricket. As an underarm bowler Ward had modest success, and he was a competent fielder near the wicket.

Ward passed his affection for cricket – but only a portion of his talent – to two of his sons who played for Winchester, and to a third who was in the Cambridge XI of 1853. In retirement he commissioned a marble statue of a 'Cricketer in Play' from the sculptor Rossi, and in 1845, enthusiasm undimmed, he was at the Horns tavern, Kennington, to chair the famous meeting at which the Surrey County Cricket Club was formed.

Off the field, Ward had a passion for card games. Once he played uninterrupted from Monday through to Wednesday morning, when

---

* It remained the highest score at Lord's until 1925, when Percy Holmes of Yorkshire scored 315 not out against Middlesex.

the game was abandoned to enable one player to attend a funeral. A wealthy and successful businessman for most of his life, Ward sat for ten years as the Member of Parliament for the City of London, and was appointed a Director of the Bank of England. A contemporary poem sums up his prestige:

> And of all who frequent the ground named after Lord,
> On the list, first and foremost, should stand Mr Ward.
> No man will deny, I am sure, when I say
> That he's without rival first bat of the day.

The 'first bat' claim is dubious, although Ward was among the best bats of the time. A hint that he was past his prime swiftly follows:

> And although he has grown a little too stout,
> Even Mathews is bothered at bowling him out.
> He's our life-blood and soul in this noblest of games,
> And yet on our praises he's many more claims;
> No pride, although rich, condescending and free,
> And a well-informed man, and a city M.P.

With all these attributes William Ward was a powerful force in the adolescent years of cricket, and his influence lasted far beyond his playing days. In 1833 John Nyren dedicated his famous book *The Young Cricketer's Tutor* to Ward as 'the most worthy man of the day'. He was a 'walking encyclopaedia' of all there was to know about the game, and, as his prompt purchase of Lord's showed, a generous benefactor until his wealth diminished and he sold his interest in the ground to James Henry Dark in 1835.

Dark is a shadowy figure. At the age of ten he is reputed to have been employed at Lord's as a ground-boy. If so, his responsibilities would have been to field in practice matches, assist members in practice, and generally do as Thomas Lord directed. If he did begin work at such a young age he would have been familiar with all three Lord's grounds, but this is uncertain. Dark was an occasional cricketer, said to be competent with bat and ball. As a batsman he had the reputation of being a hitter, but with a porous defence. On poor wickets he would not have lasted long. An article in *Sporting*

Life in 1833 suggested that he was pugnacious in temperament 'but a good fellow' nevertheless. Four years later, the same source accounts him to be 'fair' in his dealings. It is an insubstantial picture.

We know more of Dark's activities in 1835. That year he purchased the unexpired fifty-eight years of the lease on Lord's from William Ward for £2,000 and an annuity of £425 to Ward's family. At the time, Lord's was still undeveloped and rural. It contained two ponds, often filled with rubbish, and a very rough cricket ground. It had a small wooden pavilion, but no seats for spectators. Beer was available from pot-boys, and a pen held sheep which grazed the outfield. A patent for a 'mowing machine' had been taken out in 1830, but no working machine appeared for a further twenty years. This was Dark's domain. That same year he played his only game for the Gentlemen against the Players, and was bowled by Cobbett without scoring. He also published a book, *The Principles of Scientific Batting*, written by 'A Gentleman' – it was in fact James Pycroft – and revised by J.H. Dark. It was, so far as we know, his only publishing or written venture.

For the next twenty-nine years Dark was an active proprietor of Lord's, known widely as 'the Boss'. He lived near the ground, where a small warehouse was stocked with willow stocks which he utilised in a business manufacturing bats, as well as balls. He developed Lord's, opening a court for 'real' tennis in 1838 and letting out pitches on the ground where the public could play for a shilling. He introduced a telegraph scoreboard in 1846, and a printing tent to produce scorecards two years later. Even so, in the 1850s the ground was still 'heavy clay, badly drained with a rough outfield and treacherous'. There were 'no boundaries, no stands and no fixed seats'.*

In Dark's later years he umpired, apparently well. Beyond Lord's he became the treasurer of the Cricketers' Fund Friendly Society, but his life is otherwise a closed book. Upon his retirement in 1864 he sold the remnants of his lease to Lord's, and when he died seven years later he left many questions behind him. If he was a ground-boy at ten years of age, how did he obtain the money to buy Lord's thirty

---

* Edward Rutter, *Cricket Memories* (1925).

years later? He left £30,000, a very large sum, in his will. Did he earn all this from his bat and ball business at Lord's? When did this begin? Is that how he funded Lord's? We can only surmise, but of his epitaph there is no doubt: it is Lord's.

It is a historical oddity that the most famous ground in cricket retains the name of the man who wished to develop it for housing, rather than that of one of the benefactors who saved it, William Ward and James Dark. Perhaps this is fortunate: 'Lord's' does have a finer ring to it than 'Ward's' or Dark's'!

Soon after Ward's purchase of Lord's, tragedy struck. At one o'clock in the morning of Friday, 29 July 1825, fire broke out in the wooden pavilion. In a few hours it was wholly destroyed, and with it nearly all the precious records of early cricket.* Not even the water trough, on site to refresh the sheep who chewed the outfield, could douse the blaze. Although this was an irreparable loss to the history of the game, fate would intervene, for a mere six days after the fire, on 4 August 1825, Arthur Haygarth was born, and he would spend his life assembling the *Scores and Biographies* of early cricket, which are now the bedrock of our knowledge. All that, of course, lay far ahead.

The MCC acted with aplomb over the fire. The Eton–Harrow match went ahead the following day, and within a year a new pavilion was built. The MCC was in good hands, with three men – the new ground-owner, William Ward, the Honorary Secretary, Benjamin Aislabie, and, in 1826, a new President, Lord Frederick Beauclerk – all prepared to devote their time to the well-being of the club.

Benjamin Aislabie, jovial, good-natured, relaxed and urbane, was appointed Honorary Secretary of the MCC in 1822, when the club had a mere 202 members. He remained in post for twenty years, his popularity never wavering. Like Ward, he was celebrated in rhyme:

> 'Tis Aislabie's boast to form most of the matches
> In this way at cricket; he makes but few catches,

---

* Not quite all the scorebooks were destroyed. Later, Thomas Lord sold some to the MCC. Presumably they were not in the pavilion.

> But still he's contented some money to pay
> For the sake of encouraging excellent play.
>
> He doats on the game, has played many a year,
> Weighs at least seventeen stones, on his pins rather queer;
> But he still takes the bat, and there's no better fun
> Than to see him when batting attempting to run.

Aislabie was a poor cricketer, but he had a consuming love of the game. An Etonian, he was never selected for the school eleven, but did play both for and against the Old Etonians. He was a club cricketer with Homerton, until it folded in 1808, and it was for them that he first played at Lord's, in 1802. Quite slim as a youth, he grew into a huge man – at one time over twenty stone – and his appearance on the field in later life was a signal for an outburst of good-natured mirth that did not bother him in the slightest. The *Sporting Magazine* caught the flavour of the man perfectly, with a tribute from a colleague:

> As to my chief, and my jokes, he is too well known for them to wound him. Look at him, hear him and laugh *with* him, when joyous hearts are bursting bounds, and if he doesn't claim the laurel for wit, fun and good humour I know nothing ... he puts me in mind of an hippopotamus among grey-hounds.

Clearly a lovely man.

Fittingly for a man of his girth and zest for life, Aislabie was a wine merchant – with Admiral Lord Nelson his most eminent client. His celebrity was acknowledged by his appearance in Thomas Hughes's *Tom Brown's Schooldays*, in which he attends an MCC match at Rugby School:* 'Old Mr Aislabie stood by looking on in his white hat, leaning on a bat, in benevolent enjoyment.' Even in fiction Aislabie promoted the MCC, for in talking to Tom Brown the author has him say: 'I must compliment you, sir, on your eleven, and I hope we shall have you for a member if you come up to town.'

---

* The match is based on the MCC vs Rugby game of 1841.

Above Charles Lennox, second Duke of Richmond (1701–50), grandson of Charles II, was a keen gambler with a lifelong love of cricket. By employing the best players in England he created, in effect, the first professionals.

Right Sir William Gage (1695–1747), whose estate Firle in East Sussex was one of the cradles of eighteenth-century cricket. Gage's 'Sussex XI' were familiar opponents of teams raised by other early patrons including Edward Stead, the Duke of Richmond, the Earl of Middlesex, the third Duke of Dorset and the Prince of Wales.

Right Cricket being played in 1743 at its first really celebrated ground, the Artillery Ground in Finsbury, London. The ball is still being bowled, rather than pitched, and it will be more than thirty years before the third stump is added to the wicket.

Below Lionel Sackville, first Duke of Dorset (1687–1765), one of the great early patrons of the game. His 'cricketing place' at Knole near Sevenoaks was the first ground to be regularly mown, rolled and cosseted in preparation for cricket, and he employed as a gardener Valentine Romney, who at the time 'was held to be the best cricket player in the world'.

Charles Sackville, second Duke of Dorset (1711–69). Matches for large stakes between his teams and those raised by the Prince of Wales drew huge, unruly crowds in the 1730s, but by the time of his death he was disillusioned, insolvent and mad.

Above Frederick Louis, Prince of Wales (1707–51), eldest son of George II and an enthusiastic early patron of cricket. In June 1737 he and John Sackville, brother of the second Duke of Dorset, arranged what the *London Evening Post* called 'the greatest match at cricket that has ever been contested'.

Left The Duke of Cumberland (1721–65), third son of George II, loved horseracing, cards, Chelsea china, and the game of cricket, but this early patron was a better judge of a soldier than a cricketer.

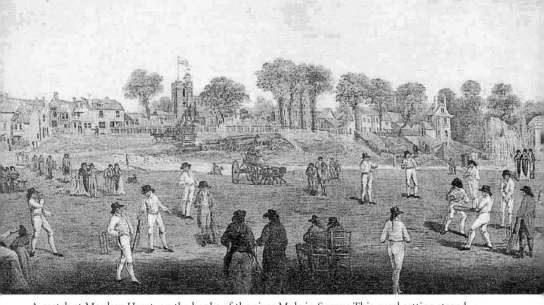

A match at Moulsey Hurst, on the banks of the river Mole in Surrey. This rural setting staged many important matches in the eighteenth century, and was a favourite venue of the early patrons of the game.

'Lumpy' Stevens (1731–1819) was a gardener for the Earl of Tankerville, and the most deadly underarm bowler of his day. After some of his deliveries passed between the two-stump wickets without dislodging the bail, a third stump was added.

Sir Horace Mann (1744–1814) was a Kentish landowner, a lifelong devotee of the game, and the most amiable of its early benefactors. His generosity did much to promote the growth of cricket before his eventual bankruptcy in 1808.

John Frederick Sackville, third Duke
of Dorset (1745–99), and the third in a
line of great cricketing patrons.

Although hardly dressed for it, the Countess of Derby plays cricket with other ladies at
The Oaks, in Surrey, in 1779.

Left John Nyren, whose memories of cricket at Hambledon were recorded in *The Young Cricketer's Tutor* in 1833. His recollections have given us a vivid picture of early cricket that is unavailable elsewhere.

Below It would be easy to imagine that this much-loved painting gives us a glimpse of cricket at Hambledon, but its date and venue are uncertain.

Right A page from a sketchbook has survived to give us a unique glance of some of the Hambledon cricketers. George Shepheard, an occasional Surrey cricketer, jotted these impressions while watching them in action.

Right below The Bat and Ball Inn on Broadhalfpenny Down, where Richard Nyren sold the cricketers of Hambledon 'punch to make hair curl' at twopence a pint.

This ninety-one-year-old, in a smock, was once the most accomplished batsman cricket had yet known. 'Silver Billy' Beldam joined the Hambledon club in 1785, and lifted the art of batting to a new level of style and elegance.

An etching of *Cricket Played by the Gentlemen's Club, White Conduit House, Islington* in 1784. A third stump has been added to the wicket, and the bat, once curved, is now straighter, with a backward arch. Three years later, some of these players became founder members of the MCC.

Lord Winchilsea (1752–1826) was a nobleman of the old school. Although President of the Hambledon Club, this confirmed bachelor would be a key founder of the MCC, and encouraged Thomas Lord to acquire its first ground.

In his prime Aislabie lived at Lee in Kent, where he took a lively interest in the parish. Generous and kindly, he employed additional labourers to tend his grounds when casual jobs were hard to obtain because the weather was severe. It was the type of endearing gesture that explains his general popularity. Despite his bulk he was fit, and he walked and rode with ease the fourteen miles of his parish bounds. When the lease on his home expired in 1823 he and his family moved to Sevenoaks, where they lived for the remaining nineteen years of his life. When he died he was universally mourned, and a memorial inscription was erected in the churchyard at Sevenoaks; but Aislabie was buried where he would have wished, close to his beloved Lord's, in St Marylebone parish church.

Aislabie's spirit lives on. In the late 1980s I was idling away a wet hour in the Long Room at Lord's with the cricket writer and broadcaster E.W. 'Jim' Swanton, when he pointed to a portrait high up on the wall and asked me if I knew who it was. The subject was a rosy-cheeked man in a black top hat and long red coat, and as a pure guess I replied, 'Surely that's old Ben Aislabie.' Swanton positively glowed. 'No one's ever got that right before,' he told me. 'It's an early portrait, you see, before Aislabie became fat.' My guess was a sheer fluke, but from that moment on Jim Swanton greatly overrated my knowledge of cricket history. The portrait has since been relegated to a nearby stairwell, but one day I hope Aislabie will return to the site he deserves, from where, once again, he can gaze out onto the ground whose welfare was the love of his life.

Lord Frederick Beauclerk was appointed President of the MCC in 1826. History has never warmed to him – nor, I think, ever will. Beauclerk is seen as avaricious, ill-tempered, hypocritical and a gamester adept at sharp practice. It is a damning charge sheet. Some criticisms may be overstated, but his own behaviour offers little reason to make one disbelieve them. Beauclerk's reputation is poor because the judgement of his detractors lives on, while his devotion to cricket, and his contribution to it, are often overlooked.

Beauclerk was born in May 1773, the fourth son of the fifth Duke of St Albans – a direct descendant of the romps of Charles II and

Nell Gwynne. While at Cambridge University he was selected to play for the MCC against Kent at Lord's, his precocious eighteen-year-old talent having been spotted by Lord Winchilsea. From the outset he was a free-scoring, graceful batsman, noted for strong off-side play, and if his average of 27 in top-class cricket seems low by modern standards, it was prodigious on the rough and unprepared wickets of the day. He was a formidable bowler, too, and one of the first cricketers to appreciate the importance of fielding and to work hard to reach a high standard. Winchilsea was first attracted by Beauclerk's slow underarm lobs, which deceived many batsmen with their accuracy and disconcerting lift and bounce. We do not know the scale of his success as a bowler, since at that time wickets were credited only if the batsman was clean bowled; but we do know that he was a leading wicket-taker throughout his career.

Beauclerk was pitched into first-class cricket at a time when gambling on matches was commonplace. In 1791, at eighteen years of age, he took part in a handful of games, each of which had a stake in the range of five hundred to a thousand guineas. This youthful experience alerted him to the fact that money could be made from the game, and he was later to boast that he earned six hundred guineas a year from wagers on cricket alone. Such behaviour may have seedy connotations today, but would not have done so at the time.

The young Beauclerk was born into an age in which the younger sons of the gentry had meagre prospects, and were foisted onto the army or the Church, whether or not they had a vocation for either. There was little alternative. Beauclerk chose the Church, and took Deacon's Orders at Norwich in 1795. He was ordained two years later, and offered the living at Kimpton, where he was to be an absentee vicar for the next thirty years. His priorities were clear from the outset. In his first summer as vicar he delegated his pastoral duties to a poorly-paid curate and abandoned the parish to play cricket. In the winter he hunted, preferring to destroy foxes rather than save souls.

Beauclerk left us no personal recollections, so we can only see him through the eyes of his contemporaries. They do not reveal a pretty picture. In one match at Lord's, in a sweepstake on which batsman would score the highest number of runs, he drew himself and, to ensure he won, refused to run for any hits from a fellow batsman, the left-handed John Bowyer, who was matching him run for run. Interviewed sixty years later by the *Illustrated Sporting and Dramatic News*, Bowyer recalled Beauclerk running back and forth to the scorers to count his notches. By this stratagem he won the sweep by a mere four runs, cheating Lord Ponsonby, who had drawn Bowyer, of the stake money. Ponsonby's reaction is not known, but Bowyer, who had been promised two guineas if he won, was not impressed when Beauclerk offered him a guinea as a consolation. 'I call that cheating,' was his view, 'no more or less.'

Beauclerk's social status and eminence as a cricketer gave him huge influence at Lord's; no one would gainsay him. A later critic, Andrew Lang, mocked his powers:

> I am the batsman and the bat
> I am the bowler and the ball
> The umpire, the pavilion cat
> The roller, pitch and stumps and all.

His power was not appreciated by everyone. On 23 June 1808, when a fellow cleric, the Reverend Dr Nathaniel Highmore, visited Lord's, he reported as follows:

> I noticed a man coming out from the booth, dressed in a white hat, a coloured handkerchief about his neck, striped trousers, and a square kind of coat . . . This person seemed to possess considerable power in regulating the gambling match, which was about to commence and which I had given sixpence to see. He called to one named Beldham, gave order about the wickets etc. and appeared so much as one having authority, that I felt a wish to know who and what he was. I therefore asked a civil-looking gentleman . . . The gentleman . . . stared at me with a look expressive, if not of contempt, at least of astonishment. His surprise at my ignorance did not, however, prevent him from gratifying my curiosity by saying,
> 'That there? Why, that's Lord Frederick.'

'What, Lord Frederick Beauclerk?' I said.

'Aye, for sure,' was the gentleman's reply.

Greatly amazed, and supposing myself to have been misinformed as to his Lordship being in holy orders and holding a very large cure of souls, I continued my intrusion by saying . . .

'I had thought, Sir, that Lord Frederick Beauclerk was a clergyman?'

'A clergyman?' said the gentleman, 'why, so he is; but he ne'er preaches once of a twelvemonth.'

Dr Highmore, in high dudgeon, wrote an outraged letter to the Archbishop of Canterbury. He may have been activated by dismay that Beauclerk was so carefree of his clerical duties, but he had a personal grievance that coloured his view. Dr Highmore had been refused permission by the Church to be an advocate in ecclesiastical courts and a stipendiary clergyman, whereas it appeared that Beauclerk could be an absentee cleric and a cricketer. Was this special privilege? Dr Highmore thought so, and he didn't like it. A week after his first letter, his fury heightened when he learned that Lord Frederick's team had won a thousand guineas in the game he had witnessed. He picked up his pen again – and again – but history does not tell us how, or if, the Archbishop reacted.

Beauclerk was imperious and often avaricious. In July 1810, in company with Thomas Howard, a fast underarm bowler, he entered into a wager over a single-wicket match against William Lambert and George Osbaldeston. It was a brave bet. Osbaldeston was a top-class all-rounder, and seven years later Lambert would become the first man to score two hundreds in a single game – 107 not out and 157 for Sussex against Epsom.* Beauclerk refused to postpone the game, upon which £100 rested, when Osbaldeston was too ill to play. 'Pay or play' was the Beauclerk creed. Osbaldeston batted briefly to score one run (in order to qualify for a substitute fielder), after which Lambert, who, said Billy Beldham, 'would hit what no man could meddle with' played alone. He won by 15 runs after purposely bowling wide balls to Lord Frederick 'to put him out of temper' when he was

* Lambert was a Surrey man playing as a 'given' man for Sussex.

batting well. Beauclerk's fiery temperament ensured that the ploy succeeded, and Lambert won both the stake money and a parcel-wrapped gift, the contents of which he never disclosed, from Osbaldeston's mother. It was victory, total and complete, for Lambert, but soon folly would put him at Beauclerk's mercy – and it would not be forthcoming. This game was excluded from the early scores kept by Harry Bentley because, it was widely believed, an irritated Beauclerk paid him to keep it out. A year later the laws were amended to impose a one-run penalty for any ball a batsman could not reach. It is highly likely that Beauclerk, still smarting, was behind the change.

If Osbaldeston and Lambert celebrated, as surely they did, Beauclerk would soon enjoy his revenge. Lambert delivered himself up by apparently allowing himself to have been bribed by the 'legs' – bookmakers' runners – to 'fix' an England vs Nottingham match in 1817. If he had, this was foolish, because 'once sold' a player was at the mercy of the 'legs', who would not scruple to blackmail him. But it was not uncommon. During a match at Lord's the following season, Lambert became involved in a heated discussion about his action with John Bennett, a fellow professional who had also been involved, when Beauclerk overheard the commotion. Both players were hauled before the committee and summarily banned from cricket in 1818. It was a cruel piece of bad luck for them,* for the practice was widespread, but their ill-fortune did help to curb the evil of crooked results. Beauclerk's peremptory discipline was justified, but given his own earnings and reputation for sharp practice, it carried a whiff of hypocrisy.

Beauclerk's relationship with Osbaldeston never recovered. Osbaldeston, widely admired as the 'Squire of England', was a contemporary John Peel who loved hunting, shooting, fishing, riding, boxing and billiards, at all of which he excelled. Small in stature, he was larger than life. In 1800 he had fought a duel over a debt with Lord George Bentinck; he won a wager by riding two hundred miles in under ten hours; and he served in Parliament for one session, after

---

* Doubly bad luck for Lambert. He had dedicated *The Cricketer's Guide* to the MCC the previous year.

which, unsurprisingly for such an individualist, he found it 'not to his taste'.

Osbaldeston had scored his hundreds as a batsman, but he was most proud of his fast bowling, so much so that when he was teased that George Brown of Brighton was quicker, a 'four-' against 'two-' wicket contest was swiftly arranged. Brown, supported by E.H. Budd, Thomas Howard and James Thumwood, defeated Osbaldeston and William Lambert. In his disappointment the impetuous Osbaldeston scratched out his name from the membership list of the MCC. Beauclerk was delighted at his rival's discomfort, and when his lifelong friend Budd suggested that Osbaldeston be reinstated, the vindictive Beauclerk said no. This graceless behaviour was typical of Beauclerk, and as Osbaldeston was widely liked, fuelled much resentment. Little Beauclerk cared. Osbaldeston was never readmitted to the MCC, and thereafter only rarely played cricket. The squire returned to his field sports and served as a Master of Foxhounds and High Sheriff of Yorkshire.

Beauclerk was not without courage. In 1817, in the game at Nottingham that Lambert allegedly 'fixed', he spoke sharply to a professional who, irritated at being dressed down, threw the ball so violently to Beauclerk that he broke the middle finger of his right hand in gathering it. The finger was bound up and Beauclerk played on, batting with one hand. The injury seemed minor, but it became inflamed and the infection spread to his throat and chest. The *Sporting Magazine* reported that 'there were three days during which his life was in danger, a mortification being apprehended', and praised Beauclerk as 'for thirty [actually twenty-five] years indisputably the first gentleman player', but added – with a sting in the tail – 'after this accident, Mr Osbaldeston, a much younger man, can no longer be denied [that] status'. Osbaldeston must have relished that judgement.

One anti-Beauclerk cameo does not convince. He was bowling to Tom Walker, that phlegmatic old rustic, who simply dropped each ball to his feet – he was not known as 'Old Everlasting' without cause. Beauclerk threw his white hat to the ground, muttering, 'Confounded old beast.' This incident is often used to suggest a lack of sportsmanship by Beauclerk, but it seems no more than frustration, and far milder than the sledging in modern Test cricket. Be that as it may, if Beauclerk intended it as intimidation of a social inferior, it failed. 'I doant care what ee zays,' said Tom, and batted on, unconcerned.

A rounded view of Beauclerk is elusive, but there is no doubt of his cricketing ability. His highest score was 170 for Homerton vs Montpelier in 1806, and as late as 1824, when he was over fifty years of age, he was still able to score 99 against an England eleven. A further three years later the grand old veteran faced William Ashby, one of the new breed of round-arm bowlers, and scored 78.

In 1827, the year after Beauclerk was elected President of the MCC, he was appointed vicar of St Michael's in St Albans and of St Mary's, Redbourn – two livings in the gift of the cricket-loving Earl of Verulam. Neither of these appointments, nor their source, encouraged Beauclerk to take his clerical duties seriously. Parishioners at Redbourn were informed by the parish clerk, 'Old Moody', that 'The Vicar is going on Friday to the throwing off of the Leicester hounds, consequently he will not be back till Monday next week. Therefore, there will be no service in the church next Sunday.'

Beauclerk did not give a fig for convention – a hereditary trait, given his ancestry – but even so, he took eccentricity to the brink. On at least one occasion he adopted the novel practice of preaching to his congregation from a saddle fitted in the pulpit, although in more placatory vein he did race his horses in local point-to-point meetings under a friend's name to avoid a dispute with his Bishop, who would have thought such an activity improper in a cleric.

The Reverend Lord Frederick Beauclerk, Doctor of Divinity, vicar, huntsman, cricketer and President of the MCC, was summed up by the Regency courtesan Harriette Wilson as 'a sly, shy, odd man, not very communicative unless one talks of cricket'. Beauclerk got off lightly. Harriette Wilson was an early 'kiss and tell' girl who offered to remove her victims from her memoirs if they paid her to do so, causing Wellington to mutter, 'Publish and be damned.' She did – and was.

Beauclerk was the foremost amateur of his day, and often the only one to merit selection for representing England in teams otherwise dominated by professional players. He batted for England over eighty times. As a player and as President of the MCC, he was an elemental force in cricket. Without reference to the opinions of others he selected representative teams and adjudicated on disputes. The laws of the game were determined upon his word. He remained a towering figure in cricket throughout the first half of the nineteenth century. His two sons, Charles and Aubrey, played for Hertfordshire, and Charles on one occasion for England, against Kent in 1835. Lord's still drew Beauclerk as an old man to all the great games, and he sat there, his white dog at his feet, observing all in solitary reflection of a life devoted to cricket and, in character to the last, totally indifferent to the verdict of history.

8

The Rise and Fall of Single-Wicket

In the early decades of the nineteenth century, as cricket moved towards the game we know today, an earlier form, with erratic rules carved out of convention, continued to flourish, albeit intermittently. Single-wicket cricket long predated the first known eleven-a-side match in 1697: when the teams were named at Coxheath in 1646, the match was between two players on one side and four on the other. Similarly, two matches in Berkshire in 1712 were contested between two players on either side.

The 'rules' of early single-wicket cricket – the term was taken to cover games of up to five players a side – were probably agreed on a match-by-match basis, but by the nineteenth century a settled format had evolved (for the rules as drawn up in 1831, see Appendix 3, page 403). If the ball passed behind the wicket it was 'dead'. Batsmen were expected to play the bowling with one foot anchored within the crease – no striding forward to drive the ball Beldham fashion – and to score a single run they had to touch the bowling stump *and* return to their wicket. If the batsman left his crease to hit the ball, any runs were disallowed. These rules were not codified until 1831, but they were generally applied far earlier. A lost ball entitled the batsman to three runs – a poor return for what must have been an extravagant hit; and if a fielder stopped the ball with his hat, a similar score was awarded.

Whenever games were between fewer than five players on either side, byes and overthrows were disallowed, and the batsman could not be stumped or caught out behind the wicket. Runs could only be scored in front of 'bounds' placed adjacent to the wickets, which put back-foot players at a great disadvantage. If the game was between five or more players a side, all hits, byes and overthrows were allowed to count towards the batsman's score. The nature of the rules – and the physical strain on the solitary bowler (which was eased by allowing him up to a minute between each ball) – ensured that single-wicket cricket was a slow game. The rate of progress may have been pedestrian, but the element of one-to-one combat, so redolent of boxing, jousting or duelling, appealed to the British instinct. Contests between leading players attracted large crowds.

A code for betting was common, since many single-wicket games were staged to facilitate gambling. In a two-innings contest – fully completed – the total number of runs scored by each side determined the winner. If only one innings was possible – with the second being abandoned – then, to prevent the bets being voided, the outcome could be decided by the single completed innings. These laws were intended to be straightforward and unarguable, but with money at stake, as in the famous Beauclerk/Howard against Osbaldeston/Lambert spat, often they were not.

Single-wicket games became more spasmodic as eleven-a-side cricket grew, and by 1850 this form of cricket had largely died out. In the intervening years fewer than a hundred significant games were played (see Appendix 4, page 404), and the rarity of such contests has ensured that they entered the folklore of cricket. In the 1790s players as diverse as Noah Mann, Andrew Freemantle, Richard Lawrence and Robert Brudenell (Lord Cardigan) featured in contests.

The attraction of single-wicket matches was that they pitched the finest players of the day in competition, amid rivalries that sometimes led to skulduggery. When Three of Surrey (Lambert, Robinson and Beldham) played Three of England (Bennett, Fennex and Lord Frederick Beauclerk) in June 1806, Beldham 'took a lump of wet dirt and sawdust, and stuck it onto the ball which, pitching favourably, made an extraordinary twist and took Lord Frederick's wicket'. 'Silver Billy' was not the first, nor the last, to doctor a cricket ball to encourage it to misbehave. But no one seemed to mind. As ever, Beauclerk was not a man to attract sympathy. Nor was Beldham ashamed: he boasted of his subterfuge over drinks at the Green Man and Still in Oxford Street, a favourite haunt of thirsty cricketers.*

Single-wicket challenges often led to mismatches. At Lord's in 1820 the formidable E.H. Budd beat J. Brand, amassing a total of 101 runs in two innings while poor Brand scored 0 and 0. To add to Brand's embarrassment, Budd deliberately knocked down his own wicket in both his innings to enable the match to progress. He may have simply been exhausted. To amass 101 runs, each of which involved running to the far wicket and back, Budd must have run nearly three miles. Many challenge matches attracted a large gallery; side bets held the spectators' interest even during tedious contests. When the Nottingham pace bowler Sam Redgate played Tom Heath at Nottingham in July 1831 he took nearly an hour to open his score, and then – to the relief of those spectators who had not bet on his success – he was run out by an eighty-seven-yard throw that flattened the middle stump.

In July and August 1833 Tom Marsden and Fuller Pilch met in two matches that were marketed as being for the Championship of England. Pilch won both games easily, scoring 73, 78 and 100 in successive innings; the left-handed Marsden never seemed likely to win, though he batted well for 25 and 31 in the return game.** Nonetheless, Marsden was a formidable hitter, supreme in the north, and the game must have been thought to be competitive, for Pilch's brother Nathaniel remembered in old age 'how pleased we were when Fuller beat [Marsden]'. Despite winning the accolade of Champion, Pilch disliked single-wicket games and rarely played them, even though he was by common consent the finest batsman in the land between 1828 and 1845.

The youngest of three cricketing brothers, Fuller Pilch was born on 17 March 1804. His elder siblings, Nathaniel and William, were

---

* Recalled in W.W. Read, *Annals of Cricket* (1896).
** The figures given are the runs scored off the bat. Extras boosted them to 77, 82 and 106 for Pilch, and 26 and 35 for Marsden.

fine players but not in Fuller's class. The three boys, born in Brinton (not Horningtoft as usually stated), three miles from Holt, where their father kept a tailor's shop, all played cricket for Holt – which masqueraded as 'Norfolk', as in 1820 at Lord's when William Ward scored his famous 278.

Pilch, long-legged and elegant, was a front-foot player with an impeccable defence and a reach that enabled him to stride forward to smother the ball. He used a bat with a short handle, played in a top hat and had an upright stance at the wicket, keeping 'both legs very straight' according to the Surrey batsman William Caffyn, with a favourite shot through the covers. He was in prime form in 1834, scoring 153 not out against Yorkshire in a rain-interrupted match that ended in a draw only because the Holt team could not afford to stay another night in their lodgings. Squire Rippingall, a sponsor and enthusiastic amateur player, was 'hopping mad' that the team left, recalled Nathaniel, but not mad enough to offer to cover their extra expenses. That season Fuller averaged over 43 (next highest was 18), including scores of 87 not out and 73 against Yorkshire, and 105 not out for England against Sussex.

In 1835 Pilch was poached by Kent with an offer of £100 a year to 'come into the County', where he joined the famous eleven that boasted Felix, Wenman, Hillyer, Alfred and Walter Mynn: unsurprisingly, they dominated cricket. At Kent, Pilch – who was a fine slow underarm bowler – found that talent redundant. As the team already had Mynn, Hillyer ('who could put the ball on a sixpence') and Adams, his bowling skills were rarely needed. Even so, analyses of 6 for 21 and 8 for 16 for Manchester against Liverpool in 1845 reveal that he did not lose the art. In the early 1850s Pilch kept a winter cricket ground at Oxford, near Christ Church, where he coached young players in the nets. And later, following in the footsteps of Richard Nyren – and preceding many other fine cricketers – he became a publican, being host of the Saracen's Head Inn at Canterbury, and later an umpire.

In the pre-Grace era of round-arm bowling on dodgy wickets this easy-natured, popular cricketer had an outstanding career. He scored a total of 13,600 runs (average 19.5), including ten centuries and sixty-three half centuries, with a top score of 160, as well as capturing 537 wickets. He was a fine fielder who took many catches, and his throwing from cover point ran out many batsmen who underestimated his accuracy. But there is one oddity in his career. In an age in which batting orders were chaotic and haphazard he batted, with rare exceptions, at second wicket down. It is the first illustration of a trait that affects many cricketers: Pilch, I suspect, was superstitious.

In August 1838, five years after Pilch became single-wicket 'Champion', the title was resurrected for a two-match contest between Alfred Mynn and James Dearman, ironically on Fuller Pilch's home ground at Town Malling, Kent. Mynn won the first game easily by 112 runs, and in the return match scored 46 runs in as many balls, an outstanding feat with an unsprung, unspliced bat. Mynn, it was reported, 'was always a tremendous punisher', although his rate of scoring seems modest today.

It would be a further eight years before the most famous of all single-wicket challenges was staged, between Mynn and Nicholas Felix at Lord's in June 1846. Virtue sat comfortably on the shoulders of Mynn, who with Nicholas Felix and Fuller Pilch was one of the three great cricketers in the second quarter of the nineteenth century. All were friends, with Mynn and Felix, who had met on their debuts for Kent at Lord's in 1834, remaining especially close throughout their lives. The hop merchant Mynn, huge and muscular, and the diminutive and cerebral head teacher Felix were an odd couple, but their gentle natures were in perfect harmony, and the image of Felix playing the flute for Mynn in evening repose is an enduring one. Both were amateurs – of a sort – who received 'expenses' for playing cricket. Neither ever achieved financial security.

In cricket's long march from obscurity Pilch, Mynn and Felix were among the select few whose talent left a lasting memory; they were in the mould of Nyren, who pioneered the skills of a captain, Harris and old John Small of the early Hambledon teams, and Beldham and Beauclerk. Over these formative years a handful of individual performances electrified the game – Ward's 278 and William Lambert's two 100s in a single match – and set benchmarks for the future.

The primitive nature of early cricket had evolved by the 1830s. Willes and Knight had won the battle to legalise round-arm bowling. Bowlers no longer trundled the ball along the ground but bowled subtle underarm on a length or, increasingly, pitched round-arm on a length, seeking to defeat the batsman with guile, speed or spin. Beauclerk had now retired from top-class cricket, but the importance he gave to fielding had helped raise the general standard. Even so, the sensation caused by Heath's massive throw to run out Redgate in 1831 shows that this was not yet universal.

As the nineteenth century advanced, gambling became more sporadic, bets often token, and the finances of the game no longer depended upon it. Statistics began to be collected by amateur enthusiasts, among them Fuller Pilch's nephew William. The press reported the cricket more than the antics of patrons and celebrities. The game was developing a hinterland. Affection for it was being passed down the generations and across the country; and a great acceleration was imminent. It had been embraced by nobility, adopted by their sons at the finest schools and universities, and was a growing enthusiasm for the working man. British servicemen carried the game overseas, where it would take root and grow, and outlast an empire which at its height extended to every corner of the world.

The cricket-loving public were hungry for a superstar, and Alfred Mynn, born at Goudhurst in Kent in 1807, captured their imagination. Mynn's skill took years to blossom. He made an unremarkable debut for the Leeds Club against Gravesend in June 1829, and played only in minor games for the next two years. He had other preoccupations, for he had married a local girl, Sarah Powell, at the end of 1828, and five daughters followed within the next six years. By 1832, the year in which the great Reform Bill split the country, even the diehards had accepted round-arm bowling, and Alfred Mynn began to make an impact on cricket. After a game against Hawkhurst in June of that year *Bell's Life* commented that he was 'promising to become equal to the first rate bowlers of the day'. Two months later, at the end of August, he made a memorable debut at Lord's for the Gentlemen against the Players, taking five wickets including the prized scalps of four top-class batsmen, Pilch, Beagley, Searle and Marsden.

For Mynn, events were moving fast. The previous week he had won his first single-wicket encounter, beating Tom Hills of Malling, who bore the title 'Champion of Kent'. Hills had reason for grievance, since for some reason wides were not counted as runs in the contest, and the inaccurate Mynn bowled a hatful of them. However, a return match a fortnight later confirmed Mynn's superiority when he won comfortably by an innings and 21 runs in a famous victory. Fifty years earlier, players were known as 'Lambert the farmer', or 'Waymark the miller', or 'Rumney the gardener'. After this victory, Mynn did better: he was labelled 'the Lion of Kent'.

Mynn's rise to eminence followed an agonising time for him. Both his parents died within a year, and he nearly lost a leg as a result of injuries sustained while playing at Leicester in the inaugural South vs North match in 1836. It was a fixture destined to become the most important game of the season, and on this first encounter the non-playing captains, watching from a boundary tent, were Beauclerk and Aislabie, President and Secretary respectively of the MCC. During pre-match practice on the first morning Mynn was hit on the ankle and it swelled up, leaving him a hobbling spectator on the first day. He batted with a runner early the following morning and scored an undefeated 21, but his bruised ankle flared up again, and was extremely painful. Nevertheless, on the third day he batted again in an epic contest with the pace bowler Sam Redgate, who hit him repeatedly on the inside of his right knee. It must have been a memorable sight: Redgate, in knee breeches and stockings (he was one of the few players who did not favour the unpressed long trousers and broad braces that were then fashionable), bowling at fierce speed to Mynn, playing the innings of his life while his unprotected legs took a battering.

Mynn batted on for his highest ever score, 125 not out, but at the end of his innings he could barely limp from the field. Lord Frederick

Beauclerk, that arch-opponent of leg guards, shocked by his appalling injuries, laid him on the roof of a coach and sent him swiftly to London for treatment. As Redgate praised him – '. . . that was Mr Mynn's day, that was, it mattered not what length I bowled him, the better I bowled the harder he hit me away' – surgeons speculated that Mynn would lose his right leg as he lay in agony at the Angel tavern, St Martin's Lane, and later at St Bartholomew's Hospital. Eventually the surgeons decided not to amputate, and when Felix visited his friend the following day, Mynn, smiling, passed on the news. The kind and gentle Felix observed later that 'with his gigantic stature, unequalled in symmetry, there was combined the docility of a child'. It is an evocative picture. Mynn took a long time to recover, although the death of his parents the following year may have slowed his return to cricket. His ordeal had one beneficial effect: leg guards became more acceptable.

Alfred Mynn had become a force in the land, and the most popular of cricketers. The reminiscences of his contemporaries conjure up a picture of a huge figure wearing a top hat (occasionally a broad-brimmed straw hat) bowling from a short run, or rather a walk, up to the wicket before using his immense strength of shoulder and arm to propel the ball at such speed that the longstop twenty yards behind the wicket – often his brother Walter – would wear protective shin pads beneath his wide-legged flannel trousers. Another testament to his skill comes from Fuller Pilch:

> I never liked playing against Alfred Mynn, for he and I were like brothers in the first place; and, in the second, he would drop 'em short and put all the steam on if the ground was hard, for he knew my play. And people mayn't think it, but a short pitched ball, cutting right across from the on to the off, is about the nastiest stuff you can have; for if she shoots she wants a deal of play to stop her, and if she jumps 'knuckle high' it is a job to keep her away from short slip, or from popping up.

It is easy to see why Mynn was the centre of attention whenever he played. He was never to lose a single-wicket game, and after twice defeating James Dearman of Yorkshire in August 1838 was acknowledged as the Champion of England. The games with Dearman came about in an odd fashion. On 16 June 1835 a letter appeared in *Bell's Life*, purporting to have been written by Mynn, that challenged Fuller Pilch to a contest. The letter proved to be a forgery, as *Bell's* swiftly acknowledged, and although many wished to see a match between Pilch and Mynn, none was ever staged. In the absence of a Mynn–Pilch confrontation the vacuum was filled when Dearman was offered by a backer to play 'any man in England' for £100. Mr Thomas Selby, a solicitor from Town Malling in Kent, took up the challenge, offering Pilch as his player, and when a reluctant Pilch withdrew, Mynn replaced him. He won both games with ease in front of large crowds. At Town Malling, wearing a close-fitting jersey bound in red ribbon, a red belt and a straw hat rimmed with red ribbon, Mynn won by 123 runs to 11, ending the game in spectacular fashion by ripping out the diminutive Dearman's middle stump and sending it cartwheeling through the air. In the return match Mynn was an even more comfortable victor, by an innings and 36 runs. It was to be eight years before he was challenged again in the most famous single-wicket encounter of all: Mynn against Felix.

Nicholas Felix was one of the most engaging characters ever to play cricket, with natural gifts that seemed endless. He was a classical scholar, linguist, head teacher, ventriloquist, musician – 'Able,' said Pilch, 'to make music on anything from a church organ to tongs' – artist, author and inventor. He was a gifted water-colourist, painted portraits of his fellow cricketers, wrote charmingly about cricket, *Felix on the Bat*, published in 1845, being his masterpiece, and invented primitive batting gloves comprised of rubber strips, and a bowling machine he christened 'the catapulta'. He casually let others benefit financially from his innovations, and made not a penny from them himself. Felix did not subscribe to the sado-virility school of hard knocks, and advocated batsmen protecting their legs by wearing rubber padding beneath long socks.

As a batsman, Felix was in the front rank. Pilch, no mean judge, thought him the most attractive batsman in England, although he conceded that he was not as safe as Nottinghamshire's Joe Guy or the Kent wicketkeeper Ned Wenman – or, mused Pilch immodestly, himself. Felix was a left-handed batsman who batted '*en garde*' as though about to fence, with his knees slightly bent and a backlift that carried the bat well over his shoulder. He was famed for cutting the ball backward of square and for driving forcefully through the covers. He bowled rarely, fielded 'wonderfully' at point, and was a distinctive figure in his tall white hat. His top score was 113 for Kent vs Sussex in 1847, although his 105 for England against MCC at Lord's in 1843, and his 88 in 1842 to help the Gentlemen beat the Players for the first time in twenty years, were equally famous innings.

As a young man Felix, whose real name was Nicholas Wanostrocht, inherited a school from his father, and it was not until he was twenty-seven, when he moved the school to Blackheath in 1832, that he began to play first-class cricket. Even then his scholastic duties meant he rarely played before the end of June. As cricket was not thought to be an entirely respectable pursuit for a schoolmaster he adopted the pseudonym of 'Felix' to separate his participation in the game from his professional responsibilities. It was a poor subterfuge, for people soon realised the two men were one and the same, but it served Felix's purpose.

His single-wicket match with Mynn at Lord's on 18 June 1846 seemed an odd contest. The thirty-nine-year-old Mynn was a genuine all-rounder, one of the greatest in all cricket history and ideally suited for single-wicket contests, whereas the forty-one-year-old Felix, a specialist batsman, rarely bowled his slow lobs, and took only a handful of wickets for Kent in a long career. The match was, once again, billed as being for the title 'Champion of England'. There was of course no such 'Championship' – as on previous occasions the billing was merely a ploy to attract a large crowd, which it did. Unsurprisingly, Mynn was the odds-on favourite with the gamblers, and there was a side bet of two hundred guineas a side.

The stately Mynn bowled at pace off a short run – sadly, we can never know how fast, but it was said to be 'terrific' – and Felix found it hard to score in his first innings. Both players had two 'given' fieldsmen, and to score a run, it must be remembered, the batsman had to run to the far wicket and back. Felix's speciality was leg hits and cuts behind the wicket, but these were disallowed in single-wicket contests, and Mynn was hard to drive in front of the wicket. Despite Felix's 'scientific approach' – a term denoting grace and style – a rapid delivery splintered his unspliced bat, and the next bowled him out before he had scored.

It was a bad day for bats. After scoring only five runs from Felix's slow lobs, Mynn's bat broke too as he attempted a straight drive and Felix held a return catch that, had he missed it, would have flattened his nose. 'It came to me like a cannon-shot,' said Felix. 'I only had time to put up my hand to save my life. Fortunately the ball lighted exactly in the centre of the palm of my hand.' The catch did, he added, give 'all the appearance of design'.

What followed was a monumental tribute to the stamina, skill and courage of two players no longer young. In his second innings Felix faced 247 balls from Mynn. He hit 175 of them, but scored only 3 runs, since once more the vast majority of his strokes fell 'out of bounds' behind the wicket, and were inadmissible as runs. Mynn did bowl one wide, which in the contest counted as one run. Felix was then bowled out, and by 5.30 in the afternoon Mynn was the victor by an innings and one run.

One would imagine that a game of several hours in which only a handful of runs were scored would have been dull. Yet the crowd were enthralled. There was much to admire: Mynn's strength and athleticism in bowling 247 successive balls at pace was extraordinary. So too was the bravery of the diminutive Felix in facing them without pads or other protection. The David and Goliath aspect of the tiny Felix and the mighty Mynn in opposition added spice to the spectacle, and the crowd, seasoned observers including Mynn's benefactor and tutor John Willes, remained absorbed. It was an epic encounter, and a return match was swiftly decided upon.

This was held on 29 and 30 September 1846, on the ground adjacent to the White Hart, Bromley, owned by a Mr Pawley. Marquees were erected for the gentry, and huge crowds flocked to the contest. Once again Mynn won. Felix scored 12 runs (10 wides, 1 no ball and 1 run off the bat), and Mynn passed this total undefeated in his second innings, with both players demonstrating once again the virtues they had shown in the earlier game. All Mynn's runs came from the bat, with no extras. This was the last great single-wicket match. Other contests would take place,* but they would be second-feature events at the conclusion of an eleven-a-side game. Never again would such contests capture the imagination of large crowds. Soon travelling elevens of professional players would provide a spectacle in which many of the prominent players of the day could be seen in a single game. The single-wicket genre fell out of favour.

Even at a distance of nearly two hundred years, it is easy to see why Mynn was so popular. A gentle giant, simple and uncomplicated, he was pre-eminent as a great fast bowler, and was a fierce hitter in the front rank of batsmen. As a fieldsman he was a safe catcher in the slips, where his huge hands swallowed the ball. A.J. Lowth, who bowled often with Mynn, tells us that he could swing the ball in the air. Mynn bowled with skill as well as pace, and it is little wonder that many batsmen could not cope. His skills show an uncanny similarity to those with which Ian Botham would thrill crowds 140 years later.

All the stories of Mynn are laced with affection. None carries any suggestion of Beauclerk-like sharp practice. His cricket reflected his open-hearted and honest nature. 'My boy,' he once chaffed William Caffyn, who was drinking tea, 'beef and beer are the things to play cricket on.' His on-field alter-ego Botham – 'Beefy' to his friends – would have recognised the philosophy.

Off the field, Mynn's life did not follow an even course. In the 1830s his five daughters attended Bearsted Seminary, which must have been costly, and suggests that Mynn had either inherited a significant sum from his father's will or was earning a high income from cricket.

---

* For example: in 1851 F.P. Miller (31) beat G. Gilbert (5 and 10) at The Oval; in 1861 Bob Carpenter and Tom Hayward (33 and 82) beat Tom Darnton, Tom Robinson and Tom Hardy (28 and 32); in 1862 Bob Carpenter, Tom Hayward and George Tarrant (1) lost to John Jackson, Richard Daft and Alfred Clarke (12) ; in 1864 Tom Bignall (1 and 24) beat Harry Crook (12 and 1) at Radcliffe. This list is not exhaustive.

I suspect the former, since despite his successful cricket career Mynn appears to have been bankrupted at least once, and to have spent brief spells in gaol when warrants were served. The clearest evidence of his money troubles comes from the *Bristol Mirror* in its report on 23 August 1845 of the Western Counties vs MCC match at Bath, which notes that a sheriff appeared with a warrant 'for taking the person of Mr Mynn' over a London debt. The sheriff desisted during the game, but upon its conclusion Mynn was taken to Wilton gaol. He was declared bankrupt, and the 'Statement of Affairs', dated 29 August 1845, makes it clear that he had been in prison briefly at Maidstone and in Surrey (twice), as well as Wilton. Mynn's physical assets were less than £20, including the value of his wife's and children's clothes. He had, in cash, £7.10s. and a further £5 received from friends. If he ever had enjoyed ample funds, they were no more.

One debt for which Mynn was pursued – though clearly there were others – was for £127.12s., owed to a Mr John Wyatt of Alverstoke, Hants. This resulted from Mynn's signature on a bill of exchange for £100 (the balance presumably being interest), which was discounted by his brother John and for which Mynn received only £35 and his brother £65. Beyond that bare information, nothing is known of Mynn's financial tribulations, or how and why he fell into debt. However, he was discharged from bankruptcy at Exeter court on 9 September 1845.

The following year a one-eyed veteran cricketer of irascible nature would launch an idea that would carry cricket far and wide, and Mynn and Felix, although past their cricketing prime, would be leading members of his travelling cricket circus.

9

The Missionary and the Mercenaries

The first cricket journalist of any note was William Denison. In 1846 he published profiles of some of the principal players of the day. They were not comprehensive: he missed out Felix, among others. All those he included were from Cambridgeshire, Surrey, Sussex, Nottinghamshire and Kent, aptly reflecting the fact that the most fertile breeding ground of cricket was still in the south and east.

At that time teams often played under the guise of a county – the Wellesbourne Club styled itself as Warwickshire – but only four of what would become the familiar county clubs had been formed: Sussex in 1839, Nottinghamshire in 1841, Kent in 1842 and Surrey in 1845. All that would soon change after the subject of one of Denison's profiles, a forty-six-year-old ex-bricklayer and publican who bowled old-fashioned underarm lobs, took the game to every part of the country. William Clarke was his name.

Clarke was an unlikely missionary for cricket, being portly, one-eyed, short-tempered and not above sharp practice. He was born in Nottingham on Christmas Eve 1798, and little is known of his youth except that as a teenager he followed his father to become an apprentice bricklayer, and at seventeen he was a sufficiently talented cricketer to make his debut for a Nottingham eleven against Ripon. At the age of twenty he married Jane Wigley, who kept the Bell Inn at Angel Row, Nottingham. Children soon followed – Francis, John, Matilda, William, Jane and finally Alfred (born in 1831), who as an adult toured Australia with George Parr in 1863–64. At some point Clarke lost the sight of his right eye while playing fives, but his marriage appears to have been happy, cricket filled his life, and the Bell inn became a centre for Nottingham cricketers.

The glory days of most cricketers fall between the ages of eighteen and thirty-five, but as with so much else, Clarke defied the trend, and his top-class cricketing career was to span forty-one years. From his debut he was a regular member of the Nottingham Old Club side, was captain for many years, and missed only two recorded games in his thirty-year career for the county. He gained a grounding in slow lob bowling from Tom Warsop of Nottingham, and learned the value of varying his pace under the tuition of Beauclerk's old adversary, William Lambert of Surrey.

For the first twenty years of his career, from 1815 to 1835, nearly all his cricket was played in Nottingham or nearby. Cricket records were haphazard and there is no comprehensive documentation of his performances with bat or ball, but those that exist from later years are impressive: for Nottinghamshire in 1842 he took 7 wickets for 98 runs against England; in 1843, 8 for 28 against MCC; the same year, 6 for 17 against Sussex; and two years later, his finest analysis, 9 for 29 against Kent – all at Trent Bridge. Contemporaries put Clarke in the front rank of bowlers, but his greatest successes were to come in the twilight years of his career, when his guile grew and as batsmen became more familiar with the new style of round-arm bowling and less accustomed to Clarke's slow underarm lobs. Not that they were always *that* slow. William Caffyn, who played with and against Clarke, believed that his faster ball was the key to his success, as it deterred batsmen from going forward to attack him. Yet speed is relative. One poet wrote of Clarke:

> He did not bowl to break one's leg,
> Nor yet to smash one's jaw,
> He dropped 'em dead on the middle peg
> Like Southerton and Shaw.

Caffyn and Richard Daft were among many fine cricketers who batted against Clarke and left recollections that bring him to life. He was an acute observer of batsmen, swift to spot any weakness, seldom bowled a similar delivery twice in succession, varied his pitch and pace, was skilful in setting the field to his bowling, and could both curve the ball and spin it, sometimes savagely. He used the crease well, often bowling from the very edge of it. Daft observed:

> ... his delivery was a peculiar one. He came up to the crease with the usual trot which normally all slow under-hand bowlers adopt, but instead of delivering the ball from the height of the hip, he at the last moment bent back his elbow, bringing the ball almost under his right armpit and delivered the ball thus from as great a height as it was possible to attain and still be underhand.

This vivid description, worthy of the great civil servant that Daft's great-grandson Robin Butler (Secretary to the Cabinet 1988–98) was to be, explains how Clarke made the ball lift from a length to discomfort even the finest batsmen. He took malicious pleasure in trapping their fingers against the handle of the bat and causing them to send for protective gloves. The ghost of David Harris would have cheered.

Nor was this the only similarity between Clarke and his predecessors from that earlier age, for he showed great skill at single-wicket challenge matches. In August 1834, on the Forest Ground at Nottingham, entirely unaided, he played against and defeated eleven publicans, scoring 39 runs in one innings against a meagre total of only 27 amassed by his eleven opponents, who each batted twice. However ineffective his opponents might have been – *must* have been – it shows extraordinary accuracy to take twenty-two wickets for so few runs. There were no boundaries in the 1830s, and all runs were literally run: Clarke scored his 39 from a handful of hits as butterfingered fielders fumbled around. Nor was this an isolated win against the odds. In 1836 he defeated Fourteen Victuallers, scoring 19 runs in one innings against a total of 17 by his opponents in their twenty-eight innings. These were farcical contests, but the astute Clarke observed that poor cricketers were keen to pit themselves against the stars. Years later, that knowledge was to make his fortune.

It was not until 1836 that Clarke made his debut – for North vs South – at Lord's, where in later years he was to enjoy great success. Shortly afterwards, tragedy was to strike his private life. In September 1837, after nineteen years of marriage, his wife Jane died, leaving him with a young family. It was a misfortune soon overcome. Three months later Clarke married Mary Chapman, a widow ten years his senior and proprietress of the Trent Bridge Inn, a quaint and comfortable hostelry of modest size with splendid views over the open land of King's Meadows, ablaze each spring with the purple of crocus bloom. Such a rush to matrimony seems almost indecent, and suggests either a prior liaison, love at first sight or a cosy marriage of convenience. Given Clarke's practical nature, it was most probably the latter.

The inn offered an additional enticement. Beside it lay land that Clarke acquired, enclosed and laid out as a cricket ground, paying special attention to the quality of the wicket. Trent Bridge was born. Within a year its attraction was such that Nottinghamshire – as Nottingham Old Club came to be known – began to play there regularly. The first of Clarke's legacies to cricket, a future Test match ground, was in place.

As Trent Bridge opened, the Forest Ground faded into history. A contemporary letter gives a memorable flavour of the old ground:

> . . . the cricket ground, which lies about a mile from the town, on the Forest, as it is still called though not a tree is left upon it – a long, furzy common, crowned on the top by about twenty windmills, and descending in a steep slope to a fine level, round which the race-course runs. Within the race-course lies the Cricket ground, which was enclosed at each end with booths; and all up the Foresthill were scattered booths, and tents with flags flying, fires burning, pots boiling, ale barrels standing, and asses, carts and people bringing still more good things. There were plenty of apple and ginger-beer stalls, and lads going round with nuts, and with waggish looks crying, 'Nuts, lads! nuts, lads!' In little hollows the nine-pin and will-peg men had fixed themselves to occupy loiterers; and in short, there was all the appearance of a fair. Standing

at the farther side of the Cricket-ground, it gave me the most vivid idea possible of an amphitheatre filled with people. In fact it was an amphitheatre. Along each side of the ground ran a bank sloping down to it, and the booths and tents at the ends were occupied with a dense mass of people, all as silent as the ground beneath them; and all up the hill were groups, and on the race-stand an eager forward-leaning throng. There were said to be twenty thousand people, all hushed as death, except when some exploit of the players produced a thunder of applause.*

It is a colourful description, full of life and atmosphere, and recalls the early days of Hambledon half a century earlier. The end of a game, too, is vividly described:

... nothing was so beautiful as the sudden shout, the rush, the breaking up of the crowd, when the last decisive notch was gained. To see the scorers suddenly snatch up their chairs, and run off with them towards the players' tent; to see the bat of Bart. Good, the batsman on whom the fate of the game depended, spinning up in the air, where he had sent it in the ecstasy of the moment; and the crowd, that before was fixed and silent as the world itself, spreading all over the green space where the white figures of the players had till then been so gravely and, apparently, calmly contending – spreading with a murmur as of the sea; and over their heads, amid the deafening clamour and confusion, the carrier pigeon, with a red ribbon tied to its tail, the signal of loss, beating round and round to ascertain its precise position, and then flying off to bear the tidings to Brighton – it was a beautiful sight and one that the most sedate person must have delighted to see.

With its maturity, cricket would gain a great deal, but this letter suggests that much may have been lost as well.

Contemporary cricketers welcomed the excellent conditions of the new Trent Bridge ground, but spectators did not relish the six-pence entry fee, and Clarke was roundly abused for it: in the early

---

* Quoted in William Howitt, *The Rural Life of England* (1838).

matches in 1838 the crowd cheered every hit off his bowling, as they did his dismissal when batting. During the first game on the new ground his pantomime reaction to the restive crowd was to pretend to be caught off a 'bump' ball; as his dismissal was being celebrated, he took guard for the next ball. The boos were wasted, and Clarke being Clarke, the money was pocketed. His cricketing skills, including a maiden century for Holme Lane against Bingham, soon won the crowd over again – not that the hard-headed Clarke would have been much bothered either way.

By the early 1840s *Bell's Life* was reporting matches at schools and clubs, and between representative sides. Cricket was blossoming. But as yet there were few top-class teams offering truly competitive matches. Between 1840 and 1851 Nottinghamshire met Sheffield seven times, Sussex five, Kent four, England three, MCC and Hampshire twice, and Surrey only once. All this would change during the Victorian era.

In 1837 a diminutive eighteen-year-old had succeeded to the throne. She became Queen at a time of turmoil and change, but would live to rule over the most powerful empire the world had seen. Agitation for reform had been growing for forty years, and opposition to change was crumbling. Five years earlier, the 1832 Reform Act had begun the task of cleaning up an unrepresentative and corrupt electoral system. The long march to a universal adult franchise had begun. Legislation, including the Factory Act of 1833, had been passed to improve the terrible working conditions of children in textile factories. Children under nine could no longer work legally, and maximum hours were set for older children. Other reforms were well-intentioned but less successful. The new Poor Law of 1834 turned out to be monstrous, with the manner in which applicants for help were treated being brutal. Harsh decisions divided families, leaving children in care. Dickens's Mr Bumble in *Oliver Twist* (1838) was fiction, but his real-life alter-egos were not.

Science was contributing to the new age. In 1834 Michael Faraday discovered electromagnetic induction, in 1836 John Daniell invented the battery, in 1837 Isaac Pitman introduced shorthand, and in 1839

Fox Talbot pioneered photographic images and William Cooke and Charles Wheatstone invented the first telegraph.

Workers at looms, furnaces and coal faces were growing increasingly impatient with their lot. In town and country, contrasting social systems were emerging. Power tilted to new entrepreneurs in the towns, while the country gentlemen held sway in the counties. The physical environment was changing everywhere. As new building increased in the towns, common land was enclosed for farming in the countryside. One happy reform for the small tenant farmer was the abolition in 1836 of the bitterly resented tithes that had been paid to the Church for centuries. Out of the hearing of their Good Shepherd, the harvesters chorused:

> We've cheated the Parson, we'll cheat him again,
> For why should the Vicar have one in ten?

Prosperity had been widening for a hundred years. Now rising wealth opened up new opportunities. Artisans, skilled workers, senior clerks, lawyers, bankers – all were required and were rewarded, thus enriching a demand that hoteliers, shopkeepers, tailors and hatters rushed to meet. The growth of prosperity fuelled aspirations – if you had it, flaunt it – creating a wider demand for butlers, footmen, cooks, maids and other domestic staff that had previously been the prerogative of the privileged few.

It was a time of growing national self-confidence, from which cricket would benefit. Wider prosperity created a market that William Clarke would exploit. And as the Victorians took their convictions around the world, cricket travelled with them. *Tom Brown's Schooldays*, the most famous school story of all, was published in 1857, although it was set in the late 1830s. Towards the end of the novel, Tom Brown, captain of the first eleven, is sitting on the boundary talking to a master as he watches his team bat. 'It's more than a game. It's an institution,' says Tom. The master replies: 'The discipline and reliance on one another which it teaches is so valuable I think . . . It merges the individual in the eleven, he doesn't play that he may win, but that his side may.' The sentiments reflect the mores of the decade in which the book was written, rather than that in which it is set. Victorian moralists had the ambition of trying to impose their own code of conduct on the nation as a whole. It was artificial, often hypocritical, and ran against human nature, but it seared deeply into the national psyche. The virtues that the master saw in cricket were to be the sporting ideal of the Victorians. Unsurprisingly, cricketing terms passed into commonplace use in the language. Shabby behaviour was 'not cricket', whereas to 'play with a straight bat' was a high tribute. The English language, always mobile, effortlessly absorbed these new expressions, and they live on.

Even so, it is a bit premature for Hughes to claim such virtues for the late 1830s. Nor is Tom Brown justified in claiming cricket at that time as an institution, for it would not become one for two more decades. And even then, it is likely that had he still been alive that shrewd individualist William Clarke would not have agreed with the master's pious pronouncements about the primacy of the team. That was a gentleman's creed, not a player's, and in real life the players almost always won.

Tangible improvements in daily life benefited cricket. The penny post enabled fixtures to be arranged more easily, and reports and scores carried swiftly to the sporting press. *Bell's Life* enlarged its cricket coverage to meet the demands of its readers. Cricket statistics fascinated from the outset; a century later the mathematician G.H. Hardy spoke for all cricket-lovers when he said that if he knew he was to die that day, he would still want to know the close of play scores.

One further ingredient was necessary to spread cricket across the country, and it was about to come. From the mid-1820s, travel became simpler and less expensive. John Macadam pioneered a new system of road-building. Thomas Telford improved the burgeoning system of canals, and inland navigation became far easier. George Shillibeer's horse-drawn omnibus appeared on the streets and, most important of all, the first commercial railway service, between Stockton and Darlington, opened on 27 December 1825.

The potential of rail travel was far-reaching, but it faced the seething resentment of workers who feared that all new technology would cost them their jobs. Tragedy and farce accompanied the opening of the Liverpool to Manchester line in 1830. When the first train on the new line stopped to take on water, William Huskisson, a prominent Tory politician, left his carriage for some fresh air and, hampered by his ill-health, failed to move swiftly enough as an oncoming train approached. His leg was crushed, and he died of shock and loss of blood. When the train reached Manchester, instead of the anticipated warm welcome it was greeted by an angry crowd demonstrating against the onrush of technology. None of this would halt the railway's advance. Within a year the line was carrying thirty thousand passengers a month, and doing so four times faster than a coach could travel. Thereafter, the spread of rail was frantic. In 1837, Euston terminal was built in London. A year later, passengers could travel from London to Liverpool, changing at Birmingham and Warrington. Mr Pickwick's world was dying. By 1848 there were five thousand miles of track, and double that two years later.

The new mode of travel was safe and swift – trains routinely averaged the incredible speed of fifty miles per hour – but not always comfortable. First-class was fine, second-class bearable but third-class passengers travelled in nothing better than open-topped cattle trucks, unprotected from the elements. However, wet or dry, there was for the first time easy communication between town and country. Rural and coastal England were opened up, and new towns arose from nothing. Crewe did not even feature in the census of 1841, but its position as a key railway junction saw it grow to a sizeable town in a decade. Other hitherto insignificant villages such as Swindon also exploded in size. And so did the possibilities for cricket, as the fixture list spread widely.

As the conversation from *Tom Brown* illustrates, the rustics' game was now socially acceptable. Cricket encouraged gentlemanly virtues, and was firmly established in the universities and public schools. In 1841, public policy gave it a further boost. General Lord Hill, keen to improve army recruitment and the fitness of the troops, instructed all major barracks to lay out cricket grounds. As the number of grounds grew, so did the interest of players and spectators. Cricket was beginning to conquer all classes, and a growing press was there to report it. *Punch* was born in 1841, followed two years later by the *News of the World* and the short-lived *Daily News*, edited for a few months in 1846 by Charles Dickens. The growing press corps carried cricket as well as news and social commentary to a wide audience. Some were not impressed. An article in 1842 opined: 'the majority of newspapers print pure lies', but such a sweeping denunciation could not apply to cricket scores. A virtuous circle began to turn a minority interest into a national pastime.

It is easy in retrospect to see how events came together to create a surge of interest in cricket, but they were so disparate that it must have been less evident at the time. The 1840s was a decade of depressed trade, poor harvests and social unrest. The Chartist movement demanded reform but fizzled out, destroyed by its own excesses. Fiscal reforms lifted trade and the repeal of the Corn Laws cut the price of bread. In the midst of these events, the further growth of cricket needed a catalyst, and once again, as with the establishment of the ground at Trent Bridge, the financially astute William Clarke saw an opportunity that others missed. Clarke was now approaching his mid-forties, and was nearly fourteen stone in weight. His cricket career should have been drawing to its natural close, but he had plans to ensure that it did not. His combination of cricketing skills and business acumen was soon to promote the game he loved more widely than any man had done before him.

History can be frustrating when a primary source has been lost. So it is with William Clarke's diary. We know that he kept one, but it has never been found, and may be lost forever. Thus we do not know precisely when he realised that money could be made from the rising enthusiasm for cricket. But we can conjecture: there are clues. After his debut for the Players at Lord's in 1836, Clarke rarely travelled southwards from Nottingham. But in 1844 and 1845 he did so, to play for the North vs MCC at Lord's and for England vs Kent at Canterbury in both years. In these four games he captured forty-one wickets, but more importantly he observed the size and enthusiasm of the crowds, and their willingness to pay to watch top-class players. It whetted his appetite for a new venture.

So too did another game that may have been a trial balloon. In 1845 Clarke wagered £200 to encourage Fuller Pilch to bring a team designated as 'England' to play at Trent Bridge. The game was a success, and Clarke saw the prospect of financial gain from an enthusiastic public if he presented them with a travelling team of first-class players. This may have been decisive. In 1846 he uprooted his life and moved to London. His departure from Nottingham was disastrous for the county's cricket team. That year they played no games at all, and in the next two seasons a miserly three, all of which they lost. 'Old' Clarke, as he had become known, or sometimes 'the General', was not easily replaceable.

In London, to help maintain his income while he planned his venture, Clarke was employed to bowl to MCC members at Lord's. It seems an odd role for one of the finest cricketers of the day, but it was commonplace in the social structure of the 1840s – indeed it remained so for another hundred years: Surrey bowlers were paid to bowl to members in the nets in the 1930s. Practice bowler or not, Clarke, at the age of forty-seven, was now resident in London and on the spot to turn out for the Players against the Gentlemen. He was selected to do so in 1846, and 5 wickets for 30 runs was evidence that age had not withered his skills. The mature bowler was a natural entrepreneur too, and in both capacities he was about to prove he was at the top of his game.

The countrywide demand to see top-class cricket was growing, and Clarke was the first to cater to it. In 1846, even as he continued to play cricket, act as a practice bowler, lay out new cricket grounds, run Trent Bridge ground and manage the Trent Bridge inn from a distance,* he was hatching the plan that would make him a rich man and cricket a national game. Clarke's inspiration was to form a peripatetic team of the cream of professional players to tour the country and play against all-comers. In a stroke of pure marketing

---

* He managed the inn until 1847, and the ground until 1848, when his stepson John Chapman took it over.

genius he named it the Eleven of England, but more colloquially it became known as the All-England Eleven.

Clarke's timing was perfect. The railways were facilitating long-distance travel, interest in cricket was high, and the professional cricketers, with few exceptions, were working men of modest means, keen to add to their income while their fame and skills lasted. A study of seventy-one professionals between 1827 and 1840 shows their backgrounds as:

> 22 craftsmen in light industry
> 17 trade workers and shopkeepers
> 14 agricultural workers
> 14 clothing and textile workers
> 2 clerical (1 clerk and 1 schoolmaster)
> 1 college servant
> 1 coachman*

None of these jobs offered high income or status. These men were, in the terminology of the day, 'working class', though many had artisan skills that lifted them socially above mere labourers. When their cricketing days were over, only a small minority returned to their trade. Uneasy economic conditions offered them few other jobs. The more successful became publicans, but others found employment as ground bowlers or coaches at clubs or universities. Yet others coached boys at preparatory or public schools. Some became private coaches: even forty years later, Ranjitsinhji, when at Cambridge, employed professionals to bowl at him. But many ex-cricketers found life hard, and some, such as the left-handed batsman Thomas Beagley, who was fêted in his prime, died in poverty. Very few enjoyed ongoing reward for their cricketing skills: a ground-staff bowler at Lord's or The Oval earned only thirty to fifty shillings a week. For Clarke, it was a buyer's market: the perfect scenario to attract the players he needed. The select members of the All-England Eleven were elite professionals, hired as mercenaries, the forerunners of Kerry Packer's

---

* W.F. Mandle, 'The Professional Cricketer in England in the Nineteenth Century', *Labour History*, November 1972.

cricket circus one and a quarter centuries later. All would have been grateful for the opportunity. Two of those who became regular players, Alfred Mynn and Nicholas Felix, were nominally 'amateurs', but neither had an independent income and both received 'expenses' that were indistinguishable from the match fees paid to the professionals.

The team played its first competitive game against Twenty of Sheffield at the Hyde Park Ground, Sheffield, on 31 August 1846 – and were beaten by five wickets. Clarke, who hated to lose, had made a rare mistake: he had underestimated his opponents. In addition to the numerical advantage he conceded to them, he had permitted Sheffield to play three professionals, Chatterton, Sampson and Wright, as 'given' men. All three were sufficiently high-quality players to be picked to play against the Gentlemen at Lord's, the premier fixture of the year. It was not an error Clarke would repeat. He knew that if it was to be marketable, his team had to win.

Clarke used the end of the 1846 season as a trial run for his new venture. The team dressed nattily in white shirts with small red spots or stripes, white trousers, black or brown boots, neckerchiefs and fashionable tall hats, some black and some pale with a crêpe surround. Nicholas Felix and James 'Jemmy' Dean wore their trademark yachting caps. Cricket-lovers flocked to see them. The All-England Eleven was a colourful sight and a popular novelty.

Although predominantly professional, the first eleven included one quasi-amateur, the veteran Alfred Mynn, and one genuine amateur, the youthful Villiers Smith, captain of Oxford University. The balance of the team were nine of the best professionals around – Clarke himself, Jemmy Dean, William Dorrinton, Fuller Pilch, Joseph Guy, William Martingell, Thomas Sewell Senior, George Butler and William Hillyer. Apart from Smith, only Martingell was under thirty years of age, and the two cricketing legends, Mynn and Pilch, were well past their prime. But the team was excellent box-office.

Hillyer and Martingell were medium-pace round-arm bowlers. Hillyer, said Denison, pitched on the off stump and moved the ball sharply towards the slips. His immense stamina and easy action enabled him to bowl for long periods. Martingell was an all-rounder who batted especially well against fast bowling. His ability was acknowledged by Kent, which from 1840 had paid him £60 a year to live in the county and play for the team. Jemmy Dean ran to fat and tended to waddle as he approached the wicket, but when he got there he was a fast and accurate bowler and a secure batsman. Joe Guy, a stylish bat with a strong defence, was, eulogised Clarke, 'all ease and elegance, fit to play before Her Majesty in her drawing room'.

One omission from the first game was the young Nottingham farmer's son George Parr, who had been playing at Trent Bridge for two years and was building a reputation as an exciting batsman. It is a typical Clarke story: four days before the opening match Clarke had organised a benefit match – the beneficiary being himself – between his embryonic All-England Eleven and Five Gentlemen of the Southwell Club in Nottinghamshire, supplemented by Five Players of Nottinghamshire (including Clarke himself), with Alfred Mynn as a 'given' man. Parr, who was playing for Southwell, arrived late, having decided to row to the game from his home in Radcliffe. Worse, Mynn was a passenger in his boat. Parr then compounded his felony by top-scoring with 51 runs against Clarke's team. Clarke, ever the disciplinarian, excluded him from the first match.

Only two further games were played that first season, against Eighteen of Manchester and Eighteen of Yorkshire, both in September, and unsurprisingly, given the talent available to Clarke, the Eleven won both games comfortably. The final game set a pattern for many clashes that were to follow. The Yorkshire bowler J.R. Ibbetson took twelve wickets in the two innings, but when the umpires no-balled him for an illegal action the game descended into rancour and could only be concluded when two more sympathetic umpires were found. It would not be the last squabble. Nonetheless, in business terms, Clarke's new venture was off to a promising start.

It was to grow. In 1847 the Eleven played ten games at prime venues in Leicester, York, Manchester, Birmingham, Liverpool, Sheffield, Leeds, Newcastle upon Tyne, Stockton and Stourbridge, and a year later added Derby, Bradford, Coventry, Sunderland, Darlington,

Chelmsford and Southampton to their itinerary. New players were drafted in: George Parr, John Wisden, William Lillywhite and Nicholas Felix in 1847, the wicketkeeper Tom Box in 1848, William Caffyn in 1850 and Julius Caesar and George Anderson in 1851. The very best of early Victorian cricket became members of Clarke's cricketing circus.

George Parr was now growing into his immense natural talent. Tall, strong and muscular, with a crouching stance at the wicket, he burst into the Eleven with a hundred against Twenty-Two of Leicester, and followed it with an undefeated 78 against Eighteen of York. He used his feet to drive, could cut savagely and hit powerfully to leg. On all wickets, he gained the reputation of being the best bat in England. Caffyn was not far behind. Tom Box – 'sharp as a ferret', said Felix – was the best wicketkeeper in the country, although like all stumpers at the time, with the possible exception of Wenman of Kent, he only took the ball on the off stump, and left leg-side deliveries to be gathered by the longstop. He was also a useful batsman, and often contributed valuable runs.

The diminutive John Wisden, who was a potboy to Box as a twelve-year-old, made only one appearance in 1847, but played more often in later years. Despite his small stature he bowled fast and batted well, specialising in the 'draw' shot, in which the ball was played between the batsman's legs, which would become defunct when pads were worn. In 1850 Wisden took 340 wickets in thirty-eight matches, including all ten in one innings for North vs South. He scored centuries for Sussex against Kent in 1850 and Yorkshire in 1855. He was a good businessman and, as Clarke would discover, not easily cowed. The droll Julius Caesar was a brilliant hitter to the on-side, with a stubborn defence and a partiality for slow bowling. George Anderson had the invaluable gift of making runs on a poor wicket when his colleagues failed. Against Manchester he scored 43 of the Eleven's total of 80, with 8 being the next highest score.

William Lillywhite's epithet, 'the Nonpareil', aptly summarises his status as a bowler. He was well aware of his reputation, and his observation 'Me bowling, Pilch batting and Tom Box keeping wicket

– that's cricket,' suggests that he was not a modest man. Small and stout, he was still playing at the age of sixty-one, his tall hat and wide braces a familiar sight on cricket fields. Nicholas Felix not only brought fine batting to the team, but became President of the Eleven and its spokesman and peacekeeper. Since Clarke's gruff nature often caused offence, this was no sinecure.

The demand to see this team of all-stars was colossal, especially in the north, where top-class cricket was less well-established, and the All-England Eleven travelled widely. The spectacle of a game against Clarke's superstars was very enticing. Moreover, in an echo of early cricket traditions, the matches attracted huge betting on their outcomes: in one game at Manchester, £40,000 was said to have been staked. Nor were the bets all one-way – teams such as Manchester, Bradford, Leeds and Birmingham nurtured fine players and had rich backers. To satisfy the demand to play against Clarke's all-conquering team, the Eleven often played inferior teams, bolstered in number, usually to twenty-two players, keen to pit themselves against the finest cricketers of the day. Sometimes the second-rate players were supplemented by professional bowlers to even the odds. Whoever they played, the team generally won: of fifty-one games between 1846 and 1849 they only lost eleven, with thirteen drawn or rained off.

Such was the prestige of the Eleven that opponents often held a 'rehearsal' to select the best twenty players from local teams to meet them. Sometimes this benefited Clarke. In 1848 the Burton upon Trent Club selected a professional, (Robert) Crispin Tinley, to face the Eleven. Although the fixture was ruined by rain, 'Cris' Tinley, a fine fielder close to the wicket and a destructive batsman, later joined the All-England Eleven. He began as a fast round-arm bowler but subsequently became a lob bowler to equal Clarke.

By 1851 the fame of the Eleven had boosted its fixture list to thirty-four games, the highest they ever achieved, and from that date to the late 1870s they played at least twenty matches a year. Their role in promoting the game north of Nottingham was pivotal, and as William Caffyn and Richard Daft were later to testify in their memoirs, the team was overwhelmed with invitations. 'Owing to the exertions of Clarke,' said Frederick Lillywhite in 1851, 'cricket has become a very popular game in the North, even as far as Scotland.'

The success of the Eleven made Clarke a wealthy man. He contracted his team to play for appearance money of around £70, although sometimes he pocketed the gate receipts in payment. Out of these funds he would pay each player between three and five guineas, depending on their reputation and performance, but a large portion of the money ended up in his own pocket. If individual players were offered a bonus by admiring sponsors, Clarke took a share. Since a refusal of this 'request' risked non-selection for future fixtures, most players complied.

The All-England Eleven was a travelling caravan for commerce. Wherever they went there were tents to be erected, cricket gear to be sold and food and drink to be consumed. The merchants flocked around. On and off the field, the Eleven were treated royally. Before their arrival, often months before, committees were set up to oversee the match and plan the entertainment. The team was greeted at railway or coach stations by admiring crowds, and sometimes even with a welcoming peal of the local church bells. Huge numbers of spectators flocked to the games, often walking miles to do so, and post-match receptions, banquets and balls were customary. The team's visit might be accompanied by galas, fêtes, fireworks and balloons – everywhere they went, their arrival was an event that had to be celebrated, and the players were celebrities who had to be cosseted:

> Their breakfast, in fact, and the best they could get,
> Was a sort of déjeuner à fauchette;
> Instead of our slops, they had cutlets and chops,
> And sack-possets, and ale in stoups, tankards, and pots;
> And they wound up the meal with rump-steaks and 'schlots'.

To round it off after dinner, wrote William Caffyn in his autobiography *Seventy-One Not Out* fifty years later, 'churchwarden pipes were the order'.

It sounds idyllic, and it was, up to a point. But it was hard work, and precarious, for the celebrity of the team depended upon its continuing success. The celebrations accorded the players flattered their egos and boosted their reputations, but were not always welcome, since even with the growing convenience of trains, travelling was extensive, frustrating and tiring. This emerges very clearly from a manuscript, 'The Doings of the Eleven', written by Felix about the team's travels in 1851 and 1852, and the later recollections of the amiable Yorkshire batsman George Anderson. Looking back, Anderson wrote:

> Cricketers who now go about the country in saloons and express trains have a much easier life than we of the All-England Eleven had to grow accustomed to. Dublin to London, London to Glasgow and Edinburgh, and so on – these were the journeys we had to do, often in one night, to be ready for the next day's match . . . Was there any wonder that I should have to be roused up out of sleep to go in to bat?

Anderson also recalls a coach journey in which the team was lost in rural Lincolnshire on a moonless night, arriving at their destination without sleep at 6 a.m., with play beginning at noon. It was not all good cheer, good fare and Caffyn's churchwarden pipes.

Felix concurs. He recalls Alfred Mynn losing his luggage on a train journey, and bearing the misfortune with his customary good nature. More taxing were coach journeys burdened with luggage and cricket equipment. Felix writes of leaving Hereford for Gloucester after a dinner as crowds 'stand in an admiring gaze around the coach as it heaped upon its roof the trunks, the portmanteau's . . . then came the stirrup cup, then the fond farewell, then the loud huzza, with waving of hats' – then 'on towards Gloucester'. The trip was long and supremely uncomfortable before Felix found a 'welcome bed' in Gloucester in which to rest the aches and pains of his journey. After one night the team travelled on through Bristol to Exeter, where they spent the night before heading off at first light to Teignmouth to play Devonshire. It was a tiring life.

The team was a collection of diverse personalities. Felix, mild-mannered, artistic and cerebral. Pilch, taciturn and likely to hide silently behind his churchwarden pipe. Parr was 'queer tempered' and fond of gin and water, with Caesar his regular drinking companion. Caesar, nervous and depressive, with a fear of fire and of being in a room alone, was, surprisingly in view of his timidity, a good boxer. Hillyer suffered from gout, and was teased constantly by his colleagues threatening to stamp on his painful toes. Box was dapper, with unfashionably long hair and a smashed nose courtesy of a lively Lord's wicket. Collectively, they drew the crowds and carried top-class cricket across the country.

The cricket was less strenuous than today, but more hazardous. An over comprised four balls, mostly round-arm or traditional lobs, but occasionally underarm length bowling. There were no sightscreens, and the ball might come to the batsman at speed, out of the gloom or a background of darkly clothed spectators. With few exceptions, batsmen played from the crease, both for self-preservation and because, in the stately cricket of the day, moving aggressively down the wicket was thought to be unethical. By the standards of the modern game, fielding was sedate. No one threw himself full-length to save runs or dived to take a catch. Apart from being unfashionable conduct, the high hats and the clumsy boots and shoes ruled out such athleticism.

But the cricketers had to be fit, for with no boundaries, every score had to be run. Batsmen, Caffyn remembered, were run out through sheer exhaustion. The bats were little better than blocks of willow, though some by now were crudely spliced, protective gear was primitive and the wickets were pitted, uneven, overgrassed and dangerous. Lord's, despite its pre-eminence, had a venomous wicket. Prudence dictated that many batsmen stayed on the back foot for safety; in so doing they were easy prey for skilled bowlers like Clarke. Scores were low, and a batting average in double figures was considered creditable.

William Clarke was the heart and soul of the All-England enterprise. Nominally, the Eleven was run by a committee, with Felix as President, but in all important matters Clarke's writ ran on and off the field. He was Manager, Secretary and Treasurer, and was unwilling to share control of the golden goose. On the field he captained the Eleven and bowled incessantly, always believing he was about to capture the next wicket. Often he was right. In seven seasons between 1848 and 1854 he took 2,327 wickets (an average of over 330 each year) at a modest cost apiece. The majority of his victims were in games against 'odds', facing teams of fourteen, eighteen or twenty-two players, some of whom would have been inferior cricketers, but nonetheless it remains a formidable total.

Clarke was not an easy man or, so far as we can judge, a very nice one. History has left us a life rich in anecdote, not all of it to his credit. He was often unlovable and boorish: once on a train, when given the unwelcome instruction to extinguish his cigar, he stubbed the lighted end out on the porter's hand. His wit was sardonic. Felix tells of seeing a rustic cricketer take a severe blow to the head:

'Did you see that, Muster Felix?' asked Clarke.

'I did,' replied Felix.

'Whoy, then that's juist as folk ought to play me!'

'How is that?' asked Felix.

'Whoy, with the head,' said Clarke.

There was truth in that remark, and one that Clarke himself practised. He was a 'foxy' cricketer. But his temper and his high-handed behaviour led to resentment among his team, and feuds were frequent. Caffyn, frustrated by Clarke's treatment of him, left the All-England Eleven at the end of 1854 for a coaching engagement at Eton. Discontent and controversy had been close to the Eleven from the outset. The mercenary professionalism of Clarke's brainchild was widely disliked. Furthermore, the team attracted the opposition that so often follows successful innovation. Such carping was merely the chattering backcloth to deeper friction.

Clarke was partly responsible. In almost all circumstances his behaviour was dictatorial, and he inspired resentment more than affection. He was not generous to the team. Guy did not wish to return to being a baker, or Martingell a shoemaker, or Caesar a carpenter, or Hillyer a gamekeeper – and Clarke used that knowledge.

He paid his players the sums he promised, but as they had to meet their own expenses, part of their match fee was eaten up before it reached their pockets. Moreover, their earnings were far less than Clarke's – and they knew it. Clarke could argue, justifiably, that the Eleven was his idea, that he organised all the games, and that without him no one would earn anything at all. Even so, as his players lined up to receive their £4 or £5 from coins set out on a table in front of Clarke, it must have irked them to see him sweep much larger sums into his own hands with the tactless comment, 'And this is for me.'

Some of the ill-feeling was unavoidable. As the fixtures piled up, the larger squad Clarke accumulated meant that some players had to be omitted from each game. They resented this, and the resulting loss of income. On-field issues, such as Clarke persistently overbowling himself, added to the frustration. So too did the squabbles that occur whenever a group of highly talented individuals spend too much time in each other's company.

The success of the Eleven posed a further dilemma: the demand to see them in action was greater than their capacity to meet it. Some spectators had a keen eye. In 1852 an old man of eighty-six donned his tall hat and smock to walk the seven miles from Farnham to Godalming to see the day's play: it was 'Silver Billy' Beldham. But frustrations piled up, and as the appetite for more games grew, some of the players acted on the obvious solution. In the middle of the 1852 season,* John Wisden, who had deserted Clarke at the end of the previous season, and Jemmy Dean, who had only occasionally played for him, established a rival: the United All-England Eleven. Wisden felt he was justified. He had spoken to Clarke about the disproportion between his earnings and the professionals' fees, and had been rebuffed. The rival eleven was his response.

Most of Wisden's recruits had never, or only rarely, played for Clarke – some may have been angry that they were never invited to do so – but they were players of a sufficient quality to end Clarke's monopoly of the only travelling top-class team. The distaste for

---

* For the first half of the season Wisden was fully occupied as cricket coach at Harrow School.

Clarke among the new eleven was evident at a meeting held at the Adelphi Hotel, Sheffield, on 7 September 1852, when they resolved never to play for or against Clarke if Clarke had arranged the game. Among the signatories, with Wisden at their head, were Tom Lockyer, Tom Adams, Jemmy Grundy, Thomas Hunt, John Lillywhite and Thomas Nixon, who had played for the All-England Eleven, and George Pickwell, who had not. All of them were familiar with Clarke and his fearsome reputation. Clarke was enraged, but powerless: he had no means of preventing others following the lead he had set. He attempted to dissuade Wisden, but it was a hopeless task. No meeting of minds was possible. Clarke was not bereft of allies. His key players – Mynn, Felix, Pilch, Parr – stayed loyal, but this did not prevent a rancorous dispute from emerging in the columns of *Bell's Life*.

Clarke and, surprisingly, the iconic Mynn, who had played nearly a hundred matches for the Eleven between 1846 and 1852, were the targets of this correspondence. 'A Lover of Cricket', whose identity was never positively established, initiated it with a full-blooded, and very personal, attack on Clarke. He was accused of being arrogant, stingy, paying his players too little and too late, and of misrepresenting the quality of the All-England Eleven, because some of the players' best years were behind them. The 'Lover of Cricket' targeted Alfred Mynn, admittedly past his prime, who was 'useless now at any point of the game'. This was unfair: there are glimpses of Mynn at this time striking sixes over square leg and into the beer cellar of an adjacent pub. Some of the charges were true – Clarke *was* arrogant and mean* – but overall the criticism was unbalanced and partial: no mention was made of Clarke's contribution to cricket, or of the widespread public demand to see Mynn.

As President of the Eleven, Felix replied courteously defending the quality of the team, very probably at Clarke's instigation, for Clarke was astute enough to recognise the marketing danger if the status of the team were undermined. Pilch, more bluntly, broke his customary silence to decry the criticism as 'sickly prattle'. Others

* He was not always mean. When Caffyn scored 28 not out in a total of only 41 for the All-England eleven at Lynn in 1852 he was presented with a box of cigars by Clarke.

weighed in supportively. Clarke himself wrote a fierce defence, refer-ring to 'malicious fabrications' and, without naming him, making it clear that he was aware of the identity of his critic. In a curious passage Clarke wrote: 'I knew his name to be not *Sorrywether* but something like it, a portly barrister, noted for his old Dando qualifi-cations.' From this, the cricket historian G.D. West, in *The Elevens of England* (1988), identified the anonymous scribe as an MCC and Surrey member, Charles Merewether QC, although the chaotic draft-ing of the letter to *Bell's Life* suggested a man less educated than a Queen's Counsel.* We may never know the identity of the letter's author for certain. In any event, whoever he was, he renewed his attacks on Clarke and Mynn in a further long letter that drew a dignified and moderate response from Mynn's elder brother William, who mocked the anonymity of the critic and refuted some of his allegations. Mynn himself, placid as ever, endured Clarke's tantrums equably, pocketed his fees and kept clear of controversy. The corre-spondence then ceased – or at least, ceased to be published – and the two rival All-England teams played on with their enmity unresolved.

But in Clarke's case not for long, although even in his later years he provided memories that lasted. In 1854 he took his team to play against Twenty-Two of Bristol in a field behind the Full Moon hotel, Stokes Croft. The All-England Eleven fielded a strong team, including Clarke, Parr, Caffyn, Caesar, Box, Anderson and Willsher, and won by 149 runs: a five-year-old boy, William Gilbert Grace, was at the match, and remembered only that the team wore top hats. They returned the following year, winning this time by 165 runs, and young William's elder brother, fourteen-year-old Edward Mills Grace, was presented with a bat by Clarke for fielding well at longstop. The bat was an object of pride to the whole Grace family.

The man in the high white hat with crêpe around it played his final game against Twenty-Two of Whitehaven in June 1856, bowing out with a wicket with his last ball. Two months later William Clarke was dead, at the age of fifty-seven. In death he received the plaudits

---

* Merewether advised Anthony Trollope on legal matters for *The Eustace Diamonds* (1873), the third novel in the Palliser series.

denied him in life. He was, said *Bell's Life*, 'the Man who won games in his Head' – an acute judgement. He had passed on his accumulated wisdom in articles offering 'Practical Hints on Cricket' that merit reading even now. With the All-England Eleven he had offered a showcase for the greatest cricketers of the day. After he died his Eleven and its rival were reconciled, and played charity matches at Lord's for the benefit of the Cricketers' Fund Friendly Society. Clarke was buried at Norwood Cemetery; no headstone marked his grave until 2005 when, due to the efforts of Alex Picker, a latterday admirer, one was finally erected.

Alfred Mynn did not long survive Clarke. Despite his increasing bulk he played on until 1857, beloved by the crowds to the end. Within his massive frame not all was well, and this most popular of cricketers died in 1861, at only fifty-four, of ill-health brought on by diabetes. At his death Felix said of him, '[He was] one of the noblest specimens of manliness and courage combined with all that was becoming in a man.' It was a touching tribute from a friend, but another admirer, W.J. Prowse, once Felix's pupil at school, composed 'In Memoriam', verses that even today remain the finest ever penned to honour a cricketer:

> With his tall and stately presence, with his nobly moulded form,
> His broad hand was ever open, his brave heart was ever warm;
> All were proud of him, all loved him. As the changing seasons pass,
> As our champion lies a-sleeping underneath the Kentish grass,
> Proudly, sadly will we name him – to forget him were a sin.
> Lightly lie the turf upon thee, kind and manly Alfred Mynn!*

Cricket, with its love of heroes, would never have forgotten Mynn, but Prowse's tribute fixed him firmly and forever in the pantheon of the game's greats.

He is joined there by Nicholas Felix, who played his final game for the All-England Eleven at Torquay in 1853, ending, sadly, with a nought. The following season, suffering from rheumatism, he played only one club game and then retired. Never rich, or wise with money,

---

* For the verses in full, see Appendix 5, page 411.

he began to earn his living as an artist,* but three years later a stroke paralysed his right arm and hand, drawing from him the mild response that he was 'most kindly admonished by Almighty God'. His lovable nature attracted support from his friends. The Reverend James Pycroft, his neighbour in Sussex, set in train help that paid his medical bills and left a small gratuity. After partial recovery from his stroke, Felix retired to paint at Wimborne in Dorset. Penury always hovered nearby, but subscriptions raised by admirers alleviated some of the hardships of later life for this enduringly popular cricketer, until his death in 1876.

Without Clarke, Mynn and Felix, and with the rising interest in county sides, the itinerant teams diminished in importance, although they increased in number. Wisden's United All-England Eleven had broken Clarke's monopoly, and the competition intensified. In 1858 Sherman and Chadband sponsored the New All-England Eleven, and four years later Fred Caesar's New All-England Eleven made its appearance. The United South of England Eleven, largely a Surrey offshoot with W.G. Grace, appeared in 1864 and greatly increased the hostility between northern and southern professional players. In all, nearly twenty such sides can be traced, some of which played on until the 1880s before finally fading into history. Traditionalists like Pycroft loathed the travelling professional elevens, believing that they stifled amateur talent. But the mature judgement of Lord Harris is kinder: he felt that the elevens sustained and widened interest in cricket, and were the midwives to the county system. For that, we owe much to them.

---

* A portrait of William Hallett, Mayor of Brighton and an old cricket companion, shows that he had talent in oils as well as watercolours.

10

Wider Still and Wider: Cricket Goes Abroad

Cricket is an English game that has grown in character since it was carried to far-flung posts of the world by the servants of Empire. In Australia, India, South Africa, the West Indies and Sri Lanka, it began as a leisure-time pursuit of the conquerors. Empires are never loved by those whose lands they occupy, whose assets they exploit, and whose people they control. Nor was the British. And yet, uniquely among empires, England left behind a language, a system of law, civil administration – and cricket. An imperial legacy was not new – Romans, Persians, Ottomans, Hapsburgs, even Mongols, all left them, and sometimes they were benevolent – but none bequeathed a game that furnished a common bond between nations which had the ability to help put aside, or bind up, political differences.

The first cricket on the Indian subcontinent was played by British sailors stationed in the Bay of Cambay, a huge inlet north of Bombay. Dispatches from 1721 suggest it was their favourite diversion. So far as we know, their occasional games made no impact upon the Indian population, but perhaps it sowed a seed: the game would fascinate later generations. The expatriate community expanded towards the end of the eighteenth century, and cricket became a major part of the sporting and social scene. Military officers, civil servants and merchants, all looking for a taste of home recreation, set up clubs in the coastal centres. While their servants served tea and delicacies in tents beyond the boundary, the expatriates did not foresee that the charm of cricket would so catch the imagination of the local population that two hundred years later more than half the games in the world would be played in India, and by Indians.

Calcutta was an immensely important economic and military centre, and it was there, in 1792, that the Calcutta Cricket Club was established, on the site of the present-day mega-stadium Eden Gardens. It is probably the oldest cricket club outside Britain.* It was here on 18–19 January 1804 that the earliest full scores of a game in India were recorded: hilariously, between Old Etonians and the Rest of Calcutta. But it was Bombay where Indian cricket – cricket played by Indians, not sahibs – really began, albeit from a rather oblique part of the native population: the Parsees. Originally émigrés from Islamic Iran, the Parsees settled in large numbers on the western seaboard of India, and for over five hundred years had been established there as traders and merchants. Despite their importance to the economy they were never fully assimilated into Indian society, especially by the Hindu elite, but their mercantile prowess was grudgingly respected. Their community included some of Bombay's wealthiest individuals, which would prove to be a great boon to cricket.

No one knows why the Parsees took to cricket with such enthusiasm A cynical interpretation would be that they saw the game as an effective way to steal a march on the haughty Hindus by ingratiating themselves with the ruling British. Early matches must have been an ungainly spectacle, as the Parsees' traditional tunic shirts impeded batting and bowling alike; but whatever their motivation, they became devoted to the game.

As they were unable to join European clubs (a ban which, disgracefully, lasted until Independence in 1947), the Parsees were quick

---

* There have been various claims about the date that the club was founded. The most widely accepted date is 1792. However, there is a reference in a local newspaper to the club having been in existence in 1780. If this is true, it would make the Calcutta Cricket Club older than even the MCC.

to establish the Oriental Cricket Club, in 1848 in Guha. This was superseded two years later by the Zoroastrian Cricket Club, with a further thirty others set up between 1850 and 1860. The eccentric names chosen for these clubs, a mixture of Greek classical references and British icons, support the contention that the Parsees wished to appeal to the British: Spartan, Elphinstone and Gladstone were among them.

The Parsees played on the *maidan* (or field) that lay in front of the fortified British headquarters, Fort George. The space provided a huge open area, nearly forty acres in size, for recreation, since it had been cleared of roads and buildings in 1772 to give an uninterrupted line of fire against attackers. It was similar to the defensive area in front of Fort William in Calcutta where the Calcutta Club played and where Eden Gardens now stands. The Bombay Maidan was known as the Parade Ground or the Esplanade, and hosted a plethora of European sporting activities – and Parsee cricket. It is now known as the Azad (Hindi for 'free') Maidan, and a million cricket dreams are still set up there every Sunday afternoon.

Once the success of the Parsee adoption of cricket became obvious the Hindus began to take an interest too, and soon formed their own club, the Bombay Hindu Union Cricket Club, in 1867, or possibly 1866. Inter-racial rivalry was fierce, and contemporary accounts tell of the Hindu elders' dismay at the superior skill of their Parsee opponents. Both Parsees and Hindus restricted membership of their clubs to the upper-classes. Low-caste Indians were not welcome. Snobbery and exclusivity were not solely the prerogative of the British.

The Maidan became a focus for tension after the formation of the European-only Bombay Gymkhana (Hindi for 'club') in 1875. This brought all the sporting activities of the ruling elite – cricket, archery, football, tennis and rifle-shooting – into one social club, all of them being conducted on one ground, the Maidan. The Gymkhana was granted exclusive use of one-third of its area, leaving Parsees, Hindus and Muslims to play their matches in the remaining two-thirds. Thus, three thousand Europeans had control of a third of the area, with the rest of it being available to the remaining non-commissioned whites and the 650,000-strong Indian population. The situation was tolerated initially, and the first match between the Parsees and the Bombay Gymkhana was played two years later: the Parsees, scoffed at by the white cricketers, played well but lost the game.

The simmering tensions over the division of the Maidan burst open in 1879, when two English polo clubs merged with the Bombay Gymkhana and were given permission to play two evenings a week on the non-Gymkhana part of the land. It was a cruelly unfair decision which not only gave the English *de facto* use of two-thirds of the entire area, but ruined the playing surface of the non-Gymkhana cricketers. The ill-feeling this caused gave rise to a bitter dispute which led to a titanic and closely argued bureaucratic exchange between the club, Parsee civic leaders and the Bombay government, which eventually found in favour of the Parsees in 1882. Subsequent appeals, and a change of Governor, however, gave the area back to the polo players in 1884, to renewed local outrage.

Undaunted, the Parsees formed the very well-funded Parsee Gymkhana in 1886, and petitioned the government for a designated part of the Maidan. A further erudite exchange of petitions brought about a deft solution: recently reclaimed land from the sea, a mile or so from the Maidan, was made available, so long as 'all costs' were met by the Parsee Gymkhana. This may have been graceless, but it was not a practical problem to the Parsees, as the President of the Gymkhana was the fabulously wealthy Sir Jamsetjee Jeejebhoy. So, eventually, the native cricketers of Bombay were able to play without having to dodge the holes left by the hooves of their colonial masters' polo ponies.

The Parsee Gymkhana soon grew in strength. It toured England in 1886, losing nineteen games and drawing eight. The captain, D.H. Patel, modestly said in his farewell speech that 'It was not with the object of gaining victories that we made the voyage to England.' However, a second tour in 1888 did bring eight wins to offset eleven defeats. Both tours were organised by Charles Alcock of Surrey (see pages 349–53), whose mark can be found on so much of Victorian sport. The Parsee tour improved playing skills, for in 1889 they finally beat the Bombay Gymkhana themselves, by three runs. The following year the Parsee Gymkhana met G.F. Vernon's touring eleven, an amateur side featuring Lord Hawke. The tourists had won six and drawn one of their games by the time they reached Bombay, and they thrashed the Bombay Gymkhana by an innings. On 30 January they played the Parsee Gymkhana. In a nail-biting two-day match the Parsee side won by four wickets, with their fast bowler Mehallasha Pavri taking 7 colonial wickets for 34. It was the first high-water mark of Indian cricket.

Indian cricket enjoyed a further psychological fillip later that year when Lord Harris became Governor of Bombay (see pages 315–17). After a shaky start, during which he dismissed Indian petitions that sought the return of the land appropriated by British polo players, he became a great supporter and patron of the game, and permitted reclaimed land on the seafront to be rented to provide open space for cricket for Hindus, Parsees and Muslims. Harris also inaugurated the Presidency Match, the leading domestic competition until the Ranji Trophy began in 1934–35, a two-game series, sited in Bombay and Poona, between Europeans and Parsees. The first fixture in 1892 ended in a rain-ruined draw, but over the next fourteen years twenty-six matches were played, of which the Parsees won eleven, the Europeans won ten, and three were drawn for various reasons. The remaining two matches were abandoned, one for monsoon, one for plague. Bowing to pressure from other communities, the Presidency tournament expanded to become a national competition. The Hindus joined in 1907, making it the Triangular Tournament, and it became the Quadrangular Tournament when the Muslims took part in 1912. Years later, in 1937, it became the Pentangular Tournament due to the inclusion of a new side called 'The Rest', made up of Indian Christians and Jews. It continued until 1945, when it was stopped because of fears that its openly sectarian structure might be inflammatory. Mahatma Gandhi, the spiritual guide of the nation, was one of those who were deeply critical of its structure.

Cricket among Indians became less exclusive and more open to different castes from the 1880s. Baloo Palwankar, one of four cricketing brothers, and Mehallasha Pavri, who starred in the defeat of Vernon's team, were the most notable of the early players. Ranjitsinhji was, of course, Indian, but he was not domiciled in the country, and in any event wanted to play for England. When he played for the Maharajah of Patiala's Eleven at Eden Park and Kolkata in June 1899, huge crowds flocked to see him. But in cricketing terms, ethnicity notwithstanding, Ranji was not an Indian, and later Duleepsinhji and the elder Nawab of Pataudi became honorary Englishmen too.

Baloo Palwankar was the first of the long line of great left-arm Indian spinners. As he was an 'Untouchable' he was initially overlooked by the Hindus for whom he was employed as a groundsman in Poona. But the ever-watchful Parsees, eager for every advantage, saw his potential and enticed him to play for them. Because of his prowess the Hindus swiftly admitted him as a club member, although caste taboos meant that he was left to eat and drink outside the pavilion. Indian caste restrictions mirrored Victorian social exclusion in an extreme form, but Baloo's cricketing skills prised open the barriers. As he became more invaluable on the field, the Bombay Hindu Gymkhana graciously permitted him to dine with his higher-caste team-mates.

Parsee cricket's brightest star was Mehallasha Pavri, the destroyer of Vernon's eleven, who captured 170 wickets at a cost of 11.66 each in the second Parsee tour of England in 1888. England suited him, and his bowling, and he settled there to play for Forest Hill, Surrey Club and Ground, and Middlesex.

Cricket in India did not die out after independence was gained in 1947. At the time the British departed fooball was equally popular, especially inland, yet it was cricket that captured the primary affection of a billion Indians. Why was it that a nation newly free from the shackles of British rule eagerly adopted a sport so closely linked with the hated imperialists? The answer may lie in the general feeling that it was worth keeping some aspects of British rule, and that alongside the legacies in law, administration and education, cricket was worth promoting. So thought Gandhi, whose power base was in the cricket-loving Bombay area, and who encouraged his followers to celebrate the good things about British rule. This had a huge influence. But the true reason for cricket's enduring popularity is simpler: it captured the heart of India, and it has never let go.

Old Boys of Eton College crop up time and again in the story of cricket's journey around the world, and it is an Old Etonian civil servant, Charles Anguish, who *may* have been the prime mover in introducing cricket to South Africa – or, as it was then known, Cape Colony. His role cannot be proven, but it is highly likely. Anguish was a talented cricketer who was sent to Cape Colony in 1797 to take post as Comptroller of Customs. He had played for Eton, MCC, Surrey and the Earl of Winchilsea's Eleven, and it is safe to assume he was an avid devotee of the game. Anguish spent only a brief time in Cape Town, but the suspicion – as yet unproven – lingers that he was the first man to pitch stumps in Africa. Tragically, he lived up to his surname, and committed suicide after only a few months in the colony.

Eleven years later, and two years after Cape Colony, dizzy with having changed hands three times during the Napoleonic Wars, once again became British, the first documentary evidence of cricket appears. An advertisement in the 2 January 1808 edition of the *Cape Town Gazette and Africa Advertiser* publicised a match between the 60th Regiment and Officers of the colony. No venue is given and no match report was published, but two years later another advertisement gives details of a game to be played between the Ordnance Department and the 87th Regiment at Green Point – making this the oldest cricket field in South Africa. The oldest cricket club is Port Elizabeth, which was founded in 1843, followed by Wynberg in 1844, Cape Town in 1857, and Western Province in 1864. As the servicemen and civil servants moved inland, so did cricket, and by 1870 clubs had been formed in Pietermaritzburg, Bloemfontein, Kimberley, Pretoria and Johannesburg.

There is evidence of Bantus and Hottentots playing cricket as early as 1854, but the game was really a white man's pastime, at least from a documented point of view, and the writer H. Rider Haggard suggested that it became something of an obsession for them. Commenting disparagingly on the disastrous military blunder at Isandhlwana in January 1879, he wrote: 'Our generals entered into it with the lightest of hearts; notwithstanding the difficulties and scarcity of transport they even took with them their cricketing outfits into Zululand. This I know as I was commissioned to bring home a wicket that was found on the field of Isandhlwana, and return it to the HQ of a regiment to which it belonged, to be kept as a relic.' It is a story that puts a fresh complexion on Newbolt's celebrated 'Vitaï Lampada' (see pages 297–9).

More often than not, pitches in the early days were little more than flat dustbowls, but the game quickly became a popular part of life in the colony. Players were so hungry for action that games were arranged between the most frivolous of ad hoc teams: Married vs Single, Right vs Left Handers, Ladies vs Gentlemen, Beautiful vs Hideous and Six Footers vs The Rest. Such games may have been light-hearted fun, and of variable quality, but serious cricket was near at hand.

The first organised competition was the Champion Bat Tournament at Port Elizabeth in January 1876. Four teams competed: King William's Town, Grahamstown, Cape Town and Port Elizabeth. King William's Town were the victors, and they repeated their success in 1880 on home ground. Port Elizabeth triumphed in 1884, Kimberley in 1887 and Western Province in 1890. The 1890 tournament was its swansong – and the only one to be granted first-class status – as the competition gave way to the Currie Cup, which to this day remains the leading tournament in South Africa.

The Currie Cup itself was the gift of the Scottish shipping magnate Sir Donald Currie, and accompanied the first English team to visit the colony in 1888. At a leaving dinner in England, Sir Donald entrusted the Cup to the tour manager, with instructions to present it to the best domestic side they played. He selected Kimberley. In 1890 Transvaal challenged Kimberley and defeated them by a convincing six wickets, kicking off the tournament proper. Following this game the South African Cricket Association was founded to become the ruling body of South African cricket. Thereafter, the Cup was the subject of fierce competition between the provinces.

That first England tour proved more significant in retrospect than it seemed at the time. Eight years later, some of the matches of Major Robert Gardner Warton's team were granted Test-match status, which makes the first eleven-a-side match of the tour, played on matting at Port Elizabeth on 12 and 13 March 1889, the first Test match to be played in South Africa. England won comfortably by eight wickets on the second afternoon. The England captain was C.A. Smith, later Sir C. Aubrey Smith, who became Hollywood central casting's archetypal bluff English cove, appearing in countless films, including *Rebecca* and *The Prisoner of Zenda*. The Second Test, at Cape Town, delivered a world first when South Africa's A.B. Tancred became the first batsman to 'carry his bat' through a Test innings. The South Africans were all out for 47, with Tancred undefeated on 26. For England, Johnny Briggs was unplayable, with match figures of 15 wickets for 28 runs. When England batted, the diminutive Surrey opener Bobby Abel, with 120, was far too good for the South African bowlers.

Victory was again elusive for the home side when Walter Read of Surrey captained the England tourists in 1891–92. In the only Test, a massive English win by an innings and 189 runs, the composition of the teams was distinctly odd. England fielded the former Australian Test players J.J. Ferris and Billy Murdoch, while Frank Hearne, once of England, opened the batting for South Africa. Read's team won thirteen games on the tour and drew seven, usually against odds. The left-handed Ferris took 235 wickets at low cost, little knowing that nine years later he would die in Durban at only thirty-three years of age while serving in the British Army during the Boer War.

Lord Hawke's tourists of 1895–96 won all three Test matches by huge margins. George Lohmann of Surrey swept the opposition aside, taking 35 wickets at under 6 runs each and becoming the first bowler to take 9 wickets (for only 28 runs) in a Test innings. Among the South African batsmen was R.M. Poore, Lord Harris's old ADC in

India, who would later play for Hampshire. Hawke returned in 1898–99, winning both Test matches, the first by only 32 runs after 'Plum' Warner, with an undefeated 132, became the first man to carry his bat on debut through an England innings.

South Africa's first tour of England in 1894 raised the spectre of racial controversy. Non-white players were rarely given the opportunity to play for the colony's premier clubs, but Western Province's Malay fast bowler Krom Hendricks was selected in the team. However, colonial giant Cecil Rhodes, the Prime Minister of Cape Colony, vetoed his inclusion on the spurious grounds that he didn't want Hendricks to be subjected to insulting native stereotyping, such as the endless requests for demonstrations of spear-throwing that had beset the Australian Aboriginal tour of England a quarter of a century before. He was quoted as saying, 'They would have expected him to throw boomerangs during the lunch interval.' Hendricks could have declined to do so, of course, but Rhodes's real intention was to enable an all-white team to travel, and Hendricks was excluded.

During the tour the South Africans played the MCC, who included W.G. Grace. They won twelve, lost five and drew seven of their matches, but poor weather, poor publicity and poor gates made the tour a financial flop. After the game against Lord Sheffield's Eleven at Sheffield Park, cabbies blocked their way to the railway station as a protest against the team using a bus for transport. This caused another financial setback, for they had to use the taxis to catch their trains.

In April 1900, during the height of the Boer War, a British patrol picked up a letter addressed to Colonel Robert Baden-Powell, the British commander of the besieged town of Mafeking, from Sarel Eloff, Transvaal President Paul Kruger's grandson and Commandant of the Johannesburg Commando. It invited Baden-Powell to a cricket match, inspired by the ones Eloff had understood the British liked to play on Sunday afternoons in Mafeking, in the spirit of 'friendship and unity'. Baden-Powell, who may have remembered Isandhlwana, replied:

Sir,

I beg to thank you for your letter of yesterday, in which you propose that your men should come and play cricket with us. I should like nothing better – after the match in which we are at present engaged is over. Just now we are having our innings, and have so far scored 200 days, not out against the bowling of Cronje, Snyman, Botha and Eloff; and we are having a very enjoyable game.

Once military conflict ended, cricket flourished. The South Africans toured England in 1901, 1904 and 1907, while 'Plum' Warner led the first official MCC tour in 1905–06. Five Tests were played, and South Africa won four of them, notching their first-ever Test victory at the Old Wanderers Ground, Johannesburg. Four years later 'Shrimp' Leveson Gower's MCC team was beaten by three Tests to two, and in their first tour of Australia in 1910–11 the South Africans lost the series four games to one, but narrowly won the Third Test by 38 runs. Zulch, Snooke and Faulkner all scored hundreds for the tourists, although none matched the brilliance of Victor Trumper's undefeated double century for Australia.

Test wins, albeit against below-strength English sides, greatly boosted South African cricket, although a rude awakening awaited them in England in 1912 in a triangular tournament with England and Australia. In foul weather, South Africa were convincingly beaten in the series. England returned to South Africa in 1913–14, winning four of the five Tests, with Sydney Barnes taking forty-nine wickets at 10.93 in only four Tests. Typically, after a row, Barnes refused to play in the final Test, but his record for the highest number of wickets taken in a Test series still stands. The First World War then intervened, and Test cricket closed down for over six years. Barnes never played another Test match.

In 1979 a belt buckle was found on the banks of the River Tweed in Scotland. Upon examination, it appeared to depict a mulatto slave batting in the style of the eighteenth century, and the Barbadian palm tree (*Roystonea oleracea*) in the background identified the site. The straight, one-piece unspliced bat and the three stumps supported the likely date of the buckle. It is the earliest evidence yet uncovered that cricket was being played on the island before the nineteenth century.

This discovery apart, the first reliable reference to cricket in the West Indies appeared in a Barbados newspaper on 17 January 1807, soliciting interest for a dinner to be held after a game at St Anne's Cricket Club. The club itself had been set up the previous year. At the time the West Indies was embroiled in the Napoleonic Wars, one of the world's first truly global conflicts. A massive military population was resident there to defend Britain's lucrative interests in the chain of islands from Jamaica in the north-west down through the Leeward and Windward Islands as far as the north-east coast of South America at Demerara (now Guyana). Unsurprisingly, the first recorded matches were between British soldiers: the *Bridgetown Gazette* tells us of a game to be played on 19 September 1809 on the Grand Parade between officers of the Royal West Indies Rangers and officers of the 3rd West Indian Regiment 'for 55 guineas'. The result is not recorded.

As was the experience elsewhere in the Empire, the local civilian elite soon joined in. The *Barbadian* newspaper reported in 1849 that two clubs 'for gentlemen' had been set up in Bridgetown, the City and the St Michael Clubs. They were, the paper assured its readers, 'well organised', and their games were 'watched by highly respectable ladies and gentlemen'. On the field there is evidence of the social inclusiveness of cricket, as officers and men played together in the same teams. A report on a game between St Ann's Garrison and the 78th Regiment in 1838 specifically mentions the 'good feeling' generated by officers and men as equals on the pitch. There was, however, a limit to inclusion. No black faces appeared as either participants or club members.

Clubs soon proliferated. The St Jago, Vere and Clarendon Clubs were founded in Jamaica in 1857, with several others following in the 1860s and seventies. The early centres were Barbados, Demerara and Trinidad. At the time the West Indies was only a series of islands and colonies, each with its own clubs and rivalries. The first step towards a broader competitive coalition came in 1865, when Barbados arranged a fixture with Demerara at Garrison Savannah in Bridgetown on 15 and 16 February. The event was a huge success, and the local interest was so great that employers released their employees to attend the game in the afternoon. It was a happy result for the huge crowd: the home side beat Demerara by 138 runs. In September of that year with home advantage, Demerara avenged their defeat in the return match. The two sides met again in 1871 in Bridgetown, where Barbados won by eight wickets.

Competition spurred expansion as cricket took root. Trinidad joined a triangular 'Cricket Festival' held at the Wanderers Ground, Barbados in 1891, which the hosts won. Jamaica became part of the touring network that year, followed swiftly by Antigua in 1893, and St Vincent and St Lucia in 1896. A challenge cup was introduced in Barbados in 1892, and in Jamaica the following year. The Intercolonial Challenge Cup, featuring Barbados, Trinidad and Demerara, was inaugurated in 1893.

By the mid-1890s exceptional black players were being included in teams, especially for their extraordinary bowling. We do not know the names of these individuals, but they were largely gleaned from ground staff for 'friendly' games only. For most of the black population the experience of cricket was literally on the sidelines. Yet their interest in watching cricket was astounding – eighty Bridgetown firms agreed to close 'on all four days when Barbados entertained the visiting colonies' in 1891. Contemporary accounts refer to excited crowds being so noisy during a game against the English tourists in 1895 that the visiting captain had to use a whistle to attract the attention of his fieldsmen.

The first (all-white) West Indian tour was to America and Canada in 1886, led by George Wyatt of the Georgetown Cricket Club of Demerara. They played thirteen matches, winning six, losing five and drawing two. The MCC resisted requests in both 1888 and 1889 from Wyatt and other West Indian cricket leaders to allow a tour of England, but an English touring team under Slade Lucas did come to play in the region in 1895. It was a second-rate side even by amateur standards, but the sixteen matches, of which the tourists won ten and lost four, drew massive crowds. In one match Barbados scored 517 runs in an innings, and even though they lost the match, their performance was of great encouragement to the West Indians. The successful tour boosted the self-esteem of the host territories.

After Lucas's team had left there was jubilation at the news that not one but two touring sides were planning to come the following year. One side, invited by Barbados and Jamaica, was to be led by Sir Arthur Priestley; the other, invited by Demerara, by that perennial tourist Lord Hawke. Hawke's team played fourteen matches, winning nine, losing two (to Trinidad) and drawing three. The real emergence of black players is seen here for the first time. Pelham Warner, a member of Hawke's Eleven, ascribed Trinidad's victories to two black professional bowlers, Wood and Cumberbatch. Warner, originally from Trinidad himself,* identified the 'illiberalism' of the whites-only policy of Barbados and Demerara clubs as a huge factor holding back the quality and spread of cricket in the islands. He urged the inclusion of black players to 'make the game more popular locally'. Furthermore, he insisted that any touring side going to England must include 'four or five' black players if it was to stand any hope against the counties. Not to do so, he asserted, would be 'absurd'.

Warner's brave and far-sighted advocacy of racial inclusion is a refreshing example of the kind of enlightened attitudes that allowed Britain to rule its Empire with dexterity, and to give up its colonial possessions so deftly when the time arose. They are in sharp contrast to the all-too familiar depiction of privileged Victorians as self-deluding supremacists. Such people existed, but so did their opposites. What makes Warner doubly interesting is that he was an 'insider' from the West Indian white cricket administrators' point of view, and also had blue-chip 'mother country' credentials to boot. He was someone who should have wanted black people firmly put in their place, but didn't. The episode shows Warner as being far from the establishment crony he sometimes appeared to be. Results would

---

* His father was Attorney General of Trinidad.

vindicate his progressive view. When a Trinidadian side went to Barbados in 1897 without its black bowlers, because Barbados would not play against them, they were thrashed. Warner's case was further reinforced in 1899, when Spartan, an all-black side, won Barbados's Challenge Cup.

There was much debate, especially in Barbados, about what the inclusion of black players would signify in the West Indian social context, and how the wider world would react if black players were selected for an international side. But whatever the whites' fears may have been, when the time came to pick the team for the first tour of England in 1900 a healthy dose of practicality prevailed, and five black players were included: Fritz Hinds, W.J. Burton, C.A. Olliviere, S. Woods and Lebrun Constantine.

Constantine (whose son Learie, born the following year, would be one of the West Indies' greatest cricketers) nearly missed the trip. He was seen kicking his heels on the shore after the boat had left for England. He said he couldn't afford the trip, so a whip-round was hastily arranged and he was put on a motor launch and sent off in the wake of the rapidly diminishing ship. He scrambled aboard before the vessel left the Gulf of Paria, and went on to score the first century in England for the West Indians, against MCC at Lord's. Old Harry Jupp of Surrey might have sympathised, although his excuse for missing the ship to Australia in 1876 was less excusable (see page 352).

The first West Indies touring side was not awarded first-class status. This was not on racial grounds, but was a legitimate quality judgement. *Wisden* described the tour as an 'experiment', but experimental or not, the tourists beat Surrey by an innings and 34 runs, which, although they no longer dominated the County Championship as they had done between 1887 and 1895, was a huge scalp. The main significance of the tour, however, was that it made it impossible for black players to be omitted from any part of the domestic game in the West Indies. If they were good enough to play the best club sides in the world, in England, they could not be denied the right to play at home on equal terms.

Lord Brackley led a tour of the islands in 1905, and the West Indians were back in England in 1906. On this occasion six black players were in the team. Once more they enjoyed few wins, but one was outstanding: they beat a very strong Yorkshire side that included Rhodes, Denton, Tunnicliffe and the former Cambridge University captain Tom Taylor. This win was indicative of a promise that was not speedily realised, as the West Indies did not return until the 1923 tour of England, and did not play a Test until the series of 1928. A long apprenticeship then followed before they established themselves as one of the dominant nations in cricket, with a style that was – and is – distinctive.

'Now we are one people,' claimed New Zealand's Lieutenant-Governor William Hobson after the Treaty of Waitangi signalled the formal entry of the country into the British Empire in 1840, only a year after organised emigration to Wellington had begun with the sailing of the *Aurora*. Cricket had preceded it. The journal of one Henry Williams makes a passing reference to missionaries and children playing at Horotutu beach, Pahai, on 20 December 1832. A similar journal by Edwin Fairbairn suggests that another game was played in late 1833 or early 1834. And Charles Darwin's famous *Voyage of the Beagle* refers to a game at a missionary station at Waimate in the Bay of Islands on 21 December 1835.

The non-Maori portion of the Lieutenant-Governor's 'one people' was a mere ten thousand, a third of whom lived in Wellington, and on 28 December 1842 the leading social and sports club of the city, the Wellington Club, arranged a cricket match. It was played on the Te Aro Flat, one of the few flat areas between the steeply rising mountains that surround the city and the sea, and 'the Blues' beat 'the Reds' (the significance, if any, of this nomenclature does not survive) by 2 runs, or as it was noted at the time, by '126 to 124 notches'. After the game the teams sat down together at the Ship hotel for a late Christmas dinner of roast beef and plum pudding.

The spiritual home of New Zealand cricket is still in the Te Aro area of Wellington. It is the home of the famous Basin Reserve ground, which came into existence after an earthquake in 1855 made a planned harbour 'basin' development redundant by pushing up the 'basin' and its surrounds over six feet above sea level, making it useless to shipping. Local residents quickly applied for the area to become a public park, and once this was agreed it was drained and levelled, using the labour of convicts from nearby Mount Cook gaol. The first game of cricket on the new ground was played in 1868 between the Wellington Volunteers and the Officers and Men of HMS *Falcon*.

With a growing immigrant population made up of energetic middle-class British pioneers, cricket spread rapidly throughout New Zealand. The game was central to the tough lives of the settlers; when Christchurch was founded in 1851, five hundred acres were set aside specifically for recreation. In Auckland, the Domain ground was established in 1862 although Eden Park would supersede it forty years later as the premier ground in the city.

The first international side to visit was George Parr's glittering All-England Eleven in 1864, with E.M. Grace, Julius Caesar, Robert Carpenter, Tom Hayward and John Jackson. Four games were played in Otago and Canterbury against teams of twenty-two men, and were easily won. Thirteen years later, in 1877, James Lillywhite brought his touring side after having just played what was later designated as the first ever official Test match in Australia. The next year the Australians sent a side to their near neighbours and, seeking parity with England, insisted on using the 2:1 handicap system too. Even then, Antipodean rivalry was so fierce that at Canterbury the locals were too proud to have this imposed on them by their colonial cousins from across the Tasman Sea. A compromise was agreed at fifteen members of Canterbury vs eleven Australians – and Canterbury won!

For England, a tour to New Zealand was generally tacked onto a visit to Australia, as in 1864, 1877, 1879 and 1882. But New Zealand cricket was thriving, and the domestic Cricket Council was founded in Christchurch in 1894. Huge time and effort was put into improving the game by bringing coaches over from England, developing the grounds and making cricket (and rugby) a core part of the educational life of New Zealanders – especially in the cricket-mad South Island provinces. A domestic competition began in the 1906–07 season with a shield given by Lord Plunket, the Governor-General, to the victorious side, Canterbury. The challenge nature of the competition ensured that the shield was held by either Auckland or Canterbury for most years, although Wellington and Otago were also recognised as first-class teams.

New Zealand began to tour overseas in 1898–99, when a visit to Australia led to defeats by Victoria and New South Wales, but not by the national team, as no Test matches were arranged. Inward visits continued. In 1902 Lord Hawke planned to tour, but fell ill, and Pelham Warner led an English side that included B.J.T. Bosanquet, soon to unleash his 'googly' upon unprepared batsmen. Australia toured also, and players such as Spofforth, Trumper, Armstrong and Hill displayed their talents. In 1914 Victor Trumper scored 293 in three hours at Canterbury, in an innings New Zealand has never forgotten. It was a glorious prelude to an inglorious war. Nevertheless, old colonial rivalries died hard. The Australian cricket authorities were unwilling to grant Test status to games against New Zealand, and the two countries would not play their first official Test until 1946. New Zealand were heavily defeated, and would not meet Australia again in a Test match until 1973.

Cricket was slow to come to Sri Lanka, and was played mostly by expatriates up to the Great War. Ceylon (as it then was) is one of the most culturally diverse islands in the world, having been colonised successively by the Portuguese (1505–1658), the Dutch (1658–1796) and the British (1796–1948). The coastal areas became a British Crown Colony in 1802, and after the fall of the Kandy kingdom in 1815 this was swiftly unified for ease of administration.

As a hugely fertile staging post to the Far East, the colony swiftly developed both militarily and commercially. British 'planters', of coffee and, later, tea, settled alongside a changing cast of soldiers, sailors and civil administrators. Early mentions of cricket are sparse, and the first game recorded in the *Colombo Journal* reports – inevi-

This bawdy engraving, after Thomas Rowlandson, depicts a match between the ladies of Hampshire and Surrey at Newington in 1811. Sharp-eyed readers will notice the two-stump wicket, although the third was in fact introduced thirty-five years earlier.

The canny Yorkshireman Thomas Lord. The employee who understood the needs of his masters, catered for them, and left the world's most famous cricket ground as his memorial.

Right William Ward, a prodigious run-getter in the early nineteenth century, would be a central figure in securing Lord's place as the head-quarters of cricket.

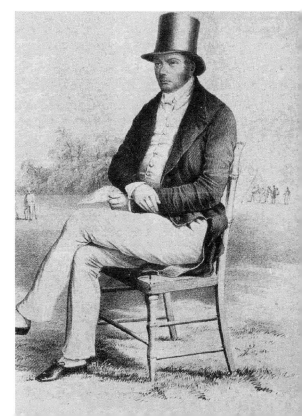

Far left The jovial and generous wine merchant Benjamin Aislabie was the first Secretary of the MCC. Although a poor cricketer, he had a consuming love of the game, and an unquenchable zest for life.

Left Despite his look of innocence, and his undoubted love of cricket, Lord Frederick Beauclerk is remembered as avaricious, ill-tempered, hypocritical, and a gamester adept at bending the rules.

The straight-legged stance and elegant forward play of Fuller Pilch were well known to bowlers of the 1830s and 1840s. This Norfolk-born all-rounder was the finest batsman of the day, and 'single-wicket champion of England'.

John Wisden, the founder of the *Almanack*, and a fast round-arm bowler. Despite his tiny build, he once took all ten wickets in an innings, and 340 wickets in a season.

Left The Scorer, by Thomas Henwood (1842). William Davies, scorer for the Lewes Priory Club, looks intent on enjoying his day. A clay pipe and a glass of claret seem more important to him than the measuring tape and match equipment which lie at his feet.

Below The odd couple. The huge and muscular Alfred Mynn and the cerebral schoolteacher Nicholas Felix before their famous single-wicket contest in 1846 for the title 'champion of England'.

Left William Clarke, an unlikely missionary for cricket, being portly, one-eyed, short-tempered, and not above sharp practice. Yet he was the finest underarm bowler of them all, and the founder of Trent Bridge cricket ground.

Top Clarke's All-England Eleven of 1847. Throughout England, spectators flocked to watch the world's leading cricketers as they took on all comers. In their midst, dressed in black, is the first eminent cricket journalist, William Denison.

Bottom The All-England Eleven on the move in 1851. This painting by Nicholas Felix shows the Eleven, with their trunks and portmanteaus, making their way by coach from Spalding to Wisbech.

Left George Parr, the 'Lion of the North', who succeeded Clarke as leader of Nottinghamshire and the All-England Eleven. He is seen here as a young man, wearing buckskin pads with twine securing them to knee, shin and ankle. His gloves have their palms cut away, and are secured by a wraparound strap.

Below The first English overseas touring team. George Parr's men look like a pirate crew as they gather on the deck of the *Nova Scotian* in 1859, before their nightmare voyage to North America.

H.H. Stephenson's English team arrives in Bourke Street, Melbourne, on Christmas Eve in 1861. The warm welcome was some consolation for a voyage of over two months.

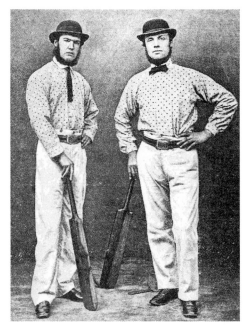

Tom Hayward (left) and Robert Carpenter were two fine Cambridgeshire batsmen of the 1860s. Hayward was a member of the All-England Eleven, while Carpenter favoured the United All-England team.

Arthur Haygarth would devote his life to assembling the five-million-word, ten-thousand-page *Cricket Scores and Biographies*. Its fourteen volumes, covering the years 1744 to 1878, with a supplement on notable players after that date, are the bedrock of our knowledge of the era.

The 1880 Australians were the first visitors to play a Test match in England. They arrived with just five county fixtures arranged, and had to advertise for opponents.

Charles Alcock in his office at The Oval. He was instrumental in organising the inaugural Test, and his immense backstage contribution to cricket warrants a higher place in the mythology of the game than history has yet given him.

This portly figure is Alfred Shaw, who bowled the first over in Test cricket. He was so accurate that, in a career of over thirty years, he bowled more overs than he conceded runs. He once bowled twenty-three consecutive four-ball maidens.

Right Edward Mills Grace. Although mainly remembered as W.G.'s elder brother, his devastating leg-side hitting made him one of the most formidable cricketers of his day.

Below W.G. Grace dominated cricket for thirty-five years, and became the emblem of Victorian England. Here he poses with Harry Jupp of Surrey. The pair were regular members of the United South of England Eleven, and Jupp faced the first ball bowled to an English batsman in Test cricket.

tably – a British regiment, the 97th, scoring 136 'notches' in a game played on 3 November 1832. In the following few years the number of clubs grew, with the Colombo Cricket Club being the first to become established, although its foundation date – some time between 1840 and 1863 – suggests that earlier clubs may have existed briefly, and collapsed. The Dikoya and Dimbula Clubs soon followed Colombo, and from 1875 combined players each year for one match when, masquerading as 'Up-Country', they played Colombo in a fixture that was the sporting highlight of the season. Numerous civil service, military and planters' clubs helped spread the popularity of the game, although, planters apart, their teams were formed wholly by expatriates.

Among the indigenous population, the Malays took to cricket most readily, and formed the Malay Cricket Club in 1872. The indigenous population founded the Colombo Colts Cricket Club the following year. The Tamils were relative latecomers to the game, with a team in 1899, and after their slow start they did not compete on equal terms with top-class local clubs until 1911–12, although they did tour India to play Madras in 1911 and 1913.

One feature of the development of cricket in Sri Lanka was the huge influence of the two leading private schools, the Royal College and St Thomas's. From 1880, the annual match between the two became the subcontinent's equivalent of the Eton and Harrow encounters. This contest was the brainchild of Ashley Walker, a former Cambridge Blue who taught at Royal College.

As cricket became more widespread, touring sides arrived. The first to do so was Ivo Bligh's team in 1882, when, en route to regain the Ashes in Australia, they stopped off to soundly beat an All-Ceylon Fifteen by an innings at Galle. Their stay was extended while their ship the *Glenroy* was repaired after a minor collision. This enabled an extra game to be played against the Royal Dublin Fusiliers. Two years later, an Australian Eleven were bundled out for a mere 75 runs against an All-Ceylon Eighteen, but retaliated by dismissing the home side for 49. The low scores probably reflected a poor wicket. Be that as it may, the match created sufficient interest for the Australians to visit regularly, and further teams arrived in 1890, 1893, 1896 and then, after a long interval, in 1909.

Ceylon began to attract English teams too. G.F. Vernon's tourists played two matches at Colombo in 1889, and were followed in 1891 by Lord Sheffield's side, which included W.G. Grace and drew a game against an All-Ceylon Eighteen. That inveterate traveller Lord Hawke sent a touring side to play Colombo, Colombo Colts and Up-Country in 1892, but he did not himself join the team until it arrived in India. MCC teams, led by Arthur Jones and 'Plum' Warner respectively, toured in 1908 and 1911, while near neighbours Singapore (then known as 'Straits') were regular opponents from 1892.

Outward tours from Ceylon were to Calcutta in 1884, from which three results survive: a victory over Terai Hockey Club and draws with Ballygunge and Calcutta. In Madras the following year a win, a draw and a defeat marked a modestly successful visit, that was bettered with two wins out of three in Bombay in 1886. Tours to Straits and Burma by All-Ceylon in 1894, 1912 and 1913, to Bombay in 1907 by the Malay Club, and to South Africa by the Tamil Union Club in 1911 and 1913–14 added to the international experience of local players. Test status lay far ahead,* but cricket was well-established in Ceylon by the beginning of the twentieth century, and would grow consistently.

In 1900 the only Test-playing nations were England, Australia and South Africa, although India, the West Indies and New Zealand were eyeing that status. Others would follow: Sri Lanka (then Ceylon), Pakistan (after the partition of India), Zimbabwe (then Rhodesia) and Bangladesh (formerly East Pakistan) as cricket's tentacles reached ever wider.

There was one continent, however, where cricket did not embed itself as a favoured sport. In 1859 George Parr captained the first overseas tour when he took twelve of England's finest players to Canada and the United States aboard the SS *Nova Scotian*. Parr, with

---

* Sri Lanka's first official Test was against England in Colombo, in 1982. England won by seven wickets.

Fred Lillywhite as chronicler and factotum, was accompanied by Surrey's Caffyn, Lockyer, H.H. Stephenson and Julius Caesar; Jackson and Grundy of Notts; Sussex's John Wisden and John Lillywhite; and Hayward, Carpenter and 'Ducky' Diver of Cambridgeshire. Despite this array of talent, cricket did not spark the imagination of North Americans. It was perhaps too leisurely a sport for such a young and thrusting nation. Even in the early 1990s, when I carefully explained the game to President George Bush, his eyes swivelled when he realised that a match could last five days and yet still not produce a winner.

In every country in which cricket has taken root the game has held up a mirror to the nation's culture. Even if all cricketers were green-skinned, no avid fan would mistake the style of play of an Indian team for that of their English or New Zealand counterparts, or Australia for the West Indies, or South Africa for Sri Lanka. All great Indian batsmen have shared, to a degree, the flowing suppleness of wrist and body that, added to keenness of eye, so gracefully show-cases the art of Indian batting. Latterday exemplars – Tendulkar, say, or Ganguly – have added the fast-moving footwork of a Fred Astaire to cope with flighted spin bowling on slow pitches baked by the sun. It is marvellous to watch, but quite distinct from the wonderfully English skills of a May or a Cowdrey, building an innings under an overcast sky and unleashing magnificent front-foot play as the clouds depart and bluer sky appears. Sometimes ethnic boundaries are crossed, as when a Gower or a Woolley is at the wicket, but even then, over a lengthy innings the essential schooling of the batsman becomes clear.

Bowlers can be equally distinctive, especially as their physical attributes supplement their cricketing skills. Indian teams, predominantly small men, do not produce many great fast bowlers, but Pakistan, part of India until the Partition of 1947, can boast Wasim Akram, Imran Khan and Shoaib Akhtar. The West Indies, of course, have a particularly rich tradition of quick men, from the fearsome Constantine and Martindale to Wes Hall and Charlie Griffith and, more recently, the elegant Michael Holding. Clive Lloyd's team in the 1980s with its four-man fast-bowling attack dominated world cricket for a decade.

The West Indians are hybrid in style, although a common attribute is the loose-hipped swagger that signals their aptitude for ball games. Some, like Learie Constantine or Vivian Richards, have the Caribbean stamped through their every movement on the field, but others – Rohan Kanhai or Alvin Kallicharran – would fit into any Asian batting line-up. Some geniuses cannot be pigeonholed. Garry Sobers batted like a dream, and bowled fast left-arm, wrist spin and finger spin. I once saw him field a ball on the boundary and bend his hand back almost parallel to his arm before flipping the ball a full seventy yards to the wicketkeeper. Only a loose-limbed Caribbean could have done that.

It is more difficult to pinpoint differences between the teams of the old Commonwealth – England, Australia, South Africa and New Zealand – where distinctions are often more of attitude than style, although the composition of the bowling attack may vary. Nonetheless, the hard wickets of Australia and the softer, more pliable tracks of England do foster different styles of bowling. Australians are more likely to field the leg spin of a Benaud or the incomparable Warne, whereas finger spin is more typically found in English teams, although nowadays there are many exceptions to such generalisations. And natural attributes vary as well: too often, over the years, Australian and South African teams seem to have harboured greater self-belief than those from England or New Zealand. Cricket being cricket, some may disagree with the illustrations I have given, but few will dispute the principle that each nation has its own characteristics on the cricket field. That is a large part of its charm.

11

The Birth of the Ashes

At the time that James Cook mapped the eastern coastline of Australia in 1770, cricket was a significant leisure pursuit in England, although there is no evidence that Cook himself had any interest in the game. In 1788 the eleven ships of the First Fleet anchored in Sydney Cove to establish a penal colony. The harsh and alien conditions experienced by the early settlers, the paucity of their numbers, and the brutality of the military and civilian administrators argued against any proper birth of Australian cricket in the first years of the new colony. Impromptu games between scratch teams – the Military against the Civilians – were arranged by colonial administrators, but these early games were affairs of the governing class. Neither the convicted felons who made up much of the small European population, nor any native Australian Aboriginals, would have been involved.

In England, the years after 1815 were full of discontent. The hardship of many people's lives led to a growth in civil unrest and crime, and the numbers sentenced to transportation rose sharply, peaking in the 1830s, then fell away. After 1840 few convicts were transported to the Australian colonies, although the practice did not end until 1868. In the early years conditions on the transport ships were appalling, but when the scandal of how prisoners were treated on board became known, improvements were enforced, and after 1815 the human cargo was delivered in far better health after their four months at sea. The Australian settlements began to grow. A veteran Scottish soldier, Lachlan Macquarie, appointed as Governor of New South Wales in 1810, was more liberal than his predecessors and is even reputed to have ordered penal workshops to manufacture cricket bats and balls. This may be true, but he cannot have done so in 1803, as some reference books state (he was not even in Australia at that time), although it is possible he did so in 1813. Be that as it may, his widespread reforms eased the hardship of life in the new colony, and emigration of free settlers from Britain began to grow. The voluntary emigrants must have been adventurous to seek a new life in a largely unpopulated continent on the far side of the world. In their restless search for something better may have lain the roots of Australian ambition on and off the sporting field. By mid-century the main population centres of the Australian colonies were settled, and civic pride was powering the growth of townships. Over the following decade the discovery of gold would further accelerate immigration.

The sheer size of the continent foreshadowed the future structure of Australian cricket, with embryonic civil administration taking root at local and colonial level. In 1845 Maitland Cricket Club was formed in the Hunter Valley, and was playing against the Australian Club at Sydney. By 1851 a Melbourne team sailed to Launceston to meet a Tasmanian Eleven. Five years later Victoria was playing against New South Wales. At Melbourne in the 1850s, the pitches in the baking climate were poor, with cattle and sheep as the only groundsmen to crop the outfield. In Sydney the main ground, the Domain, was in a public park, with no fencing or barriers to protect it. Bats and balls were primitive, grounds were uncared for, and it was common to see cricketers playing barefoot.

But as Australia grew, so did cricket. The popularity of the game spread from the main population centres to rural areas. In a subliminal tribute to the land their forebears had left behind, the continent's European settlers soon came to regard a cricket ground and a racecourse as essential components of new townships. The quality of cricket was poor, but enthusiasm for it was massive. By 1861 Victoria had seventy cricket clubs, and similar growth was apparent in South Australia, Tasmania and New South Wales. None of this was easily achieved. It was acutely difficult to prepare pitches in a hostile climate, inimical to the green fields and meadows that so enticed early crick-eters in England. The new Australians had to fight with nature to play cricket, but the pace at which the game took root was astonishing. Australian refusal to be beaten by the climate would become charac-teristic of the gritty way in which their teams gave no quarter on the cricket field.

Despite Britain's unscrupulous use of Australia as a dumping ground for surplus felons, respect for the power of the British Empire was very strong, and the reputation of English cricket was a source of pride for many expatriates living in Australia. In the late 1850s the idea arose of inviting an English team to visit Australia, although at first it proved impossible to raise the funds to do so. But good fortune was at hand. Charles Dickens was as popular in Australia as he was in the rest of the English-speaking world, and in 1861 a Melbourne catering firm, Spiers & Pond, noted that public readings of his books had been hugely successful in the United States as well as England. They saw a marketing opportunity and attempted to attract Dickens to Australia, but, tired and unwell, he turned down their invitation. Undeterred, they cast around for an alternative commercial sponsor-ship, and settled on inviting an English cricket team to tour. Their agent, Mr Mallam, travelled to England, and over dinner at the Hen and Chickens hotel in Birmingham – the South vs North match was taking place nearby, at Aston – persuaded some eminent players to travel to Australia for £150 a man – an attractive salary to professional cricketers, most of whom would normally have earned only £3 a match. Nonetheless, the offer caused friction between northern and southern professionals. The southerners accepted – seven of the team were from Surrey – but the northerners sought better terms. The seeds of a future conflict were sown.

The team arrived, to an ecstatic reception from nineteen thousand flag-waving Melbournians, in December 1861. Under the captaincy of H.H. Stephenson of Surrey, it was far from the strongest side that could have been sent – Richard Daft of Nottingham, one of the premier batsmen of the time, was among those who declined to go, perhaps because he felt that George Parr should have been captain – but it was superior to anything previously seen in Australia. The English players were here, said an adoring press, to show cricketing 'perfection' to Australia, and no Australian need feel 'humiliated if he is vanquished'. The Melbourne *Punch*, in a piece presumably written by an émigré rather than a transportee, wrote:

> Loving Old England with a child's affection,
> I'm to her fame and honour ever true,
> But then my heart has form'd a new connexion,
> Hardly less strong – I love Victoria too.

> But should 'Old England' win, we shall admire
> The height to which they've brought their noble game,
> And our Victorians, vanquished, may acquire
> A knowledge which may lead them on to fame.

Despite the dire poetry – the absent Charles Dickens would have recognised the authentic voice of Uriah Heep – Australian deference was not surprising. It was an age in which many believed that God was an Englishman, even if the formal claim was never made. Possibly it was thought unnecessary. Even forty years later, the man who should never have been Poet Laureate, Alfred Austin, wrote:

> Who dies for England, dies for God,
> Who dies for England, sleeps with God.

Lucky God. Mid-Victorian conceit believed also that English heritage was necessary to play cricket. Charles Box, writing in *The English Game of Cricket* in 1877, observed: 'Who could, for instance, picture to his imagination the phlegmatic Dutchman, with his capacious round stern, cheering or sending the ball whizzing through the air like a cannon shot, and getting a run with the speed of a roe-buck.' Box certainly couldn't, and if he took the arrogance of Empire to absurd limits, it did not seem so to many at the time. This English superiority was not yet resented in Australia, although soon it would be. Many 'new' Australians still maintained a dual allegiance to their old and new homelands. Over time, as the scales of their loyalty tipped towards Australia, the old affection would manifest itself in a fierce rivalry.

William Caffyn, one of the seven Surrey players in the team, left a colourful report of the first tour. On the outward voyage he was plagued by mosquitoes, and protected himself by wrapping his head in muslin and his arms in stockings, for which he was mocked mercilessly by his unsympathetic team-mates. Upon arriving in Australia he discovered to his dismay that the mosquitoes were on land as well. Nonetheless, his unconventional protection seems to have been effective, for he was the batting star of the tour.

The team played their first game on New Year's Day 1862, when fifteen thousand spectators saw them comfortably beat Eighteen of Melbourne by an innings and 36 runs. The eagerness to see the tourists was so great that trains into the city were overflowing, while coaches, wagons, carriages and bicycles crammed the roads from an early hour. As the teams entered the field the national anthem was heard in respectful silence by an excited crowd who, when it was over, burst into sustained cheering. The affection for England was evident, and throughout the tour the team was greeted with enthusiasm, cheers, bands and public displays. It was all exhilarating, and appreciated by the team, although the long journeys in horse-drawn coaches were tiring and uncomfortable. Nonetheless, six victories, four draws and only two defeats in games against teams of eighteen or twenty-two players showed that they survived the discomfort with aplomb.

Although there was a gulf in class between Stephenson's men and their opponents, the tour was a triumph. Spiers & Pond made a handsome profit, and wished to extend the tour by a further month, but the players, tired and perhaps homesick, pleaded domestic commitments and sailed home on the RMS Northam on 26 March. On the return voyage a happy Caffyn recorded modestly that he entertained passengers on his cornet, accompanied on the trombone by the ship's cook and by an unknown musician on the cymbals. It is a jolly image, although the trombone was played so badly that when the cook retired for refreshment, one of the players, Ned Stephenson, stuffed a towel into the instrument to muffle the sound. As the coastline of

Australia disappeared, none of the English players can have realised that it would soon become the most competitive cricket nation in the world.

The success of the tour whetted appetites, and in 1863 the Melbourne Cricket Club invited a further team. It was far stronger than its predecessor. As captain – 'There was never better,' judged Caffyn* – George Parr assembled professionals from the cream of English cricket: Caffyn, Julius Caesar, Robert Carpenter and Tom Hayward were the backbone of the batting, with the new sensation E.M. Grace as the only amateur. The bowling was equally strong, led by the fast men John Jackson and George Tarrant, supported by Cris Tinley with his slow lobs. When Surrey's William Mortlock was unable to travel he was replaced by Alfred Clarke, son of the Missionary of Cricket and a fine batsman and outstanding outfielder. Richard Daft once again declined to go, but travelled to Liverpool to wish *bon voyage* to his fellow professionals. Before boarding the boat, George Anderson of Yorkshire confided to Caffyn that his decision to go to Australia had caused ructions with his relatives, who 'think I shall never come back alive'. He did, but only just: despite a resemblance to the Ancient Mariner, Anderson was a wretched sailor, perpetually seasick, couldn't eat, and arrived in Melbourne a near skeleton. It was a daunting journey, even on Brunel's *Great Britain*, and the sixty-one days at sea must have seemed a lifetime to poor George.

Upon arrival, the team were welcomed as enthusiastically as their predecessors, but their popularity waned as the tour proceeded. On the field they performed brilliantly, and did not lose a single match, winning ten and drawing six, but their off-pitch activities let them down. Members of the team sold cricket gear at inflated prices, and displayed an avid enthusiasm for champagne and fine dinners at the expense of their hosts. This greedy behaviour was poorly regarded and long remembered, but the team's impact on Australian cricket was widely admired. One ten-year-old recalled the 'tremendous pace' of Tarrant, which sent stumps flying out of the hard ground, and

---

* Caffyn was inclined to be judgemental: he rated Pilch and Parr above Mynn as players.

occasionally split them. He vowed to copy Tarrant – and did so: the boy was Fred Spofforth.

By the early 1860s Australians had abandoned underarm lobs and grubs and were bowling round-arm or overarm, in the manner that would not be approved by the MCC until 1864. They were working to improve every aspect of their game, but no one anticipated how swiftly they would do so. They were helped by incredible luck and intelligent planning. Gold had been discovered in New South Wales and Victoria in 1851, and the magic lure of riches attracted a huge influx of immigrants, among them two Oxford cricket Blues, the Reverend E.S. Carter and S.T. Clissold. They joined other players, including W J. Hammersley, a Cambridge Blue, and Sam Cosstick and Jerry Bryant of Surrey, who were earlier immigrants. Hammersley would later become sporting editor of the *Australasian* and an important opinion-former in Australian cricket. Cosstick worked as a 'digger' in the goldfields, while Bryant became curator of the Melbourne Cricket Ground before, in typical English tradition, retiring to become mine host of the Parade Hotel. They provided Australia with a nucleus of fine players – in England, Hammersley had once taken a hat-trick with Reeves, Felix and Coltson as his victims. These were immigrants with a lot to offer to Australian cricket.

One way of assisting the development of the game in Australia was to employ eminent cricketers as coaches. At the end of the 1861–62 tour one member of the English team remained behind in Australia. Charles Lawrence of Surrey accepted an attractive salary to coach at the Albert Club in Sydney. He was a good choice. Lawrence, a former Secretary of the All-Ireland Eleven, was a high-class batsman, a fast round-arm bowler and an excellent fielder. In 1849, as a very young player, he had bowled Felix, removing all three of his stumps; the cheery Felix rewarded him with half a crown. Thirteen years later he was proving to be a gifted instructor. Lawrence made Australia his home, returning to England only once, in May 1868, bringing with him an eleven composed entirely of Aboriginal players, who played against clubs and counties and amused spectators with exhibitions of how to throw a boomerang. They did, said Grace, 'acquit themselves well', but they did not come near to challenging English supremacy. When his cricketing days ended, Lawrence returned to his old trade as a print-cutter, and in later life became a coalminer in Newcastle, New South Wales; but his legacy was in the vast improvement of Australian cricket.

After the Parr tour of 1863, a more eminent cricketer than Lawrence offered his skills to Australia. William Caffyn was engaged to coach the Melbourne Club for £300 a year, and his fiancée travelled to Australia, where they married. Caffyn coached Melbourne for a year before moving to Sydney to open a hairdressing salon with his wife, a venture which he hoped 'to rely on . . . when my cricketing abilities fail'. In Sydney, apart from renewing his acquaintance with Charles Lawrence, he coached the Warwick Club for four years, and the Caffyns enjoyed a comfortable lifestyle, although Mrs Caffyn was never at ease in the Australian climate. In 1871 Caffyn returned to England to rejoin the Surrey team; by then Australian cricket had improved beyond all expectation. Much of the credit for this belongs to Lawrence and Caffyn. They had encouraged overarm bowling, improved batting techniques, especially back-foot play, given great attention to fielding, and pioneered the preparation of better wickets. Spofforth and Billy Murdoch were foremost amongst those who testified to their influence.

The behaviour of the Parr team had left a sour taste, and for a decade only half-hearted attempts were made to arrange a further tour. Many Australians believed that a professional team would be too expensive to invite, and an amateur team too weak to be worth inviting. As 'Longstop', the *nom de plume* of the expatriate Cambridge Blue-turned-journalist W.J. Hammersley put it, writing in the *Australasian* in July 1871, an amateur team 'might have spotless flannels, gorgeous stripes and caps, snowy white shoes and flaming neckties, but what would the play be?' The robust nature of future Australian opinion was crystallising already.

And not only with 'Longstop'. Many others concurred. When the Melbourne Club invited W.G. Grace to select a team and tour in 1873–74 (see page 344), the visit was preceded by fierce controversy in the Australian press about how well their domestic cricketers would fare against an English team. Opinions were sharply divided. Some felt that an Australian eighteen, aided by the heat and unfamiliar sun-baked wickets, could beat an English eleven. Others dissented vehemently.

While the argument raged in the Australian press, Grace, after negotiating lucrative personal terms, was finding it difficult to select his team. A number of his first choices declined. Tom Emmett, 'Monkey' Hornby and Alfred Shaw all said no, as, less importantly, did Edward Pooley, George Pinder and William Yardley. Not everyone was prepared to refuse Grace, however, and when he stepped on board the P&O steamer *Mirzapore* at Southampton his brother Fred, cousin Walter Gilbert, Harry Jupp, James Lillywhite, William Oscroft and James Southerton were among the top-class players who accompanied him. So too did the former Miss Agnes Day, now Mrs Grace, whom W.G. had married a few weeks earlier and who was now going with him for an extended Australian honeymoon.

After a rapturous welcome at Melbourne, Grace's team made a poor start. Over forty thousand spectators saw Eighteen of Victoria beat an England team, not yet acclimatised, by an innings and 24 runs. All must have thought the two shillings and sixpence entry fee well spent. Stung by defeat, W.G. ruefully noted that Victoria's star players were English. Sam Cosstick was their outstanding bowler, and four years earlier B.B. Cooper, who top-scored for Victoria with 84, had shared an opening partnership of 283 with Grace for Gentlemen of the South vs Players of the South at The Oval. Grace himself, after being nearly run out first ball by Jupp, performed creditably, with scores of 33 and 51 not out as well as returning the best bowling analysis of 10 wickets (out of 17) for 58 runs. The defeat was disappointing to England, but a huge fillip for all Australia. The tourists drew their next game at Ballarat in blazing heat, with W.G. and Fred Grace scoring hundreds, before setting off on a twelve-hour journey to the mining town of Stawell. In old-fashioned traps on poor bush tracks it was not easy travelling, and when the weary travellers were met with brass bands and much ceremony, they were too tired to appreciate it. The hospitality was wonderful, but the worst possible preparation for cricket. So was the deplorable pitch on which the game was played, and England, plagued by flies, were beaten by ten wickets. The peripatetic B.B. Cooper, now one of the Twenty-Two of Stawell, scored a duck in both innings. As the tour progressed, the Englishmen found that Cooper was not to be their only regular opponent: Conway, Allan, Wills and Gaggin appeared in team after team as guest players.

After some up-country victories, Grace's team suffered an eight-wicket defeat against Eighteen of New South Wales, for whom Fred Spofforth, a lanky young quick bowler, impressed by taking 2 wickets for 16. Grace noted his talent, without realising how much he would see of him, at twenty-two yards' distance, during five Australian tours of England. As the English players became familiar with the climate and the playing conditions, they settled down to win ten and draw two of their fifteen games. Grace was very critical of the lamentable state of the wickets and the poor standard of umpiring, but neither of these deficiencies was surprising. Australia did not yet have experienced former players prepared to umpire, nor were there sufficient fixtures for the employment of groundsmen to produce quality wickets. But even without these benefits, the standard of Australian cricket was improving, although *Bell's Life* observed dismissively, 'We may one day see an Australian XI at Lord's.' 'One day' would come sooner than they thought: within three years Australia would no longer need numerical superiority to defeat the English.

The greatest shock for English pride came at Melbourne in March 1877, when, after a lengthy tour of New Zealand and Australia, James Lillywhite's professional team met a Combined Melbourne and Sydney Eleven in what can, in retrospect, be seen as the first proto-Test match. It was played without W.G. Grace, who had stayed at home to study for his medical degree. The Australian team won by 45 runs on the fourth day, largely because their opening bat Charles Bannerman – the best batsman in Australia, said Caffyn – was dropped off a sitter at the start of his innings. Rejoicing in his luck, Bannerman defied the bowling of Lillywhite, Southerton, Shaw,

Emmett and Ulyett to score 165, dwarfing the contribution of his team-mates. Even then he was undefeated, and retired hurt with a damaged finger. Another glittering talent to take part in this game was the twenty-three-year-old Australian wicketkeeper John Blackham, who broke with contemporary fashion and dispensed with longstops even to the fastest bowlers.

On the English side only Harry Jupp, with his highest Test score of 63, made runs, while Billy Midwinter (5 for 78) and Thomas Kendall (7 for 55) bowled out England in successive innings. The *Australian* reported the victory as 'no ordinary triumph', and was right to do so, for the team had won without three of their finest bowlers, Spofforth, Evans and Allan. Spofforth had refused to play when Blackham was chosen in preference to the Victorian wicketkeeper Billy Murdoch, but Evans and Allan were unfit. Soon Spofforth would appreciate Blackham's talent. Even without Spofforth, England had been beaten on equal terms, although their pride might have been assuaged by the fact that their principal tormenters, Bannerman, Kendall and Midwinter, were all born in England. It mattered not, however. Nothing thereafter would be the same. Australian confidence rose, and attitudes changed. No one would again be inhibited by English dominance, or by the absurd, and very Victorian, notion that Australian stock was 'stained' in some way by convict blood. All that was gone, although a fortnight later England won a second Test comfortably by four wickets, with George Ulyett (52 and 63) starring with the bat and Hill, Lillywhite and Southerton sharing the Australian wickets between them. On the Australian side Spofforth, now reconciled to Blackham as wicketkeeper, made his international debut, as did Billy Murdoch, and gave signs of what was to come with four English wickets.

In England, no one cared much about the First Test defeat. Lillywhite's team were professionals, it was a long way from home, and it was a fluke that was swiftly put right in the second Test. There was, thought the English, nothing to worry about. But there was. After these two encounters, Australia not only thought she could beat England, but had actually done so. Moreover, she was keen to do so

again. She would not have long to wait. The age of Australian deference was past.

It faded for wider reasons than success on the cricket field. Since
the gold influx of the 1850s, the flood of British emigrants had been
continuous, and it accelerated through the 1870s. Many emigrants
left to escape rural poverty at home, where farming was suffering
from a long depression. Harvests were poor, and incomes plummeted
as free trade brought in cheap imported corn from the prairies of
America and Russia. When millions of sheep in Britain were culled
after an outbreak of liver rot, the growing Australian wool trade
became a magnet for disaffected farmers and labourers. As they
found a brighter future in Australia, their new allegiance gave spice
to sporting rivalry with the Old Country. Having left hard times
behind them, the new immigrants became robust Australian
partisans.

In 1878 David Gregory, doyen of a formidable cricketing dynasty,
captained the first Australian touring side to visit England. It was
a profit-sharing commercial venture, with James Lillywhite as the
organiser. Only twelve players travelled, but among them were Billy
Murdoch, Charles and Alec Bannerman and Fred Spofforth. Many
spectators remembered Charles Lawrence's Aborigines of ten years
earlier, and were surprised to be confronted by a white team, having stereotyped Australians as black men. Playing up the 'joke',
the England all-rounder A.G. Steel introduced Spofforth as 'the
demon nigger bowler'. If Spofforth smiled, it would have been
bleakly.

The tourists played thirty-seven games and, mimicking England
in Australia, twenty of them were against 'odds'. It was an indication
of how far the standard of Australian cricket had improved. But this
was not immediately apparent. In their opening game, eight thousand
spectators saw them soundly beaten by Nottinghamshire. The Australians were unprepared for the wet Trent Bridge wicket, and Alfred
Shaw (11 for 55) and Fred Morley (8 for 72) demolished them in two
days. Midwinter went in first on the second day, and carried his bat
for 16 runs, the last 3 of which took him one and a half hours. It was

a comprehensive thrashing. The tourists were stung by the defeat, but retribution was to be swift, and would shatter any illusions that English play was far superior to Australian. Australia's strength lay in the bowling of Spofforth and Boyle, supported by Garrett and Allan, and a wet summer gave them every opportunity to wreak havoc. They did.

At Lord's, after yet another soggy weekend, the Australians routed a strong MCC team in only four and a half hours' cricket. It was a shattering defeat. On a saturated pitch that was then baked by the sun, MCC were bowled out for 33 and 19. The wicket, said Grace, was 'almost unplayable', and so were Spofforth (11 wickets for 20 runs) and Boyle (8 for 17). The top score in the match was Hornby's 19. Grace lasted a mere two balls in each innings, scoring 4 and 0, and Alfred Shaw and Fred Morley with five wickets each in Australia's first innings were the only Englishmen to enjoy any success. If there is one single day upon which Australian cricket emerged from the shadow of English dominance, it was at Lord's on 27 May 1878. All cricket gaped in astonishment at the Australian triumph. *Punch* rhymed:

> The Australians came down like a wolf on the fold,
> The Marylebone Club for a trifle were bowled,
> Our Grace before dinner was very soon done,
> And Grace after dinner did not get a run.

Sadly, there were no Test matches to follow up the Lord's game, and the authorities did not have the wit to arrange one speedily. This was a pity, as interest in the Australian team was sky high. Only two thousand spectators had attended the FA Cup Final that year, but a week after their victory at Lord's, thirty-one thousand spectators flocked to see them at The Oval over two days, standing many deep around the boundary. The Australian juggernaut beat Surrey, and continued to showcase their talent by rolling over the counties, winning eighteen of their thirty-seven games and drawing a further twelve. At Old Trafford the entrance fee for their game against Lancashire was doubled from sixpence to a shilling. Australia's stars were the indefatigable Spofforth, six foot three inches of wiry venom, and the wicketkeeper John Blackham, who stood up to the wicket when Spofforth and Boyle were bowling, anchoring the English batsmen to the crease. Although nervy and uncertain off the field, the shortish, dark, heavily bearded Blackham was a revelation behind the stumps. His quick eyes and hands, encased only in skin-tight, skimpy, unpadded gloves, left Pooley, Pinder and Lockyer in his wake, and carried wicketkeeping to a new dimension. At the end of his distinguished career sixteen years later – he played thirty-five Tests, ten of them as captain – Blackham could display broken and shattered fingers as a tribute to his courage as well as his ability.

The Australian tour of 1878 was an enormous financial success. After their defeat of the MCC, crowds flocked to seem them, and the Australians pocketed the bulk (generally 80 per cent) of the gate money, most of which ended up in the pockets of the 'amateur' players. This did not go unnoticed by the press or by the English professionals. When Lillywhite arranged an eleven to play the Australians at The Oval in September, nine professionals – Jupp and Pooley of Surrey and Shaw, Shrewsbury, Oscroft, Selby, Morley, Barnes and Flowers of Notts – wrote to declare that they would not play, having demanded a fee of £20 and been offered £10. The game went ahead with replacement players paid the full £20, but this embryonic strike was a pre-echo of a more famous dispute at The Oval eighteen years later. The affair would have ramifications for county cricket, and for the next Australian tourists.

As the team's successes reverberated in Australia, the Melbourne Club, scenting financial gain and English blood, invited a team to visit during the Australian summer. An amateur side supplemented by the Yorkshire stalwarts George Ulyett and Tom Emmett, and captained by Lord Harris, arrived to play thirteen games, one of which was to have serious consequences. For the game against New South Wales in Sydney, Harris hired a professional umpire from Victoria. Unfortunately for Harris, and probably unknown to him, Victoria and New South Wales were fierce rivals, ever ready to think the worst of one another. Spofforth wrote years later of that mutual dislike, and recalled being caught in a terrible storm at sea with players from both teams on board.

> 'Well,' he said to Charles Bannerman, an expert swimmer, 'suppose we are wrecked. What will you do?'
>
> 'Fine,' was the reply, 'I'll save Alec [his brother], then Murdoch, then yourself.'
>
> 'What about the Victorians?' asked Spofforth.
>
> 'Let them drown,' replied Bannerman, 'let them drown. D'you think I'm going to risk my life for *them*?'*

This may have been casual banter, but it hints at a depth of feeling that can turn swiftly to hostility. It was soon to do so. The umpire gave several controversial decisions in favour of the tourists. First he turned down an appeal against Harris, and then he upheld a hotly disputed run-out of Billy Murdoch, idol of all New South Wales. The spectators, many of whom had bet heavily on the outcome of the game, others of whom had been drinking, were outraged. Refreshed and angry, and in some cases about to see their bets lost, a mob invaded the pitch. Harris, who refused a request to change the umpire, was singled out by the mob and had to be protected by the reassuring Yorkshire bulk of George Ulyett. In the mêlée, 'Monkey' Hornby, a keen boxer, collared one rioter and marched him to the pavilion. One eye-witness reported that an English player had accused the mob of being 'nothing but sons of convicts'. If so – and it was denied – it would have added to the incendiary atmosphere. This dismal affair made an enormous stir, and although Harris exonerated penitent NSW officials from blame, he did so gracelessly. The incident was, he said, 'impossible to forget', even though the game resumed without incident on the following Monday, and Harris's team won.

Their victory against NSW was not repeated in the solitary Test in Melbourne, originally billed as 'Gentlemen of England' against 'The Australian Eleven'. The Australians won by ten wickets, with Spofforth taking 13 for 110 and Alec Bannerman scoring 73. England (113 and 160) were outclassed. Emmett, however, earned his corn

* Fred Spofforth, *Australian Cricket and Cricketer*.

throughout the tour: he took over 130 wickets, at under 9 runs each.

The riot at Sydney had repercussions for Billy Murdoch's Australian visitors to England in 1880, whose welcome was very frosty. Harris wrote in his autobiography that they had 'no one's goodwill', and at the time he made disparaging remarks about 'too frequent visits'. This disobliging intervention added to the uncomfortable atmosphere. Moreover, as Lillywhite's *Cricketer's Annual* commented: 'The recollections of the commercial spirit, which had inspired [the 1878 touring team] were still disagreeably fresh in the minds of Englishmen.' The *Annual* had clearly forgotten the 1863 Parr tour of Australia. As a result of all these comments, fixtures against counties were difficult to obtain, and the team did not play a single game at Lord's, despite Grace's attempt to arrange one in July.

The tourists, in awe of the power of the English cricket establishment, were offended but played on, drawing large crowds, mostly in matches against teams of eighteen. Between May and August only a handful of county fixtures were played. But towards the end of September the tour was rescued at the instigation of Charles Alcock, Secretary of Surrey, who saw the opportunity for an inaugural Test match in England at The Oval. An astute tactician, Alcock realised that he must first recruit Lord Harris to the idea, and, in some unknown fashion, he managed to do so. There is no evidence as to why Harris softened. It is possible that he thought the Australians had learned their lesson, but he may simply have wanted to play and beat them. In any event, that hurdle overcome, Alcock persuaded Lord Sheffield, President of Sussex, to postpone the county's match against the Australians to free up the days for the Test match. In the first of many services to Australian cricket, Sheffield agreed, and the match was arranged.

England, captained by Lord Harris, fielded a strong eleven and won comfortably. Harris won the toss and batted, scoring 52 himself, while W.G. Grace scored a century on his Test debut. England totalled 420 before Morley and Steel dismissed Australia for 149, and Harris enforced the follow-on. Billy Murdoch made an undefeated 153 in Australia's second innings, the first century ever by a Test captain, but England, after losing five cheap wickets, reached the 57 runs needed for victory.

All three Grace brothers played – with mixed fortunes. E.M. made a respectable 36 in the first innings (and nought in the second), but G.F. scored a 'pair', although he did take a memorable catch from a huge skier to dismiss George Bonnor. Poor Fred Grace: two weeks later, at the age of twenty-nine, this fit and agile athlete died of a chill, apparently caught on a draughty railway journey. For the Australians Spofforth was unfit to play, having broken a finger, and as he brooded in the pavilion he may have plotted the day when he would write his name indelibly on the history of cricket. It was, though he did not know it, not very far away. With Boyle and Palmer he had taken over nine hundred wickets that summer at fewer than 7 runs apiece. No one could doubt the advances that Australian cricket had made.

In 1881–82 Alfred Shaw led the England tourists to Australia and lost a four-match series 2–0. The tour was a financial success, but in cricketing terms it was memorable only for individual performances – the left-handed Edmund Peate took 266 wickets at 5 runs apiece – and the oddity that the English-born Billy Midwinter, who had twice played for Australia five years earlier, made his debut for England at Melbourne. Some new records were established. In the first Test over a thousand runs were scored in a tame draw, and Horan (124) and Giffen (30) recorded Australia's first-ever century partnership, 107 for the fifth wicket. Australia comfortably won the two Tests at Sydney, with Palmer taking twenty wickets at under 13 runs a time and Garrett thirteen at a little over 17 runs each. McDonnell scored 147 in the second game, putting on 199 with Alec Bannerman, while English consolations lay in the bowling of Peate (9 for 132) and Bates (9 for 199), with only Ulyett (67), Barlow (62) and Shrewsbury (82) passing half-centuries. England did better in a fourth Test (outside the series), with Ulyett scoring 149 – the first Test hundred by an Englishman in Australia – and sharing an opening partnership of 98 with Barlow in the second innings of a rain-affected draw.

Nothing in this series hinted that the scene was set for the most famous Test match of all. By the time Murdoch's 1882 Australians arrived, England should have been aware that they were formidable opponents. Of eight Tests played, admittedly seven of them in Australia, Australia had won four and England only two. Nonetheless, on their own wickets, English confidence was high despite the obvious improvement of Australian cricket. Nor were the tourists an unknown quantity. Murdoch, Alec Bannerman, Blackham, Spofforth and Boyle had all played against England in 1878 and 1880, and the team included other familiar faces: Horan, Garrett, McDonnell, Bonnor and Palmer had all appeared with success in at least one earlier series. Yet England, with their own crop of fine players, were confident, even complacent. They did not acknowledge what W.G. Grace would write, with after-knowledge, twenty years later: that this was the best team Australia had yet sent to England, or would do for the next twenty years.

After a seven-week voyage from Melbourne, the tourists landed at Plymouth on 3 May, whereupon, without practice, the giant George Bonnor illustrated their competitive impulse by throwing a cricket ball over 119 yards to win a bet. Three days later Massie, Garrett, Giffen and Jones were playing for local clubs, before the whole team assembled at Mitcham and Lord's to practise throughout the following week. The preparation paid off. In the first match, at Oxford on a bitterly cold day, Hugh Massie batted throughout the innings for a double century, scored in a little over three hours, and followed this with a second-innings 46 not out as Australia eased to a nine-wicket win.

Sussex suffered next, losing by an innings and 355 runs. Palmer (14 wickets for 110 in the match, including a hat-trick) twice bowled them out cheaply, while Billy Murdoch followed a duck in his first game with 286 not out in a mammoth total of 643, made at speed. Massie, Bannerman and Murdoch scored the first 200 in under two hours: this was cricket at its most formidable.

A check to Australian confidence was provided by the Orleans Club at Twickenham, who fielded not only W.G. and E.M. Grace but England regulars Lucas, Barlow and Steel, as well as Charles Thornton, the most formidable hitter of the day. The game was restricted to two days only (the Derby was due to be run on the third day), and the time was insufficient for a result, although Orleans had by far the best of the draw. The two titans Grace (5 for 27) and Murdoch (107 not out) had ample time to take stock of their opponents.

The Australians then beat Surrey by six wickets, before three of the Studd brothers led Cambridge University to the most famous victory in its history. C.T. Studd (118 and 17 not out, and 8 for 170) tormented the Australians, helped by notable contributions from his brothers J.E.K. (6 and 66) and G.B. (42 and 48), who opened the Cambridge innings. It was not the last time the tourists would suffer at the hands of the formidable C.T., but later in the season, when most needed, he would find himself stranded at the non-striker's end while Spofforth bowled himself into legend.

Stung by the Cambridge defeat, the tourists cut a swathe through county and representative sides, winning match after match with ease. They drew against, among others, Gloucestershire (W.G. taking 8 wickets for 93 runs) and the MCC (for whom C.T. Studd scored another hundred). They lost to Cambridge University Past and Present, while the Players of England (Maurice Read top-scoring with 130) inflicted upon them the heaviest defeat of the tour. These were rare blemishes. Twenty-four victories and only four defeats were a fair reflection of the quality of the team.

These Australian successes whetted the appetite for the Test match to come. It aroused huge interest, but a man-to-man assessment of the Australian and English teams left the Englishmen confident of victory. Barlow and Peate of England were taking wickets more cheaply than Boyle and Spofforth and, notwithstanding Murdoch, Horan and Massie, the English batting looked decidedly stronger, although Shrewsbury was omitted and Hornby, the captain, was in poor form and possibly not worth his place. Perhaps for this reason Hornby, who opened for Lancashire, batted at number ten in the first innings, but it has always been inexplicable that C.T. Studd, with two centuries against the Australians earlier in the season, should bat as low as number nine in the second innings when England needed a mere handful of runs to win.

The Test began at The Oval on a damp Monday, 28 August, before twenty thousand spectators eager to see an England victory. Murdoch won the toss and elected to bat. It was a mistake. Of the first six batsmen only he, with 13 runs, reached double figures. Amid mounting excitement the visitors lost Massie, bowled leg stump by Ulyett, with the total at 6. Grace, at point, was repeatedly applauded for his fielding as pressure mounted on the Australians, who slumped to 26 runs for 4 wickets, then 30 for 6, before a minor recovery by Blackham and Garrett saw the total rise to 48 by lunch. Rain threatened during the interval but held off, and immediately after the restart Garrett and Boyle were speedily dismissed. Blackham and Jones fell to catches by Grace and Barnes off Barlow, and the Australians were all out for a mere 63 runs, their lowest total of the entire tour. In three hours, Barlow (5 wickets for 19) and Peate (4 for 31) had undermined the hard-won reputation the Australians had gained in a season of success.

Any English cockiness had a short life. Grace was bowled leg stump by Spofforth for 4 and Barlow caught at forward point for 11 – England 18 for 2. Ulyett survived a stumping chance and was twice nearly bowled before he and Lucas batted steadily to take England to within 7 runs of the Australian total. The English batting then fell apart. Four wickets fell swiftly, including Ulyett for 26, the top score of the day, stumped by the vigilant Blackham as he danced recklessly down the wicket to drive Spofforth. Writing years later, Walter Read thought this a pivotal moment in the match, as Ulyett was set and batting well when hot blood cost him his wicket. Maurice Read and Steel hit out briefly before the innings closed for 101, a lead of 38 – slender, but potentially significant in a game in which wickets were falling for an average of 8 runs each.

After another downpour overnight, the second, momentous, morning was again showery, and Massie and Alec Bannerman opened the Australian second innings shortly after midday. Rain had taken the deadliness out of the drenched wicket, and it was bound to be easier until it dried out. Bowling conditions were difficult. The run-up was soggy, and at the point of delivery bowlers' feet were sinking in mud. The ball, reported Barlow, was 'like soap'. Another packed crowd saw Australia take full advantage of the opportunity. Massie began an onslaught on the bowling, while Bannerman defended stoutly. The arrears were eliminated at a run a minute, the 50 partnership reached in only forty minutes and Massie, dropped at long-off by Lucas on 38, scored 55 out of 66 in under an hour before, to the immense relief of the English team, Steel knocked back his leg stump. In Massie's shining hour, before the wicket dried and became more deadly and the run-up more secure, the balance of the game was altered. Lucas's butterfingers would prove fatal. Of the remaining batsmen, only Bannerman with a patient 13 and Murdoch, run out for a painstaking 29, reached double figures. Controversy and ill-humour mingled together when Jones, believing the ball was dead after a single had been run, wandered out of his crease to pat down the wicket and the predatory, if unsporting, instinct of Grace ran him out. Reports that Thoms, the umpire, in giving his decision, said: '*If you claim it, sir, – out!*' were later denied and, perhaps prompted, Thoms added later that if Grace had thrown the ball at the wicket and missed, the batsman could – and would – have run overthrows. Therefore the ball was 'live', and Jones was out. Murdoch, however, made his displeasure evident on the field, and in between innings Spofforth bluntly told Grace he was 'a cheat'.* When Jones was dismissed the total was 114, and the last three wickets added only a further 8 runs. The Australians, all out for 122 by mid-afternoon, had set England only 85 to win, but in the dressing room, still furious at Grace, they agreed with Spofforth that 'This thing can be done.'

Hornby opened the second innings with Grace, but he and his Lancashire partner Barlow were bowled by Spofforth off consecutive balls with the total at 15. At 30, Spofforth changed ends to bowl from the pavilion end and Boyle replaced Garrett. Grace and Ulyett seemed untroubled until a brilliant catch low to his right by wicketkeeper Blackham removed Ulyett at 51 – but with only 34 runs needed, and much of the cream of English batting still to come, a home victory

* Quoted in a letter written by Massie's son in 1956.

seemed certain. Grace then mis-hit Boyle straight to Bannerman at mid-off and departed for 32 (53 for 4 wickets), and the game slowed to a halt as Lucas and Lyttelton scampered a handful of runs in between maiden after maiden. Facing Spofforth, confessed Lyttelton later, was like standing on the edge of the tomb. At 66 the tomb opened, and Spofforth bowled him with an unplayable ball. With 19 runs needed and five wickets left, panic set in. Steel, wretchedly at sea, was caught and bowled by Spofforth, who then bowled Read second ball for a duck before the despairing Oval crowd. With 15 runs to win and three wickets left, tension was rising as the balance swung towards Australia. But even so, the men still to bat were not tail-end rabbits: they included C.T. Studd, who twice during the tour had been the nemesis for Australia, and that seasoned professional William Barnes of Nottingham. Barnes was no pushover: he had scored 266 for MCC against Leicestershire earlier in the season, sharing a partnership of 454 with Billy Midwinter. These men, thought The Oval crowd, must surely be able to amass the handful of runs required.

Barnes came first, and 5 precious runs were added before Lucas, who had been steady and cool, unluckily played on to Spofforth with the score at 75, leaving 10 runs to win with two wickets left. Studd – at last – came to the wicket, but only to the non-striker's end. Barnes was then promptly caught off his glove by Murdoch at point off Boyle. Peate, after a hit to square leg for 2, was comprehensively bowled by the same player. Studd, in the midst of a magical season, did not face a single ball. England were all out for 77, and Australia had won an astonishing victory by 7 runs. Spofforth's last eleven (four-ball) overs brought him ten maidens and 4 wickets, at a cost of 2 runs. Despite his epithet 'Demon', Spofforth bowled medium pace on soft England wickets, lacing his attack with the occasional very fast ball. It was brilliantly effective: in total, the 'Demon' took 14 wickets in the match (7 for 46 and 7 for 44). Boyle, also medium pace, supported him with 2 for 24 and 3 for 19. Spofforth passed from fame to legend.

In the aftermath of the game, the Australians were garlanded with praise and the Englishmen castigated for their loss of nerve. A dozen years later, Spofforth defended his opponents. 'Throughout both English innings,' he wrote in the *New Review*, 'I was breaking [the ball] back quite six inches and towards the end of the second innings the ball probably broke as much as a foot.' If that was the case, it is no wonder England collapsed. Even so, the *Sporting Times* published its famous mock obituary notice of English cricket with its postscript that 'The body will be cremated and the ashes taken to Australia.'

In retrospect, even with the genius of Spofforth, the 1882 defeat should never have happened. The Australian batting, with the exception of Murdoch and possibly Massie, was far weaker than England's, but Spofforth and Boyle were supreme on wet wickets – and the 1882 season was very wet. When the Australians sailed on to America on the *Alaska* on 28 September they left behind a nation whose sense of its own cricketing supremacy had been rudely checked. But if Australia triumphed, so did cricket. The 'Ashes' – the blue riband of cricket – were born. Test rivalry between England and Australia became an institution,* and in the twenty years following that famous Oval Test, eight England teams toured Australia and a similar number of Australian sides sailed to England. The spur of competition would bring to the fore the greatest galaxy of talent cricket had known, and raise the tenor of the game.

Over the next two decades both England and Australia enjoyed periods of success. In the fifteen years after the Oval defeat, England were dominant, and over the two decades they won twenty-seven Tests, to nineteen by Australia. They secured swift revenge in 1882–83, when an under-strength England side without Grace, Lucas, Hornby, Ulyett or Lyttelton recovered the Ashes under the captaincy of the

---

* Although the word 'Test' was applied in reference to matches between Stephenson's team and Australian state sides in 1861–62, it was first used in its modern sense about the 1882 game. *Bell's Life* noted on 2 September that year: 'At least three matches should have been arranged between England and Australia as one contest . . . can hardly be looked on as a real test.' When Bligh's team were in Australia, the *Sydney Morning Herald* (3 January 1883) referred to 'the first of the great test matches'. Thereafter, the term was in general use.

Hon. Ivo Bligh. On the outward journey they suffered a setback when their great destructive bowler Fred Morley was injured in a collision with a sailing ship. It emerged later that he had broken some ribs. He died two years later of congestion of the lungs. Few doubted that the accident was a contributory factor.

Bligh's tour gave physical reality to the *Sporting Times*'s symbol of the ashes. Soon after the team landed in Australia, Bligh replied jokily to a questioner that he had come 'to regain the ashes'. Following a friendly game at Christmas at the home of Sir William 'Big' Clarke at Sunbury in Victoria, some ladies burned something – perhaps a bail or a stump, it is not certain – and placed the ashes in a small urn, which was presented to Bligh. One of the mischievous ladies was Florence Morphy, the music tutor to the Clarke children. She and Ivo Bligh were soon engaged, and they married a year later (the romance of the Ashes has more than one meaning). Bligh's team won the third and decisive game of the series against Australia in Sydney, and the worthless little terracotta eggcup became the most fiercely fought-for trophy in world cricket.

Billy Murdoch's 1884 Australian tourists were almost as strong as the 1882 victors, even without Massie, Horan and Garrett. A defeat in the second Test at Lord's cost them a series they should have won. Murdoch took the first catch by a substitute in Test cricket – for England, catching his team-mate Scott off Steel for 75. In the first Test Australia were well on top at a rain-soaked Old Trafford, where Spofforth and Boyle ran riot, and in the third Test at The Oval, but rain saved England. The latter match was replete with oddities. Murdoch (211), McDonnell (103) and Scott (102) were the core of a massive Australian total of 551 that so demoralised England that all eleven players, including wicketkeeper Alfred Lyttelton, bowled. Lyttelton came on late with his slow lobs, and perhaps should have bowled sooner: he mopped up the Australian tail, taking 4 wickets for 19 runs. Grace, having occupied every other fielding position on the ground, replaced him behind the stumps, where he joyfully took a catch to dismiss Billy Midwinter.

For England, an angry Walter Read of Surrey, furious at batting as low as number ten, hit out so savagely that he reached his hundred in only thirty-six scoring strokes, and added 151 runs for the ninth wicket with the left-handed William Scotton of Notts. Scotton, who had opened the innings, was dismissed for 90 with the score at 332. His five-and-a-half-hour innings at The Oval was the highlight of his career, but sadly it was overshadowed by Read's spectacular hitting. England followed on, but comfortably saved the game. Years later Scotton, a sensitive man, lost his place in the Notts team and, depressed, took his own life.

After 1884, Australian cricket entered into a bleaker phase. Disputes over money soured relations with the game's administrators and irritated the public. The *Bulletin*, as ever, hit out in all directions, with England a ready target. Australians, it claimed, would 'never consent to be spat upon by dirty little cads whose soap-boiling or nigger-murdering grandfathers left enough money to get the cads' fathers "ennobled" and to enable the cad . . . to live without working'. The robust Australian press was getting into its stride.

In the tour of 1884–85 the performance of the Australian team fell away, although Arthur Shrewsbury's tourists had to battle hard to retain the Ashes in the first ever five-match series. The first two Tests, in Adelaide and Melbourne, were comfortably won by England, with Billy Barnes and Johnny Briggs scoring hundreds and Peel, Barnes and Bates sharing the wickets. Australia edged home by six runs at Sydney – the narrowest victory yet in a Test – with Spofforth dismissing Shrewsbury, Ulyett and Barnes in four balls. In the fourth Test, also at Sydney, a hundred in even time by Bonnor was the highlight of an eight-wicket Australian win that tied the series at two games each. England then won the final Test in Melbourne easily. A hundred from Arthur Shrewsbury – the first by an England captain – was followed by an Australian collapse to Ulyett, Flowers and Attewell, and the Ashes were safe.

In 1886 H.J.H. Scott's Australian team was soundly beaten 3–0 in England. It was a poor tour by an undistinguished team. Barlow, Ulyett, Briggs and Lohmann were too strong for them with the ball, and in the second Test at Lord's on a rain-damaged wicket

Shrewsbury scored 164. In the third and final Test at The Oval, 170 in the first innings by Grace gave England control of the match. Spofforth was injured early on in the tour, and ended his international career after eighteen Tests, all against England, in which he had taken 94 wickets at a cost of 18.41 runs each. In those few Tests he took ten wickets in a match four times, and five wickets in an innings on seven occasions. He was, quite simply, irresistible.

As age and poor form broke up Murdoch's team, England continued to dominate Test cricket until the late 1890s. Murdoch and Spofforth reappeared in England. Murdoch was appointed captain at Sussex in 1893, and nurtured the young Ranjitsinhji. Spofforth played for Derbyshire, and a young Repton batsman, C.B. Fry, faced him. 'It was,' said Fry, 'impossible to tell from his delivery what he would bowl.' Even in Test retirement, Spofforth was a giant of the game.

At the end of the 1880s a new generation of cricketers began to revitalise Australian prospects. C.T.B. Turner, the 'Terror', and J.J. Ferris, who later played for Gloucestershire, followed Spofforth and Boyle as high-class bowlers, although they enjoyed little support from their team-mates. In the 1888 tour of England the two of them captured 534 wickets, 482 of them in first-class matches, but their fellow bowlers could obtain only 129 between them. Two years later their haul was 430 wickets, and an admiring Grace rated Turner as one of the greatest bowlers he had faced.

Harry Trott, a future Australian captain, also rose to prominence in the late 1880s, to be followed by Syd Gregory and Hugh Trumble, who made their Test debuts in 1890. But these fine players were merely attractive outriders for a greater crop to come. Joe Darling and the fiery Ernest Jones appeared in 1894, with Harry Trott's younger brother Albert. Clem Hill and Monty Noble were followed by the genius of Victor Trumper in 1899, and two years later by Warwick Armstrong and Reggie Duff. This vast array of talent was matched in England by Stoddart, Jackson, MacLaren, Fry, Ranjitsinhji, Hirst, Rhodes, Jessop, Barnes and Blythe. It was the height of a golden age, upon which war would draw the curtain.

Despite the mutual flowering of talent, from the moment Trott's team overwhelmed the MacLaren/Stoddart* tourists 4–1 in 1897–98, Australia were the greater side. Of the next fifteen Tests, Australia, under the captaincy of Joe Darling, would win seven, while England, under Archie MacLaren, would win only two. Australian cricket had come of age.

The nation, too, had changed since the first Englishman had set foot on the continent. The press had become vigorous in a fashion modern Australians would recognise. English teams were castigated for shamateurism – a justifiable charge in the case of W.G. and A.E. Stoddart, who received substantial payments to cover their 'expenses' – and English class distinctions came in for sharp criticism. Australians were disgusted that amateur and professional members of the same team entered the field separately, ate separately and changed in different dressing rooms. It was, said the *Bulletin* in January 1895, 'everlasting snobbery . . . priggish, and out of place'. Australian teams bore their own share of criticism, the inevitable *Bulletin* commenting that the 1890 team under Murdoch, returned as captain, was weak 'except in its capacity for drink'. Free speech, without frills, became commonplace and invaded the terraces as the 'barracker' began to make his voice heard. High-volume commentary, even abuse, accompanied the play, often to the amusement of the crowd, but not to all the players. A.E. Stoddart complained after the 1897–98 tour: 'We have been insulted, hooted at, and hissed in every match and on every ground.' Like his Queen, he was not amused – but he was speaking at the end of a very unsuccessful tour.

In 1901 this vast and deserted land became the self-governing Commonwealth of Australia, with a huge growth in population and wealth. The once-convict colonies had long gone, and three and a half million expatriate Britons and Europeans made up a cosmopolitan nation. By the time the century turned, rail and steam had opened up the interior, and the discovery of gold, silver, zinc, copper, lead, tin and iron ore joined with huge agricultural growth to offer high living standards to the working man. Exports of grain, beef, dairy

---

* When Stoddart's mother died, MacLaren deputised as captain.

products and sugar made Australia an important source of food, as well as wool and minerals. Despite the inauspicious beginning of the relationship, Australia remained closely tied to Britain for men, money and markets.

Ahead for the two countries lay a partnership in war and peace, enriched by a fierce rivalry in cricket. Over the years, great cricketers would appear in abundance: Warwick Armstrong, Don Bradman – the supreme run machine – Ray Lindwall and Keith Miller were among those in an unbroken line to the Chappell brothers, Dennis Lillee, Shane Warne and Ricky Ponting. The Australian affinity to sport is such that, Ned Kelly apart, many of its national heroes are cricketers. The manner in which Australia played cricket helped to fashion the modern game. It is apt that it did so, for cricket helped to define Australia.

12

The Boom in Leisure:
Competition for Cricket

By the 1860s the options for leisure were growing, and cricket began to face wider competition for the affections of the sports-loving public. Choices would continue to increase until 1914, when the Great War changed the world forever. Bareknuckle fighting had begun to die out early in the nineteenth century, and boxing with gloves or 'muffles' had replaced it. The Queensberry Rules, published in 1867, replaced the old Prize Ring Rules of 1853, and brought order to a sport that remained hugely popular. Other more violent entertainments were ending. Public executions at Tyburn, and later outside Newgate prison, ended in 1868. Dr Johnson would not have approved. He had told Boswell a hundred years earlier: 'Sir, executions are intended to draw spectators. If they don't draw spectators, they don't serve their purpose.' But Dickens and Thackeray took a different view. Dickens, after seeing the double execution of the murderers Frederick and Maria Manning in 1849, wrote that he saw in the mob awaiting the entertainment 'the image of the Devil'. Cockfighting was discredited as a sport and rarely seen by 1870. Bear- and bull-baiting had been prohibited forty years earlier.

Some old recreations, however, retained their attraction. Archery, once a military necessity, was now a leisure activity. Field sports were still a way of life in rural areas. Horseracing had become a national obsession, with the champion jockey Fred Archer a popular hero.

The Ascot Gold Cup had been founded in 1807, and the Thousand and Two Thousand Guineas had been run at Newmarket since 1809. Steeplechasing drew huge crowds. The Grand National had been run at Aintree since 1839, and the Cesarewitch at Newmarket from the same year. By 1860 the St Leger, the Derby and the Oaks were all long-established annual events.

New sports, and non-sporting leisure activities, were rising in popularity, and would compete with cricket for the favour of the public. The railway had helped spread cricket, but it also aided alternative amusements. Excursions to seaside resorts became popular. Thomas Cook, a committed Baptist and member of the Temperance Society, invented the affordable package tour, organising an initial excursion for five hundred temperance supporters from Leicester to Loughborough by rail in 1841. Temperance is an odd parentage for the modern excursions of Thomas Cook's business, which take Britain's finest to Magaluf, Ibiza and Faliraki, where forbearance from the demon drink is most definitely not on the itinerary.

Cook's vigour in support of the temperance cause was admirable, but was plagued by misfortune. On one trip to Scotland, five hundred tourists found themselves on a train with no onboard catering or lavatories, yet from which they could not disembark. They arrived at Fleetwood 'starving and bursting', but what had been a bad situation soon became worse. The steamer they boarded on the Ayr coast had an insufficient number of cabins, and those unfortunate passengers who were not allocated one were left on deck, where they were drenched. Throughout all these privations the passengers – who must have been badly in need of a drink – endured incessant banging of the temperance drum by Cook. It is astonishing that his business thrived.

Scotland was among the destinations to which English aristocrats had taken cricket in the mid-eighteenth century, and the Scots retaliated with golf. It took root slowly but surely in England, although by the end of the 1860s only Blackheath and London Scottish on Wimbledon Common, the Royal North Devon Club at Westward Ho! and the Hoylake Club near Liverpool were established south of the border. The first 'Open' Championship was played on Prestwick's twelve-hole course on 17 October 1860. Only eight golfers contested the initial Championship, and Willie Park of Musselburgh defeated 'Old' Tom Morris by two strokes. The following year, in a slightly larger field of twelve, Morris won, and with his son 'Young' Tom went on to dominate the event over the next decade. By 1874 father and son had each won the Championship on four occasions, and 'Young' Tom, after three successive victories, was presented with the glamorous belt of red leather, adorned with a silver buckle, for which the players had been competing. Thereafter, the famous silver claret jug became the Open trophy. 'Old' Tom, who resembled a pocket W.G. Grace in face and form, outlived his son by thirty-three years and was still an active golfer at the age of eighty-three – often with W.G. as a partner. By that time the prohibitively expensive hand-made early golf balls had been phased out in favour of a new ball, made from gutta percha (a gum). The reduction in cost opened the game to many more enthusiasts, but social convention restricted the game largely to men until 1892. That year the Ladies' Golf Union was formed and the inaugural Ladies' Championship played at Lytham St Annes in Lancashire. The great British amateur Lady Margaret Scott was the first winner.

In 1869 polo, which for many years had been popular with the army in India, finally made its debut in England. It was soon widely played amongst the well-off, but the cost of maintaining ponies restricted its spread as a participatory sport.

Another, more languid, upper-class activity was about to lead to the introduction of a new game that would become a national institution. Croquet had long been a social amusement enjoyed on the manicured lawns of the leisured classes, but in 1874 a cavalry officer, Major Walter Clopton-Wingfield, devised a more active game that was a mixture of badminton and the ancient sport of court, or real, tennis that Henry VIII had enjoyed three hundred years earlier. The All-England Croquet Club, founded six years earlier, adopted the new game to boost its membership, and renamed itself the All England Croquet and Lawn Tennis Club. Three years later, in 1877, it staged the first tennis championship in England. It was held at its head-quarters in Wimbledon.

Wimbledon's entrance into the sporting calendar was a rather restrained affair. Only twenty-two contestants entered, of whom one failed to turn up, and twenty-seven-year-old Spencer Gore won a rain-delayed, and rather one-sided, final in three straight sets. The attendance was meagre: a mere two hundred spectators, paying one shilling a head, witnessed Gore's victory; just thirty of them had seats in a temporary, and probably rickety, three-plank stand. It was a far cry from the packed, enthusiastic crowds of modern Wimbledon, with its worldwide television audience of hundreds of millions. The style of play in that first competition was very old-fashioned. The service was round-arm rather than overhead, the balls were hand-sewn into flannel outer casings, the racquets were like snowshoes with handles, and to preserve maidenly modesty, gentlemen were requested 'not to play in shirtsleeves when ladies were present'. The authorities' concern for ladies was expressed more liberally seven years later when a Ladies' Championship was held, with Maud Watson the first winner.

At the time, the embryonic game of tennis was subordinate to cricket in profile and precedence. The final of the first Wimbledon tournament was suspended over a weekend to avoid a clash with the annual Eton vs Harrow cricket match at Lord's, and the MCC, as the controlling body of *real* tennis, drafted rules for the new game of lawn tennis. The All England Club, in a spasm of independence, then revised them, and since that day they have remained the sport's controlling body.

Waterways offered great opportunities for leisure, but sometimes brought tragedy in their wake. On 3 September 1878 the pleasure steamer the *Princess Alice* was returning from an excursion down the Thames when it collided with the collier *Bywell Castle* near Woolwich, broke into three pieces, and sank with the loss of over six hundred lives. This did not stop the continued popularity of boating, sailing and river trips.

The most serious sporting rival to cricket's supremacy as the national game set out its stall in the 1860s. Football had a very elevated paternity. The first rules were agreed in 1848 at Cambridge University, in an attempt to regularise the wayward fashion in which the game was played in the universities and public schools.* It was not, in its infancy, the most popular game of the working man that it would become, but more a pastime of the sons of middle- and upper-income groups. This was to change after Sheffield Football Club was formed in 1855, and Notts County, the oldest professional club, in 1862. In that year the exotically named J.C. Thring, a schoolmaster at Uppingham, noted down the rules he had helped frame at Cambridge fourteen years earlier. They were not simple, as the initial definition of offside reveals:

> A player is 'out of play' immediately he is in front of the ball, and must return behind the ball as soon as possible. If the ball is kicked by his own side past a player, he may not touch it or kick it, or advance, until one of the other side has first kicked it, or one of his own side has been able to kick it on a level with, or in front of, him . . .

A year later the Football Association was formed, with its inaugural meeting held on 26 October 1863 at the Freemasons' tavern in Great Queen Street, London. None of the famous clubs of today was represented – they did not yet exist – but those that were agreed to revise the rules during a series of meetings held in the social room of a public house. In the fifth of six meetings, two draft rules were removed which defined the future character of Association Football and promoted rugby as a distinct alternative game. The first rule-change was to prohibit any player running whilst holding the ball in his hands, and the second was to end the right to tackle the player with the ball by holding, tripping or hacking him. In future, running with the ball in hand and tackling to bring a player to the ground were restricted to rugby, and in 1871 the Rugby Football Association was formed. Over

---

* The first rules for football formally issued through the press were those of Surrey FC in 1849. In 1859 Fred Lillywhite proposed that one set of football rules be sent to him for inclusion in his *Guide to Cricketers*, while in 1863 his brother John secured the sole rights to publish the rules formulated by the new Football Association.

the years the game developed different characteristics in north and south, and in 1895 the (amateur) rugby union and (semi-professional and largely restricted to the north) rugby league went their separate ways. Two games had emerged from one.

The first football game under the new rules was played at Mortlake on 19 December 1863, between Barnes and Richmond. Sadly for such a momentous occasion, the result was a goalless draw. In 1871 the Football Association Challenge Cup was instigated as a knockout competition, with Wanderers, from south London, beating Royal Engineers by one goal to nil in the final at The Oval, where Charles Alcock (see pages 349–53) was the long-serving Honorary Secretary. On 30 November 1872 the West of Scotland Cricket Ground, Glasgow, staged the first ever football international, between Scotland and England – another 0–0 draw. From these modest beginnings, the most widely played game in the world was born. Between 1875 and 1900 football clubs were established in almost every large conurbation in the land. Many, such as Barnsley, Fulham, Aston Villa and Bolton Wanderers, sprang from church or chapel connections, while others, including Arsenal, Liverpool, West Ham, Manchester United and Coventry, began as works teams. Their popularity mushroomed, and fixtures predominated on Saturday afternoons, after factory workers ended their shifts and before church beckoned on Sundays. Football soon became commercial, with grounds fenced in and professionalism legalised in 1886.

The development of sport between 1850 and 1900 was a huge boon to fashion. All the new sports that were attracting mass support required specially-made attire, and to mark distinctions in rank the outfits became more elaborate and expensive, especially for those sports that appealed to the Upper Ten Thousand. Riding, hunting, shooting, yachting, croquet, tennis, hockey, football, ice-skating, swimming, cycling and golf all required their own kit. So did leisure pursuits such as hill-walking and mountaineering, which, as contemporary photographs confirm, attracted women as well as men. It may seem unlikely that anyone would climb the Matterhorn or Mont Blanc in bustles and bonnets, but in their own tribute to muscular

Christianity, vigorous Victorian ladies took such activities in their stride. Decorum was important in all sports, however, and, to ensure it Amelia Bloomer designed voluminous undertrousers to protect the modesty of lady cyclists.

Social convention added to the growth of new attire. In smart society a different outfit was required for every social or sporting occasion, thus requiring the purchase of an ever-increasing variety of clothes. All this was a bonanza for the fashion entrepreneurs. Dr Gustav Jaeger, Arthur Liberty, Henry Harrod, John Lewis and Thomas Dickins all saw their stores become household names. They were not alone in profiting from the boom in leisure. The Army & Navy, Freeman, Hardy & Willis and countless lesser-known High Street outlets also cashed in as demand rose.

Fashion being fashion – and commerce – guaranteed that the styles changed, thus ensuring that the market didn't flag. In men's fashions, garish colours to denote social class were phased out and replaced by the quality of fit and cut – and Savile Row grew. The Regency fashion icon Beau Brummel, who pioneered well-cut clothes and clean linen, would have approved. More sober suits became stylish. Coats moved away from the colourful 'dandy' style to masculine frock coats and morning coats as the practical Victorians turned to more businesslike clothing. There were other changes too: woollen underclothes became popular as, out of sight, comfort and warmth captured the market. Even nightshirts became unfashionable and were replaced by sleep suits and pyjamas.

In one respect the middle and upper classes aped their social inferiors: jackets, formerly the preserve of working- and lower-middle-class men, emerged as sporting fashion in the form of blazers or Norfolk jackets, and smoking and lounging jackets accompanied them for indoor evening wear. Blazers became an essential cricket accessory. Hats – a largely alien concept in modern days – proliferated. Silk top hats were required for formal use, with new styles emerging for casual wear – the trilby, the bowler (named after its inventor, Thomas Bowler), the homburg and the boater for watersports and all-purpose leisure wear. Cricketers adopted caps.

As men's fashions became more sober, women's clothing became more feminine, with endless frills, flowers, trimmings, ribbons and embroidery that delighted the haberdashery trade. Women suffered agonies to enhance their appearance. The invention of the crinoline frame in 1856 cut down on heavy layers of petticoats, but the fashionable bell shape required painful corseting. Even when the crinoline gave way to the bustle, tiny waists still required splayed corsets. It must have been a huge relief – literally – when straighter and more practical skirts became fashionable late in the century. It was part of a trend in which women, whether suffragettes or not, sought a wider role in society beyond that of being required to be decorative. Many of these bewildering changes in fashion moved through the income scales as mass-produced ready-to-wear clothes became widely available, and paper patterns and the invention of the sewing machine enabled stylish clothes to be made at home. And looking stylish was important, for even beyond the need for specially designed clothing for sport, other recreations required dressing up as visits to the theatre and music halls became ever more popular.

In the Victorian theatre the big change – as with so much – came as a result of the ever-growing railway network. This had two beneficial effects: theatre-lovers could now travel from the provinces to the towns and cities to see popular productions, and impresarios could send whole companies out on nationwide tours. This brought about the practices of trying out new material on less influential provincial audiences and sending successful (usually London) productions out on tour once West End audiences began to dwindle. It also had one unfortunate side-effect – it spelled the end for some venerable old companies, often attached to regional theatres, that could trace their lineage back to Shakespearean times.

Queen Victoria was an avid theatre-goer, much as Elizabeth I and James I had been so many years before, and her royal patronage brought respectability to what Charles Churchill called that 'strolling tribe, the despicable race' of actors. Respectability for the theatre brought docility to audiences. Once noisy and ribald, they now sat in a silent and respectful admiration that was aided by the new practice of dimming house lights, setting seats in the stalls, and the introduction, in the 1860s and 1870s, of the 'dress' circle with its implied requirement for Sunday-best outfits and restrained behaviour. These changes were supplemented by the high quality of the entertainment. The dominant figures on stage were Sir Henry Irving, Dame Ellen Terry, Sir Herbert Beerbohm-Tree and Sarah Bernhardt. Surprisingly, given the boom in theatre, only the Irish wit Oscar Wilde emerged as a major new playwright during this period. Crowds flocked to laugh and cheer as Wilde poked fun at convention and social mores. His wit even turned on cricket, which he condemned because the batsman 'assumed such an indecent posture'. It was a droll observation, given his intimate association with Lord Alfred Douglas and the fact that he would be sentenced to two years' hard labour for gross indecency, although we should perhaps be grateful that the savage sentence gave rise to Wilde's brilliant 'Ballad of Reading Gaol'.

More boisterous entertainment, with audience participation, could be found in the music halls that had sprung up in urban centres across the country. These shows mushroomed as soon as they were permitted to sell food and drink, and patrons were allowed to smoke, on the premises. Some of the new venues offered irreverent entertainment. The Coal Hole, off The Strand, staged mock trials which featured men in drag, obscene comedy and explicit dancing. It was all too much for the Victorians to permit, and the Coal Hole lost its licence in 1862.

The man who developed the new genre of entertainment was Charles Morton, 'the father of the halls'. Morton bought the ancient Canterbury Arms in Lambeth in 1848, and turned it into a temple to light entertainment. His marketing was shrewd. He offered 'one quality – the best' in all his shows, and enticed audiences by selling piping-hot baked potatoes straight out of ovens which were wheeled around the theatre. Morton saw that fun and culture could mix in a society dedicated to self-improvement, and charged an entrance fee of sixpence to the main hall and a further threepence to visit the gallery, which featured a permanent art exhibition. The success of Morton's innovation prompted the growth of many similar establishments that ignored the culture but offered popular, if low-brow, entertainment at a modest price. By the early 1870s, in London alone there were over three hundred music halls of varying size and quality. Some were seedy dens, but others offered riotous and hugely popular entertainment. They merged into variety theatres after new regulations restricted the sale of alcohol unless the auditorium was divided from the stalls which had replaced the tables of thirty years earlier. But the mixed fare of entertainment – song, dance, comedy, acrobatic and speciality acts – continued largely unchanged.

Many of the stars of these shows became much-loved celebrities, often performing at several theatres during the same evening. Some of them entered show-business history: Harry Lauder, who was knighted; the diminutive Dan Leno, with, said Marie Lloyd, 'the saddest eyes in the world'; George Robey, the self-styled Prime Minister of Mirth; Bernie Bellwood; John Nash and Gertie Gitana were all huge crowd-pullers. Leotard – 'the Daring Young Man on the Flying Trapeze' – delighted the crowds and gave his name to the garment he wore during his act. Many of the music-hall songs long outlasted temporary popularity. Marie Lloyd will forever be linked with 'Don't Dilly Dally' and 'Oh! Mr Porter', George Leybourne with 'Champagne Charlie', Lottie Collins with 'Ta-Ra-Ra-Boom-de-ay!' and Charles Coburn with 'The Man who Broke the Bank at Monte Carlo'.

I grew up with these songs sixty or seventy years after they were first performed. In 1901 my father, then twenty-two, began working the variety theatres as a singer, comedian and (occasionally) magician, and soon formed his own variety company that criss-crossed the country for thirty years as well as appearing in Canada and North and South America. As an old man, near-blind and bedridden, he would talk to me, then a boy, of those days, the artistes he worked with and the songs they sang. Often he would sing them as his eyes misted with memory. My mother, although far younger, had worked as a dancer in my father's company, and shared many of his memories. To me the Marie Lloyds, Dan Lenos and Vesta Tilleys were flesh and blood, and not cardboard figures from an era long gone. I grew up with them long after they had died.

As my father lay sick, old men and women, show-business friends who had worked with and for him fifty years earlier, came to visit. They would sit on the bed, often in shabby clothes, and reminisce about a life that had given them little except memories that lingered and a past they hungered for still. My father would tell of a theatre in a northern colliery district where the miners and waterside men in the gallery were audibly and luridly critical of the performance. The manager appeared on stage to announce: 'Ladies and gentlemen, this is a place of refinement, and it's jolly well going to be, and if those noisy ——— don't shut up I'll come up myself and chuck them into the ——— street!'

It is hard to fathom why the manager regarded the theatre as a 'place of refinement' when the most popular star of the time, Marie Lloyd, was the antithesis of decorum. My father appeared with most of the music-hall stars, including Marie Lloyd at the Hackney Empire, and he had a fund of racy stories about her. When she ran into theatrical disapproval with the lyrics 'She sits among the cabbages and leeks', she offered to change them. She did – but 'She sits among the cabbages and peas' was not thought to be an improvement. My father and his guests chortled over stories like this, happy again in the past. I was told how tough the Saturday-night audiences were in Glasgow, how the Brixton Empire was always packed and jolly. As they spoke I could almost hear the Victorian audience belting out the choruses of the popular songs they so enjoyed. I loved the visits from these warm-hearted exotics, who lived to entertain and who had lived lives in which they had basked in the applause of the crowd one day, and found themselves out of work the next. It was, it seems to me now, rather like politics. It was certainly like cricket in the way it offered transient fame followed by years of obscurity.

Other forms of entertainment often mocked politics. In 1871 *Thespis*, the first collaboration between the successful conductor and arranger Arthur Sullivan and the aspiring playwright William Gilbert, aroused little attention. Real success did not come until *HMS Pinafore* in 1878, which ran for seven hundred nights in London. Over the next decade Gilbert and Sullivan exploited the rich seam of their complementary talents as *The Pirates of Penzance, Patience, Iolanthe, The Mikado, Ruddigore* and *The Yeomen of the Guard* packed in the crowds at the newly-built Savoy Theatre in The Strand.

In 1857 Edward Elgar, the grand old man of English music, was born in the tiny Worcestershire village of Lower Broadheath. I empathise with Elgar since, like me, he was forced through his family's lowly circumstances to leave school at only fifteen. Clerical work in a lawyers' office was a misery, and he began to earn a living teaching the violin and cello and playing in local bands. His early compositions were for family gatherings and the nearby church, although before long his work began to be performed in larger halls at Birmingham and Crystal Palace. Well-received early compositions such as the oratorios *The Black Knight* (1896) and *Caractacus* (1898) were followed by *The Enigma Variations* (1899), which was an instant sensation. He wrote Britain's alternative national anthem 'Land of Hope and Glory' as simply the first part of a series of marches called *Pomp and Circumstance* (1901–30), little knowing it would become, at Edward VII's request, the Coronation Ode for the new King. This postdated the Victorian era, but Elgar's popularity was earned from Victorian music-lovers, and performances of his works provided leisure competition for cricket.

Cinema and its child, television, would one day carry cricket to millions who would never see the game played in the flesh. Its first flickerings were seen in the dimmed artificial lights of the Grand Café, avenue des Capucines, Paris, on 28 December 1895, when the brothers Auguste and Louis Lumière introduced the cinematograph, and it captured imaginations so swiftly that crowds flocked to see it. On 21 February 1896 Felicien Trewey demonstrated the new technology to a handful of spectators at the Marlborough Hall in Regent Street, and within a month the Empire Theatre began showing cinematographic shows, and innovative music halls spiced up their programmes with short presentations.

In England in 1899 an early pioneer, Robert Paul, built the first British film studio in Sydney Road, New Southgate. By then he had been making films for four years of such sporting events as the Oxford and Cambridge boat race, the Derby and boxing matches, as well as *Arrest of a Pickpocket*, the first drama filmed in Britain, and more general entertainment such as *Dancing Girls*, *Comic Shoe Black* and *Boxing Kangaroo*. By 1900 film length had stretched to as much as ten minutes. In February 1907 the former magic-lantern showman Joshua Duckworth opened Britain's first purpose-built cinema in Colne, Lancashire. The death knell of the variety theatre could be dimly heard. New stars such as Mary Pickford and Charlie Chaplin soon appeared on the screen. At the time of the Great War cinema's most lavish days still lay ahead, but it had already transformed the leisure choices of millions.

None of this growing range of leisure options held back the growth of cricket, supported as it was by the mighty personality of W.G. Grace. In an age that predated radio, cinema and television, leisure was an active rather than a passive activity, and the fun-seekers expected to contribute to their own pleasure. The Victorians knew how to enjoy themselves. Within one lifetime's memory lay far harsher social and working conditions, in which pleasure was a rare option for the working man or woman – and folk memory still recalled a time in which it barely existed at all. It is no wonder, despite an existence for many that was still harsh by the standards of today, that the Victorians enjoyed themselves with gusto whenever they could, and used every precious free moment to celebrate the increasing opportunities of the age.

The Victorians' determination to contribute helped cricket. So did the social climate that promoted the game and the press that widely reported it. The public's expectation of success, and their general belief – occasional Australian upsets notwithstanding – that English cricket was the benchmark to which others should aspire, kept the crowds flowing to the grounds to enjoy the excellence on offer. Cricket was not threatened by the competition it faced, but drew strength from it. And ahead lay what was to become known as the 'Golden Age'.

13

The Cricketers and the Counties

As William Clarke's travelling eleven were touring England, disparate threads were drawing together on and off the field. On the field, the evolution of cricket had been accelerating for twenty-five years. Batting, bowling, fielding, laws, clothing and equipment had all moved on from the heyday of Beauclerk and Pilch. The players' fashions of the early nineteenth century had departed: top hats in black or white beaver, high-collared shirts and bow ties, with wide braces supporting flannel trousers – all had gone. The practical demands of round-arm bowling had brought about the demise for braces, and the top hat had passed into cricket history, condemned by greater athleticism. Coloured shirts, often spotted or striped, with white trousers and belts were in vogue for a while in mid-century. Blazers became the norm, and blue or brown cricketing boots replaced shoes a few years later. Caps, often in garish designs, appeared about 1860. Ahead lay self-supporting trousers and white buckskin boots with spikes, to bring cricketing dress to a style familiar today.

Despite diehard opposition, the move towards affording batsmen greater protection from injury was relentless. It began as early as the 1820s, when batsmen began to wear shin pads beneath their flannels to protect themselves against the greater pace of round-arm bowling. Primitive pads also made their debut, although their provenance is debatable. James Pycroft and Arthur Haygarth credit Tom Nixon, the Nottingham slow bowler. Whoever was responsible, pads were very slow to come into widespread use, and remained unpopular with

former players for many years: it was not until the 1860s that they
became common apparel, and even then batsmen such as the great
hitter C.I. Thornton scorned them. Early batting gloves appeared in
the 1830s, but were little more than ineffective finger-stalls until the
innovative and safety-conscious Felix invented tubular protection. At
Lord's, with its wicked turf, Felix wore padding to protect his right
elbow as well as his hands and legs. Wicketkeepers wore only primitive gloves with inadequate reinforcement, and most stood well
behind the wicket, with longstops being positioned behind them to
limit the leakage of runs. By the 1850s bats had evolved from the
one-piece block of willow, with cane handles being spliced into the
body of the bat to give it greater 'spring'. Sometime in the late
1830s or early 1840s scorecards originated, although Fred Lillywhite's
printed cards, updated throughout the day, did not appear until 1848.

All aspects of cricket were in flux. As 'grubbers' died out and 'lob'
bowling faded, round-arm bowling reached its peak in mid-century
with Jackson, Tarrant and Willsher. John Jackson (1833–1901) was
one of the finest of all pre-overarm bowlers, and at his best, between
1855 and 1866, was unsurpassed. On ill-prepared wickets his devastating performances earned him the soubriquet 'Demon' many years
before Spofforth. It was not his only nickname: others knew him as
'Jim Crow'. Even less attractively, Robert Carpenter christened him
'Foghorn' because he blew his nose like a trumpet whenever he took
a wicket. Jackson's nose was a focus for anecdote. Once he was hit
on it whilst batting in the nets, and brandy was sent for to rub into
the wound. Jackson thought this a waste, and drank it, treating his
nose by bathing it with warm water instead. Six-foot and well-set,
perfectly built for fast bowling, Jackson was not only fast, but controlled the ball well, and varied his pitch and pace. E.M. Grace
credited him with breaking the ball both ways as it reared rapidly
from the pitch. It is not surprising that he was so deadly, and so
feared. One anonymous victim rhymed:

> The first ball hit me on the hand,
> The next I played in doubt,

> The third ball smashed my fingers,
> And the fourth ball bowled me out.

Jackson twice took his skills abroad, to America with his Nottinghamshire team-mate George Parr in 1859, and to Australia, also with Parr, in 1863–64. Sadly, his retirement following an injury picked up when playing Yorkshire in 1866 predated Test cricket, or he would surely have become a greater figure in cricket folklore. Against all opposition his record was formidable, with many outstanding analyses, but his own favourite was eight wickets and one catch for the North against the South at Northampton in 1857, with the tenth man, John Wisden, lamed – by Jackson. In the grim humour of the fast bowler, this was all ten. Jackson has secured a place in history as the most fearsome bowler of his time. In his prime he was astute, too: he demanded payment in gold sovereigns.

George Tarrant (1838–70) of Cambridgeshire, who had provided Spofforth with such inspiration on the Parr tour of Australia, was not far behind. Tarrant (full name George Tarrant Wood, although he never used 'Wood') was a slight man of below average height; even so, bowling round the wicket, his pace generated from an exceptionally long run, he was as fast as Jackson. When Tarrant died at only thirty-one, Richard Daft opined that 'Tear-'em' Tarrant wore out his good health with the sheer physical effort of his bowling. He loathed being hit by batsmen, and reacted badly to it.

The only left-arm bowler in the trio of great fast round-armers was Ned Willsher (1828–85), whose lean frame, sunken cheeks and protruding chin, decorated with fashionable whiskers, lent him a forbidding demeanour. 'Lanky and cadaverous', remembered Daft. 'Consumptive looking', judged Lord Harris. Willsher had cause to look gloomy, as he had only one lung, although this deficiency did not impair his athleticism. Unlike Tarrant, he was gracious to batsmen. He admired the ease with which Richard Daft played him, commenting: 'I always feel as if he said, "If that's the best you can do, Ned, you'd better put someone else on."' Willsher's reputation as a destructive bowler was earned for Kent and the All-England Eleven, for whom his combination of pace with accuracy captured many wickets. In 1861, against Eighteen of Manchester he bowled twenty-five overs of four balls each while conceding only one run. 'He was,' eulogised Grace, 'one of the most difficult [of all] left-armed bowlers.'

Round-arm bowling did not disappear with the passage of the law legalising overarm, but co-existed with the new style. For a further thirty years the terms 'high arm' and 'low arm' were used to describe bowlers, which suggests that styles of delivery between round-arm and overarm were practised in England. In Australia, by contrast, overarm was common, and all the Australian bowlers from 1878 invariably used a 'high' action. One reason Spofforth was so destructive in England was that batsmen were unused to facing fast bowlers with very high actions. As a result, when he had a helpful wicket, as against the MCC in 1878 or England in 1882, Spofforth was virtually unplayable.

The thesis that batsmen were unfamiliar with overarm bowling is reinforced by a little-known article by James Pycroft in *London Society* in October 1876, in which he writes:

> The alteration of that law and the liberty to raise the hand as high as you please have, I think, made bad, worse. The state of things under the old law was bad because it was conventionally disobeyed; still the law made every young bowler aim at something like a low and horizontal delivery; whereas now the hand is always higher than even Willsher's was when John Lillywhite no-balled him [see page 266] . . . In the last University Match, Mr Patterson's delivery, which was vertical right over the crown of his head, though quite fair by law, was in no sense bowling at all, and an abuse which the law never was supposed to suggest, and I was sorry indeed to see in this most interesting match of the season, such a libel on all decent cricket. There may be other cases as bad . . .

Kindly old Pycroft was a crusty traditionalist who never liked overarm bowling. In many ways he mirrors Nyren's belief, many years before, that round-arm bowling would ruin the game he loved. Nonetheless, Pycroft's observation that 'There may be other cases as bad' suggests that, twelve years after the law was amended, few English bowlers were overarm specialists, and most adhered to the round-arm style of an earlier generation. Certainly, round-arm fought a long rearguard action. W.G. Grace bowled round-arm to the end of his long career, and when Willsher was no-balled to usher in the legalisation of overarm bowling, Grace was a mere boy of fourteen years of age.

One fundamental change that proceeded slowly at first and then accelerated was in the care and maintenance of pitches, although some, notably Lord's, were still in very poor condition in the 1860s. It could have been so much better. Edwin Budding patented a 'grass cutting machine' as early as 1830, and Alexander Shanks of Arbroath had manufactured a horse-drawn mower (Shanks's pony) in 1842. Mechanical lawnmowers were available from 1850, but slow to come into use. Lord's did not use one until the 1880s, when it also introduced a heavy cast-iron roller pulled by a horse called Jumbo. Such techniques were anathema to diehards like Robert Grimston, President of the MCC in 1882. Grimston was never reconciled to overarm bowling either.

The result of such conservatism was that in the 1860s and 1870s W.G. Grace faced 'two or three shooters' each over when batting at Lord's, and recalled that the batting creases were physically cut into the turf until Alfred Shaw suggested whitewashing them as a better option in about 1865. The Lord's pitch must have been dreadful to bat on. Sussex believed it to be so hazardous that they refused to play there in 1864, and the new MCC Secretary, R.A. Fitzgerald, had the ground returfed. It looked better, but did not turn out to be much of an improvement for batsmen. Lord Harris was still receiving 'three shooters every eight balls' at Lord's in 1868, which suggests that it was still venomous. Corroborating evidence comes from a tragedy in 1870. George Summers, a rising twenty-five-year-old playing for Nottingham, died a few days after a ball hit a stone on the wicket, rose sharply and crashed into his head. Richard Daft, who followed him to the wicket, wrapped a towel around his own head for protection and scored 53 to follow his first-innings 117. Two years later MCC were bowled out by Surrey for 16, having been no runs for

7 wickets; the pitch must have been a stinker. Spectators fared better, with two wings added to the pavilion in 1865, the erection of a grandstand in 1866 and the Taverners' Stand the following year. But away from Lord's, pitches were improving: Fenner's, The Oval, Hove and Canterbury were among those that offered a fairer contest between bat and ball.

By mid-century the population of England had risen to over twenty-seven million. Most of them continued to work on the land, but the balance was changing as the growth of the towns and cities powered ahead. Everyone was trying to come to terms with the onrush of the Industrial Revolution. The visible benefits – railways, bridges, roads and municipal buildings – were in stark contrast to the medieval conditions experienced by some workers. The writings of John Stuart Mill, Karl Marx and Friedrich Engels were beginning to raise uneasy questions about the social and economic organisation of industrialised nations. Marx began to put his masterpiece *Das Kapital* onto paper, unaware that it would spill blood for a hundred years. Marx's mother was unimpressed, commenting that she would rather he *made* capital than wrote about it; Irving Berlin later rhymed:

> The world wouldn't be in such a snarl,
> If Marx had been Groucho instead of Karl.

The contrast between hardship and greater opportunity was everywhere. Mrs Gaskell's *Mary Barton* (1848) exposed the feudal relationship between master and men in a northern mill town, but even as she wrote, non-industrial employment was rising. Twice as many people found employment in domestic service as in the cotton industry. Most employees worked a five-and-a-half-day week, and were entitled to Saturday afternoons and Sundays as the days of rest. Weekend freedom opened a wider window for leisure and recreation.

Priorities varied in different strata of society. Middle- and upper-class women, with rare exceptions, devoted themselves to family and charity. Poorly educated working-class women were less fortunate. Economic necessity left them in domestic service, textile mills, shops, doing piecework and other forms of low-paid drudgery. For many life was getting better. For others it was not.

1848 was a crucial year. On the Continent, revolution brought turmoil to France, Austria, Germany, Italy and Hungary. Yet this violent carnage bypassed Britain, despite huge Chartist meetings on Kennington Common. No one can be certain why it did so, but many explanations suggest themselves. The British aristocracy had better relationships with their social 'inferiors' than did their European cousins: it would have been inconceivable for a French aristocrat to play cricket with his gardener. Personal freedoms were widening, parliamentary reform had begun, the monarchy was popular and Britain's power was in the ascendant. The downtrodden had advocates – reformers, writers, politicians – arguing their cause. Many were improving their circumstances, or saw the opportunities to do so. It was enough: there was no revolution, no social meltdown, in Britain. And perhaps, on top of all this, the country was just too nice a place. The Britain of Constable, Turner, the Pre-Raphaelites, Austen, Shakespeare, Browning and Tennyson, a society rich in culture and growing richer in personal options – perhaps it was all too genial to sweep away. 1848 also had one great virtue for cricket: W.G. Grace was born.

It is against this background that the Great Exhibition opened in London in 1851. It was seen as the brainchild of Queen Victoria's consort Prince Albert, who presided over the Royal Commission set up to organise it. Albert was a polymath, gifted in many ways. As Chancellor of Cambridge University, shocked at its narrow syllabus, he promoted reforms to enable it to become one of the great universities of the world. He helped plan and build Osborne House on the Isle of Wight, and was the arbiter of taste for its decor. He was a fine organist. He designed the setting for the Koh-i-noor diamond as well as the new medal for gallantry, the Victoria Cross, which as an innovation could be awarded 'for valour' to servicemen of whatever rank.* He

* The first holder of the VC was Mate Charles Lucas of the Royal Navy. The first army holder was an Irish NCO, Luke O'Conner, decorated for his gallantry at the Battle of the Alma in the Crimean War. He became a Major-General.

was also Patron of the MCC from 1843. But the Great Exhibition was his crowning glory.

The Prince did not conceive the idea – that was the Civil Servant Henry Cole – but it was he who drove the project forward. It was a huge success, as British industry and technology were displayed in competition with those of other great nations. The Exhibition attracted six million visitors, many brought by the enterprising new travel agent Thomas Cook, to view fourteen thousand exhibits housed within a giant 'Crystal Palace', an innovative structure of glass and cast iron erected in Hyde Park. Charlotte Brontë caught the atmosphere of the Exhibition when she wrote in admiration: 'Whatever human industry has created you will find there . . . it seems as if only magic could have gathered this mass of wealth from all the ends of the earth.' The enthusiastic and nationalistic crowds paid homage to the new technologies with a jingoistic joy at the affirmation of British industrial success. It was a turning point. Fear of revolution had gone. Pride in Britain had supplanted it.

More confidence, more leisure and more disposable income were contributory factors to the further growth of cricket. The game had long since moved beyond its earlier days as a plaything of wealthy individuals, but the Victorian eye for business would enable it to develop a commercial aspect of its own. The combination of wider interest, more spectators and ease of travel were essential preconditions for the next phase of cricket, the birth of a County Championship. But it would be a long time coming.

The county system of cricket in England is now so embedded that it is easy to assume that it was always there. But it wasn't, and, appropriately for a game whose birth date is unknown, the gestation of county cricket was prolonged and messy. Teams designated as a 'county' had contested games since the eighteenth century, but the names were fakes, mere 'cover-alls' for groups of scratch players brought together for a particular contest. When the *Postman* newspaper of June 1709 advertised a game between 'Kent' and 'Surrey', no such clubs existed. Nor did the members of the two teams play together on a regular basis. The names were concoctions, the players mercenaries, mere vehicles for a wager between men of wealth and influence. And yet, these early *ad hoc* contests were to influence the later structure of cricket.

The fallacious naming of 'county' clubs was an ancient tradition that became entrenched when teams masquerading as county sides began to dominate their eras. In the early nineteenth century 'Kent' were in the ascendancy, later 'Sussex' with the influence of the round-arm bowling of Lillywhite and Broadbridge, followed by the great 'Kent' teams built around Mynn, Pilch, Felix, Wenman and Hillyer; but in each case no such county club had been formed. The cricket historian Peter Wynne-Thomas brought together research on cricket between the 1820s and the 1860s to suggest nominal 'county champions' during that period: Sussex, Kent and Surrey are the only counties to feature up to 1852, when Nottinghamshire began to upset the early dominance of the south-eastern counties.*

By 1860 four county clubs – Sussex (1839), Nottinghamshire (1841), Surrey (1845) and Kent (1859) – had been established. They were private clubs. They did not distribute profit. They were owned by their members. Their ethos was that of the amateur, and they were fiercely independent. The MCC, by right of history, was *primus inter pares* and the accepted lawmaker for cricket, but it had no legitimate authority over the county clubs, which had their own priorities, employed their own staffs, arranged their own fixtures and were often unbiddable. The question of a formal County Championship was not even a gleam in a visionary's eye.

Other clubs joined the four pioneers, but only in a leisurely fashion. Yorkshire and Hampshire were founded in 1863, followed by Middlesex and Lancashire (1864) and Worcestershire (1865). Derbyshire (1870), Gloucestershire (1871), Somerset (1875), Essex (1876) and Leicestershire (1879) appeared in the next decade with Warwickshire (1882) and Glamorgan (1888) bringing up the rear. There are three oddities in this progression: an Essex Club existed in 1790, but faded away; Northamptonshire founded a club in 1820, but did not enter

---

* *The Cricket Statistician*, December 1980.

the County Championship until 1905; and Glamorgan did not do so until 1921. The seventeen counties would become eighteen in 1992, with the addition of Durham.

As county clubs formed, inter-county fixtures rose in number, although by 1870, when eight clubs – Surrey, Lancashire, Gloucestershire, Nottinghamshire, Middlesex, Sussex, Yorkshire and Kent – were in existence, only Surrey played all seven other counties, and even by 1880 only forty-six inter-county games were played. To a later generation, familiar with the county game, it seems odd that its advantages were not seized more swiftly. But it did not seem odd in 1860, or for the following quarter of a century. The paucity of clubs and the difficulties of travel argued against it. So did their parochialism. None favoured ceding their power to the central control that would be necessary. Nor was there any mechanism to thrash out such objections to see if they could be overcome. A County Championship was simply not on the agenda. Moreover, the amateur touring sides, I Zingari ('The Gypsies') first among them, and the professional mercenary teams had captured the public imagination. All this would change only slowly.

Meanwhile the All-England Eleven and its many imitators – up to twenty at one time – carried cricket around the country. Games were predominantly in the north of England, although Scotland and Ireland were additions to this itinerary. Games in London or the south, where there was more competition and less demand for them, were a rarity. The allure of the travelling elevens remained huge, and the cream of contemporary talent – Richard Daft, Bob Carpenter, George Parr, Tom Hayward, George Tarrant, John Jackson and Jemmy Shaw – turned out for them regularly. These players' commitments reduced their availability to the counties, and cut down the number of inter-county fixtures.

Cricket in the 1860s was played against a background of turbulence and ill-feeling. As we have seen (see pages 187–9), pay, and William Clarke's imperious style, had caused unseemly rows within, and between, the travelling mercenary teams, but other professionals were worried about money too, fearful of the future as they neared the end of their cricketing years. This concern manifested itself in resentment by the (largely professional) north of the (much more amateur) south, and between individual professionals and amateurs. Many petty disputes, accompanied by much petulant behaviour, soured the game. Jealousy erupted in the north when H.H. Stephenson of Surrey was appointed captain of the England side to tour Australia in 1861–62.* Central to the unpleasantness were disputes between northern and southern players, in particular the counties of Surrey and Nottingham.

This was given a focus in 1862 following a match between Surrey and England at The Oval. For over ten years, round-arm bowlers had raised their arm above shoulder height, and although still illegal, this had been tacitly accepted by umpires. But flouting of the law was unsatisfactory, and was about to come to a head. England's Ned Willsher, whose action was 'high', was warned for throwing by his close friend, umpire John Lillywhite, and then no-balled for six successive deliveries. Willsher stalked off, followed by his professional colleagues, who believed, or affected to believe, that the umpire was acting upon the instruction of the Surrey Club. Some northern professionals, notably Nottinghamshire's often queer-tempered George Parr, reacted very badly, and refused to play either against Surrey or in the two most important representative fixtures of the year, North vs South and Gentlemen vs Players. For a while Surrey and Nottinghamshire refused to play one another.

The atmosphere worsened two years later when the United South of England Eleven was formed, largely at the instigation of Surrey professionals led by Julius Caesar. Its formation was a direct result of the schism between northern and southern players, and did nothing to heal it. The new eleven drew players from the All-England Eleven and the United All-England Eleven, and further infuriated professionals who feared, with cause, that their livelihood was at risk.

One problem was soon resolved. John Lillywhite's no-balling of

---

* This was unlikely to have been a protest against Stephenson personally, who was an easy-natured, popular professional. It was probably caused more by frustration that the opportunity had gone to the south.

Willsher brought common practice and cricket law into collision, and overarm bowling was legalised, with the arm permitted to be extended as high as the bowler wished. Willsher's action became legitimate. It is an irony that it was Lillywhite who brought the matter to a head, for it was his father William, forty years earlier, who had been one of the foremost advocates of legalising round-arm bowling. Times had changed, but the Lillywhites were consistent in their gift for revolution.

To add to all this pent-up frustration there was significant agitation in 1864, fuelled by anonymous letters to the *Sporting Life* which advocated a cricket 'Parliament' to replace the authority of the MCC. No doubt the letters were mischievous, but they did reflect concern that the MCC's control over cricket was feeble. The club had sanction over the game's laws, but not over the conduct of its players. The commercially inspired professional elevens were their own masters, and their behaviour could be anarchic. More happily, that year the *Wisden Cricketer's Almanack* was born, and the sixteen-year-old W.G. Grace entered top-class cricket.

The instinct for reform that had dominated the politics of the first half of the eighteenth century was also alive in cricket. Indeed, so active was it that the moneyed and patrician Henry Hyndman, a Sussex cricketer from 1863 to 1868, would become an intimate of Marx and a leading advocate of socialism. Radical passion was not excluded from the dressing rooms of cricket.

In the midst of squabbles, new players were emerging to enrich the game. The quality of batting was improving. University and schools cricket was thriving. On the field, professional players comfortably outperformed amateurs. In the Gentlemen vs Players fixture, which had begun in 1806, the Players had won thirty-nine victories to only fourteen by the Gentlemen, and some of the latter's successes had only been won with teams of more than eleven players. W.G. Grace would soon balance the scales.

As cricket moved at pedestrian pace towards the structure we know today, games between counties remained occasional, although they began to increase towards the end of the 1860s. The shortage of fixtures make comparisons odious, but Nottinghamshire, Yorkshire and Surrey appear to have been the strongest sides. The game remained very Victorian in its attitudes. The distinction between 'amateurs' – respectfully addressed as 'Mr' – and paid professionals – known only by their surnames – remained stark, especially in the south. In the north the situation was less clear-cut: Tom Emmett, a professional, captained Yorkshire, but even he offered to stand down as soon as the amateur Lord Hawke became available. Hawke declined, not out of modesty, but to learn the trade under Emmett so that he could replace him (see page 325). It was a feudal arrangement, and Yorkshire were fortunate that the sharp eye of Mrs Gaskell was not around. Nottinghamshire were more democratic. For more than fifty years, from 1838 to 1889, the county was successively captained by William Clarke, George Parr, Richard Daft, William Oscroft, Alfred Shaw and Mordecai Sherwin – all professionals.

Amateurs changed in separate dressing rooms, entered the playing area through separate gates, and ate apart from the professionals. The great Lancashire openers Hornby (a dashing amateur bat) and Barlow (a stonewalling professional but a deadly bowler) would only meet on the pitch at the start of their innings. If Barlow resented this, there were consolations: if Hornby ran him out, as he did the first time they batted together, he would present Barlow with a sovereign. The distinctions were absurd and insulting, but in Victorian England they were commonplace. Irritation flared up from time to time. There was an especially serious outbreak of discontent when the Australian tourists of 1878 were treated with the social courtesies due to amateurs, and paid more generously than the English professionals. Half a century later, even after the egalitarian impact of the First World War, the old prejudice lingered on. When Percy Fender led his Surrey team, amateurs and professionals alike, onto the field at Lord's together, he was summoned by an irate Lord Harris and informed curtly 'we don't want that sort of thing at Lord's, Fender'. By 'that sort of thing' he meant that Fender should not flout convention, and amongst the class conscious in post-war England convention ruled that birth, blood and wealth bestowed natural advantages that a wise society should not challenge. To those who thought in this way, it was evident that only amateurs were 'gentlemen'. This attitude was reinforced when professionals deferred to amateurs even when their cricketing skills were inferior. The preference for amateurs as captain remained ingrained in some counties until all distinctions between amateurs and professionals were abolished in 1963. Some genuine cricket-lovers believe in it still, however. Fashions sometimes move faster than instincts.

The pay of professionals did not compensate them for their inferior status. They had cause to be aggrieved. In the 1860s, Surrey professionals – and Surrey was among the richer clubs – were paid £3 a game, with a win bonus of a further £1. Ten years later they only commanded £5 a game, with the win bonus unchanged. Moreover, out of this modest income professionals had to pay their travel costs and hotel bills, which swallowed part, and occasionally all, of their match fees. In 'great' games the pay rose: £10 was the fee for Players in the annual match against the Gentlemen, and £6 for representing the North against the South. Over a full season of six months – April to September – an average county professional might earn around £80, although the very best of them might double that sum.

It was a modest salary for a high skill when compared to the £85 per annum of an unskilled labourer, although those professional cricketers fortunate enough to find winter employment were able to add to their income. The modesty of cricketers' resources was illustrated by Charles Alcock, Honorary Secretary of Surrey, when he observed that professional Surrey players in the early 1880s had one pair of flannels each for the entire season. By 1890 the basic professional salary had risen to about £275 per annum (far exceeding unskilled wages of £95 per annum), made up of match fees supplemented in many cases by coaching and ground staff positions. But even after this increase the average professional's pay only matched Alfred Mynn's income in the 1840s – and Mynn once, and possibly twice, went bankrupt without enjoying a lavish lifestyle.

Nonetheless, salaries did improve, and bonuses, testimonials and 'talent money' further boosted income for the fortunate few. So did benefit matches for loyal players as they neared retirement. Ned Willsher received £794 from his benefit in 1872, Tom Emmett £616 in 1878, George Ulyett £1,000 six years later and Edward Pooley £400 in 1883. Such sums were valuable, but not life-changing. Cricketers did not leave the game with their futures secure.

Coaching opportunities were available for elite professionals at universities, schools and county clubs, and occasionally as private tutors, even to royal princes. When F.W. Bell coached the Royal Princes at Windsor he 'couldn't make a job of them at all'. William Caffyn of Surrey was more successful, coaching at Oxford University in 1853–54 with Pilch, Willsher, Grundy, Hinkly and Buttress. The professionals were paid £1 a week, plus one shilling and sixpence for each hour of coaching. They often earned up to eighteen shillings by bowling out their pupils, who placed a shilling on their stumps that was forfeit if it was knocked off. This was lucrative fun for an elite few, but most professionals faced an uncertain future, and many drifted into obscurity and destitution.

Despite the Cricketers' Friendly Society, set up by professionals in 1862, even eminent players were at risk of poverty when their playing days were over. As we have seen, Nicholas Felix had fallen on hard times by the end of his life, and others fared even worse. Despite two benefit matches, Julius Caesar died alone and penniless in a tavern in Godalming. John Jackson died in a workhouse, lonely and shrunken, his magnificent physique gone, having been living on five shillings and sixpence a week. Jack Crossland died in such poor circumstances that Lancashire paid for his funeral. Tom Box, penniless, collapsed and died while changing a scoreboard at Prince's Cricket Ground during a game between Middlesex and Nottinghamshire in 1876. Surrey wicketkeeper Edward Pooley drifted from billiard saloons to building sites to the workhouse, explaining: 'It was the workhouse, sir, or the river.' He died in the workhouse. Harry Jupp, Fred Morley, Cris Tinley and George Anderson all fell into poverty. They were not alone. These are poignant stories. All these men had enjoyed their fame and enriched cricket, but cricket had not enriched them. Sometimes, at their death, clubs belatedly met their responsibilities. When Jupp died in 1889, Surrey paid his funeral expenses, made a grant of money to his widow and gave small sums to his son and two sisters. It was late – but welcome.

Some former players were successful in their after-cricket life. The enterprising William Gunn and Richard Barlow were among the minority to become well-off. So was Roger Iddison, a more run-of-the-mill professional who in the pre-qualification days scored hundreds for both Yorkshire (122 against Cambridgeshire in 1869) and Lancashire (106 against Surrey in 1866), as well as captaining both sides and playing regularly for the professional touring teams. Iddison was an energetic man with a William Clarke-type eye for a profit. In 1867, while still playing, he set up Roger Iddison & Co., and advertised the 'best cricket stock in the North of England', which he sold with liberal discounts to clubs, colleges and schools. In later years he was a salesman, commission agent and auctioneer, but he never returned to his youthful trade as a butcher. The quick-witted and financially astute Iddison was among a small minority. For most professionals, life was bleak when cricket ended.

Despite the tentacles of the travelling elevens, the cricket-watching public's allegiance to 'their' county sides grew from their formation as they became a nursery for new talent. Nottinghamshire, a constant irritant to the dominance of the southern counties, was especially successful in discovering players to follow Joseph Guy, Samuel Redgate and William Clarke. A new generation, led by George Parr, began their careers in the 1840s and 1850s, and bridged the gap to formal inter-county matches a quarter of a century later.

Parr was the forerunner of Richard Daft and, later, Arthur Shrewsbury and William Gunn, in a Nottinghamshire lineage of pure batting class. He had a sound defence, and was a shot-maker to all parts of the ground, but mainly to the leg side: an elm standing outside the Trent Bridge boundary was so peppered with his sweeps and pulls that it became known as 'Parr's tree', and upon his death a limb was lopped from it and placed on the coffin at his funeral. In his twenty-seven-year first-class career Parr toured America in 1859, and captained the second English tour to Australia that performed memorably on the pitch and so shamefully off it. When William Clarke retired as captain and Secretary of the All-England Eleven the shrewd and businesslike Parr succeeded him, and he retained the position until 1870, despite also captaining Nottinghamshire for much of that time.

A decade after Parr began came Richard Daft, whose first-class career stretched from 1858 to 1891. Uniquely, Daft began and ended as an amateur, but played as a professional for most of his illustrious career. This enabled him to be one of only two players to represent both the Gentlemen and the Players, the other being Edwin Diver of Warwickshire. Daft batted in the classic upright style seen a hundred years later in Ted Dexter at his best. He used his feet to drive the ball, excelled at the now-defunct 'draw' shot, and was masterly, as Ned Willsher acknowledged, at facing fast bowling on poor wickets.

Cambridgeshire were a major force in cricket in the 1860s, when Robert Carpenter and Tom Hayward (uncle of the later Surrey batsman of the same name) led the batting and George Tarrant was the main strike bowler. Oddly, Carpenter played for the United Eleven and Hayward for the All-England Eleven, so in commercial matches they often played against one another, although they toured America in 1859 and Australia in 1863–64 together. They were also on the same side in the notorious Surrey vs England match in 1862 in which Willsher was no-balled and the schism between north and south took root, Carpenter contributing 94 and Hayward 117 to England's then record score of 503. After their departure from cricket Cambridgeshire faded, and it never again became a first-class county.

The great mid-century bowlers, apart from Jackson, Tarrant and Willsher, were Cris Tinley and the left-arm Billy Buttress. In 1847 Tinley made his debut for Nottinghamshire against an England Eleven as a sixteen-year-old fast round-arm bowler. As a batsman he had a quick eye and could hit bowlers off a length, but his cross-batted technique was too vulnerable to make him a heavy run-scorer. Later he converted to a slow lob bowler of sufficient deadliness to take over 2,300 wickets for the All-England Eleven. Buttress, like Tarrant, bowled round-arm for Cambridgeshire, but neither of them enjoyed a long life. Over-fond of drink, the fun-loving Buttress, known as a joker and ventriloquist, died at thirty-eight years of age; but even so he outlived Tarrant, who died of pleurisy at only thirty-one. When wholly sober and at his best, Buttress bowled medium-pace, breaking the ball sharply from leg to off in a delivery that appears similar to Alec Bedser's great leg cutter. All these bowlers operated on poor wickets, but even so their career records and contemporary reports show them to be formidable cricketers.

By the early 1870s the allure of the travelling elevens was fading, and inter-county cricket accelerated towards becoming the mainstay of the first-class game. A galaxy of talent began to appear as Arthur Shrewsbury, Walter Read, Lord Harris, Richard Barlow, A.N. Hornby, Cuthbert Ottaway, Ivo Bligh, the Studd brothers,* Charles Thornton, A.G. Steel, the Walker brothers and A.P. Lucas all made their debuts in inter-county fixtures. In the dry summer of 1874 more first-class games were played than ever before, but the bowlers held the whip hand, and only a minority of matches lasted through to a third day.

This was a good age for the press. Newspapers' circulations, and thus their influence, had grown as a result of wider literacy and a reduction in price, as taxes on newsprint and advertising were dropped. Obtaining news copy had been eased by the founding of the Reuters press agency in 1851. *The Times*, the premier paper, cut its price from seven pence to three pence, and saw its daily sales rise by 75 per cent to seventy thousand copies between 1851 and 1861. The *Standard*, published morning and evening, sold 130,000 copies daily, and the *Telegraph* 150,000 in the evening alone.

All of these papers reported cricket, and they began to add drama to the informal games by constructing an artificial 'Championship'. This was based on inconsistent fixture lists (some counties arranged fixtures against weak opponents, whereas others chose stronger teams so as to maximise gate receipts) and haphazard points systems. Nonetheless, although unscientific, a consensus often emerged, as one team was so dominant that its pre-eminence was widely acknowl-

* The six remarkable Studd brothers were: A.H. (Middlesex), C.T. (Middlesex), G.B. (Middlesex), H.W. (Middlesex and Hampshire), J.E.K. (Middlesex) and R.A. (Hampshire).

edged: in the previous decade Surrey (1864), Nottinghamshire (1865), Middlesex (1866) and Yorkshire (1867 and 1870) all had strong claims to the 'unofficial' County Championship. In the 1870s Gloucestershire and Nottinghamshire generally dominated, with Lancashire emerging in the second half of the decade.

In 1872 the infant Football Association, prompted by its Honorary Secretary Charles Alcock, Secretary of Surrey Cricket Club, inaugurated the FA Cup as a knockout competition. Its appeal was obvious, and the following year the MCC proposed a similar competition for cricket. Despite hostility from Surrey, who didn't want their fixtures disturbed by an MCC-inspired competition, and W.G. Grace, who didn't want his purse disturbed by United South of England players turning out for their counties, the competition went ahead. It began at Lord's with a Kent–Sussex encounter. Sadly, it ended there too. Upon the usual wretched Lord's wicket several Sussex players were injured, and *Wisden* recorded one batsman's demise as 'not out (retired, hurt by Mr Coles' bowling)'. Kent won by 52 runs in a little over a day, but it was an empty victory, and the competition was abandoned.

As inter-county fixtures grew, the clubs began to band together informally to regulate cricket. The term 'first-class' began to be commonly used to describe top-class cricket,* and old-fashioned terms such as 'great' or 'grand' matches fell away. In May 1873, at the instigation of Surrey (once more prompted by C.W. Alcock), rules were introduced to prevent mercenary players from turning out for counties for which they had no residency qualifications. This had been a long-standing irritation to Surrey. A few years earlier, in 1866, Charles Payne had scored 135 not out against them as a Kent player, and in the very next match a further 95 playing for Sussex. Surrey had not forgotten, or forgiven. In their view, some qualifications were paper-thin: 'A man need only sleep one night in London to be qualified for Middlesex,' was the acid judgement of one Surrey

---

* *Bell's Life* first used the term in 1849, describing a player as 'barely good enough for a first-class match'. In 1856 it published a table of 'first' and 'second' class batting. But not until the 1870s was the term widely used.

Right Three of the remarkable Studd brothers. From left, J.E.K, C.T. and G.B. They captained Cambridge University in consecutive seasons, and C.T and G.B. played Test cricket for England. Later two became missionaries, and one (J.E.K.) became Lord Mayor of London.

Below 'The Demon' – Frederick Spofforth, the first of the great Australian bowlers. Tall, lithe and lean, it was said that his satanic looks gained him as many wickets as his devilish accuracy.

Below right The Hon. Ivo Bligh led the English team which recovered the Ashes in Australia in 1882–83. He was a genial, kindly man, whose widow presented the Ashes urn to the MCC.

Lord Harris batting at Lord's for the Lords and Commons Eleven against the touring Canadians in 1922. Seventy-one years old, he scored a useful fifteen runs.

Right A.S. Wortley's portrait of W.G. was commissioned by the MCC through £1 subscriptions between 1888 and 1890. Grace is portrayed in an MCC cap and brown boots, with the old Lord's tennis court as background.

Below Lillie Langtry turns her back as the Prince of Wales arrives at Lord's for an imaginary Test match in 1887. W.G. Grace keeps his mind on the cricket and takes a single.

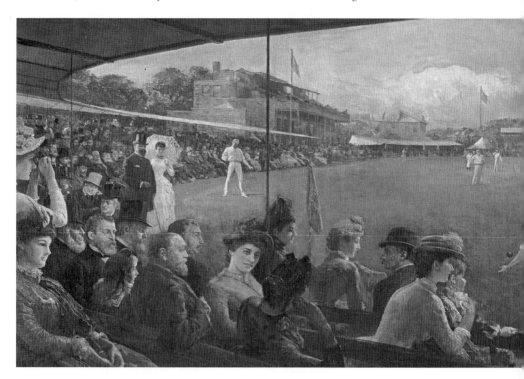

Below The Surrey batsman
W.E. Roller on his way to bat at
The Oval, painted by his brother
George in 1883.

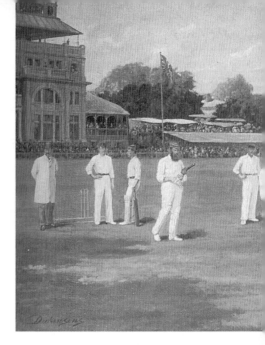

William Scotton was a noted stonewaller. Twice he batted for an hour without scoring, but in 1893 he committed suicide after his cricket career ended.

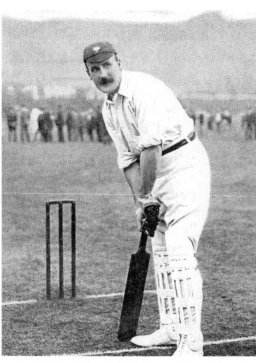

Lord Hawke, seen here while captain of Yorkshire, was a formidable leader. Self-confident, opinionated and haughty, he once said, 'Pray God no professional shall ever captain England.'

Arthur Shrewsbury, one of the greatest batsmen in Victorian England for over two decades. Firm and confident on the field, but haunted by insecurities off it, he shot himself in 1903.

Gentlemen vs Players at Lord's is an imaginary composition of the famous players of 1895. W.G. Grace comes in to partner Andrew Stoddart, while the Players' wicketkeeper Sherwin chats to the umpire.

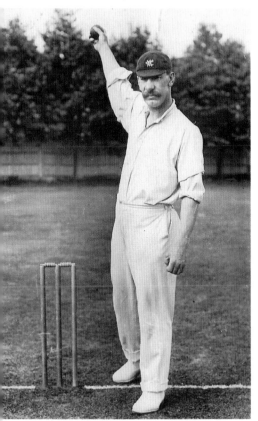

The magnificent all-rounder Albert Trott is the only man to have hit a ball over the pavilion at Lord's. He found life more difficult than cricket, and shot himself in 1914.

Ranjitsinhji, of whom Neville Cardus wrote, 'All other batsmen are labourers in comparison.' This Indian prince enchanted spectators with his wristy technique, and his torrent of runs for Sussex and England.

Stanley Jackson, born to the purple, son of a Cabinet Minister, and blessed with sublime cricketing skills. 'Jacker', who captained England, but never his county Yorkshire, was the first man to score five centuries against Australia in England.

Below Victor Trumper unfolded his full genius on the Australian tour of England in 1902. As a man he was mild-mannered and generous to a fault, but the majesty of his batting left spectators awe-struck. After his death, aged thirty-seven, he became a cult figure in Australian cricket.

The mightiest of all of cricket's great entertainers was Gilbert 'the Croucher' Jessop. He was never a 'slogger', but an instinctive, scientific destroyer of bowling. Some of his scoring feats seem to belong to the realms of fiction.

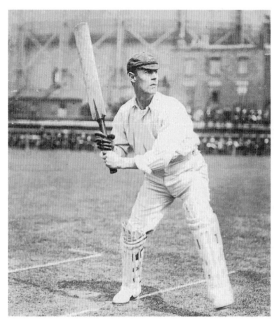

Left Three giants of Victorian cricket: William Murdoch, C.B. Fry and W.G. Grace. This photograph was taken in 1901 at Crystal Palace, where all three were playing for the newly formed London County.

Albert Chevallier Tayler's marvellous *Kent vs Lancashire at Canterbury* celebrates Kent's first official championship, in 1906. Colin Blythe bowls to Johnny Tyldesley of Lancashire from wide on the crease, in a match which Kent won by an innings.

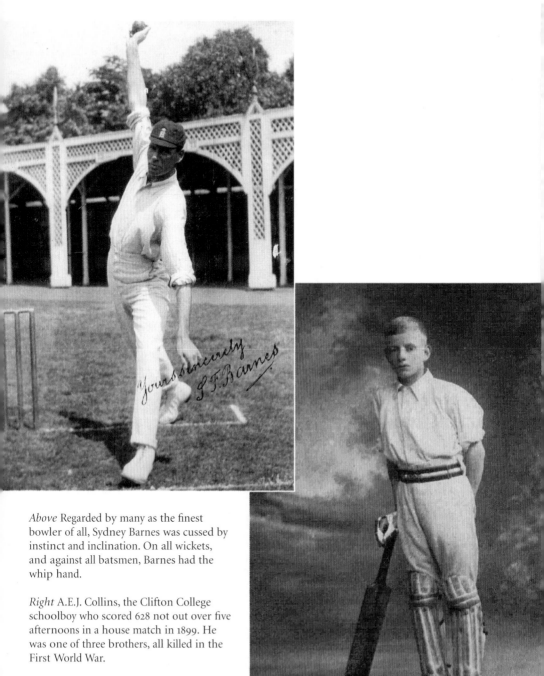

Above Regarded by many as the finest
bowler of all, Sydney Barnes was cussed by
instinct and inclination. On all wickets,
and against all batsmen, Barnes had the
whip hand.

Right A.E.J. Collins, the Clifton College
schoolboy who scored 628 not out over five
afternoons in a house match in 1899. He
was one of three brothers, all killed in the
First World War.

member, apparently forgetting that, prior to 1873, Surrey had happily shared Southerton with Sussex. Nevertheless, with the indefatigable Charles Alcock as Secretary of their meetings, the principal counties – Surrey, Yorkshire, Sussex, Nottinghamshire, Lancashire, Kent, Middlesex, Derbyshire and Gloucestershire – determined a qualification of birth or two years' residence before a player could represent a county, and restricted individuals to one county only in a given season. In an acknowledgement of its influence, the MCC was invited to adjudicate in any dispute.

Although the new counties jealously guarded their independence, they accepted the right of the MCC to preside over important amendments to cricket laws, to encourage positive results and enhance the free flow of the game. From 1870 bowlers were permitted to change ends twice, not once, in an innings, although to prohibit abuse they could not bowl two successive overs. In 1883 the MCC ruled that the batting side could have the wicket rolled before play began on the second and third days of a match. The purpose of this innovation was to remove the disadvantage to the batting team if overnight rain, or heavy dew, had affected the uncovered wicket. That same season, umpires were forbidden to stand in any game in which their native county was playing, thus removing an old suspicion of preference that had caused many an upset.

The decade ended with the successful Australian tour of 1878, a continuing rise in the number of inter-county fixtures, and the appalling summer of 1879, with a huge number of rain-affected matches being abandoned. Those that were completed were often swiftly decided upon wet and sticky wickets.

From 1882 the county club secretaries began to meet annually. The teams of the early part of the decade were Nottinghamshire and Lancashire, but in the latter half Surrey came to the fore. Nottinghamshire were indisputably the team of 1880, despite squabbles over pay with their professional players, who had been unsettled by the Australian tourists receiving a share of their tour proceeds that exceeded the fees paid to English professionals. It would not be the last dispute of its kind, as professionals enviously eyed the earnings of 'amateurs' such as Grace and, later, Walter Read of Surrey and Andrew Stoddart of Middlesex. Read was even receiving £120 a year from a fake job as Assistant Secretary of Surrey, as well as an annual bonus that was twice that offered to Surrey's professionals.

The powerful Nottinghamshire side had a seemingly unending supply of talented local players. The finest of them all was Arthur Shrewsbury, who played for the county for twenty-seven seasons. Technically gifted, with a perfect defence, he reached a peak in the mid-1880s, and sustained it. His life, however, is a paradox, and it is doubtful if he was a happy man. Quiet and retiring by nature, he was a prominent supporter of professional militancy. Yet he was so sensitive about his premature baldness that he was never seen bareheaded even when changing for cricket. A lifelong bachelor, he was perpetually worried about his indifferent health, ultimately with a tragic outcome. Yet in the 1880s he was probably, Grace included, the finest bat in the country. In 1887 he totalled 1,653 runs, with eight centuries, including 267 against Middlesex at Trent Bridge, and an average for the season of a little over 78.

Shrewsbury's run-scoring companion for Nottinghamshire was the giant William Gunn. Before joining the county Gunn was employed by Richard Daft, but his graceful batting ensured his career as a professional. A double century for MCC against Yorkshire at Lord's in 1885 made his reputation, and he remained at the top for twenty years. He scored forty-eight first-class centuries, and five times in his career was part of a partnership of over 300 runs, three of them with Shrewsbury.* With Shrewsbury and Gunn supported by the great stonewaller William Scotton, William Barnes and Harry Daft, son of Richard, Nottinghamshire had a powerful batting line-up. In their (unofficial) Championship years of 1883–86, the county lost only two games. Fred Morley died in 1883, but Alfred Shaw, Charles Wright and Wilfred Flowers were still around to take the wickets.

* 398 (Gunn 196, Shrewsbury 267) for Nottinghamshire vs Sussex, Trent Bridge, 1890; 369 (Gunn 139, J. Gunn 294) for Nottinghamshire vs Leicestershire, Trent Bridge, 1903; 330 (Gunn 203, Barnes 140 not out) for MCC and Ground vs Yorkshire, Lord's, 1885; 312 (Gunn 161, Shrewsbury 165) for Nottinghamshire vs Sussex, Brighton, 1891; 310 (Gunn 150, Shrewsbury 236) for Non-Smokers vs Smokers, East Melbourne, 1886–87

While the Nottinghamshire side was predominantly made up of local players. Lancashire was not. Their great opening batsmen, Hornby, who captained England at cricket and rugby, and Barlow, the first man to open both the batting and the bowling in a Test match, were home-bred, but the suspected 'throwers' who led the attack, Jack Crossland, Alec Watson and George Nash, were all imports. The rows about the legality of their actions were intense (see pages 312–13), and created friction with Kent, Surrey and Nottingham, but the quality of the team was undoubted. With the cadaverous Dick Pilling* behind the stumps and Allan Steel and Johnny Briggs as all-rounders, they were a formidable side. Steel played relatively few games for Lancashire, but the small and chubby Briggs made his debut at sixteen, and 2,000 wickets and 14,000 runs made him the most successful all-rounder in the county's history. His gift of quoting lengthy extracts from Shakespeare suggests he was among the most erudite as well. One minor weakness was Hornby's running between the wickets. He ran out Barlow for nought the first time they batted together, and thereafter paid him a sovereign for every transgression. Shrewsbury once recorded that he was sorry when Hornby was out, as 'otherwise he would have run everyone else out'.

Surrey began the decade in decline as Jupp, Humphrey and Pooley drew to the end of their careers. But W.W. Read, Maurice Read, Bobby Abel, William Roller, Kingsmill Key and, in mid-decade, George Lohmann, transformed Surrey into a Championship side which dominated the county scene as surely as Jack the Ripper terrorised the East End. In 1886, an appalling summer that left many games unfinished, Surrey twice beat the touring Australians, with Maurice Read scoring 186 in the second game. It was a fitting prelude to six successive Championships, one shared, between 1887 and 1892.

The main engine of success was George Lohmann. In 1888 he took 142 wickets in fourteen county games at less than 9 runs a wicket. Lancashire were beaten in a day at Old Trafford, Lohmann

---

* Pilling was a sick man from the early 1880s. He died of consumption, aged thirty-five, in 1891.

taking 13 wickets for 51 runs. John Beaumont, a Yorkshireman, took 8 for 40 against his home county, and with Thomas Bowley gave Surrey a devastating strike force. Sussex suffered one of the worst defeats in history at The Oval, where they were beaten by an innings and 485 runs.

Other teams fell well behind the three leaders. Kent, despite the efforts of Lord Harris, had only limited success in the 1880s. Gloucestershire, the Graces notwithstanding, were well off the pace. Middlesex had powerful batting, but no bowling attack to capitalise on the runs scored. They suffered an irreplaceable loss when Charles Studd, the best-known of the six brothers, left cricket to become a missionary, as, later, did his brother George. His mother was horrified and his family dismayed, but Studd had an ambition 'to run a rescue shop within a yard of hell'. He did so in China and Africa for the next forty-six years. Yorkshire, despite the prime of Hall and Ulyett, the efforts of Emmett, Peate and Peel, and the appointment of Lord Hawke as captain in 1883, did not emerge as county champions for another ten years.

Even apart from W.G. Grace, there were some memorable individual performances. Shrewsbury scored 164 at Lord's for England against Australia on a foul wicket with Spofforth in full cry. It was the innings of the decade. In 1887 Walter Read made 247 and 244 in successive matches against Lancashire and Cambridge University, and a year later 338 against Oxford University and three successive hundreds. Such scoring was Grace-like in its abundance. In 1882 G.F. Vernon and A.H. Trevor put on 603 for the second wicket for the Orleans Club. Poor Rickling Green, their opponents, were dismissed for 94 against Orleans's total of 903.

In 1888 the short-lived County Cricket Council, set up at the initiative of Lord Harris the previous year (see page 313), faced an awkward motion from Nottinghamshire, who wished to prevent players qualified for one county from playing for any other if their home county required them. Yorkshire, in the formidable person of their autocratic and traditionalist Chairman M.J. Ellison, agreed – and so did W.G. Grace. Lord Harris, displaying the liberal-conservative element of his nature, argued that professional players should be able to move their talents, and after fierce debate he won the vote 7–5. It was to be his last contribution to the Council he founded before he decamped to govern Bombay, and with it he won an important freedom for professional players.

It was also a wise decision. The Nottingham motion represented a restraint of trade entirely out of touch with contemporary opinion. Beyond cricket, pressure groups such as the Fabian Society were advocating practical socialism, and trying to persuade the radical Liberals, and moderate Conservatives of the Harris mould, to adopt it. George Bernard Shaw's observation that 'The middle and upper classes are the revolutionary element in society; the proletariat is the conservative element,' explained this wooing of the major parties. As the tributaries of socialism came together in the late 1880s, public support for labour reform and the working man was widespread. If Harris had not prevailed, a cricketers' strike might have received the same mass endorsement offered to strikes by match girls in 1888 and dockers a year later. As the dockers' strike began, Henry Hyndman, late of Sussex Cricket Club, was a prominent speaker at the dock gates. Both the dockers and the match girls had good cause for grievance, and public support forced employers to meet their demands. The heyday of naked capitalism was past its peak. The cricket establishment owed Harris their thanks: they would not have enjoyed losing a pitched battle with the cricketers.

Some old enemies of the game were still alive. Sunday cricket, which had been such anathema to the Puritans, continued to suffer from ecclesiastical opponents and perverse laws. The issue surfaced intermittently throughout the nineteenth century. A week before Victoria succeeded to the throne, the vicar at West Malling, Kent, denounced as sinners all those who attended a match between Kent and Sussex, including neighbouring clergymen. Six years later, in 1843, seven boys were fined three shillings (plus costs of twelve shillings) for playing cricket on their village green at Hurley in Berkshire on the Sabbath. *Bell's Life* denounced the complainant as a 'saintly person with the name of religion on his tongue, but with a heart wholly destitute of its true principles'. Lord John Manners raised the issue in Parliament, asking the Attorney General – amid loud cries of support – whether 'it was illegal for the working classes ... to play cricket on Sunday after Divine Service'. His question had a sting in its tail: 'If so, is it legal for the rich to drive out in their carriages on that day?'

The absurdity of the situation was exposed by the Attorney General's reply. He advised that, under existing statute law, the boys were not liable to punishment for playing in their own parish, but would be if they played outside it. The boys' fines were paid anonymously, but similar cases continued to arise. In 1858, at East Burnham in Buckinghamshire, fines of fifteen shillings *or six weeks in Aylesbury gaol* were handed down from the bench. Such sour justice may have curbed cricket, but it left would-be cricketers to while away their time in beer shops or public houses, while the public common was left empty. Some cricket clubs banned Sunday play, while others existed to play only on Sundays.

In the mid-1880s a correspondent to *Bell's Life* reported that in London 'football and cricket was taboo'ed on all public grounds' on Sundays, along with swimming, dancing and music. He also referred to a Sunday game in Leicester in June 1885 between a scratch team and the Secular Club. The police permitted the match to proceed, but pro- and anti-Sunday play demonstrators clashed, the pitch was stormed and the players were threatened with being thrown into the river. Their ball *was* thrown into the river, but a cricket-lover's dog retrieved it. The game, however, was abandoned. Such scenes suggested that not much had changed in two and a half centuries.

In 1889 there were further changes to cricket law, although not to the laws relating to cricket. An over was increased from four balls to five, and bowlers were permitted to change the end from which they bowled as often as they wished, provided they did not bowl two overs in succession. Finally, the batting side was permitted to declare its innings closed whenever the captain wished in a one-day game, or on the last day of a three-day game. This last amendment was to end the farcical situation in which captains were not permitted to declare an innings closed, and so instructed their batsmen to throw away their wickets in order to end the innings as quickly as possible, a tactic which John Shuter of Surrey did not hesitate to use. All these modifications balanced the game better, cut down on the frequency of drawn matches and encouraged positive results.

In the twenty-year span of these innovations the number of inter-county matches multiplied dramatically from the mere handful played in 1870, and as a consequence the number of old-fashioned commercial games declined. The time was ripe to set up a formal County Championship, although the birth pains would be severe for some counties. After a controversial debate the County Cricket Council decided to classify county sides and place them in three separate divisions. The top eight teams, Yorkshire, Surrey, Kent, Gloucestershire, Lancashire, Middlesex, Nottinghamshire and Sussex, formed the top division, with Derbyshire, Warwickshire, Essex, Leicestershire, Staffordshire, Somerset, Cheshire and Hampshire in the second tier. A third tier would consist of Norfolk, Northants, Northumberland, Durham, Devonshire, Hertfordshire, Lincolnshire and Glamorgan. These largely arbitrary designations were widely resented, but the principle of a County Championship was agreed. Once again the railways had a role in cricket history. The county sides that came together to form the championship were all linked to the primary rail network from London. Other early cricket centres – Hertford, Bedford, Ipswich, Cambridge, Buckingham – were not. None of these were included in the initial Championship, and none has since broken into it.

The organisation of cricket differentiated it starkly from football. Cricket was based on counties, whereas football teams, formed in the same era, were based on towns. Superficially this is odd, since until 1900 spectators were twice as likely to watch cricket as to attend football matches, and logic suggests therefore that of the two sports it is cricket that should have been organised upon units with a smaller population. Yet history dictated otherwise. Football's origins were urban, but cricket had begun as a rural pastime, and the assumption of 'counties' seemed a familiar and natural basis for the organisation of the game. The creation of county councils in 1888 may have reinforced that instinct. Whether so or not, the county system was to form a lasting basis of the game in England.

14

The Chroniclers and the Scribes

They tell us who played. Who batted. And bowled. And caught. To the dispassionate eye their records are mere jumbles of names and numbers, but to the cricket-lover they are a gateway to games long gone and days that, if they cannot be relived, can be reconstructed. The men who kept the scores, and bequeathed them to us, are the archaeologists of cricket, the chroniclers who reopen the past and make it vivid for today – and forever.

With a scorebook every ball of a game can be relived, and the drama of a long-dead match can be experienced again. The aficionado will speak gaily of 'Fowler's match' (Eton vs Harrow, Lord's, 1910) or 'Spofforth's match' (England vs Australia, The Oval, 1882), 'Cobden's match' (F.C. Cobden took a hat-trick with the last three balls of the game as Cambridge University beat Oxford by 3 runs in 1870), or individual innings or analyses, and will know the games and their outcomes almost as if he had been there. Almost. The knowledge we have lacks some of the incident, some of the flesh of the actual encounter, but the bones are there, reconstructed as a skeleton that offers more information to the enquiring eye than a well-preserved Egyptian mummy. The chroniclers have told us much about cricket, but little of themselves. But they too deserve their story to be told, for they are few in number and our debt to them is very great.

When cricket was young, runs were 'notches' carved on sticks by innumerate peasants and overs (once a pattern was established) were of four balls each, but analyses of bowling were not kept and batsmen were dismissed without acknowledgement to the skills of the bowler. Out of this statistical wilderness order was established and, slowly but inexorably, more information began to be recorded, until in the fullness of time a line of statisticians appeared that stretches now from Samuel Britcher and William Epps to Bill Frindall.

These days the cricket enthusiast will turn to *Wisden* to refresh his memory of games gone by, or to look up career records or any detail, however remote, that intrigues him. *Wisden* is indispensable to settle arguments, and a comfort to cricket-lovers in the bleak months when the game is abroad for the winter. But cricket has been played for over five centuries, and *Wisden*, however invaluable it may be, only began its life in 1864, and for records of the game before then, we must look elsewhere.

Three men who died long before John Wisden published his first *Almanack* – a mystery man, a would-be politician and an eminent former cricketer – helped cast a light on the history of the game when nothing, or at least very little, was known of it. None of their records is as complete or as accurate as *Wisden* would later become, and each contains errors and omissions. Nonetheless, they are an invaluable insight into cricket in an age of which we know too little and wish to know more. A fourth man, a cricketer and a contemporary of the new *Almanack*, would dwarf all previous chroniclers after a lifetime of research into the early days of cricket.

Very little is known about the mystery man, Samuel Britcher, except that between 1790 and 1805 he compiled the scores of matches played each year. Tantalisingly, his name appears only in passing in contemporary references. It seems he did not merit anecdote or flesh-and-blood description, so he remains a shadowy figure, dimly lit up only by conjecture.

We can be almost certain that Britcher was the first official scorer for the MCC, and that his publications largely relate to the games he attended. We can picture him sitting alongside Aislabie and Beau-clerk, pencil in hand, as he records cricket at Lord's, either from a seat in the old wooden pavilion or sitting on the edge of the field of play. A great deal of research by cricket historians, notably David

Rayvern Allen in *Britcher's Scores* (2003), makes it probable that Britcher was born in 1744 at Linton, near Maidstone, which is suggestively near to the Linton Estate of the early cricket patron Sir Horace Mann. It is possible, but not provable, that Sir Horace, a leading figure in the MCC, encouraged Britcher to score for the team, much as Thomas Lord had been commissioned by Lord Winchilsea to find a ground for the old White Conduit Club.

But we can't be positive of this without more specific contemporary references which, if they exist, remain hidden. Nor, since Britcher was a not uncommon name in Kent at the time, can we be absolutely certain that the Samuel Britcher born in Linton is the scorer, although it is likely. A further clue is that the first volume of his *Principal Matches* was printed in Maidstone. None of this, however, is conclusive, and if no further information is uncovered in some dusty garret, we must simply be grateful that a light was cast on early cricket by the diligence of an anonymous man.

There is nothing anonymous in the colourful personality of William Epps, who in 1799 published *A Collection of All the Grand Matches of Cricket played in England within Twenty Years, viz. from 1771 to 1791*. He noted that it was unnecessary to record later years, as Samuel Britcher was doing so on an annual basis. At the time, of course, the market for such scores would have been very restricted, and the cost of printing small numbers of scorebooks would have been correspondingly large. Duplicating Britcher's work was unlikely to be a commercial proposition, and Epps saw no point in it. Nonetheless, his two decades of pre-Britcher scores are invaluable.

Epps collected his scores from the papers of 'several gentlemen', which presumably implies enthusiasts who had played in the games. Rustic cricketers are likely to have been illiterate, and in any case would not have been referred to as 'gentlemen', so it was probably the familiar figures of Dorset, Winchilsea, Tankerville and Horace Mann who provided the raw material which Epps collated and 'carefully corrected'. As he did not dedicate his volume to a patron it is safe to assume that it was not subsidised, and nor was the information from a single source, which would surely have been acknowledged.

It is not clear whether Epps undertook his research in the hope of making a profit, or whether, as is equally likely, it was a labour of love by a cricketing enthusiast and inveterate pamphleteer. Unsurprisingly, later research has revealed that Epps's records are not comprehensive, and they ignore matches outside the south-east. Nonetheless, they provide a glimpse into late-eighteenth-century cricket that otherwise would be missing.

Cricket was not the only passion in Epps's life. He twice unsuccessfully contested the Rochester parliamentary seat, as well as the mayoralty of the town. He was a man with a social conscience and a radical turn of mind, with opinions that he had no wish to keep to himself. Pamphlets such as *Truth Unmasked*, written by C. Larkin and published by Epps, and *An Antidote to Electioneering Calumny* (probably written by Epps) reveal him to be the sort of rumbustious controversialist who overstates his case and rarely becomes a serious politician. Such men as Epps frighten off more conformist minds. He is the sort of individual who has views too eccentric to be taken seriously, but who in modern times might become an irreverent, sometimes scurrilous and probably widely read, columnist in a national newspaper.

Unlike Britcher and Epps, the next chronicler, Henry Bentley, was a notable cricketer and a participant in some of the matches he recorded. He was born in Cavendish Square, London, on 19 February 1782, and first played at Lord's for the MCC against London in May 1798, at the age of sixteen. A safe batsman and occasional change bowler, he settled comfortably into the top flight of cricket. In the first ever eleven-a-side game on the present-day Lord's ground (earlier single-wicket games had been played) he opened the batting and top-scored as a given player for Hertfordshire against the MCC with 33 not out in a total of 79 in the first innings. He played with all the top players of the early nineteenth century, and was a popular figure. When he was given run out while playing for All-England against Nottinghamshire in 1815, having clearly gained his ground before the stumps were broken, Billy Beldham remarked, 'Why, he has been home long enough to take a pinch of snuff.' It mattered not: Bentley was out, although the erring umpire was replaced. Bentley was phlegmatic about it all: this man of 'abstentious habits and steady and sober disposition'* played for England, MCC, Hampshire, Hertfordshire and Middlesex, ending his first-class career for the Players against the Gentlemen at Lord's in 1822 – again run out, this time for 5. It was the first time the Gentlemen beat the Players on even terms; nor did they do so again for twenty years.

For most of this time Bentley lived in Lisson Grove, then as now adjacent to the Lord's ground. Upon his retirement he swiftly published, in 1823, a book covering scores between 1786 and 1822, a far longer period than either Epps or Britcher. He followed this with contemporary appendices covering the seasons 1823–25.

In 1826 Bentley moved to Norwich, where he became groundsman, coach and veteran player of the Norwich Club. In January 1827 a Norfolk County Cricket Club was formed at a meeting in the Rampant Horse inn, and in April the club took a lease on a field at Lakenham, where Bentley supervised the laying-down of a cricket pitch claimed to be 'one of the best in the Kingdom'. He continued to play for Norwich for three more years before settling in Hereford, where he was landlord of the Cricketers' Arms, Widemarsh, and from 1838, at the age of fifty-six, groundsman, coach and ground bowler to Hereford Cricket Club. He was soon a local institution, and the ground was considered to be 'an ornament to the City of Hereford'.** Controversy engulfed Bentley in 1847 when, as umpire, he gave a disputed decision in favour of Hereford, and their opponents, Shropshire, walked off the pitch hurling abuse at him.

This local squabble spread widely, and William Ward, saviour of Lord's and Governor of the Bank of England, came to the defence of his old cricketing colleague. It was, said Ward, 'impossible to doubt Bentley's competence', as 'a more honest cricketer never set foot on a greensward'. This was high praise, even hyperbole, from an eminent figure, and the dispute faded away. As Bentley aged, his health failed, and whether it is coincidence or not, so did that of the Hereford

* According to Arthur Haygarth, *Scores and Biographies*, Vol. I.
** Letter to *Hereford Times*, October 1845.

Club. In 1857 an ailing Bentley was admitted as an almsman to Coningsby Hospital in Hereford – Anthony Trollope's model for Hiram's Hospital in *The Warden* – and there he died, aged seventy-five, in September 1857. Bentley's scores, completed in 1826, one year after the Lord's fire destroyed all the records held there, were used (not always accurately) to recreate the MCC match book, and assumed a cricketing value their author could never have imagined. But even as his records were being copied, a greater compiler of cricket statistics had made his entrance.

It is an irony of history that Arthur Haygarth was born in Hastings on 4 August 1825, within days of the fire that destroyed the Lord's pavilion and all the ancient records of cricket held within it. He would die seventy-eight years later, having written five million words, covering ten thousand pages, about cricketers and the matches they played. In all he published fourteen volumes of *Cricket Scores and Biographies*, covering the years 1744 to 1878, with a supplement on notable players after that date. It was a lifetime's work of sixty years, undertaken for love of the game, that began as the enthusiasm of a boy. Aged fourteen, Haygarth, then at Harrow, bought a copy of Henry Bentley's scores, published in 1823. Two years later he began collating scores himself, and never stopped.

Haygarth was not only a scribe. He played for Harrow in their two victories over Eton at Lord's in 1842 and 1843. In 1844, he became a playing member of the MCC, and over the next twenty years he took part in over 150 games, mostly at Lord's. He batted first wicket down, and had a near impenetrable defence, but only a small battery of attacking shots. Although good enough to be selected for the Gentlemen against the Players on sixteen occasions, Haygarth was never an example of brighter cricket; he occupied the crease for a long time, often on vile wickets, and compiled his runs, mostly singles, with the same methodical persistence that he applied to gathering cricket records. In 1846 he took four hours to score 26 for the Gentlemen at Lord's. Even that was speedy when compared to his 16 in three hours for MCC against Hampshire. The sight of this tall, thin, dark-complexioned man crouching over his bat must have driven bowlers to despair. His highest score was 97 for MCC against Surrey Club and Ground in 1855, but his most famous innings was in 1857, again for the Gentlemen against the Players, when, coming in first wicket down, he made an undefeated 53 in an innings of 194. As he was facing Wisden, Jackson and Caffyn, it was a notable effort, although it was overshadowed by a whirlwind 70 from Reginald Hankey. In his final game, in 1861, he scored 46 against Hampshire for the MCC, and in 1864 he was elected a life member of the club.

By then he had spent over twenty years collecting scores, and he would continue to do so for nearly four decades more. It was a phenomenal effort, undertaken entirely for pleasure. But it was hard work. Epps, Britcher and Bentley had recorded only the batsman's score and mode of dismissal – scanty information and far less than we would wish to know – whereas Haygarth prepared both a full record of matches and exhaustive information about the players. In all he covered 8,500 matches and over 3,100 biographies, and in doing so enriched cricket history.

His achievement is even more extraordinary in an age that pre-dated databases, telephones, faxes and speedy travel. Haygarth visited the principal centres of cricket, often many times, and handwrote thousands of letters. His persistence rivals that of Sonya Tolstoy, who repeatedly rewrote amended drafts of her husband's epic *War and Peace*. There are of course mistakes in Haygarth's finished work, but surprisingly few.

The publication of his research led to many frustrations for Haygarth, not least because of the cost. The Surrey captain, F.P. Miller, helped finance early volumes, the first four of which were published between 1862 and 1863 by Fred Lillywhite. But this relationship foundered when Lillywhite untruthfully attempted to claim credit for the compilation of the scores for himself and his late father William. Haygarth promptly corrected him, and Lillywhite withdrew from further publication.

The dilemma Haygarth faced was that only the hyper-enthusiast sought all the information he offered, while other less expensive publications pandered to the mass audience. Publication of exhaustive cricket records was a loss-making enterprise, invaluable to history but costly to the publisher. A sponsor was needed. Finally the MCC stepped in, and fourteen years after the publication of the previous volume, further volumes began to appear in 1876, continuing until 1895. This too was an unhappy collaboration – 'They treat me badly,' grumbled Haygarth – but history was the beneficiary. Volume XV was not published until long after Haygarth's death in 1903, when the cricket historian F.S. Ashley-Cooper supervised its production. It consists of a thousand biographies covering eminent cricketers between 1879 and 1898, and index references to the earlier fourteen volumes. Haygarth's full contribution, in its immensity, makes him the greatest of all cricket chroniclers. It is sad that he died somewhat embittered, never realising the value posterity would place on his life's work. Volume XVI was finally published in 2003.

Apart from Haygarth's endeavours, mass-audience publications began to appear from the middle of the nineteenth century. William Denison's *Cricketer's Companion* (1844–47) provided scores and a review of each season, while *Lillywhite's Guide to Cricketers* (1849–66), a paperback which was absorbed into *Lillywhite's Companion* (1865–85) and *James Lillywhite's Annual* (1872–1900), was the most popular contemporary publication. The modern bible of cricket, *Wisden*, made its debut at a cost of one shilling in 1864 as *The Cricketer's Almanack*, and has been published annually ever since. Despite its name, and the fact that the first issue was published and sold by John Wisden & Co., there is little or no evidence that the great cricketer took an active part in its preparation. Nor was the first edition exclusively about cricket, but it included such irrelevancies as the dates of the Wars of the Roses and information about the length of British canals. It was an inauspicious debut. But over the generations successive editors and staff made *Wisden* an indispensable part of any cricket-lover's library, with its familiar yellow binding offering the promise of memories of great deeds and days in the sun. In 1867 lists of the births and deaths of cricketers first appeared, followed three years later by the first accounts of matches played. In 1872 W.H. Knight began a county-by-county introduction to the forthcoming season. The 1886 volume was delayed by a year, and Charles Pardon became editor until 1890, when his brother Sydney succeeded him and remained in post for thirty-five years. Sydney Pardon made *Wisden* indispensable as the record of cricket, as well as a formidable voice of opinion about the game and those who played it.

Wisden owes much to earlier chroniclers, especially Haygarth, although it was only in its twenty-eighth edition, in 1892, that it finally emulated him and began to incorporate obituaries. In the beginning many of them were perfunctory, although over the years they grew into a great catalogue of cricket history. All human life is in the obituary pages, from the monumental entry upon W.G. Grace's death in 1915 to the acknowledgement that Edward Rae (died June 1923) introduced cricket into Russian Lapland. There are humour and poignancy aplenty in the lives that are recalled. George Remnant, a friend of Charles Dickens, batting in a field beside the novelist's home at Gads Hill, hit a ball out of the ground into a pony and trap carrying Dickens's children and governess. The ponies bolted, and Remnant cast down his bat to pursue and halt the vehicle. Albert Trott, the only man to hit a ball over the present Lord's pavilion, sick and with no hope of recovery, shot himself in his lodgings. Edward Pooley, who refused to tour Australia with Grace and was 'in many ways his own worst enemy', died penniless in a workhouse. Billy Murdoch had a fatal seizure at Melbourne while watching Australia play South Africa. And Archie Jackson, a young Australian batsman touched by genius and hailed as the 'second Victor Trumper', died at only twenty-three years of age, having married on his deathbed. Life hands out both harsh and kindly fates, and *Wisden*'s obituaries cover them all.

Much of the lore of cricket is gathered in stories and memoirs, and we owe a debt to those writers whose work offers posterity a glimpse of cricket as they saw it in their time. Among those offering this literary inheritance, a handful stand out. Neville Cardus was born in Manchester in 1890, and his writing does not strictly fall within the compass of this book, except in one respect: Cardus did not shrink from writing in emotional terms about the game he loved. In doing so he evoked the magic and romance of the game as no man before or after. To read Cardus, as to read Dickens, is to have your emotions stirred. It was reading Cardus that encouraged me to look back to earlier ages to discover if his heroes – there were few, if any, villains – had earlier counterparts. I fancy that Cardus often gave reality a little help from his charitable imagination, but if he did the beneficiary was cricket.

No one but Cardus could have added to the game's folklore as he did. Is it really true that the eccentric Cecil Parkin of Lancashire sang 'Little Dolly Daydream' as he ambled up to bowl his off-breaks? Possibly he did, on occasion, if his bowling was good, his life settled and the sun shone. But on a wet and windy day at Old Trafford, I doubt it. Nonetheless, I love the story. And more recently, did school-boys outside Lord's really decline to watch the cricket because 'There are no more Denis Comptons, are there?' The story is wonderfully evocative of the genius of Compton, but it seems to me to be the product more of the romantic instinct of a gifted writer than the thought processes of a London urchin. If Cardus did give truth a hand, he was not alone. So, I fancy, did Nyren in his memories of Hambledon. So did James Love in his first heroic poem of cricket. Cardus was an original in the depth of his talent, but his habit of exaggeration was in an old tradition.

Not every writer was cavalier with facts. Later scribes such as John Arlott and Jim Swanton dealt in reality, albeit in Arlott's case often in purple prose. In Victorian times, W.H. Knight wrote in a florid style that would be mocked today, but which was knowledgeable, and Sydney Pardon enlivened *Wisden*, *Bell's Life* and *The Times* with the highest quality of factual writing. Pardon's obituaries in *Wisden* were models of gentle judgement, although he was fierce in denouncing 'unfair' bowling actions and in his hostility to two-day, as opposed to three-day, cricket.

A handful of Victorian books provide a portrait of early cricket, among them *The Cricket Field* (1851) by the Reverend James Pycroft. *The English Game of Cricket* (1877) by Charles Box and W.W. Read's *Annals of Cricket* (1896) are lively portraits of later days. Three autobiographies, *Seventy-One Not Out* (1899) by William Caffyn, Richard Daft's *Kings of Cricket* (1893) and W.G. Grace's *Cricket* (1891) stand above all others in their evocation of cricketing life, while Nicholas Felix's *Felix on the Bat* (1845), with its charming illustrations, remains a classic exposition of the batsman's art.

The Church, so hostile to early cricket, mellowed to provide both great players and strong advocates of the game. The Reverend Henry Hutchinson Montgomery (1847–1932), father of the Field Marshal who 'hit Rommel for six', opened the batting for Harrow and never lost his love of cricket. His *History of Kennington* (1889) – he was vicar of the parish for many years – focuses on early cricket as 'the greatest outdoor game in the world' and claims it as 'the nursery for healthful, unselfish, open-handed and generous-hearted young men'. From his vicarage Montgomery would have heard vast crowds at The Oval cheering cricket success and bemoaning failure. His predecessor Blue Dick of Minster (see page 26) would have flung himself from his own church steeple at such clerical misbehaviour. His successor the Reverend David Sheppard, captain of Englandand Bishop of Liverpool, would have had Montgomery cheering his play.

But cricket is a dreamer's game, and fiction too has added its tribute. Among poets, Byron played cricket and, as we have seen, misreported the runs he scored. In February 1819, two years after writing 'A thing of beauty is a joy forever', John Keats wrote more prosaically to his brother and sister to tell them of his being hit in the eye by a cricket ball: 'Yesterday, I got a black eye – the first time I took a cricket bat ... and there is no inflammation this morning . . .'twas a white ball.' Keats was lucky – it was a soft practice ball: the first genuine white cricket ball had to await the Kerry Packer revolution 150 years later. The poets' bloodline provided excellent cricketers fifty years later, in the form of Charles Wordsworth and Lionel Tennyson, nephew and grandson respectively of the great poets. We know, too, the delight of playwright Frederick Reynolds when he became an early member of MCC (see page 120). And the impressionist Camille Pissarro, writing to his son, said: 'I'm going to take the house in L'Isle Adam [in south London]. Unhappily, it is right next to the cemetery, but the garden is six or seven times bigger than ours, we shall be able to play cricket . . .'

Sir Arthur Conan Doyle, creator of Sherlock Holmes, both played and wrote about cricket. 'The Story of Spedegue's Dropper' (1928) is a delightful tale of an asthmatic schoolmaster who tosses the ball high in the air, over the batsman's head and onto the top of his wicket, thus winning the Ashes for England. This had in fact once happened, at The Oval in September 1865, when E.M. Grace, with the family gift of stretching the laws of cricket to the utmost, frustrated by Harry Jupp's stonewalling, lobbed the ball over Jupp's head and onto his stumps. The game was held up for nearly an hour as spectators protested, but Jupp was out.

Conan Doyle played ten first-class matches for MCC between 1900 and 1907. He took only one wicket, but magically it was, as he recalled in his poem 'A Reminiscence of Cricket', the 'greatest, the grandest of all', W.G. Grace at the height of his powers. Conan Doyle bowled three balls to him: a sitter, a long hop, and:

> The third was a gift – or it looked it –
> A foot off the wicket or so;
> His huge figure swooped as he hooked it,
> His great body swung to the blow.

> Up, up, like a towering game-bird,
> Up, up, to a speck in the blue,
> And then coming down like the same bird,
> Dead straight on the line that it flew.

But, gloves outstretched for the catch, Derbyshire wicketkeeper Storer was below it:

> I stood with my two eyes fixed on it,
> Paralysed, helpless, inert;
> There was 'plunk' as the glove shut upon it,
> And he cuddled it up to his shirt.

It was, for Conan Doyle, a great moment.

Dickens made innumerable references to cricket, from his earliest work to his last, unfinished novel, *The Mystery of Edwin Drood*. Most famous, of course, is the great All-Muggleton against Dingley Dell game that so entertained Mr Pickwick, and at which Mr Jingle's tall tale of his single-wicket contest against Colonel Blazo carried fiction to unlikely limits. At Muggleton the players wore 'straw hats, flannel jackets and white trousers', and, Mr Pickwick is informed, 'they notch in a tent'. A mere 54 notches secured victory for All-Muggleton. Other mentions in Dickens are more peripheral. In *The Old Curiosity Shop* a child dies with his bat beside his bed. The headstrong Steerforth in *David Copperfield* was 'the best cricketer you ever saw', and dear, lovable Joe Gargery in *Great Expectations* would catch his hat as it fell from the chimneypiece with 'a quickness of the eye and hand, very like that exacted by wicketkeeping'. For Barnaby Rudge, attending a No-Popery rally in St George's Fields, 'the smell of the grass brought back his old days at cricket'.

Anthony Trollope regretted not playing cricket in his unhappy schooldays, but in *The Fixed Period* (1882) he is at his most satirical in describing a colonial match featuring Sir Kennington Oval and Sir Lords Longstop opening the batting for England against an Australian team captained by the suitably named Jack Neverbend.

Conan Doyle, Dickens and Trollope were not alone. Apart from Thomas Hughes's praise of the virtues of cricket in *Tom Brown's Schooldays*, John Galsworthy wrote of it in *To Let* (1921), the final volume of the Forsyte Saga, and Iris Murdoch in *The Sandcastle* (1957). Thackeray wrote of cricket, but only passingly, in *The Newcomes* (1855), but A.A. Milne and J.M. Barrie featured the game more substantially in their writing. Barrie believed cricket was an idea of the gods, and formed his own team, the 'Allahakbarries', derived from the Muslim call to prayer 'Allahu Akbar'. Siegfried Sassoon's description of a village match in *Memoirs of a Fox-Hunting Man* (1928) is as enchanting as Hugh de Selincourt's *The Cricket Match* (1924) or A.G. MacDonnell's *England, Their England* (1933). P.G. Wodehouse, who had opened the bowling when at Dulwich College, wrote sufficiently about the game to justify his own anthology,

Wodehouse at the Wicket. Dorothy L. Sayers's aristocratic sleuth Lord Peter Wimsey was a fine cricketer, as was John Creasy's Toff and, more recently, George MacDonald Fraser's roguish Flashman.

The art of fiction has added to the romance of cricket – no other sport features so much in literature – with nostalgia often at the core of the story. But it is a poet, Francis Thompson (1859–1907), who best epitomises the wistful memory any elderly cricket-lover has of games past. In 'At Lord's' he remembers a match from 1878 between Gloucestershire and his own beloved Lancashire:

> For the field is full of shades as I near the shadowy coast,
> And a ghostly batsman plays to the bowling of a ghost,
> And I look through my tears on a soundless-clapping host
> As the run-stealers flicker to and fro,
> To and fro:
> O my Hornby and my Barlow long ago!

Much cricket poetry is in praise of famous men – Prowse's obituary tribute to Mynn, for instance (see page 411), Burnby's eulogies to patrons or much of the output of Albert Craig, 'the Surrey poet', who composed his verse during the day's play and sold it to the Oval crowd. Craig was a Sheffield man who came to London on an excursion ticket and 'never used the return half'. His verses may have been execrable, but they were contemporary, and, as Craig once pointed out to a critic, 'They sold.'

Of course, not all poets were enamoured of cricket, notably the short-sighted Kipling, who in 1902 derided sportsmen and sports-lovers in 'The Islanders':

> Then ye returned to your trinkets;
> Then ye contented your souls
> With the flannelled fools at the wicket
> Or the muddied oafs at the goals.

Kipling was not irreconcilable, however, and with the coming of the First World War his feeling for the young softened his view:

> No Lord's this year: no silken lawns on which
> A dignified and daily throng meanders,

> The schools take guard upon a fierier pitch
> Somewhere in Flanders.

It was a melancholy reflection, no doubt made more so when his only son, John, was killed in action a few weeks later, at the age of eighteen. As Kipling had campaigned publicly for young men to enlist, John's loss was a harrowing blow from which the great poet never recovered.

Occasionally, cruelty makes an appearance in verse. *Punch*'s 1886 parody, in the style of Tennyson, of the highly-strung depressive William Scotton after he had scored only 34 in an opening stand of 170 with Grace in the Oval Test against Australia, must have hurt such a delicate mind:

> Block, block, block
> At the foot of thy wicket, O Scotton!
> And I would that my tongue would utter
> My boredom. You *won't* put the pot on!

> . . . Block, block, block.
> At the foot of thy wicket, ah do!
> But one hour of Grace or Walter Read
> Were worth a week of you!

I hope poor Scotton never read this, or if he did, that he was consoled by the knowledge that he could bat all day and his literary assailant could not. He had, after all, helped Walter Read save a Test against Australia only two years earlier. Cricket and politics have many similarities: one is that the critic always believes himself to be wiser and more gifted than the protagonist. But Scotton can be brought to life before us still, while his critic is long-dead dust and ashes.

The notion that cricket exemplified desirable virtues was very Victorian, but in fact the idea predated the Victorian era. The opening line of the earliest-known cricket poem, James Love's 'Hail cricket! glorious manly British Game!' (1744), conveys the same message. Perhaps the Victorians overdid it. Towards the end of the era, Sir Henry Newbolt's 'Vitaï Lampada' (1897) went way over the top when it drew together the lessons learned on a cricket field and applied them to man's grimmest game, war. Newbolt sets the scene at a school cricket match:

> There's a breathless hush in the Close tonight
> Ten to make and the match to win
> A bumping pitch and a blinding light,
> An hour to play and the last man in.
> And it's not for the sake of a ribboned coat,
> Or the selfish hope of a season's fame,
> But his Captain's hand on his shoulder smote
> 'Play up! play up! and play the game!'

Having grown up, many of the second sons of the gentry, who inherited very little and needed a profession, joined the army and were sent to defend the outposts of Empire. Newbolt continues:

> The sand of the desert is sodden red,
> Red with the wreck of a square that broke;
> The Gatling's jammed and the Colonel dead,
> And the regiment blind with dust and smoke.
> The river of death has brimmed his banks,
> And England's far, and Honour a name,
> But the voice of a schoolboy rallies the ranks:
> 'Play up! play up! and play the game!'

It is a glorious sentiment, but is it real? For some impressionable young men, inculcated with the Victorian ethic, it may have been, as their pith-helmeted regiments marched to Egypt to discipline the Mahdi. But if it was, it was a generosity of outlook that died long before the First World War.

Yet Newbolt was not just writing sentimental mock-heroic twaddle, for the *true* Victorian message lay in the third, and least well-known, stanza of the poem, which could serve as a guide for life:

> This is the word that year by year,
> While in her place the School is set
> Every one of her sons must hear,
> And none that hears it dare forget.

This they all with a joyful mind
Bear through life like a torch in flame,
And falling fling to the host behind
'Play up! play up! and play the game.'

'Vitaï Lampada' translates as 'They pass on the torch of life'. The message is very clear: the young must be taught to pass on the values that matter. We may scoff at the Victorian zeal for improving on common nature, but it is surely preferable to much of today's cynicism.

The image cricket imprints on the eye is generally attractive, and has been an enticement to artists from the first half of the eighteenth century. The first known cricket engraving – ironically by a Frenchman, Thomas Gainsborough's teacher Hubert Gravelot (1699–1773) – is *Youth Playing Cricket* (1739), but Francis Hayman's *Cricket in Marylebone Fields* (1747) is a far more interesting composition, and a finer model for later paintings.

In the years to come, many great artists would include cricket in their works, including Turner's *Cricket Match* and *Wells Cathedral with a Game of Cricket*, and *Cricket on Hampton Court Green* by the impressionist Camille Pissarro. Thomas Rowlandson illustrated the game faithfully in *Cricket in White Conduit Fields* around 1790, but more typical of his style is the slightly bizarre *A Cricket Match Extraordinary* from 1811, with plump maidens gaily rushing around. Intriguingly, the earlier work shows a wicket with three stumps, which is correct, and the later with only two, which is not.

And yet, notwithstanding the work of great artists from Rowlandson to Lowry, high-quality cricket art is limited. To my eye, many of the paintings fail to inspire because the wide panorama of the field often leaves the cricketers as insignificant figures on the canvas. The game itself is not captured, and such paintings can leave an overall effect that is flat and unpleasing. But this is not invariably so. Frederick Batson's *Playing out Time in an Awkward Light* (c.1900) and John Robertson Reid's *A County Cricket Match* (1878) are lovely compositions, despite the anonymity of the players.

In many of the early paintings cricket is an incidental theme, most famously in the portraits of Walter Hawkesworth Fawkes as *Boy with a Bat* (c.1760), probably by Thomas Hudson, and *Miss Wicket and Miss Trigger* (1778) by John Collett. Hudson, a leading portraitist, included bats in the hands of boys in a number of family portraits, although whether this was simply a prop, or represented a genuine enthusiasm of the boys, is impossible now to know. One subject of interest to cricket historians in these paintings is the nature of the bats and, in the Fawkes portrait, the two stumps notched for one single bail. Francis Cotes's *Wicket and Ball* (1768) is a detail of his painting of *Lewis Cage as a Batsman*, and is of interest for its accurate portrayal of early equipment, while W.R. Coates's *Batsman, Wicket Keeper and Umpire* and *Bowler, Non-Striker and Umpire** are both enlarged details from his *A Cricket Match* (c.1740), which in turn is thought to be derived from an engraving by H. Roberts after L. Boitard. It is of interest because it gives cameo close-ups of both ends of the pitch. Other paintings such as *Village Cricket* (1855) by John Ritchie are really landscapes featuring cricket in the foreground or the background, but not as the primary feature.

Paintings sometimes expose the artist to be ignorant of cricket. The cover of an issue of the *Sporting Magazine* from 1793 features a *Grand Cricket Match* – so called because it was played for a thousand-guinea side bet between Lords Winchilsea and Darnley – at Lord's, but it shows only two stumps at the wicket, many years after three stumps were commonplace. Although nominally an 'action' picture of a game, it gives the impression of players frozen in still life, unlike later, and finer, pictures. George Shepheard's watercolour sketch *Twelve Cricketers in Characteristic Attitudes* (c.1790) gives us an all-too-brief, but precious, glimpse of the styles of David Harris, Thomas Lord, Charles Lennox, and other contemporaries. Other cricketers of that time live on in portraits. 'Lumpy' Stevens, by Almond, and 'Silver Billy' Beldham (from a photograph taken in his old age) represent the Hambledon era, with 'Squire' Osbaldeston and

---

* Francis Cotes's *Wicket and Ball*, and W.R. Coates's *Batsman, Wicket Keeper and Umpire* and *Bowler, Non-Striker and Umpire* are not paintings but merely convenient descriptions of details first used in *John Player's Art of Cricket*.

Lord Frederick Beauclerk, cherub-faced and ruthless, leading the next generation.

By the mid-nineteenth century, as interest in cricket increased, so did its representation in the arts. Staffordshire figurines began to appear of players such as George Parr and Julius Caesar. *The Captain of the Eleven* (1882) by Philip Hermogenes Calderon, showing a curly-headed boy playing forward, could only have been a Victorian study. William Evans, the art master at Eton, painted *Cricket on Eton College Field* (c.1843), combining cricket and the attraction of the college. The game also produced its first artist-player in Nicholas Felix; others, notably the great Australian spin bowler Arthur Mailey and the England wicketkeeper Jack Russell, would follow years later. Felix was, among his other gifts, a talented artist in pastels, watercolour and oils, and his *Felix on the Bat* contains delightful lithographs. His portrait of *The Eleven of England in 1847* is technically efficient as well as historically important. Felix also features as a batsman in some lithographs by George F. Watts, once a pupil at Felix's school, illustrating cricket strokes.

Sussex vs Kent at Brighton (c.1851), an engraving by Drummond/Basèbe, which became a popular print by W.H. Mason, depicts players famous in the years either side of 1850, but unlike Albert Chevallier Tayler's *Kent vs Lancashire at Canterbury* (1906, see below) it does not record a real match, although all the players represented – including Fuller Pilch, William Lillywhite, Alfred Mynn and his brother Walter, and Nicholas Felix – did play in similar fixtures at some time. It is a lovely scene, but a figment of the imagination, not reality. A lovely composition by Sir Robert Ponsonby Staples from 1887 purports to show an incident in a Test match at Lord's, but it incorporates notables in the crowd who would not have been present in reality. The Prince and Princess of Wales are seen walking on the outfield, he in top hat and she with parasol, while Lillie Langtry, the Prince's mistress, delicately averts her gaze, and others of his *amours* can be glimpsed among the crowd. It is a sly cameo, but not a truthful one.

The age of Grace encouraged many portraits in honour of the

great player, one of which, a head-and-shoulders painted by Archibald Stuart Wortley in 1890, was loaned to me by the National Portrait Gallery and hung on my study wall at 10 Downing Street as a sublime respite from politics. Among many others, a full-length oil of Grace standing at the wicket in golden light, also by Wortley, is one of the most evocative, while a 1905 head-and-shoulders by Henry Scott Tuke is an attractive representation of the ageing lion. Sometimes ancillary figures were captured. *The Scorer* (1842) by Thomas Henwood shows the elderly William Davies of Lewes Priory, behatted, bespectacled and portly as he records the progress of an unknown match, with stumps, bats and ball cluttered together beneath the table at which he sits. An empty bottle lies on the ground, with a companion and a full glass on the table. This painting became a delightful print that is still reproduced and that adorns many houses, including my own.

Towards the end of the century many portraits were commissioned, with the full-length picture of the Surrey batsman W.E. Roller walking down the pavilion steps on his way to bat at The Oval being among the best. It was lovingly painted by Roller's brother George in 1883. Caricatures of cricketers by 'Spy' (Sir Leslie Ward) and 'Ape' (Carlo Pellegrini) decorated *Vanity Fair* from time to time, with those of Prince Ranjitsinhji, Lord Harris and the 'demon' Frederick Spofforth helping to form the memory that history has of them.

Albert Chevallier Tayler's *Kent vs Lancashire at Canterbury* (1906) is the most lovely illustration of an 'action' cricket painting in oils. It depicts Colin Blythe bowling to J.T. Tyldesley as Kent close in on the victory that would make them county champions. The pavilion clock stands at seven minutes past five, and the day is drawing to a close. The painting was commissioned by Kent's man-for-all-seasons Lord Harris, and Chevallier Tayler's fee of two hundred guineas was amply covered by the sale of prints signed by the two men. In 2006 Kent sold it at Sotheby's for £600,000, and the purchaser kindly agreed that it could remain on view to the public, at Lord's.

This famous painting was preceded a year earlier by a series of drawings of *The Empire's Cricketers* by Chevallier Tayler that were based on photographs taken by an enthusiastic amateur cricketer who was to make an imperishable contribution to the history of the game as a chronicler on film. The first photograph of a cricket match was taken on 25 July 1857 by Roger Fenton, who had recently returned (with 150 pounds of photographic paraphernalia) from capturing images of the Crimean War. It shows a local match between the Royal Artillery and the village of Hunsdonbury in Hertfordshire, in which the cricketers appear to be rooted to the spot. Photographic portraits began to appear, often the work of Robert Adamson or David Octavius Hill, and the images of Fuller Pilch, John Wisden and 'Silver Billy' Beldham were captured for immortality. So were club sides (I Zingari), touring sides (George Parr's team to North America in 1859) and county sides (Sussex, 1864), all of which left to posterity a vision of young men with beards, moustaches, muttonchop sideburns, hats and coloured accessories to their clothing. They look stiff and posed as they gaze into the future, a generation unfamiliar with photography and unsure how to relax in front of a camera. Other photographs of the game being played in Australia, Hong Kong, South Africa, Japan, India, Mexico and North America are incontrovertible evidence of the speed at which cricket was spreading around the world.

As shutter speeds increased, so did the action the camera could capture, but many so-called 'action' shots, as in Archie MacLaren's 1896 book *Cricket for Beginners*, were posed. Primitive motion photography began, but the advent of serious sporting images had to await one of the towering figures of photographic innovation, George W. Beldam. Beldam was a privileged man. He had the time and the financial security to indulge his interests, and the intellectual persistence and dedication to use that freedom in a good cause. He was the embodiment of the gentleman amateur and talented polymath, an engineer, watercolourist and sportsman. In his leisure, Beldam knew how to enjoy life. He shot game, fished for trout and salmon, played tennis and golf, and was a sufficiently fine cricketer to represent Middlesex for eight seasons. Another leisure interest was women – he had three wives. Photography was not a new art when Beldam took his first photographs in 1895, but it was still limited.

Nonetheless, he used it not only to capture precious images but to display the techniques that made some players stand out.

Beldam took sporting photography to a new level, and left portraits that capture the magic of late Victorian and early Edwardian times. His were the finest sporting photographs of cricket and golf that had yet been seen. His social position, wealth, and a long friendship with W.G. Grace gave him access that would have been denied others. Atypically for a man of his background, he learned his cricket on Ealing Common. He played for his college at Oxford, but not for the university, and for Middlesex's second eleven from 1894 until 1899, when he topped the batting and bowling averages and scored ten centuries, two of them over 200, in club cricket.

The following year, at the age of thirty-two, he was brought into the Middlesex side by the captain, A.J. Webbe, and in his subsequent career for the county he scored nearly 5,000 runs at an average of 30.16 and took 76 wickets at 27.14 each. His highest score was 155 not out against Surrey at Lord's in 1902. His bowling victims, albeit few, included some of high quality: Hayward, Gunn, Hobbs, Jessop, Shrewsbury, Ranjitsinhji and the Australians Gregory, Hill, Armstrong and Noble were among them. As a familiar figure in top-class cricket, Beldam had every opportunity to know and to photograph some of the finest players of his time. He did so with skill and innovation, being the first sporting photographer to use a really fast shutter. His favoured camera was an Adams Videx with five-by-four-inch glass-print negatives, before he graduated to one fitted with a motor drive, using celluloid with a shutter speed of $^1/_{250}$ second. Beldam used his photography to try to capture the unique talent of the great players of his age. He often bowled to batsmen, taking their picture at the same time using a long shutter cable which he operated with his left hand. It was an erratic procedure, but the results were memorable. The technical leaps forward that allowed close-up action shots would not come until the First World War, when the military's need for high-quality portable cameras and telephoto lenses would, incidentally, enable fans to understand and enjoy cricketers' styles as never before.

The images Beldam left behind are evocative of an age now gone. There is something inexpressibly sad in many of his wonderful photographs. Depicted in them are young men, gifted at cricket, fit and healthy, who gaze clear-eyed, and with a touch of wonder, into the newfangled camera. In the prime of life, they are full of hope; and yet, as we look at them today, history tells us their futures, their successes, their failures and the span of their lives. All are gone now, except in memory, even the longest-lived of them. Beldam's images leave them frozen in time, as the leading sportsmen of a generation, hurtling unknowingly towards a war that would end their world and, in far too many cases, their lives as well.

15

The Autocrats

One sunny morning in 1873, at the high noon of Empire, a twenty-two-year-old Oxford cricket Blue was waiting patiently at Faversham station for a train to London, where he was due to play for the Lords and Commons Eleven against the wandering amateur side, I Zingari. He intended to watch cricket at Lord's the following day, where his old school, Eton, would play Harrow. It was a pleasant prospect, but it was not to be. On the platform he was greeted by Herbert Knatchbull-Hugessen, a mandarin of Kent cricket, who chatted amiably to him in the belief that he was on his way to Gravesend to play for the county against Lancashire. It was a reasonable assumption. The young man was a promising batsman, and the son of the first President of the Kent County Cricket Club, newly formed by the amalgamation of the old Kent and Beverley Clubs in 1870. Upon learning his true plans, Knatchbull-Hugessen tried to persuade him that a 'county' game for Kent should take priority, and that he should telegraph his withdrawal from the Lords and Commons, forgo Eton vs Harrow, and head for the Bat and Ball ground to make himself available for Kent. To do so would be an uncomfortable breach of a prior commitment, and the Blue demurred. Knatchbull-Hugessen pressed his case, and, overwhelmed by argument and filial loyalty, the young man finally agreed.

At Gravesend a professional who had expected to play was left out of the team to make way for the young amateur. In that far-off game his scores were modest, only 26 and 6, but he set his mind upon a career with Kent. A year later he had succeeded the veteran W. de Chair Baker as Honorary Secretary to the club, and in 1875 he was appealing in the county newspapers, with great success, for funds to promote Kent cricket. That summer, at the age of twenty-four, he was appointed captain of the county eleven, and remained so for fifteen years until political responsibilities curtailed his cricket. Thereafter, despite a five-year break for colonial duties, he dominated the council chambers of cricket with unrivalled authority. The young cricketer was the Hon. George Robert Canning, better known to history as the 4th Lord Harris.

It is not easy, 120 years after his prime, to set Harris in the context of his time and portray him fairly. Autocrats attract lavish praise or unremitting hostility, and there is seldom a consensus. There is evidence aplenty that depicts Harris as either benevolent and paternalist or narrow-minded and bigoted. Both caricatures have their supporters. His contemporaries, by and large, tended to a favourable view, while revisionist historians such as Derek Birley have poked fun at a man who now seems ludicrously out of date.

Harris was born to privilege. At only ten years of age, in 1861, his father took him to the small pavilion at Lord's to see Middlesex play Kent, but he arrived in time only to absorb the atmosphere. The game had ended, with Kent defeated. He was more fortunate the following season at Hove, when Kent's Joseph Wells (father of the writer H.G. Wells) and Ned Willsher, a cricketing hero of the young boy, exploited a sticky wicket, damp but drying as the wind blew in from the sea, and twice bowled out Sussex. It was not the only fragment of memory that young George carried away from that game: he never forgot the 'red uppers' that adorned the Kent amateur all-rounder G.M. Kelson's cricket boots. In his maturity he remembered other sartorial affectations from that season. At Lord's, Robert Carpenter and Tom Hayward of Cambridgeshire took the field in black 'Billycock' hats with matching black-and-white check shirts. Harris drank in the scene. Off the field, a red-faced potman, in white jacket and apron, cried 'Give us your orders, gents,' as he served thirsty spectators with beer poured from large pewter cans he wheeled around the boundary. And not only spectators: even fieldsmen in need of refreshment would take a pot from him and drink it in the outfield. Tonbridge the potman was a familiar figure at Lord's until 1866, when he died of cholera. The whole atmosphere germinated a lifelong love of cricket in the young Harris.

He was educated at Eton, where he fell under the cricketing influence of R.A.H. 'Mike' Mitchell, a polished batsman and former captain of Eton and Oxford. Mitchell was a talented coach and an advocate of orthodox batting. His pupils played correctly, or they did not play at all. Under his guidance Harris was selected for the eleven for three years from 1868 to 1870, in a team rich with promise. It included the Hon. Ivo Bligh and C.T. and G.B. Studd, all of whom would play for England, and C.J. Ottaway and C.I. Thornton, who were to make a mark on first-class cricket. An early vignette, unflattering to Harris, is of him running out a batsman who was backing up too enthusiastically in the 1870 Eton vs Harrow match. Harrow supporters were furious. Even as a boy Harris was a stickler for the strict laws of cricket.

Harris went up to Oxford in 1871, won his Blue as a freshman, and was a regular member of the team for three years. As a young man he was so in love with cricket – or, perhaps, with the joy of the good life he was leading – that his exuberance could grate. In one match for Kent he was so boisterous at point that Richard Daft refused to bat on until he shut up. 'His Lordship talks and distracts my attention,' scolded the great batsman. Harris was aware that his hot-headed temperament could let him down, and when his blood cooled he was keen to make amends. Batting for Kent with a young George Hearne, Harris – well set and in good form – called for a sharp single. Hearne, seeing no chance of a run, hesitated, but ran when he saw Harris charging towards him down the wicket, and was easily run out. As he turned to the pavilion, Harris muttered to him, 'Damn little fool. Serves you jolly well right. Why the devil don't you come when you're called?' Hearne was aggrieved, but deference (and politeness) stilled any caustic response. At the end of the day Harris came up to him.

'George,' he said, 'that was no run.'

'No, my Lord,' replied Hearne, 'I didn't think it was.'

'Why, then, did you come?'

'Well, I saw you coming and thought your wicket was worth more than mine.'

'Another time I do a silly thing like that, don't you come,' said Harris. 'I beg your pardon.'

It was a handsome apology, offered in the hearing of other professional players, and shows the gracious side of Harris's character.

Harris matured early, and never shirked responsibility. His precocious talents were appreciated. In 1882, when he was only thirty-one, grateful Kent supporters subscribed four hundred guineas to present him with a pair of engraved silver candelabra during Kent Cricket Week at Canterbury to mark his services to Kent cricket. It was an astonishing tribute to one so young. The eight hundred donors offered also a silver inkstand to Lady Harris, no doubt as a consolation for her husband's preoccupation with the county side.

His writ ran on and off the field. On the field, he once caught Harry Jupp of Surrey at ankle height, but Jupp, a notorious non-walker, stayed defiantly at the crease. Harris bridled: 'Go out, Jupp. I'm not asking for that!' Obediently, head down and suitably admonished, off Jupp went. This was a mini triumph for Harris, for Jupp was not always so pliable. When bowled first ball in a country game, he calmly replaced the bails and settled down for the next ball. 'Ain't you going out, Juppy?' asked the opposing captain. 'Not at Dorking I ain't,' said Jupp. And he didn't.

In the early 1870s many amateurs opted to play for wandering teams such as I Zingari, but by persuasion and his own commitment to Kent, Harris made it fashionable to play in inter-county games. At the time that Harris joined the county, Kent were in decline. From 1700 to 1750 their supremacy had been unchallenged, and from 1750 to 1800 only Hambledon were their equal. In the early nineteenth century John Willes and Herbert Jenner (later Herbert Jenner-Fust) were notable figures, and from 1834 to 1850 the 'good old Kent XI' was dominant:

> With five such mighty cricketers 'twas but natural to win
> As Felix, Wenman, Hillyer, Fuller Pilch and Alfred Mynn.

Those days were long gone, and after that great team broke up in the early 1850s, only Ned Willsher was in the front rank of cricketers.

Harris, the new captain, had much to do. His career record for Kent was respectable but far from Olympian. He played 156 games, scoring 7,806 runs at an average of 30.02, including a glorious innings of 176 against Sussex in 1882 – one of nine centuries. In 1883 he opened against Yorkshire and carried his bat for an undefeated 80 out of a total of 148. In his best year, 1884, he totalled 1,417 runs in forty-two innings. In all first-class cricket, including Tests, he amassed 9,990 runs at an average of 26.85. His fast round-arm bowling captured seventy-five wickets at 25.11,* and he held 190 catches, nearly all close to the wicket. Harris played in only four Test matches, each time as captain, and all against Australia, scoring 145 runs, with a top score of 52 and an average of 29. In these games he bowled a mere thirty-two balls, conceding 29 runs without taking a wicket. He took only two catches. It was a comparatively modest record.

As a batsman Harris was an uncertain starter, and was never in the very highest class, but when set he was stylish, with a strong defence and a forcing technique, hitting especially well in front of the wicket. He was courageous too, and played some of his most memorable innings on bad wickets against quick bowling. George Hearne, who played with Harris at Kent, mused that he had rarely seen fast bowlers require fieldsmen at both long off and long on, but with Harris they did. Ironically, given events to come, he made that remark while watching Harris score 118 against Jack Crossland of Lancashire in 1883. It seems that on his very best days Harris fought fire with fire, and the image of a finer batsman in a later era, Ted Dexter, comes to mind.

Harris loved the game, 'preferring', as W.G. Grace noted, 'a close finish to over-whelming victory'. Grace, who played often with Harris

---

* Harris's seventy-five wickets include five for which no analysis is known. The average shown of 25.11 refers to the other seventy wickets.

at home and abroad, became a lifelong friend after they met on a tour to Canada and North America under R.A. Fitzgerald in 1872. The trip, in Grace's view, was 'a prolonged and happy picnic', and Harris, accompanied by his Old Etonian team-mate C.J. Ottaway, agreed. Certainly he enjoyed himself hugely, and forged a strong bond of mutual respect with the great cricketer. It was a friendship that was useful to them both. At Clifton in 1887 a Kent vs Gloucester game was petering out on the last afternoon, with Grace twenty runs short of a second century in the match. In a quixotic gesture, and in sharp contrast to the Eton–Harrow imbroglio of his schooldays, Harris put on a slow underarm bowler to help Grace reach his landmark, and was the first to applaud when he did. Was this deference to Grace, whom he had worshipped as a schoolboy, the fruits of friendship, or the Corinthian behaviour of a sports-lover? We shall never know, but in a sense it is irrelevant, for it is Harris's contribution to cricket off the field that left a lasting mark.

The span of his career was remarkable. In 1862, at the age of eleven, he was practising at Lord's, and his final innings was played sixty-eight years later on a return to his beloved Eton. Throughout most of those seven decades he was the single most powerful voice in cricket. His enthusiasm never waned. Two days before he died, in March 1932, he was wondering whether his ailing health would recover sufficiently to enable him to address the AGM of the MCC at Lord's. Sadly, it did not.

Harris was a Victorian to the bone. He saw cricket as embodying a value system, and insisted that it was a school of the greatest social importance. 'Cricket,' he declared, drawing on his experiences at the Indian and War Offices, and as Governor of Bombay, 'has done more to consolidate the Empire than any other influence, and it is certainly the means of consolidating agreeable friendships and originating pleasant re-unions.' This was, of course, a very Victorian view, echoing Thomas Hughes's aphorism that cricket was more than a game.

Harris's involvement in the Sydney riot in 1879 and the first Test match at The Oval in 1880 (see pages 229 and 230–1) were not the only controversial incidents in his career. In the early 1880s unfair bowling, with a bent arm, was prevalent, and was in danger of becoming accepted. In December 1883, county secretaries met and tried to get an agreement that counties would not select 'throwers', but Lancashire would not agree. Nor were the MCC, or umpires, keen to challenge suspect actions. Often the umpires were timid creatures, deferential by instinct and unwilling to make contentious decisions. Some were former players tutored not to upset their social 'betters'. Others were simple, uncomplicated souls. Billy Goodhew, after umpiring at Old Trafford, was typical: 'If you pleath, thir,' he said to Harris, 'I am very glad to be back in England again.' This is not the self-confident tone of voice of a man prepared to court unpopularity in order to uphold the law. Umpires needed a lead if they were to make controversial rulings. Harris was soon to give them one.

Lancashire had two professionals, their fast bowler Jack Crossland, and George Nash, a slow left-hander. It was widely believed that Crossland bowled his fastest deliveries with a bent elbow, and that Nash's action was wholly illegal. In essence, they both 'threw' the ball. After making a duck, bowled third ball by Crossland at Old Trafford in 1885, Harris thought so too – and took action. When confronted, the Lancashire captain A.N. Hornby, a dominant personality unlikely to be faced down by Harris, was chilly and non-committal.* Crossland took a lot of wickets for Lancashire, and Hornby did not wish to sacrifice a man who had never been no-balled. Although he was an amateur and a 'gentleman', Hornby was also a Lancastrian and a fierce competitor. This did not satisfy Harris, who persuaded Kent to refuse to play Lancashire in the return fixture at Tonbridge. Lancashire were shocked. They were inured to complaints about their bowlers' actions – rows with Surrey had been particularly bitter as spectators demonstrated against Crossland** – but no one had ever proposed unilateral action. And yet Harris had justification on his side. W.G. Grace thought Crossland had the 'most doubtful

---

* Hornby was a formidable character. A piano piece, 'Hornby Schottische', was written and published in his honour in the 1880s.
** Lancashire beat Surrey by an innings in August 1882 after Crossland took 11 for 79 (ten clean-bowled). Surrey spectators hurled abuse at the umpire for failing to no-ball him.

action' and 'ought to have been no-balled in every over'. He was also frighteningly quick. Even *Wisden*, although noting that Hornby must have thought Crossland's action was fair, observed that many others did not.

The scene was set for confrontation. But then Nash lost his place in the Lancashire team to Johnny Briggs, and after a formal complaint by Nottinghamshire the MCC ruled that Crossland no longer possessed a residential qualification to play for the county.* It was an accurate, but convenient, ruling. The Kent–Lancashire dispute dissolved into a crisis that never was, but the evil of throwing had been highlighted, and for a while it began to fade away, although the ill-feeling between Lancashire and Harris was to persist.

Harris was an innovative administrator. In 1886 he attempted to reduce the residential qualification to play for a county side from two years to twelve months, but in a rare rebuff he failed to persuade the counties to do so. In this initiative, Harris was ahead of his time: fifty-two years later, and six years after his death, his proposal was adopted. In July 1887 he was the prime mover in a decision to form a County Cricket Council, which he was to chair. It grew out of the practice, begun five years earlier, of the county secretaries meeting annually. It differed from the cricket 'parliament' that the *Sporting Times* had advocated in 1864 in that the council did not seek to replace the MCC as the highest body, but focused on county matters, not lawmaking for the game overall. Its role was to oversee tours and to decide questions about the laws, but on the understanding that the MCC was the highest court of appeal.

The big question facing cricket at that time was league classification, and the CCC placed itself (fatally) at the heart of the debate. A subcommittee meeting in August 1890, chaired by John Shuter of Surrey and including W.G. Grace, proposed setting up a first division consisting of Gloucestershire, Kent, Lancashire, Middlesex, Nottinghamshire, Surrey, Sussex and Yorkshire, with a second division of Derbyshire, Essex, Warwickshire, Leicestershire, Stafford-

* It appears that Crossland lived in Nottingham from October 1884 to April 1885.

shire, Somerset, Hampshire and Cheshire. A third division made up of Northamptonshire, Norfolk, Lincolnshire, Northumberland, Durham, Glamorgan, Devonshire and Hertfordshire was also proposed. There was much wailing and gnashing of teeth over a couple of important fundamentals: there was no agreed mechanism for entry into the league, or much more importantly a simple and clearly understood mechanism for promotion or relegation. The subcommittee thrashed out proposals, but trouble lay ahead. Many of the counties did not like to have their fixtures passed down from above, as a division system was bound to do. Other grievances also surfaced.

Fears were voiced at a meeting of second-class counties on 25 October 1890, and were reiterated when the CCC met at Lord's on 8 December. Here, argument was fierce, and a formula to satisfy everyone (especially the second-class county representatives) could not be found. Amid hopeless confusion, a vote was taken not on the issue of classification, but on the very existence of the CCC. That vote was inconclusive, and no majority decision emerged until the new Chairman, M.J. Ellison of Yorkshire, dramatically put the dissolutionists into a majority by casting his vote to suspend the CCC *sine die*. That was the end of the CCC. It was never revived.

It is easy to see Harris as an old-fashioned figure, a product of his social class, an advocate of muscular Christianity, an authoritarian exercising the privilege of power to which he was born. He was all of that. As he matured as captain of Kent his team were wary of his fearsome reputation as a martinet. One professional fled the dressing room, explaining, 'I've run myself out . . . and his Lordship is coming in.' Nonetheless, such cameos offer only an incomplete portrait. Harris had humour and grace in his make-up too. He frequently related the tale of a conversation with W. de Chair Baker, the organiser of the Kent Cricket Week at Canterbury:

'Good morning, Mr Baker.'

'Morning, morning.'

'It is a lovely day for cricket.'

'Fine day, fine day.'

'I hope you are well?'

'Well, well.'

'I hope your brother is, too?'

'Dead, dead.'

When Harris was appointed Governor of Bombay in 1890, at the age of thirty-nine, he believed, wrongly as it turned out, 'My cricket book is closed.' W.G. Grace thought so too, and commented on Harris's decision to leave cricket that 'It is the only bad thing I know of him.' In fact much lay ahead of Harris, not least in India, where he had lived as a child when his father was Governor of Madras (he was also Governor of Trinidad). He sailed for the subcontinent on 27 February 1890 in the P&O steamer *Thames* with his wife and five-month-old son, arriving six weeks later on 11 April. Harris served as Governor of Bombay for five years before returning to England, where admirers laid on triumphal receptions to welcome him back. In India, however, his governorship was both praised and damned. One critic published a selection of contemporary newspaper reports, observing: 'Never during the last one hundred years has a Governor of Bombay been so strongly criticised and never has he met with such widespread unpopularity on account of his administration as Lord Harris.'

This is unfair. Harris's manner may have grated – Victorian attitudes to those they governed were high-handed – but his intentions were admirable. He sought to introduce better sanitation, improved education and more up-to-date agricultural methods. These were benevolent policies, long overdue and much needed, and it is hard to see why he attracted such hostility. Experience of politics suggests that it may have been unavoidable. If his critics were Indian nationalists, avid for political self-determination, there was bound to be a clash with *any* Governor who believed in the Victorian right to rule. Folk memory may also have recalled that in 1799 Harris's great-grandfather, General Lord George Harris, had helped defeat Tipu Sultan, an implacable opponent of British rule. If so, it is unsurprising if tolerance and goodwill towards Harris were hard to find.

Whatever the truth of this matter, it is clear that Harris saw cricket as a means to promote his policy, minimise intercommunal strife and implant Victorian ideals. He instigated games between local teams and European sides, and encouraged the upper classes to patronise the game, despite being roundly abused in the press for doing so.

Soon after he arrived, in a poor start for his governorship, Harris flunked a controversial decision when he was presented with a petition to evict European polo players from the Bombay Esplanade so that Indians could play cricket on it. This was a dispute with a long pedigree, and the former Governor, Lord Reay, had sided with the Indians (see page 196). Nonetheless, the polo players had recolonised the ground, and the Indian petitioners looked to Harris, with his known love of cricket, to return the land to them. His refusal to do so upset many petitioners. Nor were their grievances assuaged when he offered to provide separate cricket plots for Parsees, Hindus and Muslims on reclaimed land, provided local clubs paid the cost of improving it. It was a grudging provision of land, in stark contrast to the speed with which Harris built himself a more splendid ground at Guneshkind, Poona, one of three residences available to him as Governor.

At first the Poona wicket was matting, as one of Harris's staff was a sufficiently lively fast bowler to be dangerous on a poor wicket. Later Harris replaced the subsoil and laid out a grass pitch. His devotion to cricket offended local critics, who claimed that he amused himself at the expense of duty. 'Would they prefer,' grumbled Harris, 'that I should lie on a sofa smoking cigarettes and reading French novels?' He did not – he played, and so did his staff. Among them were some promising sportsmen, including his ADC, Lieutenant Robert Poore, who was proficient with gun, racquet and polo stick. He turned out to be a fine batsman too, averaging over 80 in the friendly games organised by the Governor. Five years later Poore was to be a thorn in the side of Lord Hawke's tourists in South Africa, before flowering as a batsman for Hampshire.

Between 1890 and 1894 Harris played only fifty-two one-day games in India, scoring 1829 runs, with one century, at an average of 36, which does not sustain the myth of an absentee Governor indulging himself whilst his duties were ignored. Some of the criticism seems unjustified. When interracial riots broke out in 1893, with Hindus and Muslims butchering each other, Harris was accused of ignoring the carnage while he played cricket at Guneshkind for nine days. It is, I suppose, possible that he stayed at Guneshkind during these disturbances, but available records suggest that if he did so, it was not because he was playing cricket.

One accolade offered to Harris is plainly wrong: he cannot be credited with introducing cricket to India, which predated him by a hundred years, and which at the time of his arrival in Bombay was popular with Parsees, Muslims and Hindus. Nor can he justly be called the 'Father of Indian Cricket', as he was by the Indian historian Wahinddin Begg. He can, however, be credited with raising cricket's profile in the subcontinent. As part of his campaign to do so he invited his friend Lord Hawke to bring out a top-class amateur touring team in the winter of 1892–93 to play against European and Indian sides. Hawke accepted, bringing the dashing F.S. Jackson with him, and Harris royally entertained the team for fourteen days over Christmas. Jackson was the finest batsman India had yet seen, and Indian cricket looked and learned. As a result of his promotion of cricket, one well-known contemporary cricket writer in Bombay, J.M. Framjee Patel, praised Harris as 'our Guru', and many agreed with him. In India it turned out that Harris did not, as he had supposed he would do, 'close his cricket book', but merely opened another compelling chapter in a far-off land.

He was to reopen his book again upon his return to England in 1894. Although he returned to political duties in the House of Lords, accepting the post of Government Whip, it was cricket that commanded his attention. He was soon offered the chairmanship of Kent and the presidency of MCC. Ignoring any possibility of conflict, he accepted both positions. Within days of the latter appointment the MCC set up a subcommittee to investigate 'unfair bowling', about which Harris had, as he admitted, 'a mono mania'. This was not a coincidence.

It was not his only obsession. Up until 1896, English Test teams were chosen by the county upon whose ground the game was to be played. At Lord's team selection for the First Test against Australia in June that year fell to Harris, and he omitted Ranjitsinhji, who was full of runs for Sussex that season. Harris believed that Ranji, as an ethnic Indian, was not qualified to play for England. Many disagreed, and there was pandemonium at the decision. Harris, muttering darkly about 'birds of passage', stood firm. Lancashire, ever keen to embarrass Harris, chose Ranji for the second Test at Old Trafford, where he added his own comment on his exclusion at Lord's by scoring 62 and an undefeated 154 on his debut, while W.G. Grace (2 and 11), F.S. Jackson (18 and 1) and A.C. MacLaren (0 and 15) all failed. Ranji added joyfully to Harris's discomfort throughout the season, with ten sparkling hundreds. After 1896, England teams were selected by a panel.

Despite these setbacks, Harris's influence was huge, although he did not invariably prevail. In 1902 he supported a proposal to increase the width of the wicket from eight to nine inches, in order to minimise huge scores and increase the likelihood of positive results. MCC members agreed, but not by the requisite two-thirds majority, and the idea was shelved.

Harris never bowed to fashionable sentiment, and seemed sometimes deliberately to court controversy. Some of his attitudes were crass. He positively welcomed the artificial social distinctions between amateur and professional players, which seemed to him the natural order of life. Despite this dinosaur tendency he did not knowingly adopt double standards, and he supported the strict letter of cricket law. He was even prepared to criticise his former hero W.G. Grace, gently implying in *Wisden* that W.G. appealed too recklessly for decisions, especially leg before wicket, and later, in an obituary tribute, asserting that he was 'very rigid in demanding his full rights'. This was as close to saying that W.G. did not play the game in the proper spirit as he felt able to go. Since Grace was a friend, and a gentleman, Harris sugared the pill, observing that he was so popular that his transgressions only added to the fund of humorous stories about him. As a plea in mitigation, this was true. One hundred years later, in a different arena, Margaret Thatcher benefited from the same tolerance.

The tentacles of Harris's influence were widespread. At Kent, his impact as player and administrator was greater than that of any man before or since. Haygarth's *Scores and Biographies* enthused, 'No cricketer, perhaps, ever did more for a County.' A 1907 history of the county concurred: 'It would be difficult, if not impossible, to over-estimate the amount of good his Lordship has done for Kent cricket.' Even if one allows for sycophancy, these are substantial tributes.

In 1917, at the age of sixty-five, Harris became Treasurer of the MCC, where he watched expenditure with a keen eye for a further sixteen years. His creed was simple: if something was good for cricket, he approved it; if not, he stamped on it. His title, age, political career and lifelong involvement in cricket gave him a rare authority, and few challenged him. Some old obsessions lasted. His stickiness over residential qualifications delayed Walter Hammond's debut for Gloucestershire, prompting an irritated Lord Deerhurst, the son of the Earl of Coventry, to snap: 'May I congratulate you on buggering the career of another young cricketer.' Such bluntness may have startled Harris, but it did not move him. Although his reputation was formidable, Harris carried his authority with a light touch, was careful to consult, and methodical in reaching decisions. He could afford to be, since what he advocated tended to happen. He did not need to command – a suggestion was sufficient for action to follow. The hot-headed youth had grown into a steady elder statesman to whom difficult decisions were remitted for solution. Autocratic perhaps, mistaken sometimes, but effective always.

To see Harris clearly, it is necessary to make allowances for the age in which he lived. It is easy to portray him as hidebound, bigoted and stubborn, but such a judgement is too harsh, and overlooks the class-conscious temper of his times. He mellowed with age, was more kindly than irascible, and in small but important matters he was meticulous and fair-minded, for example in ensuring that staff at Lord's received their annual bonus. He was prepared to use his political clout in the interests of cricket; in particular he was persistent in encouraging the House of Lords to declare players' benefit money tax-free, as it was *ex-gratia* and an uncontracted benefit. In this he was successful, much to the chagrin of the Treasury – it was a resentment they still harboured eighty years later. As President of the Cricketers' Fund Friendly Society for many years, Harris was assiduous in caring for the welfare of professional cricketers. This is the behaviour of a patrician, not an ogre.

Cricket did not occupy all of his maturity. Harris enjoyed a successful career in the City as Chairman of Consolidated Goldfields. As an administrator, politician, businessman, churchman, landowner, cattle and sheep breeder, he lived a full life. But cricket was the core of his being. Even when he retired from his City career he did so with a cricketing analogy, reflecting whimsically upon his 'long innings' and observing, 'Now it is time to find a place among the spectators.' When, in 1932, he died and finally vacated that place among the spectators, he had, like W.G. Grace, been a dominant influence on cricket for nearly half a century.

If Lord Harris has often had a bad press from history, his fellow autocrat Lord Hawke had far worse from his contemporaries. Although Hawke was nine years younger than Harris, the two Old Etonians had a similar outlook. Both were self-confident, opinionated and rarely given to self-doubt. What Harris was to Kent, so Hawke became to Yorkshire. But Harris was subtler and cleverer than Hawke. Two incidents defined Hawke for history and relegated to the shadows his positive contribution to the game.

Bobby Peel, the senior professional at Yorkshire, was regarded by his formidable Lancashire opponent Archie MacLaren as the greatest left-handed bowler of his time. He could bat, too: he had twice scored double centuries in county cricket, and held – ironically, with Hawke – the record stand of 292 runs for the eighth wicket. An automatic choice for any England team, Peel was among the elite, and in Yorkshire he was an icon. But he had a fault: he drank, too often and too much. In August 1897, the evening before Yorkshire were due to play

Middlesex at Bradford, he overindulged yet again. At breakfast he was still tipsy and, aghast at the implications, the kindly George Hirst informed his captain, Lord Hawke, that Peel was unwell and had taken to his bed. Hirst did not hint at the cause, and Hawke was sympathetic and left him out of the eleven.

As Yorkshire took the field Peel appeared, and Hawke, believing a sick man had loyally turned up to play, went up to greet him. His sunny mood turned to ice when he saw that Peel was drunk. He ordered Peel from the field. Peel, merrily free of inhibitions, refused to go. Hawke's temper, always short, rose. At this point, legend takes over. Did Peel, as has been claimed, take the ball and bowl it against the sightscreen to show his captain he was fit to play? Even worse, did he empty his bladder on the field, and prove that he was not?* None of this is clear. What is certain is that after Hawke escorted Peel from the field, the committee met to suspend him, and the most popular Yorkshire player of the day never again turned out for the county. Shocked admirers of Peel turned their ire on Hawke.

The second defining incident, although out of the time scope of this book, is core to the poor reputation that has dogged Hawke. In 1924 the Lancashire and England bowler Cecil Parkin voiced the popular view that the captaincy of England should go to the Surrey professional Jack Hobbs (who didn't want it, and later turned it down) rather than the Sussex amateur A.E.R. Gilligan. To Hawke the idea of a professional captain was anathema. He had been the most successful amateur captain of his era, and believed that professionals could not impose discipline on 'gentlemen'. To him this was not prejudice, but logic: the manservant could not manage the master; it was against the natural order of life. A team must have a leader, and a professional could not lead. *Quod erat demonstrandum.* It was perfectly clear to Hawke. Others may have shared that narrow-minded Victorian view, but if so they were too prudent to voice it. Hawke, who had no concept of political correctness, did so. What Hawke thought, Hawke said.

* This latter charge is unlikely, not least since no eye-witnesses ever corroborated it. See 'The Unjust Slur on Bobby Peel', by Irving Rosenwater.

And so, entirely in character, Hawke offered his support to Gilligan. 'Pray God,' he told the Yorkshire Annual General Meeting, 'no professional shall ever captain England. I love and admire them all but we have always had an amateur skipper and when the day comes when we shall have no more amateurs captaining England it will be a thousand pities.' It was not the first time Hawke had expressed such archaic views. Twenty years earlier he had written in the introduction to *The History of Yorkshire County Cricket Club* (1904): 'Amateurs infuse a freshness and an enthusiasm ... which the most hard working professional cannot impart.' Even more offensively, in 1908 the *Manchester Guardian* quoted him as saying: 'Amateurs are the moral backbone of a County team.' The message could not have been clearer: amateurs were from Olympus, and professionals were made of inferior clay.

The roof now fell in on Hawke. His class-conscious world belonged to the past. Hundreds of thousands of working men had fought and died in the First World War. The Labour Party, with the ambition of representing the working class, had been elected to government in 1923, and Ramsay MacDonald, the illegitimate son of a Morayshire farm labourer and a housemaid, had become Prime Minister. Nothing was as it had been, and Hawke's maladroit utterance seemed indefensible to millions, and incomprehensible to those who realised, as he did not, how the world had changed.

Once the offending words were published, there could be no retreat. Hawke was buried in the controversy. Even pre-war, such words would have been injudicious. Post-war, they were reputational suicide. A reprint of his autobiography, *Recollections and Reminiscences* (perhaps the least modest memoirs ever published), was cancelled. To those who weren't angry with him, he became a laughing stock. His mentor, Lord Harris, and his protégé, the archetypical Establishment man 'Plum' Warner, gallantly tried to explain away 'what he really meant', but succeeded only in making themselves ridiculous without aiding Hawke. It was a public relations disaster.

How did he come to do it? There is no mystery here. Hawke was a man without guile. His self-confident persona had no perception of danger. He did not understand a world in which every public figure has a man with a sandbag waiting around every corner to flatten him. Nor did he understand that his outmoded views were no longer tenable. His rectitude, or stubbornness, or arrogance (take your pick), left him exposed to ridicule and hostility. Poor out-of-date Hawke simply did not realise that the Great War had fatally crippled the social world that was the boundary of his personal experience.

In the aftermath of the ridicule that engulfed Hawke, it is tempting to dismiss his earlier contribution to cricket. But it would be wrong to do so. His cricketing career – successively captain of Cambridge University, Yorkshire and England, President of Yorkshire and the MCC and Chairman of the Test selectors – left little room for any other interests. As a player he graced first-class cricket for thirty-one years, from his debut in 1881 to his final game in Buenos Aires against the Republic of Argentina in 1912. In those years he scored 16,749 runs, with thirteen centuries and a highest score of 166 against Warwickshire in 1896, at an average of 20.15. Hawke did not approve of 'those beastly averages', which he believed 'encouraged slow play' by those trying to 'score off their own bat', which, emphatically, was 'not cricket'. His philosophy was that of a cricketing romantic. Hawke saw cricket as a team game, and he was true to that faith. On all occasions he inspired his teams to attack, irrespective of personal glory, and it brought Yorkshire the County Championship on eight occasions. It would be foolish to deny, whatever his shortcomings, that Hawke was a formidable leader.

His tale is full of anomalies. He was Yorkshire to the core, yet was born in Lincolnshire. The second son of an obscure country vicar, he became a parody of a haughty aristocrat. Was his high-handedness innate to his character? Or was it an affectation he adopted, believing it to be appropriate to a Baron? The answer must be conjecture. Hawke may not have been cerebral, but he was complex.

The first Baron Hawke was the Admiral who scattered a potential French invasion fleet in the Battle of Quiberon Bay in 1759. It was a pivotal moment in Pitt the Elder's Year of Victories, and Henry

Newbolt, he of 'Vitaï Lampada' fame, commemorated it in his ballad 'Admirals All':

'Twas long past noon of a wild November day
When Hawke came swooping from the west;
He heard the breakers thundering in Quiberon Bay,
But he flew the flag for battle, line abreast,
Down from the quicksands, waving out of sight,
Fiercely blew the storm-wind, darkly fell the night;
But they took the foe for pilot and the cannon's glare for light,
When Hawke came swooping from the west.
The guns that should have conquered us, they rusted on the shore,
The men that should have mastered us, they drummed and
    marched no more,
For England was England and a mighty brood she bore,
When Hawke came swooping from the west.

Years later, an amended version of that poem would be a cherished tribute to Hawke.

Young Martin Bladen Hawke had every reason to be proud of his ancestry as he grew up in the modest vicarage of his father the Reverend Edward Hawke, but he had no expectation that he would inherit the barony. Fate, however, was at work. His elder brother Edward died, and when the 4th Lord Hawke died, he was succeeded by his bachelor brother. Upon his death his cousin, Martin's father, took the title. Upon his father's death in 1887 his second son, fifth in line to the barony at his birth, was swept by fate to the title, and became the 7th Lord Hawke.

Hawke was schooled for the barony at Eton, where 'Mike' Mitchell was still on hand to coach young cricketers. For Hawke, an unenthusiastic scholar, the lure of sport comfortably overwhelmed studies. Even so, he did not break into an extremely strong Eton eleven until he was seventeen. After Eton he returned to private tuition, and did not go up to Cambridge until 1881. He leavened the burden of his studies by honing his shooting and hunting skills, and beginning his long association with Yorkshire. He was introduced to the county club by the Reverend E.S. Carter, a double Cambridge Blue. At the time Yorkshire cricket was dominated by Sheffield to the exclusion of the rest of the county, and it was to remain so until 1893. Unsurprisingly, the club was racked by factions. Hawke was not joining a happy ship.

Yorkshire had no qualms about professional captains. From the foundation of the club, professionals, from Roger Iddison to Tom Emmett, had led the county eleven, but in the climate of the times the committee saw the heir to the Hawke barony as an attractive acquisition. He was a competent player with a strong personality, who could captain the club as an amateur and thus improve its social status. When Hawke played his first game as a raw recruit, the experienced Emmett offered him the captaincy, but Hawke, realising his inexperience, was astute enough to decline. But he did so only to learn. He was aware of the responsibility that lay ahead, observed how Emmett handled the team, and began to absorb the skills of captaincy. He was appointed captain at the end of 1882, although it was known that he would be virtually an absentee at Cambridge for the following three years. At university his cricketing record was mixed, but as the captain of Yorkshire he was an obvious choice to lead the university. He did so in 1885, but won only one victory that year: fortunately, it was the varsity game against Oxford at Lord's. When he returned to Yorkshire the following season his long-unbroken authority at the club was about to begin.

Emmett, the old pro, though supportive, represented a challenge to Hawke's authority simply through his former tenure as captain and his seniority as a player. To help Hawke cope with the buccaneering free spirits in the team, Louis Hall, an austere lay preacher, was appointed vice-captain, sidelining Tom Emmett to the role of senior professional. Hall's sober lifestyle was an excellent antidote to the erratic behaviour of some of Hawke's new team, unkindly described by one onlooker as 'nine drunks and a Parson'. Hawke had inherited a tough task. 'I will not affirm,' he recalled years later, 'that those men were, in every respect, satisfactory.' This was an understatement. They were, Hawke added, 'a team which suffered from injudicious hospitality'. Hawke took action. In 1887 he dismissed one of 'the drunks', the slow left-armer Edmund Peate, and having weathered the inevitable storm, his authority grew, until in due course his word became the strict letter of the law. It is this authoritarian Hawke that history recalls.

On occasion, as with his stern treatment of Peate, Hawke seemed to court unpopularity. Benefit games were vital for the post-cricket security of professional players, and in 1894 Johnny Briggs of Lancashire had nominated the Roses clash as his benefit. To guard against bad weather, not unknown at Old Trafford, Lancashire had prepared two wickets for the game, one of which had been covered. Following rain, Hawke refused to play on the covered wicket, and as a result the game ended early on the second day. Briggs, well out of pocket, was distraught. Many thought Hawke's behaviour was shabby.

It was not an isolated incident. Wilfred Rhodes had no doubt that Yorkshire were 'mean' over benefits, and he blamed Hawke. In 1899, at a meeting at Lord's, Hawke had proposed that counties should control the investment and disposal of benefit monies – a task his Lordship believed was beyond the capacity of the poor professional. Three years later, under his guidance, Yorkshire decreed that only one-third of benefit proceeds would be handed directly to the beneficiary, with the balance held in trust to 'terminate with the death of the widow'. Even if well-meaning, this aim fell short of ideal. When Schofield Haigh's widow applied to use money held in trust to buy a cottage the committee refused, instead lending her £250, upon which they charged interest. 'I can't think,' said an acid Rhodes, 'that this was right. I expect it was one of Lord Hawke's ideas.'

This is almost certainly true. Hawke was a paternalist, confident that he knew what was best for his players and determined, as he saw it, to protect them from themselves. He feared that players would 'fritter away' their benefit money on gambling or drink, and be 'reduced to beggary'.* His case, although weak, was not non-existent. Many players did indeed face hardship once they ceased playing (see

* 'Many an honest player has frittered away the substantial proceeds of his match and been reduced almost to beggary.' From Hawke's introduction to *The History of Yorkshire County Cricket Club* (1904).

for example pages 270–1). Where he could, Hawke helped. He paid a small winter allowance to 'blind, toothless and penniless' Jack Thewlis, who had scored the first ever century for Yorkshire, against Surrey in 1868. Even so, Wilfred Rhodes was surely right that it was 'a scandal that benefits were never the property of the player'. Between the views of Hawke and Rhodes lay a gap so wide that it was unbridgeable.

Even if his actions could be ham-fisted, Hawke was devoted to the welfare of his players, provided they were obedient. He set up a system of 'talent money', usually five shillings a time, paid in a lump sum at the end of the season, for outstanding performances, including fielding. The arbiter of this largesse was Hawke, and his word was final: 'I gave marks according to *my* view of the importance to the side of what was done.' He fussed over how professionals would live after their retirement, and compelled them to contribute to the Cricketers' Friendly Society. He persuaded Yorkshire to pay professionals £2 per week in the winter, although, being Hawke, he exacted a price for this concession: as Yorkshire were paying Hirst and Rhodes out of season, he refused to let them tour Australia in the winter of 1901–02. In 1905 he tried to reduce the lottery element of benefit matches, which could be ruined by rain, and Yorkshire agreed to pay up to £200 a year into a fund to augment poor benefits. These were kindly, well-meaning actions, even if, in more egalitarian days, the manner of them makes one cringe.

Hawke built up a powerful team at Yorkshire. From August 1899 to July 1901, inspired by the bowling of Hirst, Haigh and Rhodes, they were unbeaten. When they finally lost, in an astonishing game against Somerset in which Yorkshire had led by 238 runs on the first innings but were beaten by 279 runs, it was a sensation. As captain, Hawke had moments of inspiration. In the second innings of the Yorkshire match against the Australians at Leeds in 1902 he asked F.S. Jackson, rather than Rhodes, to open the bowling with Hirst, and the two men dismissed Australia for 23, their second-lowest-ever score. Jackson took 9 for 42 in the match, and four wickets in five balls in the second innings. Hawke's choice of Jackson was startling, since only a few days earlier Rhodes had taken 7 for 17 against Australia in the first innings of the Edgbaston Test match.

Yorkshire came first in Hawke's view, sometimes at the expense of England. In 1890, a pig-headed Hawke insisted that Peel and Ulyett played for Yorkshire, not England, and the Oval Test match was nearly lost. Later, Hawke became Chairman of selectors, and following Harris's example attempted to exclude Ranjitsinhji from the Test team in 1899. He failed – W.G. and C.B. Fry insisted on picking Ranji. Hawke disliked seeing an Indian in the England team but said generously of Ranji, 'There can be no possible description of his batting. It must be seen to be believed.' Three years later, in 1902, another spat arose. Hawke was still Chairman of the England selectors, and Lancashire's Archie MacLaren was captain. Their relations were poor. Yorkshire and Lancashire did not mix, and any goodwill evaporated as the Australians outplayed England. MacLaren, backed by the other selectors, wanted Haigh of Yorkshire to play in the fourth Test at Old Trafford, but Hawke refused to release him. Jackson, Hirst and Rhodes of Yorkshire were in the team, and that, he said, was sufficient. It was Yorkshire first and England second. Due to Hawke's obstinacy, Fred Tate of Sussex was picked instead of Haigh, with disastrous consequences. Tate was thrashed mercilessly by the Australian batsmen, dropped a vital catch and was bowled out when England needed only four runs to win. Poor Tate, a competent county bowler, passed into legend in the worst possible way. Hawke went marching on. Eventually, in 1910, at the age of fifty, he retired as captain of Yorkshire and moved upstairs to exercise continuing influence as President.

This new post did not deter Hawke's lifelong addiction to organising and leading overseas tours during the winter months. Between 1887 and 1912 he led tours to Australia (1887), India (1889), India and Ceylon (1892–93), the United States and Canada (1891 and 1894), South Africa (1895–96 and 1898–99), the West Indies (1896–97), New Zealand (1902–03, from which he withdrew through illness, although the tour went ahead) and Argentina (1911–12). He chose the teams personally and crammed them with 'gentleman' cricketers, predominantly Oxford and Cambridge Blues, as he believed they were best able to strengthen links across the Empire. Nonetheless, Hawke's personal behaviour ensured that there were spats with his hosts. The 1895–96 tour of South Africa throws up a classic illustration of Hawke's insensitivity. Robert Poore, formerly ADC to Lord Harris in Bombay and now a Major serving with the 7th Hussars, twice scored brilliant centuries against Hawke's eleven. Poore was a 'gentleman', and Hawke, in rather ungentlemanly fashion, tried to persuade him to desert his South African team and play for the tourists. The South African authorities were enraged at this attempted poaching, and protested vehemently. Hawke was unwilling to withdraw his offer, but the diplomatic Poore, exercising the skills he had used at Lord Harris's elbow, defused the issue by declining the invitation.

Hawke's character was a patchwork. His shortcomings were glaring, but he had virtues too. He was immensely popular in Yorkshire for his leadership of the club. One avid supporter, the Reverend Egerton Leigh, parodied Newbolt to write of Yorkshire's 1908 championship season:

> The enemy dropped catches here and there,
> When Hawke came swooping from the west;
> Some were beaten by our innings and to spare,
> Defeat by many wickets took the rest;
> The balls that should have routed us were smacked and smashed for
> four,
> The men who should have mastered us will master us no more,
> For Yorkshire was Yorkshire and a mighty brood she bore,
> When Hawke came swooping from the west.

Hawke, with his family pride, must have loved that acknowledgement. He had no jealousy or resentment in his make-up. He lived, and played, as a genuine amateur. He loved cricket, for which much may be forgiven, and he knew how to amuse himself: riding, shooting, hunting, golf and music were all favourite pursuits. Stories of his less appealing characteristics are legion. He could be obstinate and bigoted. And yet, when Pelham Warner, albeit hardly a dispassionate judge of any member of the Establishment, declared that he 'ruled by love, not fear', and was 'unselfish, with the kindest of hearts', he did touch upon a part of the complex man who was Hawke. Amid the criticisms, which are legion, much can be said to balance the negative aspects of a man who, above all, had one defect: he was born a hundred years too late.

16

The Grand Old Man and the Backroom Boy

For thirty-five years, one man dominated cricket and became an emblem of Victorian England. He was as English as Henry VIII, but gentler. His face and form were recognisable the world over, and remain so today. Some of his feats defy the imagination. He was a cricketing phenomenon who graduated to superstar, then icon. When he played in representative games, the entrance fee would rise. If true greatness is marked by dominance over contemporaries, then, with Don Bradman his only challenger, he was the greatest player of all time. He was – beyond argument – the most influential.

When he began to play cricket, Lord's was a tented field with no practice nets or heavy roller. Bowling was round-arm, and some veterans still wore high hats. The majority of batsmen – one glittering exception being his elder brother – played fast bowling predominantly on the back foot. Every hit was run out, for there were as yet no boundaries. Pitches were uncared for and often dangerous. Only animals mowed the outfield. There were no Test matches and no formal county cricket. The travelling elevens of professional players had dominated the game for almost twenty years, and *ad-hoc* representative games dwarfed the number of inter-county fixtures. From the moment he began to play first-class cricket, he was a phenomenon. In the course of his career he made every score from nought to a hundred. He posed as an amateur, but his earnings from cricket were far higher than those of all his contemporaries. He became 'the Champion' in his prime, and as his long career progressed he was known uninventively as the 'Old Man', almost certainly an echo of Gladstone, the 'Grand Old Man' of Liberal politics. It is as such that history remembers William Gilbert Grace.

W.G. Grace was born on 18 July 1848, a year of revolution across Europe. This was appropriate, although the revolution he would lead in England would be milder and more lasting. Young Gilbert, his name to the family, was born on his mother Martha's thirty-sixth birthday, into a West Country largely unspoiled by development and a family besotted by cricket. The arrival of his younger brother Fred two years later made their home, Downend House, too small for a family grown to five boys and four girls, and they moved to nearby Chestnuts, a larger property with more land and two orchards. His father, Dr Henry Grace, a general practitioner with an enthusiasm for cricket, played the game to a good standard, and set up his own village team that in time would merge into West Gloucestershire. He laid down a pitch in one of the orchards so that his boys might practise whilst their mother looked on with a keen and critical eye. Their uncle Alfred Pocock coached the boys, and their four sisters, non-players themselves, were happy to act as fieldsmen. In their absence, even the family dogs, Don, Ponto and Noble, were enlisted. The Grace cricketing gene must have leaped species, for the animals learned to catch the ball on the bounce, and Noble would retrieve it whenever it pitched into the nearby quarry full of water.

Early photographs of Grace's parents hint at strong characters. Dr Grace, stocky with a receding hairline, walrus moustache and muttonchop whiskers, looks the epitome of a dedicated general practitioner, but the impression he gives of austere Victorian paternalism does not suggest joyful enthusiasm for cricket. Mrs Grace, broad-faced, dark hair stretched ruthlessly over her scalp to hang down in ringlets upon her shoulder, looks a formidable matriarch. Other than cricket her passions are a mystery, although she looks as if she would have approved of Florence Nightingale running rings around male inefficiency in the Crimea, but not of Emily Davies co-authoring the first petition for women's suffrage. Shrewd assessments were a Grace characteristic, but an interest in politics was not.

Cricket was the core theme of the Grace home. When not being played, it was being talked about. All four of young William Gilbert's brothers – his seniors Henry, Edward and Alfred, and his younger brother Fred – were keen players, and in 1880 two of them, Edward and Fred, would play at The Oval with W.G. (as Gilbert had become in the eyes of the world) against Australia in the first ever Test in England.* Henry and Alfred were good club players, but less touched by the gifts of hand-and-eye coordination that elevated their brothers to the very top of Victorian cricket.

While Gilbert was a child his elder brother, Edward Mills, blazed the trail to fame and became one of the most exciting batsmen in Victorian cricket. E.M. had an unorthodox style that reinvented batting. In an age in which style was sometimes rated more highly than success, he spurned convention. He never bothered with the 'correct' stroke, but selected the one that would yield most runs. His keen eye enabled him, against all accepted practice, to hit across the line of the ball successfully. In reflection, years later, W.G. attributed this gift to E.M. playing as a boy with a bat that was too large for him, but whatever the cause, only the most brilliant eye-and-wrist coordination could have made this style of play so formidable.

Nor was this E.M.'s only innovation. His ease of cross-hitting enabled him to perfect the pull shot, and his aggressive instincts led him to attack fast bowling by the simple expedient of hitting it straight back over the bowler's head. He predated Ranjitsinhji's dictum, 'First, see where the ball is going to pitch, then go to it; then hit it.' His facility for playing the ball into vacant areas of the field earned him many runs. The finished product of these skills amazed his contemporaries and delighted cricket crowds. Even that giant of times past Fuller Pilch, an umpire in E.M.'s salad days, loved to see him hitting.

---

* The Graces were not unique as a cricketing family in Victorian times. The Walkers, Lytteltons, Studds, Steels, Fosters, Austen-Leighs, Rowleys and Palairets all produced more than one talented cricketer.

E.M. was a prodigy. In 1855, at the age of fourteen, he was selected for West Gloucestershire (admittedly a Grace fiefdom, for his father managed the team), and fielded so well at longstop against the all-conquering All-England Eleven that the veteran William Clarke presented him with a bat. It was a kindly act by the often crusty Clarke, and perhaps also a tribute to his gift for assessing cricket talent.

E.M. burst into top-class cricket like a meteor, and by his early twenties he had become the most feared batsman in the country. In 1862, playing for the MCC against the Gentlemen of Kent, he scored 192 not out and captured ten wickets in the Kent second innings (it was a twelve-a-side game; the remaining batsman retired hurt). It being E.M., who never did what was expected, he captured his wickets with a mixture of round-arm and lob bowling. As a fieldsman he was supreme. 'Such a point,' said William Caffyn, 'was never seen before and perhaps, never will be again.' A remarkable career was launched that, but for the advent of his younger brother, might have outshone all others in Victorian cricket.

W.G.'s ascendancy did not begin until the mid-1860s. In the years before that, E.M., small, dark and wiry, with his tiny cap perched above a luxuriantly bewhiskered face and clean-shaven chin, was among the gods of the game; thereafter, W.G. stood alone. In 1863, interspersed with medical studies at Bristol, E.M. scored over 3,000 runs in all matches before travelling with George Parr's team on the winter tour of Australia. He underperformed on the tour, having a whitlow on his finger, and, as he freely admitted, he contributed to his poor run of scores by batting even more recklessly than normal. This did not prevent him from arranging private contests for wagers* and pocketing the proceeds in an early illustration of the keen eye for financial well-being that was a Grace family trait. Despite his effervescence, E.M. did not burn himself out, but with a three-year gap to complete his qualification as a surgeon, played first-class cricket for over thirty years, and remained a stalwart of the Gloucestershire county side until 1894. Even then, at the age of fifty-three,

---

* For example, E.M. Grace and John Jackson vs Eleven of Castlemaine. Grace and Jackson (4) beat Castlemaine (2) by 2 runs.

he played on, his enthusiasm undimmed. As a club player he had once hit 295 for Thornbury out of a total of 331 in a hundred minutes. At the time, 1873, he was in his prime, but even in retirement he continued to terrorise the opposition, and as late as 1909, at the age of sixty-seven, was sufficiently agile to capture over a hundred wickets with underarm lobs. E.M. – the 'Coroner'* – was not only one of the great characters of cricket, with the sharp Grace attitude that *just* stayed within the laws of the game, but was the liveliest of personalities, with a gift for conversation and storytelling. His failure to write his memoirs is a great loss to cricket folklore, for of all Victorian players E.M. was the one most likely to break through the formality of the time to leave a vivid recollection of his experiences. With his unconventional cricket life, haphazard medical career, avaricious interest in money and four wives, his would have been a spicy story. Perhaps, as his younger brother became legend, he felt his tale was of little interest; if so, he was wrong.

The youngest Grace, Fred, died at only twenty-nine of a chill that settled on the lungs only two weeks after his first and only Test match, in which he was twice dismissed without scoring, but left behind the memory of a spectacular catch off a steepling hit by George Bonnor (see page 231). Fred was the first player, but not the last, to begin his Test career with a 'pair' (Graham Gooch, for example), and, but for his premature death, he would have played many times for England. He was an excellent forcing batsman – 6,906 runs at an average of 25.02 – and a top-class bowler who captured 329 wickets at 20.06. He was also a magnificent fieldsman. The fame of his brothers has left him rather neglected by history, but his memorable performances with bat and ball often lit up Victorian cricket.

If E.M. was a prodigy, and G.F. the forgotten Grace, W.G. would outshine them both. When he first picked up a bat as a toddler, his three elder brothers were already hooked on cricket, with E.M. developing his special talent. Throughout the year W.G. played all

* He was Coroner for West Gloucestershire.

hours on the makeshift pitch in the Downend orchard, encouraged by his parents, Uncle Pocock, sisters, friends and, when no one else was available to play with him, family servants, and stableboys too. At the age of nine, nepotism being a Victorian trait, he made his debut for the West Gloucestershire club. At that age he was merely making up the numbers, and he contributed little, but learned a great deal. Two years later, as an eleven-year-old, he scored a mere 12 runs in eleven innings, but it was his last season as a makeweight. At the age of twelve he scored 51 not out against Clifton, a mighty innings for one so young, but dwarfed by nineteen-year-old E.M.'s majestic 150. Three years later, in 1863, he scored 350 runs in nineteen innings, of which six were not out, and was ready to burst upon the first-class scene that he would dominate for thirty-five years.

W.G. and *Wisden* both entered top-class cricket in 1864. When he began, W.G. batted on poor wickets against bowlers such as Jackson, Tarrant, Tinley, Willsher and Freeman. In his latter years he faced Kortright, Richardson, Rhodes and Lockwood, while between these extremes Ulyett, Steel, Peate, Barlow, Crossland, Lohmann, Briggs, Peate and Tom Hearne strove to capture the most valuable wicket in the first-class game. In Test cricket, he faced Australians from Spofforth and Boyle to Ernest Jones and Hugh Trumble. It is a galaxy of bowling talent such as no other batsman has contended with in the long history of cricket.

Despite this array of deadly skills at twenty-two yards' distance, W.G.'s batting record soars above those of all his contemporaries. At only fifteen he was selected to play against an All-England Eleven, and the fearsome George Tarrant, in a kindly action to a young man, bowled to him during the lunch interval. When he batted, his eye in, Tarrant bowled some loose balls to help him settle, and the young W.G. scored 32 runs. He never forgot Tarrant's kindness. Before his sixteenth birthday he signalled his emergence at Hove with scores of 170 and 56 not out for South Wales against Gentlemen of Sussex. At eighteen years of age, tall, broad and powerful, he hit 224 not out for England against Surrey at The Oval. His captain, pleased by his performance, permitted him to leave the ground for the National

Olympian Association meeting at Crystal Palace, where he won the hurdles over a quarter-mile.

As a young man W.G. was lithe and supple, with every sinew trained to fitness. He could high jump five feet, run a hundred yards in under eleven seconds, and was never defeated over two hundred yards as a hurdler. Until 1870, when he gave up athletics, he was one of the fastest men in England over a quarter-mile, winning many races. He also competed in the long jump, pole vault and hop, skip and jump: Grace was an elite athlete before he turned his attention wholly to cricket. As he grew he broadened, and as he aged he fleshed out to the familiar caricature of his mature years. The twelve-and-a-half-stone young man who toured North America in 1872 – 'spare and extremely active' said Lord Harris – was eighteen stone by 1880 when he scored his famous 152 against Australia at The Oval. His black beard bushed out and dominated a strong face with sharp, twinkly eyes.

Grace's cricketing feats spanned season upon season, and occasionally flamed into successes no fiction writer would have dared to invent for his hero. In seven days in 1876 he scored 839 runs in three massive innings of 344 for MCC against Kent and, for Gloucestershire, 177 against Notts and 318 not out against Yorkshire. After his first two innings, Yorkshire were expecting him to fail. 'I'll shoot him if he makes a hundred against us,' Tom Emmett, ever the humourist, told Richard Daft. The threat, fortunately, was made in jest. Later that year Grace hit 400 not out for United South of England against Twenty-Two of Grimsby. This was not officially a first-class match, but it was still a mighty performance against twenty-two fielders. No one had ever scored such a weight of runs in such a brief period before – nor would ever do again. Year after year he topped the batting averages – twelve times between 1866 and 1880. Six times he exceeded 2,000 first-class runs in a season.* Three times he scored a hundred in each innings of the same match.** Seventeen times he

* 2,739 runs in 1871; 2,139 in 1873 (including some non-first-class games); 2,622 in 1876; 2,062 in 1887; 2,346 in 1895; 2,135 in 1896.
** 130 and 102 not out for South of Thames vs North of Thames in 1868; 101 and 103 not out for Gloucestershire vs Kent in 1887; 148 and 153 for Gloucestershire vs Yorkshire in 1888.

carried his bat through a first-class innings. In 1869 he opened with B.B. Cooper for the Gentlemen of the South vs Players of South, and together they scored 283 for the first wicket. In 1894, aged forty-six, and batting with Ranji, he amassed his highest ever score at Lord's, 196 for the MCC against Cambridge University. The following season, in a unique late flowering, he scored a thousand runs in May alone, with double hundreds against Somerset and Kent and centuries against Sussex and Middlesex. To emphasise the fact that his powers were undimmed, he scored a triple century for Gloucestershire against Sussex at the age of forty-eight. In all first-class matches W.G. scored 126 centuries in a total of 54,896 runs at an average of nearly 40, playing for much of his career on wickets that no self-respecting modern batsman would consider safe. It was an achievement beyond compare, and as if to make the point more evident, he scored a further 44,936 runs in minor matches.

As a batsman, W.G. seemed to be without a flaw. Unlike E.M., he was not a 'dasher', nor did he favour E.M.'s pull shot. He batted correctly, without risk, and within himself. He accumulated runs, with a push to leg being especially productive. He rarely lifted the ball off the ground – a characteristic Bradman shared half a century later – and hitting sixes was never part of his game plan. His defence was impeccable. Grace was a complete one-man orchestra of cricket: unlike his contemporaries he was neither a back player nor a forward player, neither hitter nor sticker. He could play any role with equal facility, although he was especially partial to fast bowling. No stroke was foreign to him, other than the leg-glance, which the wristy skills of Ranjitsinhji introduced to cricket late in W.G.'s career. Unlike many batsmen, who surrendered their wicket having accumulated a big score, Grace batted on and on. He never threw his wicket away or took unnecessary risks. He was insatiable for runs.

W.G.'s talent was not restricted to batting. He bowled round-arm – medium-paced until 1872, but rather slower thereafter, with a distinct break from leg to off – obtaining 2,809 wickets at around 18 runs a time, and a further 4,446 in minor matches. He was an enthusiastic appealer and never slow to demand a decision from the umpire. In 1873 he took 10 for 92 runs against Kent in a twelve-a-side game, and in 1886, playing for MCC, all ten Oxford University wickets for 49. Often his bowling analyses outshone the most eminent of his contemporaries. He took over eight hundred catches, mostly fielding at point, and, occasionally keeping wicket, obtained fifty-four stumpings. The figures of his onfield achievements are staggering, but they alone do not remotely tell the full tale of his contribution to cricket.* In his prime, W.G. became the very personification of the game. Many truly great players shared the field with him, but all were left in his wake in achievement and reputation. He became the father figure of cricket, the man who stood apart from all others. This was due in part to his triumphs on the field, but also to his personality. His appearance – so similar to the Victorian Prime Minister Lord Salisbury – was universally known. With Queen Victoria, Gladstone, Disraeli and Salisbury, he is one of the towering figures of the age. He popularised cricket as no man before or since.

W.G. was thirty-two years old when the first Test match was played in England in 1880. In the fifteen years preceding that game, he had topped the batting averages twelve times; he remained in the top echelon for a further twenty years, while a galaxy of batsmen – Shrewsbury, Walter Read, MacLaren, Ranji, Stoddart, Abel, Hayward, Fry – came to the fore. The 'Old Man' remained first among equals, but, sporadic feats of brilliance apart, his feats no longer towered over his contemporaries as in earlier years.

Test matches were rare events at first, and Grace played for England in only twenty-two games, scoring 1,098 runs at an average of 32.29. He scored two centuries and five 50s and captained the team for the last time at the age of fifty-one, at Trent Bridge in 1899. In that match he opened the batting with C.B. Fry, at twenty-seven young enough to be his son, and, as Grace had been in his youth, a formidable athlete. Grace's loss of pace cost many singles, and his fielding caused heckling from some of the spectators, but no one imagined it was to be his last Test match. No selector would have

---

* No one can be absolutely confident of the statistics of Grace's long career. Analyses differ. The figures which follow are those generally accepted.

dropped him – except himself. As he travelled home with F. S. Jackson he remarked, 'It's all over, Jacker; I shan't play again!' Jackson may not have taken this seriously, thinking W.G. was merely reflecting the disappointment of a below-par performance, but Grace was adamant. When the selection of the team for the next Test was being discussed, C.B. Fry arrived late at the meeting, knowing nothing of Grace's conversation with Jackson. 'Would you play Archie MacLaren?' was the innocent question put to him by W.G. 'Yes,' said Fry, unaware of the consequence of his reply, and W.G. stepped down from the captaincy and the team. It was the end of the Grace era.

The chroniclers have left a record of W.G.'s playing career that marks him out as a unique talent, but that is merely a part of the appeal that made him a figure whose fame has grown with the years. We know, too, his face and form. Tall, slim and lithe as a youth, his girth grew increasingly large despite a lifetime of intense physical activity. W.G. was never a bookworm, and had a distaste for learning: his qualification as a doctor was painstakingly achieved only at the age of twenty-nine. There was speculation that he would retire from cricket to pursue his medical career, but it was never likely. If he was not playing cricket he was golfing, or riding, or beagling, or walking – long hours of exercise in the fresh open air, twelve months a year, were a lifelong habit. And yet, his big-boned frame grew to the familiar eighteen-stone figure, with lumbering carriage and stooping shoulders, all carried atop slightly bandy legs. Dark, wary eyes looked out of his broad, bronzed and bearded face. Large brown hands greeted friend and foe with an iron grip. The superficial Grace is as clear to our vision today as it was to his contemporaries, but much else is missing. It is far more difficult to reconstruct the rounded man.

Much of what we know is appealing. Contemporaries recalled him as generous, with a breeziness of manner. He was a spontaneous countryman, modest and without vanity. He loved jokes. He was said to be boyish-hearted, boisterous, with an infectious laugh. He was simple and frank, said admirers, and often the centre of a jolly crowd. He could be wonderfully kind. For a big man, he had a high-pitched tenor voice, sometimes squeaky, and with a Gloucestershire burr, although it carried authority when he issued on-field instructions during a match. Yet, beyond cricket, the journalist Arthur Porritt, his literary ghost, thought him 'singularly inarticulate'. Bernard Darwin felt he was 'a great big schoolboy in all he did'. No recording of his voice is known to exist.* He rarely made speeches and those he could not avoid were brief and often repetitive. All this adds up to a jovial image of a sports-loving Englishman who was larger than life. But it is an incomplete portrait.

With the passage of years, it is difficult to get beyond the image to the essence of W.G. Grace. The evidence can be contradictory, and, as with all iconic figures, anecdote swamps reality: when Grace bent the spirit of cricket (but not the law) to run out Jones of Australia in the 1882 Oval Test (see page 235), even *Wisden* made excuses for him. Affection breeds tolerance, and obscures a clear picture. Yet there are too many illustrations of W.G. infringing good sportsmanship to doubt that winning was often more important to him than playing the game. When his blood was up, sharp practice stained his sporting instinct. He was once accused of obstructing James Lillywhite, who was about to take a simple catch offered by Fred Grace when W.G.'s ample body got in the way. On another occasion he ran six runs, the last three with the ball tucked into his shirt where the fielders could not reach it. These were not isolated examples. When the Australian George Bonnor was dismissed against Gloucestershire during the tour of 1882 he muttered in complaint that he was 'talked out by one of the fielders'. Grace is a likely culprit. Even his long-time friend Lord Harris admitted that 'his gamesmanship added to the fund of stories about him'. The public stature of the 'Old Man' was such that criticism was tempered to understanding, and censure was absent. Grace was lucky; for other men, some of his tricks would have heaped coals of fire on their head, but he was immune, above and beyond the common herd.

* There have been reports that one such recording does exist, probably on an old cylinder. If so, it has remained hidden despite appeals by, among others, cricket historian David Rayvern Allen.

Erratic sportsmanship was not the only debit in the Grace ledger. Although nominally an amateur and a gentleman, Grace could not claim – as Lord Hawke could, and did, with Olympian self-regard – that he never received money from cricket beyond his bare expenses. Grace had a facility for fiction, but such a claim would have met with ridicule. All his life Grace knew his commercial value, and was blatant in demanding expenses that incorporated a substantial appearance fee. Money mattered to him. His testimonial – as an amateur, he could not have a 'benefit' – in 1895 earned him an unprecedented £9,703. Two years later David Hunter, the popular Yorkshire wicket-keeper, received the highest benefit yet on record, £1,975. Grace was in a different league. There is insufficient evidence to calculate how much he earned in his career, but it is safe to assume that no one in cricket earned as much until sponsorship of players became fashion-able a hundred years after his prime. Before that, in purchasing power, the earnings of Grace, the 'amateur', dwarfed all others. And yet, in 1891, presumably with his tongue well in his cheek, he felt able to complain that cricket was 'too much of a business, like football'.

When Grace arranged teams for fixtures he charged a fee, paid the professionals their £3–£5 per man, and pocketed the balance. In an echo of William Clarke, his income from the match was often as much as that of the rest of the team added together. Grace was extremely fortunate that his 'shamateurism' did not flare into a full-blown scandal. It could, and should, have done so, but with magis-terial hypocrisy cricket's authorities looked away even though amateurs' 'expenses' far exceeded professionals' salaries. There were some tricky incidents and occasional bad publicity in the press. After Gloucestershire visited Surrey in 1878, E.M. Grace, Secretary of the county since 1871, submitted wholly inflated (and bogus) expense claims that Surrey rejected. It is unlikely that this was an isolated incident. When E.M. presented the claim to his own Gloucester committee they rejected it too, and cut it back* – and it was resubmit-

---

* Grace claimed £102.10s., which the Gloucester committee reduced to £80.10s. (*Sportsman's Magazine*).

ted to Surrey. Surrey reluctantly paid up, but the Graces pocketed the shortfall out of Gloucester's resources.

Amateurs' 'expenses', especially Grace's, were a growing scandal. In 1878 the MCC issued a note to the effect that no cricketer who received more than legitimate expenses would be selected to play in the annual Gentlemen vs Players showcase. They added, no doubt with their fingers as crossed as their facts, that they had invariably adhered to this policy. Lillywhite's *Cricket Companion* sniffed: 'Cricketers . . . know, as well as we do, this statement is, to use a mild term, hardly consistent with the facts.' In fact it was a barefaced lie. W.G., who *always* received more than his expenses (and who added thousands to the gate), was the first name in the Gentlemen's team year upon year, and his presence turned the tide of the fixture.* It was, however, consistent with a sort of logic. Grace, as an amateur, was the face of Victorian cricket.

Grace's magisterial status in England enabled him to ride out such domestic criticism with ease. It was, after all, the era of self-help, in which sturdy individualism was believed to be good for the soul as well as for the state.** Things could be less easy overseas, where his behaviour often caused resentment. When, at the age of twenty-four, he accompanied R.A. Fitzgerald's team to Canada and the United States, he was the undoubted centrepiece of the tour. It was, nominally, an all-amateur tour, with Hornby, Harris and Ottaway in the side. Yet all was not what it seemed. The 'amateurs' were paid lavish expenses and $600 in gold for each game, which was about as clear an infringement of amateur status as could be imagined. When criticism broke out in the press upon their return, Grace ignored it, and Fitzgerald, as captain, faced it down by offering an unabashed defence that persuaded no one but silenced many. No action was taken.

Nor did the fuss deter Grace from continuing to assert his worth.

---

* Before 1865 the Gentlemen had lost twenty-two of twenty-four successive games, the two exceptions being at Lord's in 1853 and at The Oval in 1862. With Grace, they were dominant for the next twenty-five years.
** Samuel Smiles published *Self-Help* in 1859, when Grace was eleven years old. Its influence lasted.

When the Melbourne Cricket Club made preliminary enquiries in 1872 about whether he would take a team to Australia the following year he agreed to do so, but requested a £1,500 fee (about £70,000 today). This unprecedented demand was rejected, but Grace was unperturbed. An English team without him would be *Hamlet* without the Prince, and he waited patiently for the further approach he was confident would come. It did so as soon as financial backers were found, but by then his terms had altered. He still demanded £1,500, but he also sought expenses for his fiancée Agnes, who was about to become his wife. Very few employees demand honeymoon expenses from their employer, but Grace had no qualms. His terms were accepted, but it is likely that his sponsors were aggrieved at his price, and events during the tour would add to their unhappiness. Grace stuck to the strict letter of his contract, but did not shy from exploiting loopholes in it. Once more, in selecting his team, he valued the professionals at only one-tenth of his self-assessment, and Emmett, Pooley and Alfred Shaw were among those who declined to go.

They were wise, for it was an unhappy tour. Grace was only twenty-five years old, and adjusting to early married life, but whatever private immaturities and distractions bedevilled him, his behaviour left a bitter taste. The professionals resented being lodged in cheaper accommodation than the amateurs. The betting fraternity, inevitably large in Australia, accused the Englishmen of conniving to lose early games, and the *Sydney Herald* claimed that one of the 'gentlemen' (unspecified) advised friends not to bet, as 'the professionals [are] not working with [us]'. The match-fixing allegation had no justification, but the professionals must have resented the allegation made against them by one of their team-mates.

Internal dissent among the team was supplemented throughout the tour by persistent adverse press criticism of on-field and off-field disputes. Whether by ill-luck or ill-judgement, Grace upset his hosts time after time. He missed receptions, refused to let the professionals attend some of them, and complained when they boycotted others. He then upset the tour promoters further by arranging extra games for 'expenses'. It was not surprising that he received hostile coverage from the Australian press, which attacked him for snobbishness (for placing the professionals and the amateurs in different hotels), hypocrisy (for claiming more expenses as an amateur than the professionals received in fees) and general bad manners towards his hosts. Even with his supreme self-confidence, Grace must have been hurt by the attacks: on one occasion he manhandled an agent of the promoters who had bad-mouthed him. This was uncharacteristic, and suggests a young man rattled by criticism. His behaviour left an uneasy relationship that would re-emerge eighteen years later, when he returned to Australia.

In the intervening years Grace earned a great deal of money, but insufficient to damp his enthusiasm for more. When Lord Sheffield invited him to lead a team to Australia in 1891–92, Grace demanded a fee of £3,000 and agreement that his wife and two youngest children could accompany him at His Lordship's expense. It was a high bid even for Grace, but it was accepted, to the dismay of the professionals, who received a mere £300 – with no relatives accompanying them. Grace may have thought his demand a normal tariff; he had, after all, taken his new wife with him to Australia at his hosts' expense, so many years earlier. His extraordinary shamateurism may have been irritating to the professionals, but it was tolerated by his admirers. Even Sydney Pardon, the long-serving editor of *Wisden*, usually punctilious about the law and practice of cricket (and brave in opposing illegal bowling actions), excused W.G. as 'anomalous', adding, 'Customs curtsey to great kings.'

Outside cricket, Grace followed the family tradition and qualified as a doctor. It was not an easy or a swift process. He enrolled in Bristol Medical School in 1868, at the age of twenty, studied intermittently at Bristol, Bart's and Westminster Hospitals, but did not pass his final examinations until 1879. He then set up as a general practitioner in an unfashionable area of Bristol where, with the help of a *locum tenens* to cover his absences in the summer, he attended the medical needs of the local community for twenty years. During the winter months he seems to have been a diligent doctor, and it is even rumoured that – uncharacteristically – he did not always submit bills to low-income families. This has the ring of truth. A kind man, blessed with good health like Grace, who had chosen to practise in a poor neighbourhood, would have understood the hardships of his poorer patients. It is a very large credit in his ledger.

And yet Grace was never recognised with a public award. In the middle of his blazing season of 1895, *The Times* mentioned 'Dr W.G. Grace whose name has been everywhere of late – except where it might well have been – on the Birthday Honours List'. *Punch* agreed:

> True, Thunderer, true. He stands the test
> Un-matched, unchallengeable Best,
> At our best game! Requite him!
> For thirty years to hold first place
> Pleases a stout, sport-loving race:
> By Jove, Sir William Gilbert Grace
> Sounds splendid. Punch says 'Knight him'.

Sadly, it never happened.

In 1898, at the age of fifty, W.G. ceased to practise as a doctor,* and a new opportunity beckoned. The Board of Crystal Palace wished to set up a new private members' cricket club that, hopefully, would enjoy county status. After much haggling, in October Grace accepted the secretaryship and management of the London County Cricket Club for £600 a year. He did not consult Gloucestershire, nor inform them of his negotiations, but planned to retain his old allegiance along with his new one. If this behaviour seems arrogant or careless, he was, after all, used to getting his own way. But fate now dealt him a crippling blow. Over the New Year of 1899 his twenty-year-old daughter Bessie, healthy and attractive, contracted typhoid fever. She fought it for nearly seven weeks, but her battle was futile, and she died in early February. It was a blow that must have destroyed Grace's peace of mind. All his life he had been indulged. Now, when he most needed help, it was denied. His distress of mind may explain the events that were to follow.

---

* After a new Health Authority was introduced Grace did not like its terms of payment, and resigned.

Despite his carefree acceptance of his new role with London County, Grace was still captain of Gloucestershire. He had played first-class cricket for them for twenty-nine years. Twenty-two thousand runs and over 1,300 wickets provided a tie to the county that seemed unbreakable. But in May the Gloucestershire committee, resentful of his high-handed ways, wrote to W.G. to ask him which matches he proposed to play for them in the forthcoming season. It was, on the face of it, a reasonable request. But it was not as straightforward as it seemed. The enquiry could easily have been made orally. The fact that it was made formally carried with it the implication that Grace had undertaken a new allegiance irrespective of the interests of the county, and that the committee wished for a formal reply from him. Grace erupted, and resigned the captaincy. Even worse, he did so in a brutal letter that expressed contempt for the Gloucestershire committee. It was a fatal breach that, even when pressed, he was unwilling to mend. It was a sad finale to a glorious show.

1899 was the season for endings. Two weeks later, at Trent Bridge, Grace played his final Test. Within a handful of days he had ceased to be captain of England and of Gloucestershire. These roles had filled his life, but they were perhaps mere bagatelles to a man coming to terms with the loss of his daughter Bessie. A giant had left the Test arena, but in the ever-moving panorama of cricket, Wilfred Rhodes, who one day would play for England at an even greater age than W.G., made his debut in Grace's last game. And, as if to stress that genius was unconfined, in the very next match a new superstar appeared. Twenty-one-year-old Australian Victor Trumper electrified Test cricket with a glorious innings of 135 not out. Cricket had moved on. So, for a few years, did W.G., but the glory days were gone. In 1905 his son 'Bert' died of appendicitis. In 1911 his brother E.M. died. So had many of his old cricketing companions: brother Fred, Shrewsbury, Pooley, Pinder, Barlow, Briggs and Scotton were all gone, some by their own hand. 'Few,' he complained 'are left to call me Gilbert.'

If Grace ever looked back in retirement, he would have done so upon the most remarkable sporting life ever recorded. His triumphs were legion, his failures few, his prestige enormous, his place in British life secure. But he might also have reflected that non-sporting life had largely passed him by. Throughout his first fifty years Britain had prospered and grown more powerful. Victorian dominance seemed permanent, and in his own sphere Grace was one of the chosen few. But all his energies had been channelled into a niche area. He had taken little, if any, interest in wider suffrage, the birth of the Labour Party, the careers of Gladstone, Disraeli or Salisbury, the evolution of Britain into an urban state. Yet his obsession had been magnificent.

According to *Wisden* W.G. played his final game on 25 July 1914, scoring 69 not out for Eltham against Grove Park. Fittingly, he was unbeaten, but his Victorian mind was about to be shocked by the onset of war against Germany. He died in October the following year after a stroke, reputedly brought on by furiously shaking his fist at a German zeppelin flying over his south London garden. He was buried at nearby Elmers End, at the side of his parents and his children, Bessie and Bert, in the shade of a hawthorn tree.

There are many criticisms that can be made of Grace, and yet, bubbling through is the affection, respect and admiration in which he was almost universally held. There is far more to be said for him than against him. That cannot be ignored. He was not perfect, but no one is. But he was the greatest cricketer of his time, perhaps of all time. There will be bids for Bradman and Sobers, and on the field there is a serious debate to be had about who was the greatest player. E.V. Lucas wrote:

> Pilch and Mynn, Carpenter, Thornton and Parr,
> These were the stalwarts who sped the ball far;
> But great though they be,
> To W.G.
> The greatest among them must ever give place
> To mighty, transcendent, unparalleled Grace!

I agree. To his contemporaries Grace was supreme and, in words used of Aristotle, the master of those who know. For longevity, for his effect on the game, for performances with bat *and* ball, for his place in history, William Gilbert Grace stands alone.

Another man, not properly an autocrat, and an approximate contemporary of Lord Harris, also left a great mark on cricket, even though his name is largely unknown. Charles Alcock casts perhaps the longest shadow of any individual connected with the organisation and competitive structures of cricket, and for that matter of football too.

Alcock was born in 1842, the second of six sons of a prosperous Sunderland shipping and insurance family. He was an undistinguished pupil at Harrow, and upon leaving the school after four years did not go to university but to London to establish a branch of the family business. Nor did he show any juvenile sporting talent: he failed to represent the school at either cricket or football. It soon became apparent that shipping held few attractions for Alcock, and he married at twenty-two and moved into journalism. In 1872, at the age of thirty he became the Secretary of Surrey County Cricket Club, a post he was to hold for the rest of his life, although always in conjunction with other interests. Using his journalistic talents he became, that same year, editor of James Lillywhite's *Cricket Annual* and John Lillywhite's *Cricket Companion*. The two publications merged in 1886, and Alcock continued to edit the new *Annual* until 1900.

The Oval had been a mere market garden before the formation of the Surrey County Cricket Club in 1845, and Alcock sought to improve the facilities for players and spectators alike. His success in drawing huge crowds to sporting events at The Oval raised the funds to build a new pavilion and tavern at a cost of £38,000. These enhanced the profile of the ground and, although Alcock did not know it at the time, laid the groundwork that ensured the future of The Oval as a venue for Test cricket. But cricket was not the only game played at The Oval: it was used for football in winter, and staged the first FA Cup Final in 1872. Rugby, athletics, lacrosse, cycling, skating and baseball were other sports that provided entertainment for the public and an income for the Surrey Club.

Alcock was a successful administrator who served the Surrey committee and then, as his authority grew, guided it. He ran an efficient club, searched for new players and cared for all those who served it. He was, as we saw earlier, the guiding force behind the first Oval Test against Australia in 1880 (see page 230). After the riot at Sydney during Lord Harris's tour to Australia the previous year, the Australians were not welcome visitors. James Lillywhite, agent for the tourists, tried to arrange a full programme against the counties but was repeatedly rebuffed. Surrey were not alone in replying that 'the programme for the season was too full to admit of the Committee making further engagements'. When Lillywhite pressed further, he was again abruptly pushed aside, and even the suggestion of a match to raise funds for charity did not elicit a positive response.

On 5 July, W.G. Grace attempted to persuade the MCC committee to stage a game at Lord's, but when that fell through Surrey reconsidered their options, and Charles Alcock began to make arrangements for what would become the first Test match in England. Lord Harris's help was solicited, and Sussex, who were due to play the Australians on the date proposed for the game, were squared. Alcock even travelled to Scotland to encourage Alfred Lyttelton and A.G. Steel to make themselves available. They agreed – and the lives of many grouse were saved. Alcock was the pivotal figure in all the preparations for the game, although Grace, Harris and Lord Sheffield, who stood Sussex down, also contributed. Harris acknowledged years later that Alcock was 'very keen about the game', but added that 'He always had an eye for the main chance,' by which he meant the income from gate receipts.

England won that inaugural Test in England by five wickets. Alcock, like everyone else, did not foresee the Australians returning two years later to demolish England at the same venue and give rise to the legend of the Ashes. He felt the pain of that defeat very badly, and after the game was seen 'sitting down on a huge iron safe, burying his head in his hands, oblivious to everything else'. It is likely, however, that once again the gate money offset his disappoint-ment. Alcock had a keen commercial sense, and founded and edited his own specialist magazines, *Cricket* and the *Football Annual*. The former was the first viable magazine devoted solely to the game, and his eagle eye for the bottom line ensured that it was a financial as well as a journalistic success. He did not hesitate to solicit advertisements, endorse products or promote other publications in which he had an interest. He was an effective businessman, but cricket benefited too: throughout the summer his magazine offered a unique weekly record of the game in England and overseas, and in the winter a monthly summary.

Alcock did not shrink from forceful editorials. Lawn tennis, a rival to cricket, was derided as 'an effeminate amusement'. 'Sport,' he declared, 'it is not.' This is a rare example of Alcock misjudging the public mood. His journalistic instinct meant that controversies were given full coverage. When the MCC changed the law to permit a captain to declare his team's innings before being bowled out, a full debate ensued in the columns of *Cricket* magazine. Much of it concentrated on how captains had formerly bypassed the strict letter of the law by instructing their batsmen to throw away their wickets. Unsurprisingly, Alcock, Secretary of Surrey, fully supported such a tactic, in the knowledge that John Shuter, captain of Surrey, had employed it whenever necessary to force a result in a game that otherwise was heading for a draw.

In his capacity as Secretary, Alcock was careful to maintain a close relationship with the Surrey players. Many of the top professionals had been courted by him and encouraged to play for the county. Tom Hayward, George Lohmann, Tom Richardson and Bobby Abel were among those who signed contracts at Alcock's behest and made Surrey the leading county side in late-Victorian England. But his personal familiarity with the players did not invariably ensure an easy relationship. When the same four professionals were selected for the third Test between England and Australia in 1896, they went on strike and demanded double their usual £10 fee for playing. A furious Alcock held firm, and two days before the match, Hayward, Richardson and

Abel backed down and apologised. Lohmann and a fifth signatory, William Gunn, did not. They should, said Alcock, have made a 'request for consideration', not a demand, but the three miscreants who apologised were reinstated to the team. Alcock was relieved, not least because simmering discontent over amateurs' expenses, especially those claimed by W.G. Grace, was an issue always likely to erupt into a public row. He may have been a friend and admirer of W.G., but as Secretary of Surrey he was only too familiar with excessive expenses claims and the public-relations time-bomb they represented.

Nonetheless, odd ructions apart, Alcock was often on hand to help the professionals as nursemaid and father figure. When a hung-over Harry Jupp missed the departure of the boat from Southampton that was taking the England team to Australia in 1876, Alcock arranged a lift in a mail tug, and caught up with the liner. Jupp scrambled aboard, but may have done so with mixed feelings. He had toured Australia with Grace three years earlier, and in heavy seas off the coast between Melbourne and Adelaide had become seriously seasick. He attempted unsuccessfully to treat himself with large quantities of brandy, with the result that he became deliriously and gloriously drunk, and raved so uncontrollably upon reaching Adelaide that he was taken to hospital and locked in a padded room. On the 1876 tour he was better-behaved, and top-scored with 63 in England's first ever Test. But his next three innings were a disappointing 4, 0 and 1, and after only two Tests he never again played for England. Alcock also attempted to keep the turbulent Surrey wicketkeeper Edmund Pooley out of trouble. This was an ongoing task, as Pooley's misdemeanours were manifold. In 1873 he was suspended for months for placing bets on a Surrey–Yorkshire match and for using coarse language: he denied an attempt at match-fixing. This was not his only scrape, or character fault: he missed the first-ever Test at Melbourne in 1877, as he had been imprisoned in New Zealand. He could also be sly. Despite his gifts, he hated to keep wicket to fast bowling, and whatever the state of the pitch would tell his captain, 'It's a slow bowler's wicket today.' But Pooley was a world-class performer behind the stumps who in 1868 dismissed twelve Sussex players in a single match, eight caught and four stumped,* and Alcock knew his value.

Astonishingly Alcock's role in developing football was even greater than his contribution to cricket. In 1859 he and his elder brother founded the Forest Football Club, which later became the Wanderers, with Alcock as captain. In 1872 the Wanderers were the first winners of the FA Cup – a competition devised by Alcock with the final (inevitably) staged at The Oval. Alcock represented England against Scotland in 1870 (at The Oval!), and captained England against the same opponents five years later. The following week he refereed the FA Cup Final, and he went on to become the first President of the Referees' Association.

Charles Alcock is set apart from his contemporaries by his dual contribution to football and cricket both on and off the pitch. Although never a top-class cricketer, he played for the Gentlemen of Essex, and was described, perhaps damningly, by Arthur Haygarth as a 'steady bat, fair change fast bowler and excellent long stop'. On a visit to Hamburg he was recruited to play as a Frenchman, under the alias A.L. Gallus, in a match against Germany, although his name was misreported as 'Earl Gaz'. 'The Earl' top-scored on an atrocious wicket – or at least he claimed to have done so in later life. He played once for the MCC, against Middlesex in 1862, batting at number eleven, and was bowled by Tom Hearne without scoring.

When Alcock died in 1906 he was buried in West Norwood cemetery. Over the decades his grave fell into disrepair, until in 1999 it was restored with donations from Surrey and the Football Association, and a marvellous new headstone was erected in his memory. His contribution to sport was enormous, and although his gift for cricket was modest, no one could belittle his backstage contribution to the game. Alcock deserves a higher place in the mythology of the game than history has yet given him.

---

* Pooley's record remained unequalled until Don Tallon of Queensland dismissed twelve New South Wales batsmen in 1938. It was finally surpassed by Zimbabwe's Wayne James, who dismissed thirteen Mashonaland batsmen while playing for Matabeleland in the 1995–96 season.

17

Your English Summer's Done

In the 1890s, England was still a nation for the few, but no longer the very few. For most of the population it was a time of optimism. As the decade began, prices fell and wages rose. Diets improved and leisure activities widened. Savings rose in value, and friendly and building societies and the Co-Operative Movement grew in size. But rural areas fared less well than the cities: wheat prices were depressed and farmers bankrupted. The rural young, whether labourers or entrepreneurs, deserted the countryside as more and more land fell out of arable use.

As Britain's population grew more urbanised, trade and commerce followed in its wake. Stores that remain familiar today began to appear in the high street. Energetic entrepreneurs established retail businesses that spread widely. John Lewis in London; Jesse and Florence Boot in Nottingham; Michael Marks and Thomas Spencer in Leeds; and John and May-Anne Sainsbury in Holborn. These were the founders of the business empires of today. Joseph Lyons opened a Corner House in Piccadilly. William Whiteley had the novel idea of importing the Franco-American concept of a luxurious one-stop shop with individual departments, catering to the more wealthy and demanding customers in fashionable areas. Out of London, most towns and cities adopted the Whiteley concept, and created their own indigenous department stores to serve the local clientele – Jenner's in Edinburgh, Jessop's in Nottingham, Brake's of Taunton and Hannington of Brighton being among them.

The first underground railway was opened between the Monument and Stockwell in London. Telephone cables linked London and Paris. Motor cars began to appear, and the first motor show was held at Tunbridge Wells. In 1896 the Red Flag Law was repealed, and cars were permitted to travel without a man walking in front waving a red flag. The speed limit was increased from four to twenty miles per hour, and 'taxi meter' cabs made their debut in London. In 1897, cabbie George Smith became the first driver to be convicted for drink-driving and a nine-year-old boy became the first motoring fatality on a public highway. In the same year, the Automobile Association of Great Britain was founded. Travel at home and abroad became more frequent, and travellers' cheques made their first appearance. Less welcome were death duties, derided as 'spiteful' by Queen Victoria when Chancellor Sir William Harcourt imposed them in 1894. Two years later, Prime Minister Lord Salisbury was equally sniffy about the birth of the *Daily Mail* – 'by office boys for office boys', opined His Lordship. Both Victoria and Salisbury, however, approved of the foundation of the National Trust, which made its first purchase, of the Clergy House in East Sussex, in mid-decade.

Elementary education became free in 1891, and local authorities were given the power to build council houses. The *Strand Magazine* was launched, and its serialisation of Conan Doyle's Sherlock Holmes stories ensured its success. Fantasy and horror were in vogue, with H.G. Wells – son of Joseph, the Kent fast bowler – publishing *The Time Machine*, *The Invisible Man* and *The War of the Worlds*, followed by Bram Stoker's *Dracula or The Undead*. Higher up the literary chain, Thomas Hardy published *Tess of the d'Urbervilles* and *Jude the Obscure*. Oscar Wilde wrote *The Picture of Dorian Gray*, *Lady Windermere's Fan*, *A Woman of no Importance*, *An Ideal Husband* and *The Importance of Being Earnest*, all in the first half of the 1890s. After being sentenced to two years' hard labour for 'gross indecency' in 1895, he wrote 'The Ballad of Reading Gaol' to expose the appalling conditions endured by prisoners. George Bernard Shaw had his first success with *The Devil's Disciple* in 1897, and remained prolific for much of the next half-century. The works of Elgar, Delius, Holst,

Puccini, Verdi and Brahms entertained classical-music lovers, while the stage talents of Sir Henry Irving, Dame Ellen Terry and Sarah Bernhardt filled the theatres.

The forces that would form the Labour Party continued to evolve, but the majority of trade unionists remained hostile to socialism as a creed. To many of them, the advocates of the new philosophy seemed alien. Most of the prominent socialists – Beatrice and Sidney Webb, William Morris, George Bernard Shaw and the Old Etonian and former Sussex cricketer Henry Hyndman – were middle-class intellectuals who had not themselves suffered the hardships of the working class. The Independent Labour Party, formed in 1893 after an especially bitter strike in Bradford, began to bring together trades unionists and socialist policy, but not sufficiently to secure electoral success. In 1895, all twenty-eight Independent Labour Party candidates in the general election finished bottom of their polls. They may have been disappointed, but they would not have to wait too much longer for their breakthrough.

When the Victorian era entered its final decade, W.G. Grace had viewed cricket from an Olympian perch for twenty-five years. As Grace surveyed cricket, so Britain surveyed the world. An empire whose prize acquisition was once Aquitaine now covered one-fifth of the surface of the globe, and Queen Victoria, Empress of India, was the monarch of four hundred million people. Close to home, Ireland, Gladstone's nemesis, was turbulent, but haphazard colonisation in Africa, the Far East and the Pacific had added tens of millions to British dominion. It was the high tide of an Empire on which, it was said, 'the sun never sets'.

Much of this colonisation had arisen by accident, or to preserve trade advantage, but the outcome was that British possessions were now five times the size of the Roman Empire, and only a portion of that was the product of military power. Conquerors from Alexander the Great to Napoleon would have been baffled at how little had been won with aggressive action, or held only by force of arms. India was governed by a small number of troops and fewer administrators. Private companies, such as the Hudson's Bay Company in Canada and the East India Company, had been proxy governments for whole countries. Smaller possessions were run on a shoestring. Ascension Island was deemed a 'ship', and governed by a Royal Navy captain. The British Consul in Egypt, Evelyn Baring, was the effective ruler of the country. Sir Stamford Raffles had acted unilaterally in founding Singapore. From across the world, the children of those who administered the Empire were sent to Britain to be educated.

In return for sovereignty of these far-off lands, Britain had put in place parliamentary systems of government, a system of law and civil administration, and had introduced what would become the dominant language of the world. Team games – cricket, football, rugby – were a further legacy.

Some of the empire-builders were adventurers or explorers. Others were rogues and hypocrites. A few were evangelical missionaries who spread the word of God. Most pioneers went about their business quietly, hoping for peace and good order, and trying to promote trade and become rich. All were forerunners to colonisation. Britain gave David Livingstone and Cecil Rhodes to Africa with equal pride. Between them, for reasons often altruistic, and sometimes selfish, the pioneers were more effective at building up these overseas territories than they knew. In the late twentieth century it was fashionable to decry the Empire. Foolish politicians, pandering to prejudice, even apologised for it. There is no doubt that there were individual acts which should be regretted. But, of all empires, the British was the most benevolent and bequeathed the most enduring legacies. Kipling and Rider Haggard celebrated the Empire in verse and story. And at the Golden Jubilee of the Queen in 1887, much of the world celebrated it as a force of nature.

In 1890, British power was at its peak. But the Empire's loose-knit structure could not last. It would soon begin to unravel. Britain had gained a foothold in southern Africa when it occupied the Cape of Good Hope in 1795, and large-scale colonisation had followed the Napoleonic Wars. Even so, the British presence was significantly smaller than the Dutch Afrikaaner population, who had migrated inland to Transvaal and the Orange Free State. Britain encircled these

Boer-administered lands. To the north, Cecil Rhodes' British South Africa Company held the territory that is now Zimbabwe, while the coastlands – the Cape, where Rhodes was Premier, and Natal – were firmly in British hands. In 1895, without – so far as is known – any sanction from the Colonial Secretary Joseph Chamberlain, Dr Leander Jameson, an ally of Rhodes, invaded Transvaal in an attempt to stir up revolt against the Boer administration. The plot failed dismally, but encouraged the Boers to arm and to prepare themselves against any such further adventures.

An uneasy period followed, with the atmosphere poisoned by the incompatibility of Bible-reading Boer farmers and profit-seeking British commercial adventurers. In the undertow of this stand-off, British citizens were denied political rights in Boer territories. Distrust grew, and when Boer commandos launched military offensives into Cape Colony and Natal in October 1899, it ignited the Boer War.

It was a bitter and expensive conflict, in both blood and gold. To achieve victory, nearly 250,000 British soldiers were deployed (over twice the size of today's army), of whom 22,000 died, two-thirds of them through disease. At home, the war was wildly supported by the majority, with music hall, as so often, catching the public mood, in songs like 'A Hot Time in the Transvaal Tonight':

> There is trouble in the Transvaal
> And England wants to know
> Whether Mister Kruger or
> John Bull shall boss the show.

There was no doubt about the answer the British nation expected. Crowds lined the streets to cheer departing troops, but there was also a strongly dissenting minority opposed to the jingoistic fervour, led by the future wartime Prime Minister David Lloyd George. When victory came in May 1902, Lord Salisbury capitalised on it with a general election and a fresh mandate; but the war was an unheeded signal that sustaining an empire now stretched beyond endurance might not be possible.

*

At home in England, cricket was building a solid foundation. In its infancy it had been a patchwork of cameos and characters, as the game showcased its charms and fought for its place in the national psyche. With the birth of county clubs and a formal Championship, that battle had been won. As the nineteenth century drew to a close, cricket enjoyed a burst of popularity, and the emergence of some epic figures.

Some old heroes left the stage in sad circumstances. William Scotton, sensitive and depressed, with his career seemingly over, quietly and undemonstratively cut his throat. He was thirty-seven. Billy Midwinter, who had played for both Australia and England, died in an asylum, grief-stricken following the death of his wife and child. Billy was only thirty-nine. His last rational conversation was about W.G. Grace, and his delight that Gloucestershire had twice defeated Notts. Grace, of course, was still an ever-present force, his skills scarcely undimmed at the age of forty-two. W.G. would play through that last decade, and, at forty-seven, enjoy a golden summer of success. In public affection and regard he stood alone, but on the cricket field his pedestal was about to become crowded.

From the mid-1890s, English cricket basked in what would later be considered its Golden Age, until a world war brought it to a close. This is perhaps an overblown view, but it was a glamorous era, lifted out of the ordinary by Grace's fading star and Shrewsbury's continuing brilliance; by the prime of Jackson, MacLaren, Ranjitsinhji, Fry and Jessop, and, among the bowlers, Lohmann, Richardson, Peel, Briggs and Rhodes. The supporting cast was scarcely less formidable. Abel, Walter Read, Gunn, Stoddart and Tom Hayward among the run-getters, with Lockwood, Attewell, Sharpe, Mold and Kortright ensuring that those runs were not too easy to achieve. As the new century dawned, other great names would come to the fore.

On 16 December 1889, as the secretaries of the county clubs met at Lord's to agree fixtures for the following season, a more significant meeting had already taken place unannounced. Representatives of Surrey, Kent, Lancashire, Middlesex, Nottinghamshire, Sussex, Gloucestershire and Yorkshire met to agree a system of calculating points to measure county success. The simple, though somewhat eccentric, system they adopted was one point for a win, minus one for a defeat, and nothing at all for drawn or abandoned games. This imperfect scoring method had so many more defects than virtues that it is astonishing it was ever agreed. Exciting games might yield no points at all for either team. No recognition was given to outstanding batting or bowling performances. There was no mechanism for promotion or relegation. No provision for initial entry into any of the divisions. Some teams were bound to end the season with a minus total. The underlying deficiencies of this botched and messy system were glaring. Nonetheless, for all its imperfections, the official County Championship was born, and would endure.

In 1891 Somerset exploited the inherent defects of the system and joined the top division through the simple expedient of arranging a sufficient number of fixtures against first-class counties. Four years later, Derbyshire, Essex, Hampshire, Leicestershire and Warwickshire were added to the top division, followed by Worcestershire in 1899. The top tier remained at sixteen county sides until after the First World War, when Glamorgan joined. These promotions were not as the result of cricketing successes on the field, but at the whim of the MCC adjudicating at the request of the counties. The MCC simply classified some counties as 'first class', and others as not. It was despotic, but effective. In this fashion, the self-appointed guardian of the laws of cricket became the accepted High Court of judgement for county cricket.

As the Championship was born, pitches were improving. Professional groundsmen were replacing unskilled labourers. The cricket 'square' had become familiar. Pitches were rolled, mowed and cut with greater skill and care than ever before. It is likely that every top-class ground used hand-pushed mowers to trim the square, and horse-drawn mowers to cut the outfield. The sheep were finally redundant. Top-dressing the wicket with binding soils became the fashion. It was a treatment pioneered by 'Fiddler' Walker (he played the violin), whose use of red Nottingham marl at Trent Bridge in the 1870s so improved the wicket that the practice was widely copied.

Previously unstable batting tracks were tamed, breaking the hearts of fast bowlers as the averages of batsmen were lifted. More happily, the absence of dents, ridges and holes in the pitch encouraged improved techniques, and the development of 'swing' bowling in overcast weather conditions. As the wrecked wickets disappeared, new skills emerged. Perfect pitches – one of the ingredients of the golden age of batting – were lovingly created by groundsmen. When the weather was changeable, bowlers still cashed in, since even good wickets, when uncovered, could be demonised by rain and sun; but in periods of hot and dry weather the flat, even surfaces were over-friendly to batsmen.

For the first time, the role of groundsman became important. Previously it had been a labourer's job, or a career post for a cricketer such as Fuller Pilch, who nurtured the pitches at West Malling and Canterbury, where he was employed as player and groundsman. Now it assumed a new importance. At The Oval, the skill was regarded as so specialist that it became hereditary. After the innovative Sam Apted came Tom Martin (1911–24), to be followed by his eccentric brother 'Bosser' Martin, who produced the dead Oval track upon which Len Hutton scored 364 in thirteen hours in a 1938 Test against Australia. It was a marvellous feat by Hutton, even on a placid pitch, but agony for bowlers and wearisome for onlookers as England amassed 903 runs for 7 wickets. 'Bosser' looked on, beaming at the excellence of his creation.

The rise in popularity of county cricket killed off some traditional games, although the ancient North vs South fixture had a dying flourish. At Lord's in 1890, playing for the South, Andrew Stoddart scored 115 out of a total of 169, facing Briggs, Peel and Attewell on a sticky wicket. It was a masterful display. In reply, Shrewsbury carried his bat for 54 out of 83, against a rampant George Lohmann who dismissed eleven batsmen for 10 runs apiece. Lohmann marvelled at Shrewsbury's skill in placing the ball for twos and threes without risk. It was a style that accumulated runs for Shrewsbury by the thousands. He was the best professional bat of the era, and though he may have lacked the dash and sparkle of some carefree amateurs, he was the man rated most highly by Grace. One representative fixture continued to thrive as a monument to the distinction between sheep and goats: Gentlemen vs Players blithely continued its rivalry until 1962. But the focus of attention moved to county cricket.

Surrey straddled the new decade in the grand manner. In the late 1880s they won the unofficial Championship for three successive seasons – taking it outright in 1887 and 1888, and sharing it with Lancashire and Nottinghamshire in 1889 – and then stretched their successful run until 1892. A stumble in 1893 was soon corrected, as they went on to become the team of the decade, with six Championships to their credit. Between 1887 and 1895, Surrey's greatest years, they won four out of every five completed games. Lord Hawke's Yorkshire, recovering from a dismal period, finished top on three occasions, whilst unlucky Lancashire, five times runners-up, had a solitary victory in 1897. Despite some dazzling stars – Sussex had Ranji, Fry and the former Australian captain Billy Murdoch; Somerset had Palairet; Middlesex had Stoddart, O'Brien and Trott; Gloucestershire had Grace, Jessop and Charles Townsend – no other teams came close to the success of the top three.

Surrey's dominance in the wet seasons of 1890 and 1891 was entirely due to the penetration of their bowling. George Lohmann, and a surprise package in John Sharpe, both captured over 100 wickets at just over 12 runs each in 1890, and the following season Lohmann increased his tally to 132 at an even cheaper tariff. Sharpe's haul fell to a still respectable 88 wickets, but Bill Lockwood signalled his arrival as a fast bowler with 11 wickets for 40 against Kent at The Oval. Nottinghamshire looked on in despair, for both Sharpe and Lockwood were refugees from Trent Bridge. Lohmann was the leading wicket-taker in 1891, and although the prolific Walter Read had a poor season, tiny Bobby Abel topped the national batting averages and comfortably outscored all other batsmen. Many games were cut short by foul weather, and Abel, with 916 runs, was the only batsman to approach the magic mark of 1,000 runs for the season.

The evergreen Abel was one of the nearly-great batsmen. He led Surrey run-scoring throughout the decade, with Walter Read as his main henchman, until the latter retired in 1897 having scored thirty-eight centuries and over 22,000 runs for the county. These were astonishing figures, but even better wickets would ensure that they were soon eclipsed. In 1893 Tom Hayward, nephew of the great 1860s Cambridgeshire batsman of the same name, joined Surrey. For the next twenty seasons he went on to score over 1,000 runs a year, and was, after Grace, the first batsman to reach a hundred first-class centuries. In between run-feasting he took 481 wickets, including two hat-tricks. Abel, Read and Hayward were the most prolific run-getters in Surrey's years of triumphs, with Bill Brockwell, Jim Street and Bill Lockwood offering strong support.

Surrey had two serious reverses in 1893. They lost the Championship to a resurgent Yorkshire, and George Lohmann to the fear of consumption. Lohmann left England to recuperate in the cleaner, fresher air of South Africa. In 1894 he was celebrated in the lyrics of a song, 'The Hope of Surrey', by Norman Gale:

> When Surrey ladled out defeat,
> Who did it?
> When Notts and Yorkshire and Kent were beat
> Who did it?
> Lohmann did – George Lohmann –
> Something like a yeoman,
> Neither fast or slow man,
> George!

The song concluded with a plea for Lohmann to return:

> Surrey wants you – come again!
> England wants you – cross the main!
> Say goodbye to
> Capetown sky, you
> Best of Georges, come again.

Lohmann obliged in 1895, but although he regained his England place he was never again quite the destructive bowler of old. A foolish squabble in 1897 ended his Surrey career in acrimony, and this great bowler returned to South Africa, this time for good, where his dread of consumption became a grim reality. Slowly and painfully, he drowned from within. It was a dreadful end. Lohmann died in 1901, at the age of thirty-six. Even in the midst of the Boer War his premature death was mourned in England and South Africa.

Lohmann, Sharpe and Lockwood had been a formidable trio. But soon after Lohmann had fallen ill, Surrey found compensation in a young talent: Tom Richardson. Fuelled on huge breakfasts and on stout for lunch, Richardson ran riot. In two seasons, 357 wickets fell to him at low cost as Surrey were champions again in 1894 and 1895. The latter win – the fifth Championship in six years – was secured against Hampshire at The Oval, when Richardson's match figures were 15 wickets for 155 runs. Yorkshire and Lancashire interrupted Surrey's dominance for the next three years, but they were back at the top in 1899, with Abel and Hayward totalling nearly 4,000 runs between them, including a partnership of 448 for the fourth wicket against Yorkshire. In that game, so good was the Oval wicket that 1,255 runs were scored in three days, for the loss of only 17 wickets. Despite the excellence of the pitch, the strength of Surrey's bowling still secured victories, and at its peak the team in the late nineteenth century was one of the great sides of all county cricket history.

Nottinghamshire and Surrey had dominated inter-county cricket for so long that Yorkshire's Championship win in 1893 was a total surprise. Lord Hawke had been leading the team for a decade without success. The county had been in the doldrums for years, and in 1891 and 1892 finished near the bottom of the Championship. As the 1893 season began, the solid stonewaller Louis Hall had retired; Ulyett and Peel were veterans; Hawke, a fine captain, was no more than an average performer; Tunnicliffe was learning his trade; and Stanley Jackson, born to the purple, son of a Cabinet Minister in Salisbury's government and blessed with sublime cricketing skills, was at Cambridge and rarely available to the county, but Yorkshire knew his value and waited eagerly for his return. They were right to do so: he had all the confidence of a man whose fag at Harrow was Winston Churchill. The scale of his loss to Yorkshire was evident when he scored 91 on his England debut, in the first Test against Australia at

Lord's in 1893, and 103 in scorching sun in the second Test at The Oval. Yorkshire looked on with envy, but also with a degree of satisfaction as their absentee talent secured his reputation.

Without Jackson, Yorkshire had no outstanding individual performances in their Championship season of 1893. Jack (J.T.) Brown established himself in the team, but neither he nor any other Yorkshire batsman was near the top of the averages. The main wicket-takers for the county were the England duo of Ted Wainwright (90) and Bobby Peel (65), and the future Test all-rounder George Hirst (59). These were creditable returns, but modest fare when compared with Lohmann's tally of victims for Surrey in earlier years, or the 137 wickets Jack Hearne captured that season for Middlesex. Yet even without outstanding individual performances, Yorkshire won the Championship. It was a true team effort for a county starved of success, and the martinet Hawke delighted in soaking up the praise.

Surrey wrestled the Championship from Yorkshire in 1894, and won more comfortably the following year, but Hawke's colts were becoming stars, and in 1896 Yorkshire were back on top. Brown scored over 1,500 runs, in a year in which Yorkshire scored 660 against Leicestershire and 543 against Sussex. Brown 'failed' against Warwickshire with only 23, but Peel (210 not out), Hawke (166), Wainwright (126) and Jackson (117) led the way as Yorkshire scored 887, a new record total in first-class cricket. That season, encouraged by Hawke, Yorkshire offered winter pay to the professionals. It was fully justified: Wainwright, Peel, Hirst and Haigh captured over 330 wickets between them.

Both Yorkshire and Surrey fell behind Lancashire in 1897, but for Yorkshire at least there were promising signs. Jackson was now available to play more regularly for the county, and supplemented his valuable batting by taking 62 wickets. Sussex suffered once again when Brown (311) and Tunnicliffe (147) put on 378 for the first wicket against them for Yorkshire at Sheffield. In 1898 Yorkshire recaptured the Championship with ease, even without the spin of Bobby Peel, whose drinking exploits had led to the dispute with Lord Hawke that ended his glittering career (see pages 320–1). Yorkshire, after Peel, had the same good luck as Surrey after Lohmann. As Peel left the team, Wilfred Rhodes stepped into it. In his first season in 1898, one of poor weather and unfinished games,* Rhodes, Wainwright and Jackson, split only by Hearne of Middlesex, nestled proudly at the top of the bowling averages. But their successes over the season paled beside one day at Chesterfield in which Brown (300) and Tunnicliffe (243) put on 554 runs when opening the innings against Derbyshire, batting through the first day to leave Yorkshire on 503 without loss. It was a breathtaking achievement, and remained a first-wicket record until Percy Holmes and Herbert Sutcliffe, also of Yorkshire, passed it in 1932 against Essex at Leyton. Brown, Tunnicliffe, Jackson, Rhodes, Hirst, Haigh, Wainwright: suddenly, the team with no stars was all stars. The Hawke formula had put Yorkshire back among the elite, and the full glory of his team was beginning to unfold. In two years' time Yorkshire would totally dominate county cricket.

Lancashire were runners-up to Surrey in 1890 and 1891, but Albert Hornby's team was breaking up. Nash and Crossland were gone. Poor, sick Richard Pilling was dead at thirty-five, another victim of consumption. It is ironic that an ailment for which the only known cure was fresh air should afflict young men who spent the whole of their working lives on a cricket field. Barlow retired, too early some said. Hornby was ending his career. Allan Steel, one of the great all-rounders, did not play in 1893 as his legal career demanded more of his time. But reinforcements were on the way. At Harrow School in 1886, Stanley Jackson had not been the only fifteen-year-old to show precocious talent. Archie MacLaren was in the same team, and naturally went to Lancashire, where his father was Honorary Treasurer. On either side of the Pennines, the two Old Harrovians prepared for battle. At only twenty-three, Archie was appointed captain of the Lancashire team, all of whose players were older than him.

He inherited a team of solid professionals, laced with outstanding talents. Arthur Mold, yet another Lancashire fast-bowler with a sus-

* There were fifty-four drawn games in the season, and eighty-two ending in definite results.

pect action – worse than Crossland, some thought – was a heavy wicket-taker. Unfair or not, Mold was fast, with a deadly break-back and sharp lift on helpful wickets. In the four seasons 1893–96, Mold took 736 wickets with some astonishing analyses. A hat-trick against Somerset at Old Trafford in 1894 was bettered by four wickets in four balls against Notts at Trent Bridge the following season. His toll that year was 213 wickets at under 16 runs a piece. Six-, seven- and eight-wicket hauls were commonplace, with 9 for 62 against Kent at Old Trafford being his best analysis. Illegal action or not, Mold was accurate and devastating. Beside him, Johnny Briggs was still quoting Shakespeare and mopping up wickets, while Albert Ward and the dashing Frank Sugg were consistent and reliable run-scorers.

MacLaren was a weighty addition to a good team. On his debut, while still at Harrow, he came to the wicket after Lancashire had lost 3 wickets for 23 runs to Sussex; when he left it he had scored a century in two hours. As a batsman he had rare talent, and his captaincy, after a shaky start, was often inspirational, although when his stubborn streak intervened he was capable of boneheaded decisions. Lancashire finished in mid-table in MacLaren's first year, largely thanks to Mold and Briggs, but the new captain, immature, imperious, dictatorial and, if thwarted, vile-tempered, nonetheless commanded respect from his team, and brighter days lay ahead.

In the winter of 1894–95 MacLaren toured Australia under Stoddart, and after modest performances in the first four Tests, scored 120 at Melbourne to help win the series by three matches to two.* MacLaren returned as a member of an Ashes-winning team, with his reputation boosted. It would soon be boosted even further.

1895 was Grace's magical year, with two double centuries and 1,000 runs in May alone. That year, a boundary off Sam Woods at Somerset took him to his hundredth century. He was not the only batsman to write himself into history. Against Somerset at Taunton, MacLaren scored 424 in a single innings after nearly being bowled

---

* In that match Brown of Yorkshire made an unforgettable 140 in the second innings. MacLaren's hundred had kept England in the game after Australia made 414 in the first innings.

for a duck,* as Lancashire amassed 801 runs in eight hours. They won by an innings and 452 runs, so the match would probably have been won easily even if MacLaren had scored nought. MacLaren topped the averages that year, supplementing his 424 with three successive centuries at the end of the season to carry Lancashire to second place behind Surrey. Briggs and Mold totalled over 300 wickets between them, and the ever-dependable Ward scored 1,486 runs. Charles Smith contributed with seventy-six dismissals, the highest total of the year by a wicketkeeper.

Although Surrey, Yorkshire and Lancashire dominated the county scene there were many fine players in other teams. Not all of them were English, and the Empire's poet, Rudyard Kipling, clearly did not have cricket in mind when he wrote:

> East is East and West is West
> And never the twain shall meet,

for they certainly did on the cricket field. The living embodiment of this encounter was Colonel His Highness Shri Sir Ranjitsinhji Vibhaji, Maharajah Jam Saheb of Nawanagar, or, as he was more simply known as a young cricketer, K.S. Ranjitsinhji – Ranji.

Ranji was a revelation to English crowds, who had seen nothing like him before. He was the personification of the silky skills that would become the emblem of Indian batting. He was all style – in appearance as well as at the wicket. His slicked-down hair, and flowing silk shirt buttoned at the wrist, enchanted spectators as he unfolded dazzling cut strokes and introduced the leg-glance – which brought him a torrent of runs from a formerly barren part of the cricket ground. Moreover, Ranji had the added mystique of being a royal prince. The whole package was box-office magic, and the crowds flocked to see him. 'All other batsmen are labourers in comparison,'

---

* Over a hundred years later only Brian Lara, with 501 not out for Warwickshire against Durham at Birmingham in 1994, has passed MacLaren's total in English county cricket, although Graeme Hick, with 405 not out for Worcester – also against poor Somerset – in 1988, came close. MacLaren's 424 has been surpassed overseas on six occasions, by Hanif Mohammed (499), Donald Bradman (452 not out), Bhausaheb Nimbalkar (443 not out), Bill Ponsford (437 and 429) and Aftab Baloch (428).

enthused one critic, while Neville Cardus – never one to miss a lyrical phrase – later wrote of 'Eastern romance and colour [being added] to cricket' from 'the land ... where beauty is subtle and not plain and unambiguous'. Ted Wainwright, himself an unambiguous York-shireman, saw it differently from the bowling crease: Ranji, he complained, 'never made a Christian stroke in his life'.

Be that as it may, he played every other sort of stroke in a career that opened English eyes to sporting genius from the East. At times the runs flowed in Bradmanesque volume: in 1900 Ranji scored over 3,000 of them at an average of 87.57, with five double centuries including two in successive innings. The runner-up, his Sussex part-ner Charles Fry, averaged 22 runs fewer, in a total of 1,830 runs. Twice, in 1896 and 1900, Ranji scored ten or more centuries in a season, including three in successive innings, and three times he scored 1,000 runs in a single calendar month. Between 1895 and 1920 he scored seventy-two centuries in a first-class career that grossed nearly 25,000 runs at an average of 56.37. It was phenomenal run-scoring, and yet it was not the quantity of runs, but Ranji's manner of scoring them, that built his reputation. Bob Thoms, one of the few umpires to be unafraid of W.G. Grace, rated Ranji the better batsman of the two, as 'he had more shots'. Thoms' reasoning is sound as a basis for judgement, but it is unfair: the young Ranji batted on far truer wickets than the young Grace had done thirty years earlier. Nonetheless, it is a powerful endorsement of Ranji's contemporary reputation.

English cricket enfolded Ranji to its bosom, and he rewarded it with an unbeaten century on his Test debut against Australia in 1896. His selection for the side at Old Trafford caused Lord Harris to have apoplexy (see page 318), but Ranji was far from the last player to represent England under a flag of convenience. If England fans were fortunate to see Ranji, then spectators at Sussex were doubly blessed, for he and Charles Fry, his exact contemporary, were on display daily as team-mates under the bibulous captaincy of Billy Murdoch.

When Charles Fry was born in 1872, the stars must have been in unique conjunction, for the gods showered him with gifts. He had good looks, a fine mind and was a formidable scholar. Physically tireless, he played football for Southampton, Portsmouth and England, and rugby for Blackheath and the Barbarians. He shared the world long-jump record, with a massive leap of over twenty-three feet. He excelled at boxing, golf, swimming, sculling, javelin-throwing and tennis. In life he was an all-rounder too. He hunted and fished, acted and wrote, nearly became a Liberal MP and might have become King of Albania, had he been sufficiently well-heeled to meet the expenses of a royal household. In company, Fry was a superb conversationalist. In an age that lauded effortless superiority, he was the most supremely gifted amateur of the day, but it was cricket that captured his full-time involvement and enshrined his reputation. In 1906 he scored six successive centuries, twice the tally of any earlier batsmen. A career that yielded 30,000 runs at an average exceeding 50 places him among the greats of the game.

It was not the least of Lord Sheffield's services to Sussex cricket that he encouraged Fry and Ranji to join the county team. It was a breathtaking partnership. The willow-as-wand skills of Ranji, partnered by the classic driving of Fry, was an enticing dish. They scored thousands of runs together, helped by the modest size of the ground at Hove and a generally benign wicket. Yorkshire were a particular victim, which may or may not have been an accident, since neither the Liberal Fry nor the ethnic Indian Ranji shared an affinity with the diehard instincts of Lord Hawke.

Other gifted players from the 1890s left reputations that are imperishable. Cricket has always warmed to great hitters, from Charles Thornton and George Bonnor to Kevin Pietersen and Shahid Afridi. Ted Alletson, otherwise a modest county player, earned undying fame with a single innings, of 189 in ninety minutes for Nottinghamshire vs Sussex at Hove in 1911. But of all the great entertainers the mightiest was Gilbert Jessop, who enlivened cricket for twenty years from 1894, and earned immortality with one Test innings at The Oval in 1902, when his 100 in seventy-five minutes won England the match by one wicket. Short, muscular, with abnormally long arms, he crouched over the bat, knees bent, resembling a coiled spring that launched itself at the ball and despatched it to the far distance throughout his long career.

Jessop was never a 'slogger', but an instinctive, scientific destroyer of bowling. He had wonderful footwork that enabled him to come down the wicket to drive the fastest of bowlers, and his sharp eyesight made him consistently the fastest scorer in every team in which he played. He could – and often did – change the direction of games within a few overs, and habitually scored two-thirds of the runs added in any lengthy partnership. His feats of fast scoring were frequent, not spasmodic, and anticipation of his batting drew huge crowds – 'Even more,' claimed Jack Hobbs 'than Bradman.'

Some of his scoring feats seem to belong to the realms of fiction, except that, for Jessop, the impossible was commonplace. In 1903 at Brighton he scored 286 out of 335 for Gloucestershire against Sussex in under three hours. In his career he scored five double centuries, and none of them took longer than two hundred minutes. In 1897 it took him only forty minutes to score a century against Yorkshire at Harrogate. Ten years later, sixty-three minutes was sufficient time for him to rattle up 150 for Gentlemen of the South against Players of the South. But Jessop was far more than a licensed entertainer. He was a brilliant fieldsman at cover point or mid-off, safe at catching, and so fleet of foot and strong of arm that wise batsmen were deterred from seeking an extra run. Nor were they threatened only by his fielding, for Jessop's fast bowling captured 851 first-class wickets at under 23 runs each, the highlight being 8 for 29 for Gloucestershire against Essex in 1900. Unconventional, sometimes erratic, but with batting governed by his magnificent obsession to hit the ball as far as he could, Jessop was an icon of cricket for two decades. If the 'Squire of England' George Osbaldeston gazed down upon him from a century before, it would have been with approval for a fellow spirit.

In many ways Jessop's hitting was freakish, but an equally outlandish talent made his debut for Gloucestershire whilst still a schoolboy at Clifton. Charles Townsend, whose father Frank had played for Gloucestershire when the Graces were at their peak, bowled leg-breaks (then a rare and novel art) and enjoyed staggering success at school.

He first appeared for Gloucestershire as a mere boy of sixteen, and that first season took a hat-trick to end Somerset's second innings – with, uniquely, all three of his victims being stumped by wicketkeeper William Brain. By 1895, still aged only eighteen, he seemed fully formed as a bowler, spinning the ball savagely and, unusually, pitching it on the line of the wicket, rather than outside the leg stump. Wickets tumbled to him, much as they had done to the bumpkin 'Farmer' Lambert (or Lamborn – his name is uncertain) of Hambledon when off-spin was new, and Townsend topped the national averages with 131 wickets at 13.94 runs each. His full-time career lasted only six seasons before his profession as a solicitor intervened, although he played spasmodically until 1922. In 1899 he emphasised his all-round abilities by scoring 2,440 runs in the season at an average of 51. An undefeated 224 against Essex that year was his career best.

The county game was enriched also by more conventional players, such as Billy Gunn, who continued his long career with heavy scores for Notts throughout the 1890s. Lionel Palairet, elegant in Harlequin cap, opened Somerset's innings with grace and powerful driving. Charles Kortright played through the decade for Essex as the fastest bowler anyone could remember – and with an honest action. The Australian Albert Trott joined Middlesex and rewarded them with 408 wickets in the last three years of the decade.* Trott was a fearsome striker of the ball, too, and – ironically, against his fellow Australians – swung his three-pound bat to hit Monty Noble over the pavilion at Lord's, a feat never yet repeated. The ball landed in a nearby garden. Other memorable players included 'Plum' Warner, the archetypal establishment man, for whom cricket was a religion; Sammy Woods, fast bowler and high-scoring batsman who played both cricket and rugby for England, and also played cricket for his native Australia; and Robert Poore, Lord Harris's ADC in India who had been Lord Hawke's elusive quarry on his tour of South Africa. Poore returned to England to play for Hampshire, and averaged 116.58 in 1899, with

---

* Trott took 580 first-class wickets in the seasons 1898–1900, but only 408 of them were for Middlesex.

a top score of 304 against Somerset. Whatever faults they may have had, Harris and Hawke were fine judges of cricketers. Even Poore's triple hundred was dwarfed by an innings in a school match played over the afternoons of a single week. A.E.J. Collins, a thirteen-year-old Clifton schoolboy, scored 628 not out in a total of 836. He then took 11 wickets for 63 as his house won by an innings and 688 runs.

During the 1890s, Test matches became an annual event. South Africa joined Australia as a Test-playing country, and others aspired to do so. Winter tours were routine. But Test cricket was a part of the season, not *apart* from it: there were no squads of elite players siphoned off for the national teams.

England played six Tests against South Africa in the 1890s, winning them all comfortably, but there was no such overwhelming superiority when facing Australia. The two teams met twenty-six times, and ten victories each, with six games drawn, suggests that they were closely matched. England's cricketers may have believed themselves to be superior, but Australia's were their equals.

The decade produced many memorable Test performances. At The Oval in 1890, the Kent left-armer Fred Martin took 12 wickets for 102 runs on his debut. At Sydney in January 1892, Bobby Abel batted throughout the England innings for an undefeated 132, while Johnny Briggs dismissed Giffen, Callaway and Blackham in successive balls. England lost that game despite these heroics, but Stoddart's 134 helped them to a record win at Adelaide.

In the 1894–95 series, Syd Gregory scored a double century in a game Australia managed to lose by ten runs after forcing England to follow on. Bobby Peel took 6 for 67 as Australia lost their last five wickets for a pitiful 19 runs. At Melbourne, Stoddart's 173 earned England a 94-run victory, while at Adelaide Albert Trott, batting at number ten on his debut for Australia, scored 110 runs in two undefeated innings and took 8 for 43 in the second England innings. Australia won comfortably.

In the Melbourne Test, famous hundreds by Archie MacLaren and Jack Brown gave England victory. At Lord's in 1896, the MCC avenged their 1878 dismissal for 19 runs by bowling out Australia even more cheaply. From 18 for 3 wickets, Australia were bowled out – for 18. In the first Test, Grace completed his 1,000 runs in Test cricket, but it was Tom Richardson's 11 for 173 that won the game for England. It was in this game that Lord Harris provoked fury by omitting Ranjitsinhji, who, selected for the following match at Old Trafford, celebrated with 62 and 154 not out, although his joy was muted when Australia won the game.

The third Test at The Oval was marked by the most famous of all cricket strikes, when nine of England's professionals demanded a match fee of £20, rather than the £10 that was on offer (see page 228). This threat to withdraw their labour was rare, although not unprecedented. But professionals' protests had been ineffective for over twenty years. The 1878 strike, when seven Nottinghamshire professionals refused to play for James Lillywhite's side against Australia, had been in demand of the same match fee of £20 still being sought by Tom Hayward and his fellow professionals eighteen years later. In the interim, disputes in 1881 and 1888 had shown that cricketers, slowly and reluctantly, were prepared to follow the increasing willingness of trade unions to take strike action over pay. It was shocking at the time, but in retrospect what is more striking is the timidity of professional cricketers in the face of great injustice. Despite the glamour of the game for the spectators, it was their livelihood, and they were right to believe that they were being treated unfairly compared to their 'amateur' colleagues.

Nor was their case unsupported. Most of the press were sympathetic, and a young lady writing in *Cricket Rhymes* set out their case:

> Now this is what the 'pros' all say,
> Why should we receive less pay
> Than those who just for pleasure play?
> 'Tis we who draw the people here
> 'Tis we who cause the crowd to cheer
> When we professionals appear.

Three stanzas later, she makes, once more, the fundamental point:

As we have reason to believe
The so-called 'Amateurs' receive
A deal more than for us they leave.

And so they did. Everyone knew that shamateurism was rife, but no one acted to end it. In due course, attention returned from the dressing room to the field of play, and nothing changed. Professionals continued to seethe, and 'amateurs' went on pocketing their expenses.

Back in Australia in 1897–98, hundreds by MacLaren and Ranjitsinhji gave England an easy win at Sydney, but Australia then swept them aside with four successive victories in which Joe Darling, Clem Hill and Frank Iredale all scored heavily.

At Trent Bridge in 1899, twenty-one-year-old Victor Trumper made his debut with a duck in a drawn game, but followed this failure with a sparkling 135 not out at Lord's in a comprehensive Australian victory. At Leeds, Johnny Briggs suffered a violent epileptic attack at the Empire music hall on the first evening of the match. He was admitted to Cheadle asylum and did not play again in the season. Though no one knew it, worse was to follow. Jackson and Hayward both scored hundreds in a record opening stand for England at The Oval, but another hundred from Syd Gregory forced a draw. The consistent public enthusiasm for these matches elevated Test cricket as the supreme form of the game.

As the importance of Test matches grew, a Board of Control was set up to administer them in England. It was not the only significant development at the end of the century. Team captains were – at last – permitted to declare their first innings closed at their discretion. The six-ball over was introduced (although eight-ball overs would become the rule in Australia, New Zealand and South Africa for part of the twentieth century), and from 1900 the captain of the fielding side could force the opposition to follow on provided they were at least 150 runs behind on the first innings. A Minor Counties Association was founded to underpin the county game. In Paris in 1900 cricket became an Olympic sport, with England, represented by the Devon Wanderers, defeating the Athletic Club of Paris to win the gold medal.

Cricket had come a long way since some anonymous yokel in the Weald made the definitive move from an ancient ball game. The modern game would continue to spread and evolve, but in all its essentials cricket reached full maturity as the Victorian age moved to a close in January 1901. The great players of the past – Small, Harris, Beauclerk, Pilch, even the young W.G. – would have been astonished at its growth and popularity. The game they had helped to build was set to become one of the dominant amusements of the world.

As the Edwardian age began, England was a mighty power on the cusp of gentle decline. Kipling, acute observer of trends, and married to an American, saw power tipping towards the West, and urged his wife's nation to 'take up the White Man's burden'. It was prescient but Kipling could hardly have foreseen that the decline of the Ottoman Empire, spilling Mesopotamia (Iraq), Syria and neighbouring territories into nation states, would lead a century later to war in Iraq and Afghanistan.

Kipling's world was changing. England had become an urban nation, in which 80 per cent of the population lived in towns, whereas fifty years earlier the town and country split had been even. London, with a population of four and a half million, was the largest city in the world. Across Europe, no passports were needed for travel or immigration, and persecuted Jews from Continental Europe and Russia poured into Britain, replacing the million Britons who emigrated to America and the dominions.*

Many of the emigrants came from the underclass of the poor, for whom the general advance in well-being had been an illusion. For millions, optimism had not led to enhanced standards of living. Disappointment led to class-consciousness, frustration and militancy. Suffragettes campaigned for the right to vote, and rebuff after rebuff turned many of them into militant campaigners. Trade union membership soared, from two million in 1901 to 4.1 million in 1913. Once organised, the workforce did not shrink from taking strike

---

* Between 1891 and 1916 the Jewish population of the United Kingdom rose from 101,000 to 257,000 (census figures).

action to obtain a fairer share of the national wealth. In the midst of hardships and discontent the political pendulum swung wildly, the young Labour Party grew and the Welfare State was born. The launch of the Zeppelin in 1900 was followed by the Wright brothers' invention of a gas-motored and manned aircraft, and a piloted helicopter by Paul Cornu. When Louis Blériot flew the Channel in 1909 it was clear that planes would add a new dimension to future conflict.

In 1906, resurgent Liberalism had given the party a huge parliamentary majority. This can now be seen as the last Liberal flowering before electoral death, but its implications at the time were far-reaching. Legislation was passed for old-age pensions (seven shillings and sixpence a week for a married couple). A National Insurance Act offered unemployment benefit to all those whose income fell below £150 a year. Lloyd George's budgets to pay for these innovations – and for re-armament – led to constitutional clashes between the Lords and Commons. In troubled times, only the imminence of war prevented a planned strike by miners, railwaymen and transport workers in 1914.

Against the background of this unrest, cricket was in full bloom. Its character was now set beyond fundamental change, although there were occasional amendments to the laws, largely in an attempt to reduce the number of drawn matches. In 1903 the bowling crease was widened from six feet eight inches to eight feet eight inches, to increase the angle of delivery for bowlers. In 1910, six runs would be awarded for a hit clearing the boundary. The innate conservatism of the game meant that some proposals were rejected. County captains twice attempted, in 1902 and 1903, to increase the width of the stumps from eight to nine inches, but Australia and South Africa objected, and the proposal failed to get the necessary two-thirds majority of MCC members. So did attempts to change the leg before wicket law to enable the batsman to be given out even if the ball did not pitch between wicket and wicket. This too was rejected in 1902 and 1903, although it was finally enacted in 1937. And the issue of players' fees rumbled on, as both on and off the field amateurs continued to enjoy a social status entirely denied their professional colleagues.

In the history of cricket, the years between 1895 and 1914 are known as the 'Golden Age', notably for batting, but also because at their conclusion a world was blown away by the Great War, the seeds of which were beginning to take root while Queen Victoria still lived. This period was the heyday of amateurism, of dashing batting, of innovation – Townsend's leg-breaks, Ranji's leg-glance, Bosanquet's googly, Barnes's development of spin and swerve. County cricket flourished, although many familiar faces departed. Arthur Mold was forced out of cricket after being repeatedly no-balled by umpire James Phillips and condemned for his bowling action by every county captain except his own. Richard Daft and Cris Tinley, once members of William Clarke's travelling elevens, died in 1900, as did Edmund Peate, who had been one of Lord Hawke's first victims at Yorkshire, Tom Hearne, and the Australian fast bowler J.J. Ferris, who had so demoralised English batting in 1888.

The mid-century stars John Jackson and Robert Carpenter died in 1901, and Johnny Briggs the following year. Briggs had been committed once more to Cheadle asylum, where he haunted the corridors by jumping out at passers-by and appealing 'Howzat? Howzat?' as his tortured mind recalled past glories. It was a sad end for a much-loved man who had been a club professional at thirteen years of age, and made his debut for Lancashire at sixteen. Two thousand wickets and 14,000 runs later, Briggs had become Lancashire's most prolific all-rounder. He died at only thirty-nine, with twenty-five thousand mourners attending his funeral.

Arthur Shrewsbury, one of the greatest batsmen in Victorian England for over two decades, shot himself fatally in 1903, having adorned cricket for thirty years. The public and private Shrewsbury were barely the same man. On the field, he was firm and confident in his cricket skills. Off it, he never feared to speak his mind or stand up for himself. In disputes between the Nottinghamshire team and the county club, Shrewsbury was often a prominent agitator. And yet, as is so often the case, Shrewsbury was often morose, and his instabilities made him a lifelong bachelor. In 1902, at the age of forty-six, he enjoyed an Indian summer of success, and averaged over

52 runs for the season. But the following year, with his cricket career over, melancholia gained a hold on his fragile peace of mind. Without any cause, he feared himself to be incurably sick. His insecurities were such that his friends were not surprised by his suicide. A first shot to the chest did not kill him, but unbelievably he fired a second, fatal, shot to the head.

Other departures were less dramatic but equally poignant. Arthur Haygarth, the great Chronicler, and Bob Thoms, the umpire, died in 1903, with Jack (J.T.) Brown of Yorkshire dying the following year of heart and brain failure at thirty-five. His Yorkshire predecessor, the ever-popular Tom Emmett, died that same year, together with the venerable old wicketkeeper Herbert Jenner-Fust, who had first played at Lord's in 1822. Richard Humphrey of Surrey drowned in the Thames in 1906: his widow Sarah believed to her dying day that he was murdered – his gold watch was apparently missing. Shrewsbury's Nottinghamshire team-mate, the balding, plump and heavily bearded Alfred Shaw, the first man to bowl a ball in Test cricket, died of natural causes in 1907. He was 'timeless', said Richard Daft in tribute, 'the Emperor of bowlers'. The old guard was changing – and passing on.

But a galaxy of memorable talent still decorated the scene as Test cricket continued to grow in importance. As yet only England, Australia and South Africa competed in Test matches, but the quality of the contests encouraged other countries to aspire to join them.

Victor Trumper unfolded his full genius on the Australian tour of England in 1902. On both wet and dry wickets he dazzled and dominated. Spectators and players alike spoke in awe of the majesty of Trumper's batting. At his heels in England came the young Jack Hobbs, the mightiest run-scorer in all cricket history, who made his Test debut in 1908. Hobbs scored 197 centuries on uncovered wickets over thirty years to become 'The Master', an epithet that is an eloquent appraisal of his place in cricket history. His technique was matchless, and a Greek epigram on Plato is equally applicable to Hobbs as a batsman: 'In whatever direction we go, we meet him coming back.' At the height of his career, *Punch* despaired:

Can nothing be done for J.B. Hobbs
To make him sometimes get out for blobs?

Other batsmen sparkled too. In 1900 R.E. Foster, one of seven cricketing brothers, became the first batsman to score a century in each innings of a Gentlemen vs Players match. On his Test debut he scored 287 at Sydney to give England a five-wicket win, despite Australian hundreds for Noble and Trumper. Frank Woolley's silky elegance adorned the game from 1906. Australia were blessed with the arrival of Warwick Armstrong, Reggie Duff and Charlie Macartney.

The irascible Sydney Barnes, perhaps the greatest bowler of all, was plucked from obscurity to Test matches by the sharp eye of Archie MacLaren. Unbiddable and unbending, Barnes lived by his own rules. He was one of life's awkward squad, cussed by instinct and inclination, but he hated batsmen most of all, and was a magnificent bowler. On all wickets, and against all batsmen, Barnes had the whip-hand.

Colin Blythe of Kent and Bernard Bosanquet of Middlesex advanced the cause of spin. Blythe, a slow left-arm bowler, emerged from the slums of Deptford with deceptive pace and spin, had enormous success for Kent and England, and can be ranked alongside Peate, Peel, Briggs and Rhodes. Bosanquet, coached by the old Surrey professionals Maurice Read and Bill Brockwell, invented the 'googly' to utterly bamboozle batsmen, and add forever a new weapon to the spin bowler's armoury. Great players appeared, batsmen and bowlers alike, as if on a conveyor belt, and the motorised movie camera invented in 1912 would soon capture glimpses of them for posterity.

Between 1900 and 1914 cricket boomed at all levels. Village, club and league cricket became ever more popular. County allegiance was very strong, and alternative summer pursuits could not compete with the drama of cricket. Some performances still stand out. In 1904 Essex lost to Derbyshire after scoring 597 in the first innings, with Percy Perrin making 343 not out. Hobbs and Rhodes put on 323 for the first wicket against Australia at Melbourne in 1912. Tom Hayward scored his hundredth century, for Surrey against Lancashire, in 1913.

Lord Hawke's Yorkshire team won the County Championship six times. Of the other teams only Kent, with four Championships, won more than a single title. Year upon year, the game grew stronger and more popular.

As cricket enjoyed its greatest days, the clock was winding down to war. Few suspected that the conflict would come, having been seduced into complacency by a European peace that had lasted since 1871. But war often has a long lead-in. As it drew closer, C.B. Fry led the Gentlemen to victory over Jack Hobbs's Players at Lord's. When they left the field an era died for Fry, Jessop and Barnes, who would never again play in the fixture. Surrey won a County Championship that was truncated by the onset of war: Hearne and Hobbs topped the batting averages, with Colin Blythe the leading bowler. In May 1914, R.E. Foster died of diabetes at thirty-six. Five days before war was declared, Albert Trott, the only man to clear the Lord's pavilion, suffering from an incurable ailment, shot himself in his lodgings at the age of forty-one.

The war that would be 'over by Christmas' was greeted with enthusiasm. Young men rushed to enlist before it was over. They need not have hurried. A generation died, and cricket was not exempt.

Kipling's words applied to cricket as they did to the country:

There's a whisper down the field where the year has shot her yield,
And the ricks stand grey to the sun
Singing: 'Over then, come over, for the bee has quit the clover,
And your English summer's done.'

For four years, it would be a very dark winter.

Afterword

The carnage of war engulfed Europe, and the Man with the Scythe set about cricket. No one will ever know how many village or club cricketers lost their lives. Nor whether, as they lay in trenches or advanced through the mud and blood of the Western Front, they talked or thought of the game they loved. Were their last moments a glimpse of home and the village green, and if so, was that able to bring them repose and peace of mind in their bleakest hour?

There was a harsh toll on first-class cricket. Lieutenant Ken Hutchings, of Kent and England, was struck by a shell in September 1916, and died instantly. In November 1917 his team-mate Sergeant Colin 'Charlie' Blythe was killed in France. This sensitive, delicate man, blessed with the gift of truly great left-arm spin, was one of three thousand fatalities in the advance on Passchendaele. His death that winter, so far removed from his triumphs amid the white tents and social gaiety of Canterbury Week, was the greatest single loss to top-class cricket.

But not the only one. Other Test players gave their lives. Australia's fast bowler Albert 'Tibby' Cotter was killed by a sniper's bullet in 1917 as he gazed over the ramparts in Palestine. Cotter apparently had a premonition of death – he had told his colleagues 'Something is going to happen.' All-rounder Major William Booth of Yorkshire, who had toured South Africa with the MCC only two years earlier, was killed in July 1916 at the age of thirty. In his last season of 1914, he had taken 141 wickets for Yorkshire at 18 runs each. The South

African all-rounder Gordon White died of wounds in October 1918, and the following month Reggie Schwarz, student of Bosanquet and master of the googly, who had twice been wounded, caught influenza and died in France seven days after the Armistice was signed.

In 1915 county cricket lost Lieutenant Guy Napier, the Middlesex medium-pacer, who died of wounds in France; Lieutenant H.F. Garrett of Somerset was killed in the Dardanelles; Alan Marshal, the Surrey and Queensland all-rounder, was struck down by enteric fever after having survived the disaster of Gallipoli; and William Tyldesley of Lancashire was killed in action. Percy Jeeves, the Warwickshire all-rounder – whose name was appropriated by P.G. Wodehouse for Bertie Wooster's peerless butler – and John Nason of Sussex and Gloucestershire, were killed in 1916. Second Lieutenant William Odell MC, the Leicestershire medium-pacer, was killed while serving with the Sherwood Foresters in October 1917, and the Lancashire left-handed batsman Captain Harold Garnett of the South Wales Borderers died on the Italian front in December of that year. Alfred Hartley, also a Lancashire batsman, was killed in France in 1918.

Others were luckier. Major A.C.G. Luther of Sussex was wounded in the Battle of Le Câteau, and lay motionless as the Germans approached, aware that wounded soldiers were often shot where they lay. His watch and wallet were removed, and then a voice spoke to him, in perfect English: 'You are a very lucky man. I see you are a member of the MCC. You can go back to your lines.' The German soldier had been a land agent in Derbyshire, where he had played cricket before the war. Luther lived until he was eighty. Frank Foster, the Warwickshire and England fast-medium left-arm bowler, survived the war, but a motorcycle injury on duty lamed him and ended his career. Foster's early dabbling with leg theory, taken to extremes by Douglas Jardine during the bodyline tour of Australia in 1932–33, would give rise to cricket's darkest hour. Another Frank, the young all-rounder Frank Chester of Worcestershire, lost his right arm at Salonika, but survived to become the greatest of umpires. In the season before the war he scored three centuries, and seemed destined for a long and successful playing career.

Lieutenant A.E.J. Collins, the schoolboy who had scored 628 not out (or thereabouts – the scorecard is messy and almost certainly a little inaccurate) for Clifton over five afternoons in 1899, was killed in November 1914, within weeks of the war beginning. Collins had sacrificed a possible career in cricket to become a professional soldier. Another Clifton cricketer, Lieutenant George Whitehead, captain of the school eleven in 1913 and 1914, and scorer of 259 not out against Liverpool, died in action with the Royal Flying Corps one month before the war ended.

James Norman Hall celebrated the role of cricketers in the war with an apt poem, 'The Cricketer of Flanders', which begins:

> The first to climb the parapet
> With 'cricket-ball' in either hand;
> The first to vanish in the smoke
> Of God-forsaken no-Man's land.
> First at the wire and soonest through,
> First at those re-mouthed hounds of hell
> The Maxims, and the first to fall, –
> They do their bit, and do it well.

And so they did; but the cost was very high.

Away from the battlefield, other tragedies took their toll on cricket. Arthur Jones of Notts, who led the MCC to Australia in 1907–08 and played twelve times for England, was yet another victim of consumption after months of acute suffering. Allan Steel, the great Lancashire and England all-rounder, who became a Queen's Counsel, died in June 1914, followed three years later by his son, on active service. Harry Trott, elder brother of Albert and a former captain of Australia, died in Melbourne in 1917 after a long illness.

In October 1915, as has been noted, W.G. Grace suffered a stroke and died quietly at the age of sixty-seven. Within days of his death, Bright's Disease* overwhelmed the thirty-seven-year-old Galahad of cricket, Victor Trumper. W.G. was in the late autumn of a magical life, but Trumper was taken away in high summer. Even amid the

---

* A chronic inflammation of the kidneys.

horrors of slaughter in France and at Gallipoli, the deaths of these two immortal cricketers stirred emotions at opposite ends of a war-torn world.

So too did the suicide in the same year of Andrew Stoddart, captain of England at cricket and rugby, batsman and wing three-quarter, scorer of 485 runs in a single day for Hampstead. His marriage and his finances were at a low ebb. He caught pneumonia and became melancholic. Whether war unbalanced him, or whether life was too bleak once his cricket days were ended, will forever be unknown. But the ghosts of Shrewsbury and Scotton suggest that the end of his cricketing days, when his skills were redundant, may have weighed heavily on his mind. Before Freud no one knew of the subconscious. After Freud, no one doubted its existence. Whatever the cause, inner turmoil led Stoddart to pull the trigger when the joy of cricket was over.

Many of the generation who died in the Great War may have become fine cricketers. George Marsden-Smedley, captain of the Harrow eleven in 1915, was killed in action only a year later. Twenty-year-old John Howell was killed at Flanders in 1915. Two double centuries for Repton and a century in a trial match at The Oval in 1914 gave promise that he was a rare talent. A greater talent, but a lesser cricketer, was twenty-seven-year-old Rupert Brooke, who died off the Greek island of Skyros in 1915, of blood poisoning caused by a mosquito bite. Brooke had been a successful bowler for Marlborough School, noted *Wisden*, adding, in masterly understatement, that he had 'gained some considerable reputation as a poet'. Brooke left a written monument. For many of the English victims of war, his famous lines from 'The Soldier' stand as a poignant reminder of a generation wasted by folly:

> If I should die, think only this of me,
> That there's some corner of a foreign field,
> That is forever England.

Cricket's long journey was interrupted, but not undone, by war. It was too entrenched to be swept away even by cataclysm. When hostilities ended the game resumed after five years of slumber, and its headquarters at Lord's ceased to be a prison camp. But the field was depleted. Jessop survived the war, but his career was ended. Barnes never again played for England, ignored more for his cussedness than any loss of form. Fry and Warner were veterans past their prime. Of the England eleven who played in South Africa in the early spring of 1914, only six took the field at Sydney for the first post-war Test against Australia in December 1920.

As if to wipe away memories they wished to erase, cricketers returned to the game without delay. Although some giants of pre-war were gone from the game, others – Hobbs, Rhodes and Woolley among them – carried on as if they had never left the crease. Nor had the crude reality of war dimmed the talent of Strudwick, Douglas or Hearne. New stars appeared, notably Patsy Hendren and Cecil Parkin. Cricket was back, but unhappily for English pride a strong Australian team with Macartney, Bardsley, Armstrong, Ryder, Gregory, Oldfield, Collins, McDonald and Mailey won the first post-war Test series by five matches to nil.

The panorama of cricket was unending. More new players with rich gifts would soon announce their arrival. Herbert Sutcliffe, Andrew Sandham, 'Tich' Freeman, Maurice Leyland and Harold Larwood were all in the wings. In Australia, Bill Ponsford, Clarrie Grimmett, Alan Kippax, Bill Woodfull and, later in the decade, Donald Bradman, all came to the fore. With Bradman, a new era began.

Sometimes an individual has gifts so finely honed that they mock the talents of even the finest contemporaries. Bradman was such a man. His record was Shakespearean in its majesty. The great playwright had a vocabulary of twenty thousand words in an age in which a Warwickshire yokel might live a long life with only three hundred words at his command. Even John Milton is thought to have had a vocabulary less than half that of Shakespeare.

In cricket, Don Bradman is beyond the reach of all. Other batsmen were more stylish, more exciting to watch, but none matched Bradman's run-scoring. He scored a century once in every three times he walked to the wicket, and amassed double and triple centuries more often than any other batsman before or since. In Test cricket he averaged 99.94. To put that into context, Bradman scored nearly 40 runs more per innings than any other great batsman in the history of the game. Herbert Sutcliffe, Walter Hammond, Len Hutton, Ken Barrington, Graeme Pollock and, at the time of writing, Ricky Ponting, are all mired at 58 to 62 runs per innings – far short of Bradman. The size of the gap is even more evident when you consider that formidable players who have earned themselves a secure place in the history of Test cricket have averaged only the difference between the Don and his following pack. Bradman was a phenomenon.

Shakespeare's contemporary Ben Jonson wrote of him that he was the greatest of all dramatists, finer even than the ancients Ovid, Sophocles, Aristophanes and Euripides: he was, Jonson declared, 'not of an age but for all time'. That contemporary judgement has held true down the centuries. No twentieth-century writer had Jonson's gift of language with which to assess Bradman, but his eulogy is as applicable to Bradman the batsman as it was to Shakespeare the playwright. In their chosen professions, as dramatist and run-getter, the Bard and the Don are alone on their pinnacles.

Bradman's pre-eminence as a run-maker was so extraordinary that it gave rise to the most shameful episode in cricket's long history. Bodyline bowling, or leg theory, was a blight on the spirit of the game. It was devised solely to curb Bradman's genius, and up to a point it succeeded. It cut down the flow of his runs, for that series alone, to the level of a Compton or a Sobers – he averaged 'only' 56.57.

Before he died, the late Bob Wyatt, who was Douglas Jardine's vice-captain on the 1932–33 tour, although no enthusiast for bodyline, told me that on one occasion Jardine, the architect of bodyline, was leaving the pitch at close of play when an Australian player, hidden beneath his baggy green cap, hissed at him, 'You bastard, Jardine.' Jardine, affronted, stormed into the home dressing room and confronted the Australian captain, Bill Woodfull. Woodfull listened to his complaint, and then barked at his team: 'Which of you bastards called this bastard a bastard?' Jardine retreated.

After Bradman retired from Test cricket at the end of Australia's 1948 tour of England, he was fêted around the world and featured on stamps, in songs and books. Plays were written about him. Streets were named after him. He has been the subject of eleven biographies, in contrast to the maximum of four about iconic Australian Prime Ministers. But, for once, Bradman was not ahead of the field: thirteen biographies have been written of Ned Kelly. Bradman died in 2001, at ninety-two, with that final elusive century beyond his reach.

Through the veil, Small, Harris, Beldham, Pilch, Mynn, Grace, Spofforth, Rhodes and Hobbs preceded the Great War. After it had ended, out of the mists of the future came many players whose genius would leave its mark: Hammond, Sutcliffe, Constantine, Hutton, Compton, Laker, Hanif, Sobers, Holding, Lara, Lillee, Hadlee, Warne, Tendulkar, Ponting, Muralitharan ... the list is incomplete, and continues to grow. All live in the recollections of those who saw them play. But so far only Grace and Bradman have defined an era.

We look back on cricket with affection, but we need to look to the future with a clear eye. The game faces many challenges. On the field, cricket has changed, and continues to do so. Some of the changes we may not like: slower over rates have not enhanced the game as a spectacle, but faster run-scoring and a spectacular improvement in fielding have done so. Overall, the quality of cricket is not in decline. A proper perspective suggests that the three greatest sides in history belong to the last sixty years. Which teams, I wonder, from any golden age, could have beaten the 1948 Australians, the 1970s–80s West Indies of the 1970s and eighties or the Australians of the late 1990s? None, I suspect: these were teams of many stars and no weak links.

Off the field, the greatest challenge to be faced is the financing of cricket. Whereas the professional game was once funded overwhelm-ingly by gate receipts, it is viable now only with the support of corporate sponsorship, television receipts and the revenues of Test matches. As a result there are more Tests than ever before, and yet there is a Catch-22: too much Test cricket, and familiarity will lessen its attraction; too little, and the finances of the game will become more fragile. No one should envy cricket administrators this conundrum.

To widen the appeal of the game we must protect those aspects that make it unique. These go far beyond simple enjoyment. The Marxist historian C.L.R. James argued that, in the West Indies, cricket had a magic that was a guiding light for the dispossessed and the disenfranchised. From a polar opposite political position, Lord Harris argued that cricket upheld the values of a nineteenth-century empire.

From their disparate viewpoints, James and Harris had instincts in common: both believed that cricket touches deep and conflicting emotions, and offers added value to society. They are right. Sport, and cricket specifically, can have a dynamic effect upon a community, and can spring from the very core of a nation. It is puzzling that the opportunities sport offers are so rarely taken advantage of, and that it so often falls off the social agenda of governments. The Ancient Greeks understood the value of games, and it is a pity that over the intervening thousands of years we have forgotten what they taught us.

Why is this? Many politicians love sport. Yet, too often, its merits are ignored by the statesman. He seems to have a puritanical instinct that relegates sport to a subordinate position, as mere entertainment, and unworthy of his attention. He misses its wider significance. He prefers gravity to gaiety. But sport matters, and we should channel its energy wisely. For sport not only uplifts, it can set an example to society – a fact I wish sledgers, false appealers and non-walkers would remember.

It will not be easy to upgrade sport within the priorities of even the most well-disposed government. Sports-lovers mustn't be naïve: governments have a responsibility to weigh sport against the creation of jobs, and the demands of health, education and social security. Their task is not easy, but I believe more can be done to help sport and thus promote the social agenda of sensible government.

Some politicians argue that governments shouldn't concern themselves with something so transitory as sport. Moreover, they argue that if the demand is there, the market will provide. This is Puritanism run wild, although up to a point it is true. But only up to a point. Policy based on such a half-truth is ideology without common sense. The market will never provide sporting facilities for children at school, or for villages or local clubs. They are simply not commercially viable. Certainly, in the UK, the market hasn't provided for the residents of the inner cities, and as a result something of real social benefit has been lost. Children immersed in sport are not causing trouble on the streets, and are less likely than others to be involved in drugs and crime. Such children can see that someone is supervising them, caring for them and making it possible for them to pursue an activity which they enjoy. Sport is a good social bargain for any community. It is healthily competitive, it channels energy into a positive force – and it is fun. Which would we prefer to see in our communities: team games or street gangs? To put the question is to know the answer.

I believe that children have a right to sport and leisure. They are equally important components of their development as literature and mathematics, and – for most children – likely to provide some of the happiest memories of their childhood.

It is a cliché to say that the future of cricket requires the affiliation of the young, but that doesn't make it untrue: we need them, both as players and spectators. Only by exposing children to the joy of cricket, even if they have no aptitude for it, can we inspire a love of the game. The long-term health of cricket requires the lifelong affection of the child who can't play as well as the skills of the one who can. And that affection must be held against the attractions not only of other sports, but of the television age and the computer revolution which offer powerful non-sporting, non-team-playing, non-character-forming challenges to outdoor recreation.

Once, cricket was a means of escape from obscurity to fame, poverty to comfort, exclusion to inclusion. Such motives are less resonant today. These days, each successive generation has a greater choice of how to spend its leisure time: once cricket and football were unchallenged recreations – but no longer. So, cricket-lovers must ask: how do we attract and develop future talent to our game?

As Prime Minister, I sought to raise money for sport and other good causes by establishing a national lottery. For doing so I was assailed on all fronts. The Churches hated it: they attacked me for encouraging gambling. The football pools hated it: they attacked me for costing them money. The press hated it: they attacked me out of habit. Very few spoke out in support. Fortunately, I got my way. My passion for sport was well known, and no one stood in the way of it. And so the lottery went ahead, and within a decade it raised around £2,000 million for sport at all levels. Within cricket, the money has gone to village greens, for nets and rollers, to youth teams and club teams, as well as to the rebuilding of our national grounds. Together with other initiatives from cricket authorities, it has helped to ensure that more people are playing cricket in England today than for genera-tions.* And this is despite the decline in school cricket. Here, I know, I did less than I should have done. I should have acted more comprehensively to restore sport to schools when I had the power to do so, and I know it now with all the clarity that comes to those who review their mistakes with honesty. Margaret Thatcher's government began selling off 'surplus' school playing fields, and I insisted that it must be shown that these were not needed before further disposals took place. The Labour government continued the policy, but as school sport diminished, more and more fields were said to be 'redun-dant', and were sold.

As I look back on it now, it would have been better not to have sold those fields at all. Open spaces, when they are gone, are hardly ever recreated. The lottery, once introduced, would have ensured that they were available to schools and the wider community. It was a mistaken policy, driven by a Treasury ethic more in tune with the value of current income than with long-term social investment. In the crush of government, I did not see this clearly enough. I should have focused on this policy, and reversed it totally.

* The first few years of the lottery were immensely successful. Sadly, the incoming 'New' Labour government of 1997 began to siphon funds away for other causes that were traditionally paid for out of taxes. It was larceny on a grand scale.

Today, a gifted sportsman leaving school and seeking either a
career or simple enjoyment has more sporting choices than ever
before – witness the upsurge in popularity of football, tennis, golf,
rugby or, in the West Indies, basketball and baseball. All of these are
an alternative to cricket, and, with the possible exception of rugby,
all offer far more financial rewards to the talented player. All these
games are of value, but I believe that cricket may offer the widest
social rewards.

To a remarkable extent, cricket is cohesive, not divisive. I saw
this myself in the mid-1990s, when Nelson Mandela invited me to
South Africa for the first post-apartheid visit of a British Prime
Minister. Following my speech to the South African Parliament, I
lunched with President Mandela alongside white Members of Parliament and former inmates of the notorious prison on Robben Island.
Our lunch was in the dining room in which Harold Macmillan had
delivered his famous 'Wind of Change' speech in 1960, and my hosts
and I broke the ice of political dispute with talk of cricket. Within
minutes an easy discussion began between men who had been bitterly
opposed politically for decades.

I invited some famous sporting personalities to accompany me
on a visit to the Alexandria township near Johannesburg. Colin
Cowdrey and Alec Stewart presided over cricket nets. That wonderful
heptathlete Judy Simpson held a master class in athletics. Bobby
Charlton demonstrated his mastery of how to kick a football. In the
nets, I bowled Steve Tshwete, the South African Sports Minister, *first
ball* – every politician's dream with a press corps in tow. All Alexandria turned out, and the sports stars were mobbed. During those
hours in the township there was sheer exuberant joy amidst hardship.
Never doubt the healing powers of sport.

The social case for cricket is convincing. It can uplift the morale
of communities, even nations. It can imprint national characteristics
favourably, even on a hostile mind. It has socially healing properties.
It touches the deepest instincts, and can provide icons for the young
to follow. A moment's reflection can demonstrate this. Are the streets
ever aflame with excitement over a politician's triumph in negotiating

a treaty, or abuzz over a businessman's success in winning a contract? No calypsos are written about such events. 'Treaty, lovely Treaty' somehow lacks the passion of the original verse written to celebrate the West Indies' defeat of England at Lord's in 1950. Nor are treaties the talk of the streets, the workplaces or the bars. They are unlikely to enter folklore. But a Test victory can be quite another matter. It is argued over endlessly, pored over, even gloated over.

Those who love cricket must help cast its spell over the future. It won't be easy: cricket faces many rivals for its eminent position in the world of sport. It is a game that, in its finest expression, takes five days to complete, and even then may end without a result. In our age of instant gratification, this is not an easy sell. And, yet, to secure cricket's future, we must attract a wider public. The Kerry Packer revolution in December 1977 showed how it can be done. Although shocking at the time, much about Packer's World Series Cricket was innovative. From it much followed, and the nature of marketing cricket changed forever; but the commercial imperatives that inspired Packer are equally true today. If interest falls, sponsorship falls, gate money falls – and so will the game. Cricket administrators, aware of this dilemma, have become ever more creative. Some of their innovations have been crowd-pullers: one-day cricket, day–night matches and the short Twenty20 version of the game have all attracted a new audience. Coloured clothing, white balls and restricted-over matches may upset the traditionalist, but such changes are securing the future of the game.

Even technology has entered the game, albeit in a haphazard fashion. Once we pretended to believe that umpires were infallible, or that their rare errors evened out over time. 'Frank Chester never made mistakes,' one old Test player once said to me. No doubt Mr Chester was a great umpire, but yes, he did make mistakes – although they were never caught on film. The pitiless eye of the slow-motion camera, its images replayed time after time, exposes the fallibility of modern umpires in a way their predecessors never faced. As a result, many important games are marked by outcries against poor decisions, especially if they turn the outcome of the match.

I used to wonder whether Steve Bucknor took so long to make a decision in the hope that the film would fade.

Pity the poor umpire: the pressure on him grows constantly, both from the players – among whom aggressive appealing has become an unattractive art form, and 'walking' a thing of the past – and from television. The philosophical argument over whether electronic aids should be used to help him seemed at the outset to be finely balanced: the traditionalist said no, the modernist said yes. Although my heart is with the traditionalist, my head says that the argument was lost the moment technology was used for the first time. There is no logic at all in a situation in which umpires are saved from having to take run-out decisions, but offered no assistance with leg-before-wicket appeals or feather-touch snicks behind the wicket.

If the umpire is entitled to verify some decisions with technological aids, why should he not, at his discretion, be able to verify them all? Anything less is simply a lottery, unsettling to the players and infuriating for the spectator, who sees within seconds on the slow-motion replay whether the correct decision was made. In recent years Test matches have been won or lost by decisions we know to have been wrong.

Some will argue that a reliance on technology belittles the authority of the umpire. Perhaps. But that authority is undermined far more by decisions that are self-evidently wrong. The best of umpires – say Aleem Dar or Simon Taufel – give a high percentage of fine decisions, but even they are not infallible, and with approximately two dozen camera positions around the ground, replays in close-up, stump cameras, microphones, snickometers and tramlines, any wrong decision is soon given massive exposure. It would take but seconds for the on-field umpire – and again, I re-emphasise at his discretion – to confer with the third umpire, who has access to the technology, and eliminate the majority of errors. The game would benefit, and spectators and players alike would be far less frustrated. It might also help to cut out the unattractive sight of on-field dissent and attempts to pressurise the umpire, which match referees should penalise.

Elsewhere, on-field umpires might be given more unfettered

power. Are the laws on bad light fair? Should the choice of whether
to leave the field continue to be offered to batsmen, since it is exercised, more often than not, upon the state of the game rather than the
state of the light? Or should the umpires be given absolute discretion?
Similar considerations apply in limited-overs games, where the side
fielding first can be penalised for a slow over-rate by having overs
deducted from its own innings. Should not the umpires also have
some sanction upon the side fielding second, if their progress is
tardy?

And should we not also look again at infringements on the
spirit of cricket? Ball-tampering, throwing, sledging, over-aggressive
appealing – often downright dishonest appealing – pressurising of
umpires; all of them are the small change of unsportsmanlike
behaviour. In these days of greater financial rewards for success, some
cricketers regard such conduct as acceptable. But of course it is not:
at its worst it's cheating, and it damages the spirit of cricket.

So, more vividly, does corruption, the impetus for which is often
to fix bets for financial gain. This is not a new phenomenon. Betting
was one of the prime motors for the growth of the game in England
for over a century, and malpractice may often have been rife. But
until recently we believed that modern cricket was clean, and it has
been shocking to discover that it is not.

All this is fatal to a sport where the spirit in which it is played is
as important to its most avid followers as the result. To retain its
reputation, cricket must root out those who mar the game. But as
they do so, the authorities around the world must beware of being
too loud in their criticism of the misdemeanours of foreign players,
yet understanding of those committed by members of their own
teams. The ICC needs to rule on this problem, publish penalties for
misbehaviour and insist that they are enforced, irrespective of the
identity of the miscreant.

Once, cricket was an English game. Now it belongs to many countries:
it is even taking root in China and Afghanistan. Around the world,
one in every two spectators is Indian – a less startling statistic than

it seems when one considers the massive population of India, which dwarfs the combined total of England, Australia, New Zealand, South Africa, the West Indies, Sri Lanka and Pakistan. The monetary implications of this will give India increasing authority in the councils of the game.

Cricket today is a far cry from the game in the age of humbug, when W.G. Grace pocketed large fees for playing at the same time that he symbolised and promoted the concept of the gentleman amateur. We have moved on from the days when, in England, the captain and the amateurs used different dressing rooms from the professional players, and stepped onto the pitch through separate gates. These images symbolise a time now past, but even in our more egalitarian age, cricket can still hold up a reflective light to society.

Throughout my life, cricket has been an abiding passion. In good times and bad it has been my constant companion, providing the perfect blend of charm, fascination, inspiration and solace. It has brought into my life some of the most decent people I will ever know, not only at home but from every corner of the world.

In writing this book there are many others, lifted from the pages of history, whose character I have come to know, admire and respect. We owe much to the early pioneers of cricket, those who broke early laws by playing it, those whose largesse funded it, those whose genius for ball games moulded the game to the sophistication we know today. My own life has been immeasurably enriched by a love of cricket. To me, and many millions of others, it has been, and I hope always will be, so very much more than just a game.

'Articles of Agreement by & between His Grace the Duke of Richmond and Mr. Brodrick (for two Cricket Matches) concluded the Eleventh of July 1727'

Imprimis. 'Tis by the aforesaid Parties agreed that the first Match shall be played some day of this Instant July in the County of Surrey; the Place to be named by Mr. Brodrick; the second Match to be played in August next in the County of Sussex, the Place to be named by the Duke of Richmond.

2nd. That the Wickets shall be pitched in a fair and even Place, at twenty three yards distance from each other.

3rd. A ball caught, cloathed or not cloathed the Striker is out.

4th. When a Ball is caught out, the Stroke counts nothing.

5th. Catching out behind the Wicket allowed.

6th. That 'tis lawful for the Duke of Richmond to choose any Gamesters, who have played in either of his Graces two last matches with Sir William Gage; and that 'tis lawful for Mr. Brodrick to choose any Gamesters within three miles of Pepperharowe, provided they actually lived there last Lady Day.

7th. that twelve Gamesters shall play on each side.

8th. that the Duke of Richmond & Mr. Brodrick shall determine the Ball or Balls to be played with.

9th. if any of the Gamesters shall be taken lame or sick after the Match is begun, their Places may be supplied by any One chose conformably to the Sixth Article, or in Case that can not be done, the other side shall be obliged to leave out one of their Gamesters, whomsoever they please.

10th. that each Match shall be for twelve Guineas of each Side; between the Duke and Mr. Brodrick.

11th. that there shall be one Umpire of each Side; & that if any of the Gamesters shall speak or give their opinion, on any point of the Game, they are to be turned out & voided in the Match; this not to extend to the Duke of Richmond and Mr. Brodrick.

12th. If any Doubt or Dispute arises on any of the aforemd. Articles, or whatever else is not settled therein, it shall be determined by the Duke of Richmond and Mr. Brodrick on their Honours; by whom the Umpires are likewise to be determined on any Difference between Them.

13th. The Duke of Richmond's Umpire shall pitch the Wickets when they play in Sussex; and Mr. Brodrick's when they play in Surrey; & Each of Them shall be obliged to conform Himself strictly to the Agreements contained in the second Article.

14th. The Batt Men for every One they count are to touch the Umpires Stick.

15th. that it shall not be lawfull to fling down the wickets, & that no Player shall be deemed out by any wicket put down, unless with the Ball in Hand.

16th. that both the Matches shall be played upon, and determined by these Articles.

Richmond
A. Brodrick

APPENDIX 2

Rules of the White Conduit Club

That the club do meet to dine, at half past five o'clock, at the Star and Garter, on the last Mondays in April and May. Members* not attending at the dinner, (if in town) to forfeit half-a-guinea each time, which shall go to the stock-purse of the club: – if out of town, to signify it in writing, to the master of the Star and Garter, two days before the dinners – One guinea to be collected at the dinners, and the rest of the reckoning paid out of the stock-purse – Members in town are particularly requested to send word to the Star and Garter, the day before the dinners, if they cannot dine, in order that dinner may be provided accordingly.

That all expences of hire of ground, umpires, bats, balls, &c. be paid out of the stock-purse.

That the meat, &c. provided on the ground, be paid for by all the players. Members of the club going into the tent, to pay half-a-crown towards the reckoning. Any member introducing visitors to pay 5s . . .

That a treasurer be elected, and a committee of five (the treasurer being one) to arrange and settle all business relative to the club;** and to serve one year. – at the end of the year, the committee to name one of the succeeding committee . . .

That none but members of the club, are permitted to play, except when there are not sufficient members present to form a match; in which case any gentleman introduced by a member of the club, may play.

None but gentlemen ever to play.

That any player being deemed out, and disputing the decision of the

---

* Membership comprises 144 names – by far the biggest of any eighteenth-century cricket club on record. It includes the Duke of Dorset and Horace Mann; altogether twenty-two lords (peers in their own right plus sons of peers with courtesy titles). Among the latter was Viscount Maynard.
** The five-man committee was made up of the Earl of Winchilsea (Treasurer), the Earl of Berkeley, the Hon. Capt. Monson, the Hon. Lionel Damer and Sir Peter Burrell.

umpires, or finding fault with them, during the match, shall forfeit one guinea to the stock-purse of the club.

No match began, to be interrupted by persons who come too late. – The match to begin at half past eleven.

That at, and after the second meeting, no new members be admitted, but by ballot; – a ballot may be held at the tent ...

That no person whatever be permitted to enter the tent, unless introduced by a member of the club.

Any player leaving the ground without paying the reckoning of the day, to forfeit half-a-guinea to the stock-purse, besides his own reckoning.

All disputes relative to forfeits incurred to the club, to be referred to the committee, and their decision to be without appeal.

All damage done in the tent, to be paid for by the person committing the offence.

No horses or carriages to be admitted on the cricket-ground.

Laws for Single Wicket (1831)

1.—When there shall be less than five players on a side, bounds shall be placed, twenty-two yards each, in a line from the off and leg stump.

2.—The ball must be hit before the bounds to entitle the striker to a run, which run cannot be obtained unless he touch the bowling stump or crease in a line with it with his bat, or some part of his person, or go beyond them, returning to the popping-crease as at double wicket, according to the 22nd Law.

3.—When the striker shall hit the ball, one of his feet must be on the ground, and behind the popping-crease; otherwise the umpire shall call 'No Hit.'

4.—When there shall be less than five players on a side, neither byes nor overthrows shall be allowed; nor shall the striker be caught out behind the wicket, nor stumped out.

5.—The fieldsman must return the ball so that it shall cross the play between the wicket and the bowling stump, or between the bowling stump and the bounds. The striker may run till the ball shall be so returned.

6.—After the striker shall have made one run, if he start again he must touch the bowling stump, and turn before the ball shall cross the play to entitle him to another.

7.—The striker shall be entitled to three runs for a lost ball, and the same number for ball stopped with hat, with reference to the 29th and 34th Laws at double wicket.

8.—When there shall be more than four players on a side, there shall be no bounds. All hits, byes, and overthrows shall then be allowed.

9.—The bowler is subject to the same laws as at double wicket.

10.—Not more than one minute shall be allowed between each ball.

Important Single-Wicket Matches 1800–1848

(Results shown where known)

16–17 September 1805
Three of Surrey (John Wells, R. Robinson and W. Beldham) *vs* Three of England (John Bennett, Lord F. Beauclerk and W. Fennex) at Lord's.

27–28 June 1806
Three of Surrey (Wm. Lambert, R. Robinson and W. Beldham) *vs* Three of England (John Bennett, W. Fennex and Lord F. Beauclerk) at Lord's.

6–7 July 1810
Wm Lambert and G. Osbaldeston *vs* Lord F. Beauclerk and T. C. Howard at Lord's. Osbaldeston retired ill in the first innings and did not bat in the second. Lambert (and Osbaldeston) won by 15 runs.

14 July 1813
Three of Mitcham (John Bowyer, John Sherman and James Sherman) *vs* Geo. Osbaldeston Esq at Lord's.

4 July 1814
Four of Hampshire (E. Carter, Thumwood, John Bennett and T. C. Howard) *vs* Four of MCC (Hon. E. Bligh, G. Osbaldeston Esq, E. H. Budd Esq and Lord F. Beauclerk) at Lord's.

28 July 1814
Three Gentlemen of MCC (G. Osbaldeston Esq, E. H. Budd Esq and Lord F. Beauclerk) *vs* Three Players of England (James Sherman, T. C. Howard and Wm Lambert) at Lord's.

21–23 August 1815
Geo Osbaldeston Esq *vs* Two of Nottingham (Humphrey Hopkin and Joseph Dennis) in the King's Meadow at Nottingham. Mr Osbaldeston won by an innings and 67 runs. Played for £50 a side.

c.1820

E. H. Budd Esq *vs* J. Brand Esq at Lord's. Budd scored 70 and 31; Brand 0 and 0.

2–3 July 1827

George Brown and Tom Marsden *vs* James and William Broadbridge on the Royal Ground at Brighton. The two Broadbridges won by two wickets.

16–17 July 1827

As above at Darnall, near Sheffield. Marsden and Brown won by one wicket.

18 July 1827

James and William Broadbridge *vs* Tom Marsden and G. Rawlins at Darnall near Sheffield. The two Broadbridges won.

5 August 1827

J. H. Dark *vs* J. Cobbett at Lord's.

30 August 1828

Three of Godalming (Oliver, W. Searle and W. Keen Esq) *vs* Three of Alton (H., T. and J. Beagley) at Godalming.

8 October 1829

Three of Winchester *vs* Three of Farringdon at Chilton Down near Winchester.

12 October 1829

Nottingham (George Jarvis) *vs* Sheffield (Tom Marsden) at Darnall near Sheffield.

19 July 1831

J. Saunders, H. E. Knatchbull Esq, J. Cobbett and W. Lillywhite *vs* C. Romilly Esq, W. Caldecourt, E. G. Wenman and James Broadbridge at Lord's.

8–9 August 1831

Three of Sheffield (G. Smith, G. Rawlings and T. Marsden) *vs* Three of Nottingham (W. Clarke, G. Jarvis and T. Barker) on the Hyde Park Ground, Sheffield.

12 August 1831

P. Gurdon's Side (Gurdon, F. Pilch, J. Cobbett and Herbert Jenner Esq) *vs* Sir St. V. Cotton's Side (Cotton, J. Saunders, E. G. Wenman and W. Lillywhite) at Dereham.

19 June 1832

James Adams *vs* Daniel Hayward at Chatteris.

30–31 July 1832

Henry Sampson *vs* Sam Bradbury on the Hyde Park Ground at Sheffield.

22 August 1832   Tom Hills *vs* Alfred Mynn at Leeds Park, Kent.

4 September 1832   Tom Hills *vs* Alfred Mynn at Town Malling, Kent.

26–27 September 1832   Nottingham (Tom Heath) *vs* Leicester (Sam Dakin) on the Forest Ground, Nottingham.

27 September 1832   Two of Nottingham (Slack and Sam Redgate) *vs* Two of Leicester (W. Shelton and Sam Dakin) on the Forest Ground, Nottingham.

28–29 May 1833   Three of Alton (John, Henry and Thomas Beagley) *vs* Three of Winchester (Windebank, Purchase and G. Freemantle) on Twyford Down near Winchester.

11–12 June 1833   Three of Alton (as above) *vs* Three of Winchester (as above) on Alton Butts.

17–19 June 1833   Three of Nottingham (W. Clarke, T. Barker and G. Jarvis) *vs* Three of Sheffield (E. Vincent, W. H. Woolhouse and T. Marsden) on the New Ground, Hulme, near Manchester.

18 July 1833   Tom Marsden *vs* Fuller Pilch at Norwich. This and the return match (5–7 August) were played for the championship of England. Pilch won.

5–7 August 1833   Fuller Pilch *vs* Tom Marsden on the Hyde Park Ground, Sheffield (return to above) (Championship of England). (Pilch 82 and 106; Marsden 26 and 35).

14 October 1833   James Dearman *vs* Tom Health on the Hyde Park Ground, Sheffield (Dearman 111 and 9; Heath 37 and 12).

26 June 1834   William Clarke *vs* Seven of West Bridgford on the Forest Ground, Nottingham. Clarke won by an innings and 6 runs.

13 August 1834   Kent *vs* England (one innings a side) at Chiselhurst, Kent (Mynn, Geo Wenman and R. Mills) *vs* England (F. Pilch, Tom Marsden and Wm Lillywhite).

26 August 1834   Three of England *vs* Three of Kent at Leeds Park, Kent (J. Cobbett, T. Marsden and J. H. Dark *vs* E. G. Wenman, A. Mynn and R. Mills).

4–5 September 1834   Two of Benenden (E. G. Wenman and R. Mills) *vs* Eleven of the Isle of Oxney at Wittersham in Kent. Wenman and Hills winning by 66 runs. (Strictly speaking, this was a double-wicket match. In 1934 a centenary match was played with the same odds.)

16 September 1834   Henry Beagley *vs* Geo Freemantle on Magdalen Hill near Winchester.

23 September 1834   Henry Beagley *vs* Geo Freemantle on Alton Butts.

18 May 1835   H. Hall and J. Cobbett *vs* A. Mynn and A. Jackson on Hall's Ground, Camberwell.

18 May 1835   H. Hall and J. Cobbett *vs* A. Mynn and A. Rich on Hall's Ground.

2 June 1835   Parnther, Caldecourt and Redgate *vs* F. P. Fenner, Saunders and F. Pilch on Parker's Piece, Cambridge.

23 June 1835   J. Cobbett and Sir St. V. Cotton *vs* Wm Lillywhite and W. Goring at Lord's.

30 June 1835   Three of Camberwell Clarence (A. Mynn, Hall and J. Heath) *vs* Three of Reigate (R. Killick, J. Allwork and T. Kent) at Reigate.

22 July 1835   S. Redgate and B. Good *vs* A. Mynn and T. Marsden on H. Hall's Ground, Camberwell.

14–15 September 1835   Two of York *vs* Two of Sheffield on the Senior Ground, North Wall, at York.

12 September 1836   Sam Redgate *vs* Eleven of Kensington Club, Forest Ground, Nottingham.

10 July 1838   Cambridge Town Club (with Caldecourt) *vs* MCC (T. Adams, E. G. Wenman and Sir F. Bathurst) at Lord's. Played at finish of MCC *vs* Cambridge Town Club (eleven a side).

25 July 1838   Tom Marsden *vs* Robert Broadbridge at Lord's.

20 August 1838   Alfred Mynn *vs* James Dearman on F. Pilch's Ground at Town Malling, Kent. This, and the return

match (27 August), were played for the championship (of England). A. Mynn won by 112 runs.

18 September 1838	Saffron Walden (A. Adams) *vs* Cambridge (F. P. Fenner) at Cambridge.
15 October 1838	Three of Eastbourne *vs* Two of Chalvington (R. and G. Picknell).
4 September 1839	John Sherman's Side (three) *vs* James Dearman's Side (three), Rochdale.
6 September 1839	Three of Mitcham (W. Martingell, T. Sewell and B. Good) *vs* Three of Town Malling (W. Mynn, W. Hillyer and A. Mynn) on Lower Mitcham Ground.
25 September 1839	Three of Rochdale *vs* Three of Manchester at ?
3 October 1839	Three of Rochdale *vs* Three of Manchester at Manchester.
5 September 1840	John Heath, W. Hillyer, W. Clifford, J. Dicker and Currey *vs* W. Martingell, W. Mynn, W. Pilch Jr, Harman and R. Groom at Bromley.
23–24 September 1840	Three of Chaddesden and Burton-on-Trent *vs* Two of Nottingham (T. Barker and J. Guy) at Leicester.
17–19 May 1841	Tom Marsden *vs* Henry Sampson at Hyde Park Ground, Sheffield.
11 July 1842	W. Waller (of Hingham) *vs* W. Pilch (of Brinton) at Norwich.
11 August 1842	W. Waller (of Hingham) *vs* W. Pilch (of Brinton) at Hingham.
18 October 1842	Sheffield (Henry Reany) *vs* Nottingham (Charles Brown) at the Hyde Park Ground, Sheffield.
20 June 1843	Three of Southampton (R. Bodle, Elliot and D. Day) *vs* Three of Winchester and Easton (Davis, Burt and G. Fremantle) at the New Ground at Winchester.
17 July 1843	Return of above on D. Day's ground at Southampton.

26–27 October 1843   Nottingham (Geo Jarvis) *vs* Dalton (Andrew Crossland), Hyde Park Ground, Sheffield.

1 November 1843   Sam Dakin *vs* Tom Hunt at Hyde Park Ground.

6 November 1843   Two of Huddersfield (Joseph and Andrew Crossland) *vs* Two of Dalton (G. Brook and Geo Berry) at Bradley, near Huddersfield.

27–28 November 1843   John Berry and Wm Wilson *vs* John Eastwood and Andrew Crossland at Lane, near Huddersfield. Yorkshire cricket was played later in the season than in any other county.

24 May 1844   F. Pilch, J. Minter and Rugby *vs* J. Sharpe, H. Bing and W. Martingell at the Beverley Ground, Canterbury ('The Lions' *vs* 'The Crowns').

3 October 1844   Three of Alresford *vs* Three of Alton at Titchbourne Down, Hants.

7 October 1844   Three of Alresford *vs* Three of Alton at Alton Butts.

23–24 October 1844   Sheffield (Tom Hunt) *vs* Nottingham (Charles Brown) at the Hyde Park Ground, Sheffield.

25 October 1844   Tom Hunt and G. Coates *vs* Henry Hall and Sam Redgate, Hyde Park Ground, Sheffield.

23 September 1845   Two of Chesterfield (inc. Tom Hunt) *vs* Two of Derby (inc. Sam Dakin) at Burton-on-Trent.

18 June 1846   Nicholas Felix *vs* Alfred Mynn at Lord's. A. Mynn won by an innings and 1 run. This (and the return match on 29 September) was for the championship of England.

18 June 1846   Taylor, Mynn and Felix *vs* Parr, Lillywhite and Dean at Lord's (Three Gentlemen *vs* Three Players). This match was got up and played at the conclusion of the match between Mynn and Felix.

24–26 September 1846   Manchester (T. Hunt and S. Baldwinson) *vs* Nottingham (W. Clarke and G. Butler) for £25 at Moss Lane, Hulme, Manchester.

28–29 September 1846   Kent (T. Adams and W. Hillyer) *vs* Sussex (G. Picknell and E. Bushby) on T. Adams' ground at Gravesend.

29–30 September 1846   N. Felix *vs* A. Mynn at Mr Pawley's, White Hart Hotel, Bromley. Return match to that earlier in the season for the championship of England.

16 September 1847   Tom Sherman of Mitcham *vs* John Wisden of Brighton at T. Box's ground, Brighton (two matches).

22 September 1847   As above, at Mitcham.

2 and 4 November 1847   Geo Chatterton and Tom Hunt *vs* Henry Sampson and Henry Wright, Hyde Park Ground, Sheffield.

27 May 1848   Arnold and Cornell *vs* Wisden and Guy at Fenner's, Cambridge.

9 June 1848   Tom Barker and Dan Hayward *vs* O. C. Pell and J. Walker, Fenner's, Cambridge.

31 August–1 September 1848   Three of England (W. Pilch, C. H. Hoare and A. Mynn) *vs* Three of Sheffield (H. Sampson, H. Wright and T. Hunt) at Hyde Park Ground, Sheffield.

'In Memoriam, Alfred Mynn 1807–1861'

WILLIAM JEFFREY PROWSE

Jackson's pace is very fearful; Willshire's hand is very high:
William Caffyn has good judgment, and an admirable eye:
Jemmy Grundy's cool and clever, almost always on the spot:
Tinsley's slows are often telling, though they sometimes catch it hot.
But however good their trundling—pitch, or pace, or break, or spin—
Still the monarch of all bowlers, to my mind, was Alfred Mynn.

Richard Daft is cool and cautious, with his safe and graceful play;
If George Griffith gets a loose one, he can send it far away.
You may bowl your best at Hayward, and whatever style you try
Will be vanquished by the master's steady hand and certain eye.
But whatever fame and glory these and other bats may win,
Still the monarch of hard hitters, to my mind, was Alfred Mynn.

You may praise the pluck of Burbidge, as he plays an uphill match;
You may thunder cheers to Miller, for a wondrous running catch;
You may join with me in wishing that the Oval once again
Shall resound with hearty plaudits to the praise of Mr. Lane;
But the gentlemen of England the match will hardly win
Till they find another bowler, such as glorious Alfred Mynn.

When the great old Kent Eleven, full of pluck and hope began
The grand battle with All England, single-handed, man to man,
How the hop-men watched their hero, massive, muscular, and tall,
As he mingled with the players, like a king among them all;
Till to some old Kent enthusiasts it would almost seem a sin
To doubt their county's triumph when led on by Alfred Mynn.

Though Sir Frederick and 'The Veteran' bowled straight and sure and well,
Though Box behind the wicket only Lockyer can excel;

Though Jemmy Dean, as long-stop, would but seldom grant a bye;
Though no novices in batting were George Parr and Joseph Guy—
Said the fine old Kentish farmers, with a fine old Kentish grin,
'Why, there ain't a man among them as can match our Alfred Mynn.'

And whatever was the issue of the frank and friendly fray,
(Aye, and often has his bowling turned the fortunes of the day),
Still the Kentish men fought bravely, never losing hope or heart,
Every man of the Eleven glad and proud to play his part.
And with five such mighty cricketers, 'twas but natural to win,
As Felix, Wenman, Hillyer, Fuller Pilch, and Alfred Mynn.

With his tall and stately presence, with his nobly moulded form,
His broad hand was ever open, his brave heart was ever warm;
All were proud of him, all loved him. As the changing seasons pass,
As our champion lies a-sleeping underneath the Kentish grass,
Proudly, sadly will we name him—to forget him were a sin.
Lightly lie the turf upon thee, kind and manly Alfred Mynn!

Index